Post-Zionism, Post-Holocaust
Three Essays on Denial, Forgetting, and the Delegitimation of Israel

This book contains three independent essays, available in English for the first time, as well as a postscript written for this English edition. The common theme of the three essays is the uses and abuses of the Holocaust as an ideological arm in anti-Zionist campaigns. The first essay examines a French group of left-wing Holocaust deniers. The second essay deals with a number of Israeli academics and intellectuals, the so-called post-Zionists, and tries to follow their use of the Holocaust in their different attempts to demonize and delegitimize Israel. The third deals with Hannah Arendt and her relations with Zionism and the State of Israel as reflected in her general work and in *Eichmann in Jerusalem*; the views that she formulates are used systematically and extensively by anti- and post-Zionists. Elhanan Yakira argues that each of these is a particular expression of an outrage: anti-Zionism and a wholesale delegitimation of Israel.

Elhanan Yakira is currently Schulman Professor of Philosophy at The Hebrew University in Jerusalem and holds a doctorate from the Sorbonne in France. His publications include *Nécessité, Contrainte et Choix – la métaphysique de la liberté chez Spinoza et Leibniz* (1989), *La causalité de Galilée à Kant* (1994), *Shlomo Ben Ami: Quel avenir pour Israël?* (with Jeffrey Barash and Yves-Charles Zarka, 2001), and *Leibniz's Theory of the Rational* (with E. Grosholz, 1998). He also translated Leibniz's *Discours de métaphysique et la correspondance avec Arnauld* into Hebrew and edited Descartes' *Meditations* and other philosophical classics.

Post-Zionism, Post-Holocaust

Three Essays on Denial, Forgetting, and the Delegitimation of Israel

ELHANAN YAKIRA
The Hebrew University, Jerusalem

Translated by
Michael Swirsky

CAMBRIDGE
UNIVERSITY PRESS

CAMBRIDGE UNIVERSITY PRESS
Cambridge, New York, Melbourne, Madrid, Cape Town, Singapore,
São Paulo, Delhi, Dubai, Tokyo

Cambridge University Press
32 Avenue of the Americas, New York, NY 10013–2473, USA

www.cambridge.org
Information on this title: www.cambridge.org/9780521127868

Published in Hebrew as *Post-Tsiyonut, post-Sho'ah* by Am Oved 2006
English edition published by Cambridge University Press 2010

Printed in the United States of America

A catalog record for this publication is available from the British Library.

Library of Congress Cataloging in Publication data
Yakira, Elhanan.
 [Post-Tsiyonut, post-Sho'ah. English]
 Post-Zionism, Post-Holocaust: three essays on denial, forgetting, and the
 delegitimation of Israel / Elhanan Yakira.
  p. cm.
 Includes bibliographical references and index.
 ISBN 978-0-521-11110-2 (hardback) – ISBN 978-0-521-12786-8 (pbk.)
 1. Post-Zionism. 2. Holocaust denial – France. 3. Arendt, Hannah,
 1906–1975. 4. Holocaust, Jewish (1939–1945) 5. Zionism. I. Title.
 DS113.4.Y3513 2009
 320.54095694–dc22   2009010231

ISBN 978-0-521-11110-2 Hardback
ISBN 978-0-521-12786-8 Paperback

Contents

Preface

The present volume comprises three more or less independent essays and a postscript written for the English edition. They share a single concern: the use of the Holocaust to advance anti-Zionist and anti-Israeli claims. Anti-Zionism has recently gained momentum and become a powerful ideological adversary of Israel. Beyond legitimate criticism of Israeli policies, the occupation, Israeli settlements in the West Bank, and so on, what is at stake in the anti-Zionist campaign is the basic legitimacy of Israel as a Jewish state, the right of the Jews to self-determination, and the fundamental morality of a Jewish polity. One of the more disturbing aspects of this ideological all-out war is the systematic use of the Holocaust as a major weapon. This is not just a curiosity, for the strategic use, or rather abuse, of the Holocaust has proved its effectiveness. The Holocaust has come to be perceived – and this is how anti-Zionism makes use of it – as the main, if not the sole, justification and explanation for the existence of Israel. In what follows, I refer to this thesis as the "master postulate," to borrow a term suggesting all-pervasiveness and longevity from an old and altogether different philosophical context. Undermining this alleged foundation and justification of the Jewish state is – in the logic of the master postulate – tantamount to a complete denial of the state's legitimacy.

According to an assumption that has become commonplace, organized Jewry, the Zionist movement, and the State of Israel have turned the Holocaust into a tool for the creation, within Israel itself, of an ethos and culture of fear, self-righteousness, and violence, as well as a basis for moral, political, and monetary claims directed outward, primarily toward Germany but, in effect, toward the international community as a whole. We are told that the Jewish establishment in general and the Israeli leadership in particular, the State of Israel, and even the people of Israel have made, are making, and will surely continue to make systematic, instrumental use of the Holocaust. The purpose of the following inquiry is to show that just the opposite is the case. More than the Holocaust serves Israel's purposes, it serves those of Israel's most strident negators and detractors. Although the anti-Israeli uses made of the Holocaust are multifaceted, taking different forms that appear at times quite contradictory, they coalesce into a single pattern of defaming Israel and Zionism. The Holocaust, or the story of the destruction of European Jewry by Nazi Germany, plays a central role in this defamation, which aims, on the one hand, to deny legitimacy to the Jewish state in principle and, on the other, to indict the state, across the board, on moral grounds.

The Hebrew version of this book appeared at the beginning of 2007. It was written completely within the Israeli context and was addressed to an Israeli audience. What was originally intended to be a short article reacting to certain phenomena that I thought merited comment – such as the appearance in some academic quarters of a new "progressive" canon comprising, notably, Hannah Arendt, Carl Schmitt, and Giorgio Agamben – became, in the end, three relatively lengthy essays. Their appearance in book form has stirred a public debate in Israel. Although I had not intended to translate the book into other languages, I was encouraged to do so by a number of people – a surprisingly large number, in fact – who thought a voice like the one this book represents should be heard abroad as well. I finally agreed. But it was necessary to adapt the book for the non-Israeli reader. As I set about doing so, a few things have become clear to me that were not so clear when I was working on the Hebrew edition: the sheer volume of anti-Israeli and anti-Zionist literature being published is astonishing, and it is growing by the day. The hostility toward Israel manifested in this literature is overwhelming. Not less surprising is the preponderant role played in this movement by Jews in general and Israelis and ex-Israelis in particular.

In Israel itself, hardly a month goes by without the appearance of some anti-Israeli book, not to speak of articles and conference papers. So much anti-Israeli literature is being produced that I quickly realized I could not deal with even a fraction of it, especially because, unlike many of the critics, I had other things to do. I have done my best to give a representative, if only partial, picture of the broad phenomenon of Western intellectual anti-Zionism. The various anti-Zionist campaigns now underway – be they on American or European campuses; among Israeli intellectuals; or in Arab, Iranian, or Palestinian propaganda – have already achieved one important strategic victory: people are no longer ashamed to speak openly of the destruction of the

State of Israel. One can now hear in polite company and read in the pages of mainstream journals that Israel should cease to exist as a Jewish state. It is, of course, not physical destruction that is contemplated in the *New York Review of Books* but "changing the regime" or annulling the Jewish character of the state. But even if it is not a question of wiping out the Jews living in Palestine, the survival of something very real and very important – in fact, unprecedented in Jewish history and unequaled in present-day Jewry – that has been built up over more than a hundred years is at stake.

In the debates and discussions held in Israel after the appearance of this book, one cardinal issue was raised again and again: "the Occupation." Supporters and opponents alike have demanded, "What do you say about the Occupation? How can you defend the basic Zionist idea, Israel's right to exist as a Jewish state, and not say anything about what goes on in Hebron?" For a number of reasons I have usually refused to engage in this discussion. First of all, the question of Israeli control over territories seized in wartime, the question of the Jewish settlements there, the question of Palestinian violence, and the question of Israeli defense strategies are all immensely complicated. The presentation of these issues in the anti-Zionist literature is usually so distorted, one-sided, and tendentious that any attempt to put them in proper perspective would demand a book-length discussion. Many such books exist, and I do not have anything new to add to them.

But there were more important reasons for my refusal to engage in a discussion of the Occupation. As the very use of the term "Occupation," with a capital O, shows, the matter has assumed mythic proportions. There are those who no longer speak of Israel but of the "Occupation Regime" (probably an allusion to the polemical term "Apartheid Regime," in use until not very long ago), as if this summed up the whole reality of Israel, the territories, and the Middle East. Nothing Israel has done to end or limit the occupation – such as the creation of the Palestinian Authority or the evacuation of the Gaza Strip – has changed anything in the anti-Zionist discourse. If anything, the latter has become only more vicious. The conclusion is plain: the real crux of anti-Zionism is not and has probably never really been the occupation, but Israel itself. The real issue, to put it differently, is not 1967 but 1948.

To set the record straight, let me say that in a general way I belong to what is called in Israel the Zionist left. This term refers, historically, to the mainstream socialist parties that were the principal factor in the building of Israel. We are not concerned here with the legal, economic, or social questions on which left and right in Israel differ, but there are two other issues that are relevant to our present discussion. One is the cardinal question of the occupation. Here, favoring a withdrawal more or less to the pre-1967 lines, the evacuation of most settlements now beyond those lines, and the creation of a sovereign Arab-Palestinian state was until recently regarded as a left-wing position. But today this position is shared by most mainstream Israeli political groups: left, center-left, center, and center-right. This is also my own personal stance on the question of the occupation.

One of the supposedly objective claims of the post- and anti-Zionists is that the so-called two-state solution is no longer possible: the situation on the ground has become irreversible, and the settlements have become an insurmountable obstacle to any solution based on the idea of partitioning the country between the two peoples inhabiting it. In truth, however, the real obstacles to peace have been the Palestinians' refusal to accept the compromises offered them (notably in the Clinton proposals of 2000) and, even more, their continual violence, internal corruption, and inability to restrain their extremists or build anything resembling a polity capable of unified political action. Israel has been conducting negotiations with the Palestinians for more than a decade now, and its basic position has been, almost without exception, an acceptance of the partition principle. The Palestinians, once again, waged a vicious war against Israel; once again, they lost it. A war is a very unpleasant thing; it is especially unpleasant for those who lose. The absence of a political solution is the main reason for the tragic situation in which the Palestinians now find themselves. It is also the condition under which the Jewish settlements in the occupied territories thrive. I think this development is most regrettable, both politically and morally. But I am also convinced that the settlements are not an insurmountable obstacle to peace. Evacuating them, or many of them, would, of course, present a huge challenge to Israeli society and to any Israeli government that agreed to do so. Like many Israelis, however, I am convinced that this will have to happen. My only advice to the skeptics – and to the Palestinians – is to put Israel to the test. What happened in the Gaza Strip is an indication that it just might work in the West Bank and the Golan Heights as well.

The other relevant political issue is that of the Jewish nature of Israel. Given the large Arab minority within its pre-1967 borders – so goes the argument – it cannot be both democratic and Jewish. As it is now, it is at best a faulty or partial democracy: an ethnic democracy, an exclusive democracy, or simply a nondemocracy. The left-wing Zionism I am talking about holds, first, that there is full justification – historically, politically, legally, and morally – for the creation and continued existence of a Jewish polity in the historic Land of Israel. In the militantly secularist view the left has traditionally espoused, the term "Land of Israel" does not connote a divine promise or anything of the sort, but a historical reality. This kind of Zionism also sees no truth – only ignorance, bad faith, or malice – in allegations that democracy and a Jewish state are incompatible. As with many such anti-Zionist claims, there exists an abundant literature of refutation. Typically, the critics pay not the slightest heed to this literature. Open-minded readers can read it and judge for themselves.[1]

One of the things that make the anti-Zionist movement so effective is that it is on the offensive. It is also strengthened by very powerful academic and intellectual trends in the West, including theories, modes of thought, methodologies, metahistorical presuppositions, and jargon that now predominate among a significant segment of the intelligentsia. The movement has succeeded to a large degree in putting Israel on trial. Hence, Israeli, Zionist, and Jewish counterdiscourse has been, more often than not, defensive and apologetic in nature. I did not think when I started writing this book, and I do not think now, that Israel, the Zionist idea, or we Israelis need offer any apologies. Thus, I did not set out to debate the protagonists of this book, be they Parisian Holocaust deniers, so-called post-Zionist Israelis, or New York professors. Such people would probably not have considered me a valid interlocutor, and, to tell the truth, I did not consider them to be worth talking to either. There has never been much point in reasoning with anti-Semites; the only thing one can do is talk *about* them. Whether anti-Zionism is or is not a form of anti-Semitism is a question much debated lately; one similarity between the two phenomena, however, is that there is not much point in talking with the anti-Zionists either. Thus, what I am trying to do in the essays published here is talk not with, but about, anti-Zionism.

Because the essays in this volume were written independently of each other, and because they were written and rewritten over a relatively long period of time, they may be somewhat repetitive. I apologize to the reader for this. However, I shall not express the polite hope that this will not spoil his or her enjoyment of the book. It is not likely to make for enjoyable reading in any case.

---

[1] I permit myself to draw the reader's attention to a book that has recently appeared in English translation and that pleads the legal-political case of Israel as both Jewish and democratic. See Alexander Yakobson and Amnon Rubinsten, *Israel and the Family of Nations* (London: Taylor and Francis, 2008).

Acknowledgments

Many people – friends, colleagues, and relatives – have read all or part of the numerous drafts that led to the present book, and I have profited greatly from their suggestions and criticisms. Shlomo Aronson, Avi Barelli, Ezra Dloomy, Hayim Goldgraber, Hayim Gouri, David Heyd, Yoash Meisler, Yehudah Melzer, Dinah Porat, Gadi Taub, Zvi Zameret, and others – all encouraged me to write this book and influenced the form it finally assumed. They also urged me to have it translated and even helped find publishers for the various versions.

Eddy Zemach, who, unfortunately, was not able to read the finished book and still cannot read these lines, played a particularly significant role in the process. He was the first to suggest that I turn what had been a short article into a longer work. More than this, he pressed me to do it, and his confidence in the value of this project was a major source of encouragement to me.

Anita Shapira, who heads the Weizmann Institute for the Study of Zionism and Israel and, together with the Tel Aviv publisher Am Oved, undertook the book's original publication, was, unlike others, undeterred by its polemical character. She and Itamar Rabinowitz also encouraged the Keshet Foundation to make the generous grant that enabled me to do the research needed to update and adapt the book for readers of English and French.

My friend Michael Swirsky did much more than translate the book into English. He spent many hours, far more than expected, revising the original text and the many additions and changes I continually made during the very long period when I was preparing the English version.

Part of the work on this version was done during a month-long residency at the Rockefeller Foundation's Bellagio Center at Lake Como, Italy. There could be no more splendid a setting for such labors than the studio at Villa Serbelloni, with its view of the lake and the surrounding mountains. The director of the center, Pillar Palacia, and the rest of the team at Bellagio made the month I spent there not only highly productive but also extremely pleasant.

Lew Bateman, Emily Spangler, and Brian MacDonald, of Cambridge University Press in New York, were not only helpful, efficient, and professional in their work on the manuscript but also encouraging and extremely friendly during the long period it was in preparation.

This version of the book could not have come into being without the extraordinary generosity, hospitality, and, above all, friendship of Noma (Nancy) and Kamal (Ken) Haron. More than anything else, it was their confidence in me and in the book, and their concrete assistance, that got the translation project underway and saw it through.

I

Holocaust Denial and the Left

A TRUE STORY, SOME FACTS, AND A BIT OF COMMENTARY

A number of years ago, I was fortunate – or unfortunate – enough to have
a unique encounter. In a Paris drenched with summer sun, under circumstances that justify the cliché about reality being stranger than fiction, I happened to speak for five or six hours with an enterprising individual named
Pierre Guillaume. Assuming that many of my readers have not heard of him,
I had better say a few words about him. When I met him, Guillaume was running a bookstore and publishing house with the interesting name La Vieille
Taupe (The Old Mole). Not far from the Pantheon, the burial place of the
great figures of the French republic, this institution, which opened and closed
and opened again over a period of many years and now no longer exists, was
the principal power base of Holocaust denial in France.[1] From the late 1960s
to the 1990s, Guillaume, his bookstore, and publishing house were the main
focus of the activities of the Holocaust deniers. The 1970s and 1980s were
their heyday, mainly by virtue of their collaboration with the Lyon literary
scholar Robert Faurisson, the best known of the French Holocaust deniers,
whose writings La Vieille Taupe published. As a result of that conversation,
and thanks to the good offices of Mr. Guillaume (for which, it should be made
clear, he received a handsome fee), the masochism section of my library was

---

[1] The inside covers of La Vieille Taupe books bear a quotation from Hegel: "Spirit often
seems to have forgotten and lost itself, but, inwardly opposed to itself, it is inwardly working ever forward, as Hamlet says of the ghost of his father, 'Well done, old mole'" (Georg
W. F. Hegel, *Lectures on the History of Philosophy*, trans. E. S. Haldane and Frances
H. Simpson [New York: Humanities Press, 1974], 3:546–547). Marx used this image to
describe the revolution being prepared underground, at the moment it emerges.

enriched by a number of Faurisson's writings as well as several other literary productions of La Vieille Taupe, all of them furnishing abundant arguments and proofs that the thing we call "the Holocaust" never happened. The story of the systematic destruction of the Jews of Europe by the Germans during the Second World War was, in truth, a colossal lie.

Apart from a few historians and experts, Israeli public opinion does not appear overly troubled by the phenomenon of Holocaust denial. A few years ago, there was some mention in the press of the libel suit brought by the English historian David Irving against the American Holocaust scholar Deborah Lipstadt, who claimed that Irving had lied when he said there had been no systematic extermination of Jews during the war. Irving lost the suit. In the verdict, he was described as a "right-wing, pro-Nazi polemicist." The Israeli media brought up the matter again, when Irving, in an Austrian court, was convicted of Holocaust denial and sentenced to three years' imprisonment. (He was released after one year.) More recently, some attention was attracted to this matter by the Teheran convention of Holocaust deniers, organized by Iran's president Mahmoud Ahmedinazad. On the whole, Holocaust denial is an activity confined to the neo-Nazi and neo-fascist right wing. At least that is how it is generally perceived by those who pay it any heed at all, scholars included, and, as such, we accord it the same significance given to other crude manifestations of old-fashioned European anti-Semitism: an ugly annoyance that belongs to a world that no longer exists. True, there has been talk here in Israel, and not only here, about the resurgence of anti-Semitism; but many think that what we are seeing is actually a new phenomenon. The violent attacks on Jews and Jewish institutions in Europe are mostly being carried out by North African and other Muslim immigrants and so appear to be an importation of the Arab-Israeli conflict rather than anti-Semitism in the old, classical, sense of the word. There is some truth in this: no doubt the wave of anti-Jewish violence in Europe in recent years is closely connected to the protracted conflict between Israel and the Palestinians. But it is less clear that the Israeli-Palestinian conflict, and especially the extreme violence of its current phase, are the *sole* cause of this new Judeophobia.[2] Even if we ignore the stubbornness with which

---

[2] The political scientist Pierre-André Taguieff suggests using the term "Judeophobia" in preference to "anti-Semitism" to describe the outburst of anti-Jewish violence, both physical and verbal, in France since 2000 and the virtual absence of opposition – political or even intellectual – to this hatred, which came mainly from North African immigrants. See Pierre-André Taguieff, *Rising from the Muck: The New Anti-Semitism in Europe* (Chicago: Ivan R. Dee, 2004). Leo Strauss had made a similar suggestion, for similar reasons: the term "anti-Semitism" could conceal the specificity and uniqueness of the hatred of Jews. The

good old-fashioned, traditional anti-Semitism continues to reassert itself, it could still be that the Middle Eastern conflict only partly explains the manifestations of anti-Jewish hostility we are now seeing from time to time and that the conflict is, in fact, serving mainly as the vehicle, or occasion, for an outburst of hatred whose sources lie elsewhere. In fact, the tendency of some experts, Israelis among them, to present what is going on in the Middle East as virtually the only cause of the new anti-Jewish sentiment and (occasionally) violence relies not on historical or political analysis but rather on ideology. At the root of this ideology is the desire, or need, to blame these events, explicitly or implicitly, on Israel. In the final analysis, this is merely an updated version of the classic rhetorical ploy of anti-Semitic propaganda, that it is the Jews themselves who are actually responsible for the hatred and violence directed against them, hence for their own suffering.

In the face of this old-new anti-Semitism, the question of Holocaust denial comes up from time to time. But what people here in Israel (and other places as well) seem not to realize fully is that in certain places, especially but not only in France, denial of the Holocaust is often associated with the left and not only the radical, neofascist right. So I spent several hours, that summer Saturday in Paris, with Pierre Guillaume. At that time, as I have said, this man was one of France's most important and effective Holocaust deniers. He could be credited with turning denial from something marginal and half-covert into a salient issue that broadly engaged French public opinion. As always happens in such cases, the very fact that denial became a public issue, and even that it was challenged and criticized, was already a strategic victory for the deniers.

Monsieur Guillaume did most of the talking at that strange encounter. He seemed a bit surprised that a foreigner like me took such an interest in the existence, or nonexistence, of gas chambers and had the kind of knowledge of the subject that my questioning revealed. (Revolutionary that he was – and perhaps still is – Guillaume was very polite and discreet and only after several hours of conversation dared to ask where I came from.) But he never lost patience with me and even took great pleasure in enlightening me about the lie of the Holocaust, where it had originated, who was responsible for disseminating it, and who was profiting from it – especially who was profiting from it. As Guillaume took pains to point out again and again, not only was he a man of the left, committed to his leftist views and to the great proletarian

Stephen Roth Institute for the Study of Contemporary Anti-Semitism and Racism monitors anti-Semitic incidents and publications all over the world, publishing annual reports as well as other material. See http://www.tau.ac.il/anti-Semitism/.

revolution, but in his view what we call "Holocaust denial" – and what he called unmasking the great lie of the annihilation of the Jews – was a decidedly left-wing activity, an expression of the revolutionary spirit. He did not deny the Holocaust *despite* his belonging to the radical left, as we might have thought, but precisely *because* of it. In fact, Holocaust denial had become, for Guillaume and his comrades, their principal activity and more or less the core of their revolutionary ideology.

This Guillaume, along with a small group of collaborators and ideological sympathizers (among them, incidentally, some Jews), was at one time part of the revolutionary ferment that took place in France in the 1960s, briefly taking political center stage in May 1968 and continuing to some extent into the 1970s and '80s. In 1965 Guillaume opened his bookstore, La Vieille Taupe; he belonged at that time to a small group calling itself Pouvoir Ouvrier (roughly, Workers' Power) and was active in another group known as Socialisme ou Barbarie, which published a journal by this name. In 1967 he left Pouvoir Ouvrier and, together with some friends, established a small opposition group – generally referred to by the name of his bookstore, which served as its base of operation – a group that located itself on the extreme ideological fringes of the world revolution. The bookstore itself became an important distribution center for revolutionary literature. In the turbulent spring of 1968, when the revolution came, Guillaume discovered the writings of Paul Rassinier, the founding thinker of left-wing Holocaust denial, and they came as a revelation to him.[3] That summer Saturday in Paris – and this was actually the occasion of my strange meeting with him – Guillaume came into a small copy shop where I was doing some business of my own to copy dozens of pages of arguments and documents for distribution to Socialist Party activists, with the aim of clearing Rassinier's name and convincing them to lift their ban on him.

---

[3] In recent years, many studies of Holocaust denial in France have been published. The most comprehensive, it seems, is Valérie Igounet, *Histoire du négationionisme en France* (Paris: Seuil, 2000). There is an interesting analysis of the denial phenomenon on the French left in Alain Finkielkraut's earlier book, *The Future of a Negation: Reflections on the Question of Genocide*, trans. Mary Byrd Kelly (Lincoln: University of Nebraska Press, 1998). A direct confrontation with the French deniers, especially Faurisson, and their arguments is to be found in Pierre Vidal-Naquet's earlier work, *The Jews: History, Memory, and the Present*, trans. and ed. David Ames Curtis (New York: Columbia University Press, 1998). For a broader perspective, locating Guillaume and his friends in a shifting scene of the radical (mostly Trotskyite) left, see Jean-Jacques Becker and Gilles Candar, *Histoire des gauches en France*, vol. 2: *XXe siècle: À l'épreuve de l'histoire*, 2nd ed. (Paris: La Découverte, 2005), esp. 119–134. See also Deborah Lipstadt, *Denying the Holocaust: The Growing Assault on Truth and Memory* (London: Penguin Books, 1994). In this comprehensive study, unfortunately, Lipstadt does not seem to fully recognize the sepecificity of the left-wing denial.

THE ORIGINS OF AN IDEOLOGICAL PERVERSION: THE ANARCHO-PACIFISM OF PAUL RASSINIER

Paul Rassinier (1906–1967) was a key figure in this affair.[4] His story is not only inherently interesting but also quite instructive. What at first glance seems merely a bizarre and meaningless curiosity is, in fact, a tale of some significance. First of all, Rassinier was widely influential; his writings, revelatory as they were to our friend Guillaume, became thereby an important factor in making Holocaust denial a public issue in France. Even more significantly, Rassinier's story, in its very dubiousness, illustrates a kind of perversion to which ideologies – in this case an ideology of what is called "the left" – are prone. It is no accident that Rassinier ended up collaborating with the radical, anti-Semitic right; no accident that he had successors like Guillaume and his friends; and no accident that the message he preached was widely accepted.

As a youth, Rassinier joined the Communist Party; he later became an activist in the Socialist Party, and all his life he held pacifist and proto-anarchist views. Despite his pacifism, he joined the Resistance in World War II, though he never took part in any activity of a violent nature. He was caught by the Gestapo, tortured, and sent first to Buchenwald. A while later, he was transferred to Dora, a work camp where thousands of slave laborers (along with German and non-German volunteers) were employed building the V1 and V2 rockets. Very few survived the terrible conditions in this camp.

After the liberation, Rassinier was politically active for a short time in the Socialist Party, even being elected to the National Assembly (the one that, immediately after the war, laid the foundations for the Fourth Republic). When his brief political career came to an end, Rassinier began to write. He composed and published a long series of books and other works dealing mainly with what we call denial of the Holocaust. In his first work, which appeared in 1948, he described his life as a camp inmate. This essay is of considerable interest as testimony to the terrible reality of the concentration camps. But we already see in it the writer's intention to provide a counterweight to other descriptions of the Nazi concentration camps, provided by other survivors as part of a literature that began to appear at this time. Rassinier, as an eyewitness, tried to show that there was nothing unique about the Nazi camps.

---

[4] On Rassinier, see Florent Brayard, *Comment l'idée vint à M. Rassinier: Naissance du révisionisme* (Paris: Fayard, 1996); and Nadine Fresco, *Fabrication d'un anti-Semite* (Paris: Seuil, 1999). What follows here relies mainly on Fresco's book.

In 1950 the book that was to prove such a revelation to Guillaume, *La mensonge d'Ulysse* (Ulysses' Lie), was published. It was here, in effect, that explicit Holocaust denial on the part of the left began.[5] In Rassinier's view, the memoirs of former prisoners and survivors of the Nazi concentration camps presented a distorted view of the phenomenon of the camps. Telling what the hardships of the camps had been like, they were like Ulysses, who, each day, embarked on another adventure in his odyssey: they painted an unnecessarily black picture. Rassinier was particularly opposed to efforts to present a Manichaean view of the modern world, to depict Nazi Germany as the incarnation of absolute evil and what had been done in the concentration camps as uniquely wicked. Rather, he sought to be precise and truthful. Among others, Rassinier took issue in his book with the interpretation of the world of the Nazi camps presented by another former Buchenwald inmate, David Rousset. Rousset's writings represent, on the whole, an important attempt, one of the first and most significant made after the war, to understand the Nazi phenomenon. Rassinier disputed Rousset's interpretation of the camps, according to which the real purpose of what went on there was the absolute destruction of whole categories of human beings whom the Nazis saw as mortal enemies. It was not only physical destruction, that is, systematic murder, but also symbolic destruction – humiliation and, in fact, eradication of the victims' humanity – that necessitated keeping them alive as prisoners over long periods of time. According to Rassinier, the camps were merely another manifestation, however extreme and cruel, of the universal logic of exploitation and enslavement. Holding prisoner masses of people who were on the verge of death, while negating their dignity and humanity, was not part of a policy of destruction (indeed, had no symbolic significance) but rather flowed from utilitarian considerations and was done according to the inexorable logic of war *qua* war. The Germans needed the prisoners' labor, and wartime conditions meant that putting masses of people to work for the good of the Reich – employment that did not differ in principle from the way all countries exploit the labor of their citizens – would result, in an

---

[5] In 1979 La Vieille Taupe published Rassinier's first two works in a single volume entitled *Mensonge d'Ulysse*. The first part, originally titled *Passage de la ligne*, was renamed *L'experience vécue*, and the second, originally titled *Mensonge d'Ulysse*, was renamed *L'expérience des autres*. An English translation of the combined work was first published as *Debunking the Genocide Myth: A Study of the Nazi Concentration Camps and the Alleged Extermination of European Jewry* (Los Angeles: Noonday, 1978) and later retitled *The Holocaust Story and the Lies of Ulysses: A Study of the German Concentration Camps and the Alleged Extermination of European Jewry* (Los Angeles: Noonday, 1978). The latter can be accessed at http://www.ihr.org/books/rassinier/debunking.shtml.

unusual way, in the death of many prisoners. But the Nazi camps, Rassinier said, were not the result or expression of any particularly murderous philosophy, different in principle from anything else produced by the state or the enslavement and exploitation upon which it depended.

Ulysses' Lie purports to be an original contribution to the debate that began in the French left after the nature of the Stalinist regime and its gulags came to light. Rassinier was opposed to presenting the Nazi camps as the embodiment of a special wickedness. He also opposed singling out the Soviet and German camps as the sole expressions of an unprecedented evil, that of totalitarianism. He had been against the tendency before the war among historians, political scientists, and other intellectuals to comprehend these two twentieth-century regimes, the National Socialist and the Soviet, under the rubric "totalitarianism." According to him, Nazi concentration camps were not really a unique historical phenomenon. Not only did they not differ from Soviet camps; they did not differ from French penal institutions either: a camp is a camp is a camp, as we were to hear fifty years later from various self-styled progressive writers.[6] It is merely an expression, more or less severe according to circumstances, of the essence of the state as such, not just of the Nazi SS state or even the totalitarian state. For Rassinier, the underlying logic of the essence of the state is the logic of war and enslavement. The task of the intellectual of the left, especially one who himself has witnessed such events, is, on the one hand, to warn against the Manichaeism that places all the blame on one side, thus provoking war, and, on the other hand, to strip the other side of its claim to moral superiority. It is war itself that is the absolute evil, not one warmongering party or another.

What makes this anarcho-pacifist argument somewhat questionable is, of course, the gas chambers. About these, Rassinier has the following to say: one of the fixed features of life in the camps was the "selection," a result of the need to distinguish between prisoners fit to work and all kinds of sick and handicapped people who could not. The brutality of the selection in certain camps was such that those who survived believed they had been saved from the gas chambers. The accepted claim that the gas chambers were used for extermination cannot, he admits, be completely denied. But, he says, if one day we discover in the Nazi archives documents showing that gas chambers were built for purposes other than extermination – and we can never

---

[6] This is the view of Giorgio Agamben, for example, a new prophet with disciples in Israel as well. See my discussion in Chapter 2. For a comprehensive history and critique of "progressive" ideologies, see Pierre-André Taguieff, *Les contre-réactionaire: Le progressisme entre illusion et imposture* (Paris: Denoël, 2007).

know what "the terrible scientific genius of the Germans" was capable of inventing – "then we shall have to admit that the use [of the gas chambers for killing] was, in certain cases, the work of one or two mad SS men" or of some camp bureaucrats. One way or the other, he adds, there is a revealing fact that must be pointed out and has never been properly stressed: "In those few camps where gas chambers were found, they were next to the sanitation facilities, used for disinfection and showering, ... and not next to the crematoria." What is more, the materials used in the gas chambers do not necessarily indicate intent to kill. Yes, thinks Rassinier, there were indeed gas chambers, and people were killed in them, but the numbers killed were much smaller than those generally given. In the last analysis, what is really bad about the gas chambers is that the rumor about them has contributed to the myth that the Nazi concentration camps were unique.

Jews are hardly mentioned in Rassinier's book, and extermination is not dealt with there as a particularly Jewish matter. The argument is on a general political level, as it were, largely within the left-wing camp. But the Jewish context is not absent from the postwar literature of denial. The first of the French deniers was Maurice Bardèche, a professor of literature, a rightist, and an avowed anti-Semite, who immediately after the war maintained that both Vichy and the collaboration had been legitimate and that the tale of extermination was a distortion and a lie. Bardèche also claimed, as early as 1948, that it was actually the Jews who had been responsible for the world war, and it was mainly they who had invented the lie that the Germans had been responsible for it, a lie they were spreading in order to win control of Palestine. What motivated Bardèche, above all, was the struggle against De Gaulle's republicanism and, especially, his sharp opposition to hunting down the *collabos*, that is, those who had collaborated with the German occupation of France, in the course of which his brother-in-law Robert Brasillach, one of the leading intellectuals of the fascist, Vichy-supporting right wing in France, had been executed.[7] Bardèche is a typical Holocaust denier, a rightist anti-Semite of the nationalist, racist, Catholic variety. He is of interest to us for two main reasons. First is the very early date – almost immediately after the war – that, in his writing and diverse public activity, he began a systematic campaign of denial that the Jews had been exterminated by the Nazis. The other, more important reason is the alliance that was quickly made between him and Rassinier. In fact, it was Bardèche who was mainly responsible for bringing Rassinier to public attention and making

---

[7] On Brasillach, see, e.g., Zeev Sternhell, *Neither Right nor Left: Fascist Ideology in France* (Princeton: Princeton University Press, 1996).

him a significant public figure in France, beginning in the early 1950s. The connection between Bardèche and Rassinier made for an alliance of radical right and radical left concerned mainly with denial of the Holocaust. Thus, by a kind of perverse osmosis, the basic themes of this denial crossed the boundary separating the two political camps, creating a shared ideology: anti-Semitism, anti-Zionism, anti-Israelism, anti-Communism, and pacifism. Rassinier himself, incidentally, was drawn more and more to the radical right, although he continued to be tied in various ways, particularly in the many articles he published, to several anarchist and pacifist groups on the radical left. Eventually, most of his left-wing friends distanced themselves from him, not so much because of his anti-Semitism, anti-Zionism, or Holocaust denial, but because of his close ties with the neofascist right; but this estrangement was never complete. The theory disputing the claim that the Jews had been exterminated gained a real foothold among some radical left-wing groups. In different guises and incarnations, it became an ideological mainstay of certain not-insignificant circles on the left, especially in France but also in Europe generally and in North and South America.

In any event, Rassinier did not rest content but continued to write books and articles on a variety of subjects. In 1962 his book *La véritable procès Eichmann ou les vainquers incorrigibles* appeared (published in English as *The Real Eichmann Trial, or The Incorrigible Victors*).[8] In this book, and in a kind of ongoing crescendo throughout his writings (Rassinier wrote and published twelve books), there was an increasing focus on two main points, between which there was an interesting dialectical relationship. On the one hand, Rassinier's opposition to the attempt to present Nazism and the concentration camps as a unique historical phenomenon became a more and more explicit rehabilitation of Germany and of Hitler. On the other hand, in a strange kind of mirror image, Rassinier found a decided uniqueness in the Jews and Zionism. More and more, his writings turned into a campaign of blame: Israel was the true enemy; it, rather than Nazism, was the embodiment of evil; and it was also different from all other countries. Rassinier's last book, published shortly before his death, is entitled *Those Responsible for the Second World War*, and its main argument is that Jewish influence (on leaders like Roosevelt, Churchill, and Leon Blum) caused the outbreak of the war. As he noted in *The Real Eichmann Trial*, "Massed at the foot of a world-sized wailing wall, day and night for fifteen years, Zionists from all over the world – all Israelis are not, happily, Zionists – have cried unceasingly,

---

[8] Paul Rassinier, *The Real Eichmann Trial, or The Incorrigible Victors* (Silver Spring, Md.: Steppingstones, 1979; Ladbroke, Southam, Warwickshire: Historical Review Press, 1979).

every day more gruesomely, every day more agonizingly. The purpose is to publicize what they consider the true and apocalyptic proportions of the horror and the tortures the Jewish world suffered from Nazism, and thereby to increase the amount of reparations which the State of Israel receives from Germany" (p. 47). Rassinier also announced on the flyleaf of his last book that he was about to publish a history of the State of Israel.

Rassinier's main factual claim, one that became the symbolic focus of the entire phenomenon of denial, was that systematic murder in the gas chambers never took place. On the basis of numerous, exhaustively documented calculations, he reached the conclusion that the number of Jews in Europe before the war was some seventeen million, of whom about a million died in the course of the war. On this basis, he posed a hermeneutical question: what conclusion may be drawn from the fact that the Jews had been concentrated in special camps? The answer was: nothing, except that this was a logical outcome of the racist character of Hitler's Germany. True, he maintained, there were no moral grounds for discriminating against the Jews, "but then, the fact that in no country in the world is an alien given a post of command is not the question" (ibid., p. 108). Hitler, whose sole objective was to protect Germany's racial purity, was prepared to allow the Jews to emigrate. But no one, including those who today attack Germany so self-righteously, was prepared to take them in. The only difference between Nazi Germany and other countries was that, in the latter, "foreignness" was determined by citizenship, whereas in Germany it was a matter of race. "But in Israel there are no Arabs who are schoolmasters, finance administrators or administrators of a kibbutz, or ministers. What takes place in Israel does not justify what took place in Germany, I repeat – if only because one cannot justify one wrong with another" (ibid.). This is worth repeating: it is not that Israeli actions cannot be justified by Nazi evil but, on the contrary, that Israel's crimes do not justify (retrospectively, of course) those of the Germans. Israel is radically evil and, indeed, the standard of evil by which other manifestations of it are to be measured.

Quite a bit has been written about Rassinier in recent years. The story of a man of the left, a member of the Resistance, who had been imprisoned in the camps and was among the few to survive the depredations of Dora, but who, when he came back from the war, became one of the chief Holocaust deniers and an associate of the extreme, fascist, anti-Semitic right wing – while continuing to view himself as a socialist and pacifist – has made him an object of curiosity and wonderment. What is ostensibly unique about this perversion but, in fact, not characteristic of it alone is the path taken by Rassinier from the pacifist, anarchist left to the radical, nationalistic, Vichyite, pro-Nazi right. The amazing fact that he had been a prisoner in Nazi concentration camps and seen with his own eyes and experienced with his own flesh the horrors of those places makes his denial of the Holocaust more than just a psychological aberration, of interest only to researchers into the human psyche. Were it merely a story of madness, Rassinier's would have been a banal one. Even his anti-Semitism, as important an element as it was in his worldview – as Nadine Persco, for example, thinks – does not fully account for it. Rassinier's story is a matter for political theorists no less than psychologists. There is an inner logic to this madness, a method, if you like, that is not incidental or peculiar to Rassinier. Rassinier's perversion illustrates how ideology – in this case, the ideology of the anarchist and pacifist left – can lose its mind, precisely because of its high degree of consistency. This method, or logic, is typical – in fact, paradigmatic. We find it in other highly consistent ideologies, including Jewish and Israeli ones, which, like Rassinier, have arrived at a position that ties the Holocaust up in an anti-Israeli, anti-Zionist Gordian knot.

Reflecting on the story of Rassinier's life and reading his writings are a lesson in the genesis of a perversion and in the mechanisms by which ideology can triumph over reality. Rassinier's ideological roots were in the pacifist, anarchist left that flourished in France in the interwar period. Rassinier belonged to a generation whose view of the world was shaped by the catastrophe brought upon France (and all of Europe) by a war whose utter stupidity was no longer questionable. The power of the state to mobilize the patriotism of millions, to exploit the readiness of an entire generation of young people to sacrifice their lives for an abstract "love of country," was regarded by many good people as unacceptable. War itself was, in their view, not only a demonstration of abysmal folly but also an unforgivable sin.[9] *Plus jamais ça* (never again), where *ça* referred to war, was the slogan of a whole generation of Frenchmen who grew up between the world wars. The slogan *paix immédiate* (peace now), later to become popular in Israel and elsewhere, was used in France, too, for example, in a manifesto written and disseminated as early as 1939 by one Louis Lecoin (for which he was arrested), the same Lecoin who, after the Second World War, founded

---

[9] One literary expression of this way of thinking is a book, famous in its day, by Nobel laureate Roger Martin Du Gard, *The Thibaults* (New York: Viking, 1939). The six volumes of this novel (in the Hebrew translation) were read avidly by many Israelis, one of whom was the present writer. The book ends with a deathbed testament written by the physician Antoine, brother of the hero Jacques (who was killed in a failed attempt to head off the war), to his brother's son. Antoine did not understand the nature of war. His testament – and the book as a whole, – ends with the words, "Do not obey!"

the proto-anarchist journal *Défense de l'homme* (Defense of Man), where
Rassinier was to publish his articles for several years.

This pacifism took various forms and was expressed in different ways.
Because patriotism and nationalism (not necessarily the same thing) were
rightly regarded as essential preconditions for the catastrophe of the First
World War, this pacifism led to a suspicion of the state as such, even the
liberal, democratic one. Although it was a worldview and political commitment of the left (and was so regarded by its devotees), it was not necessarily
connected with a Marxist or revolutionary ideology, although many of the
pacifists held socialist views and although their immediate enemy was the
right, especially the radical, fascist right. One of the most interesting manifestations of this way of thinking – at least for those interested in French
philosophy of the interwar period and the sources of contemporary French
thought, which has so many devotees, of course, in the United States as well
as in Israel – is "Alainist" pacifism. This was a view espoused by many of the
important young intellectuals of that period, students at the famous École
Normale Supérieure and the equally famous preparatory classes (*classes
préparatoires*).[10] Alain, as Émile-Auguste Chartier (1868–1951) called himself, was a well-known philosopher – some of his work is still of interest –
and an even more influential teacher. He taught in one of the better-regarded
preparatory classes and left a deep imprint on many of those who would go
on to study at the École Normale – hence, on a substantial part of the French
intellectual elite. Alain saw philosophy first and foremost as ethics, that is, a
theory of right living, and he understood his task as a philosopher in Socratic
terms, as a teacher. Among the most famous students to pass through the
elite educational institutions during that period and to be influenced by
Alain's pacifism were Jean-Paul Sartre, Maurice Merleau-Ponty, Raymond
Aron, Claude Lévi-Strauss, and many others less familiar to the non-French
reader. By the twenties and thirties, these people had already become a cultural, intellectual, and political elite, and their influence on public opinion
and political culture in France was already considerable.

Alain devoted an entire book to his pacifist ideas: *Mars, ou la guerre
jugée* (Mars, or War on Trial).[11] In this book he does not, as usual, offer a
systematic theory of pacifism but rather a long series – 113 paragraphs, to be

---

[10] A few students were accepted to the École Normale Supérieure, and only after taking the
national Concours examination. Preparation for the latter was done in special classes,
called *khagne* and *hypo-khagne*, which, while postsecondary, were usually held in the
buildings of the better-known, elite French high schools and, of course, in and around
Paris. This system is still operating today.

[11] Alain, *Mars* (London: J. Cape; New York: J. Cape & H. Smith, 1930).

exact – of sayings, notes (from his experience as a soldier in the First World War), and observations about the nature of war, militarism, the pretexts that bring people to the battlefield, relations between government and citizenry, and more. The book is a harsh, uncompromising indictment of war. It was published in 1936, at a time when many Frenchmen (and others) – among them, here and there, some graduates of the École Normale and his own students – had already begun to recognize the true nature of the National Socialist regime in Germany. Alain's pacifist disciples were to meet different fates. Some of them, like Georges Canguilhem and Raymond Aron, joined the Resistance or became active in the Free French Forces. Others, like Sartre and Merleau-Ponty, carried on with their own affairs under the German occupation, even writing some of their most important works at that time. One of his disciples, Simone Weil (not the politician and former cabinet minister of that name), was undoubtedly among the most interesting pacifist figures of the twenties and thirties. A Jew always on the verge of conversion to Christianity, detesting her own Jewishness and Judaism in general, an original philosopher, and a fascinating personality, Weil was, at one stage, a pacifist with Marxist leanings but also a person of deep religiosity. When the Second World War broke out, and she understood what was happening in occupied Europe, Weil "repented" and devoted herself entirely, in fact gave her life, to the cause of Free France, moving from the United States to London to join De Gaulle. She came to regret the political blindness that had prevented her and her pacifist comrades from, as it were, stopping the horror while there was still time.

There were also those who collaborated with the Germans and worked in the Pétain government. How does one get from pacifism to collaboration with one of the most combative and murderous of political regimes? No doubt, some were motivated by mere opportunism, weakness of will, or innate wickedness; for others, it turns out that pacifism can, under certain circumstances, turn into its diametric opposite. Pacifism views war as the ultimate evil. War can never be acceptable, and no war is just. Every war is a human act, and only fatalism (according to Alain) and moral and political helplessness lead us to think that wars are unavoidable. The young and not-so-young pacifists were, as a rule, genuinely idealistic. They believed the Kantian ideal of eternal peace was feasible. Many of them were innocently and wholeheartedly committed, out of deep conviction and truly moral, even admirable motives, to a political program that called for doing everything possible to stop war. When the true nature of the Nazi regime, especially its murderous anti-Semitism, began to emerge, the question naturally arose as to what, in precise, concrete terms, it would mean to prevent war "at all costs." For example, Bertrand Russell, himself a consistent and militant pacifist, enunciated at this time the theory of "moderate pacifism," according to which it was, nevertheless, imperative to take up arms against Nazism. Others answered the question differently, for example, by an absolute refusal to recognize the existence of any evil greater than that of war itself – seeing the latter as an evil to be fought more than any enemy. The establishment of the Vichy regime could be seen from a stubbornly pacifistic point of view as a necessary compromise with a lesser evil in order to prevent a greater one. And if the Jews had to be sacrificed in order to avoid war, it was a price consistent pacifism was prepared to pay. It was not a great leap from this to a refusal to see the destruction of the Jews as a greater evil than taking part in war or supporting it. And it is not hard to imagine how such thinking could quickly give rise to a denial of the severity of the evil eventually done to the Jews, that is, a denial of the Holocaust itself.

Rassinier's denial did, in fact, grow in the intellectual hothouse of the French left of the 1920s, with its characteristic pacifism. The French Communist Party was founded in 1920 following a split in the Socialist Party over the question of the proper relationship to the Socialist International and the Soviet Communist Party. Shortly afterward, when he was eighteen, Rassinier joined the communist ranks. The war and its consequences, and the struggle against nationalism, chauvinism, and imperialism, were the main planks in the political platform of communism during the years when Rassinier was a member of the party. The international communist movement was, even then, presenting itself as the "peace camp" and identifying the defense of the Soviet Union with the preservation of world peace. Rassinier was quite active in the party in the region of eastern France where he lived, going from one group to another, and keeping an eye on the ideological purity of his comrades, until, in 1932, he was expelled from the party. His expulsion was against the background of an ideological uproar brought on by a critique of the French party by the Communist International. Two years later, he joined the Socialist Party. These were the years of Hitler's rise to power in Germany, when the question of war and the price of preventing it became the main topic of political controversy in France and in Europe as a whole. The Socialist Party was a bastion of antiwar sentiment, of what Leon Blum, in 1945, called a "holy terror" of war.

Leon Blum and Paul Faure were the leaders of French socialism in that period. Rassinier was a disciple of Faure, who, like Alain, experienced World War I in his flesh. Faure made his pacifism and opposition to war, along with his anticommunism, his major political concern. He rejected any compromise with Bolshevism, even opposing the antifascist covenant to which the entire left subscribed. Most important in his mind was reaching an agreement with Hitler and Mussolini that would make it possible to avert war. He consistently supported all the concessions that were made to Hitler and was a fervent supporter of the Munich Agreement. In fact, even after the war, Faure did not change his mind. Leon Blum, on the other hand, opposed Munich, even though he received the agreement made with Hitler by the French Daladier and the British Chamberlain with a "cowardly relief," as he put it in another well-known statement. As the signing of the Munich Agreement approached, a great rift opened in the ranks of Blum's Socialist Party, between him and Faure's supporters. Blum opposed the agreement, in spite of the relief he felt once it was signed, while Faure supported it wholeheartedly. Incidentally, Faure also collaborated with the Vichy regime.

At the time of the rift in socialist ranks in the months preceding the Munich Agreement and the outbreak of war, one could already hear pronouncements from activists in Blum's party saying that socialism was not a ghetto, that socialists should oppose Jewish domination, and, above all, that they were not prepared to fight in a Jewish war.[12] The guilt of the Jews for having fanned the flames of World War II was, as we have seen, also a central theme for Rassinier. Like the Faurian pacifists, he thought that war was an absolute evil that must be prevented at all costs, an evil of human making and not an unavoidable natural disaster. Nazism was the outcome of the Versailles Treaty, and thus the wheel of this agreement had to be rolled back in order to prevent war. It is human beings who fight against one other, on both sides of the front, and the atrocities that take place are the direct result of war itself, not the wickedness of one side or the other. Atrocities are committed by every government that wages war. Governments – they themselves and the inherent logic of the state and of war that determines their behavior – are the source of war and its terrors; one must therefore take care not to confuse what is truly evil – war itself – with one or another of the rival camps. This is the basic pacifist doctrine to which Rassinier remained faithful all his life. This is the ideology that went mad and turned into denial of the Holocaust and hatred of Israel.

THE MEANING OF A METAPHOR: "IDEOLOGICAL PERVERSION"

It is not my intention here to question pacifist thinking. Pacifism is a legitimate philosophical and political position. It can be defended with rational arguments, and it expresses an ancient and exalted human ideal: peace.

[12] Cited in Ilan Greilsammer, *Blum* (Paris: Flammarion, 1996) (in French).

Pacifism often has respectable motives, and there is no need to doubt a priori the integrity or sincerity of those who hold pacifist views. At the same time, one can argue against pacifism, or at least certain versions of it. For example, one might question its basic assumptions about, or its interpretations of, the nature of political reality, noting that human history is not just a march of folly but also of violence, cruelty, and war. On the other hand, war's stubborn persistence in human life does not in itself negate the validity – moral, philosophical, or even political – of the ideal of "eternal peace," as Spengler, for example, thought. The validity of an idea does not depend on whether it is realized by human beings; the refusal to resort to violence is a moral imperative that is not nullified by the fact that people are violent.

But there is another claim that not only casts doubt on the philosophical and intellectual basis of pacifism but also calls it, or at least certain manifestations of it, into question on moral grounds. The history of the twentieth century shows that a pacifist approach can sometimes promote the spread of violence far worse than that which the pacifists are seeking to avoid. The best-known and most self-evident example is, of course, the appeasement of Hitler's Germany by Britain and France on the eve of the Second World War. If we stick to the French example, there is no doubt that the pacifism of large parts of French public opinion, especially on the left, greatly influenced the appeasement policy of the Daladier government on the eve of the war.

As we have pointed out, pacifists did not all react to the war in the same way. We certainly cannot say that pacifist positions inevitably led to Holocaust denial or that all pacifists became Holocaust deniers. On the contrary, only a small minority of them followed Rassinier. Nevertheless, Rassinier's Holocaust denial is not, as we have also said, just a private perversion or madness. The theoretical and ideological nature of his work, as well as its pacifist and socialist roots, is at the heart of his literary opus, and without them the latter is unintelligible. It is a kind of ideological distortion that goes beyond the particular case of Rassinier. It is the story of an ideology gone mad.

The metaphor "ideological perversion" or "ideology gone mad" has already been mentioned a number of times. We should clarify it further. In the broadest sense, "perversion" refers to a deviation from what is normal. Normalcy – and, hence, also deviation from it – can be understood empirically and statistically. Thus, for example, one might view as "normal" the way that a large part of a given population behaves. Perversion would thus be a deviation from what is perceived to be "standard" or "normal." We may associate the "normal" with the majority of the population and the "abnormal" with everything that is different from the "normal." Understood in purely statistical terms, perversion may be thought of as what moves away from the center of a distribution toward its "tails." There is a predictable distribution, for example, of certain physical traits or patterns of behavior in a given population. That which occurs most frequently is "normal." But the term "perversion," generally used to refer to deviant sexual behavior, means a deviation that is not merely statistical but "normative," a deviation from what "should" be, what is "right" or "proper" or "healthy" to do. Incidentally, it was the French philosopher Georges Canguilhem, mentioned previously as one of the Alainist pacifists who then became a hero of the Resistance, who studied the conceptual structure of the distinction between the abnormal and the pathological. He did his research during the years of the Nazi occupation.[13]

Even further removed from the merely statistical sense of "perversion" is the meaning given to the word in moral philosophy. When Kant, for example, tries to define radical evil, that is, evil that cannot be accepted, forgiven, or dismissed as stemming from natural causes, he uses the expression "die Verkehrtheit (perversitas) des menschlichen Herzens," the perversity of the human heart.[14] But perversity of the heart, its deviation from the norms of right conduct, is not just that which is to be found on the margins of what is called normalcy. Even if everyone behaved in the way described by these metaphors, it would still be a perversion of the heart, a deviation from the norm. The sole righteous man in Sodom is still righteous, even if he is the only one, and the rest, though they may be in the majority, are, from a moral point view, the "perverts." For Kant and his followers, the notion of perversity refers to an analogy and a nearly unbreakable linkage between two kinds of normativity: the moral and the clinical.

The term "ideology," too, has different meanings and, in fact, cannot be defined in a way that refers to a single phenomenon that is easy to locate objectively or is readily analyzable. It has usages that are both negative and positive, both critical and laudatory. Sometimes it is a term of disparagement, while at other times it connotes the basis of proper political action. In the broadest sense, the term refers to a connection between thought, theory, and understanding, on the one hand, and political action on the other. It applies to political programs based upon an attempt, real or imagined, to understand human social and economic reality or, at times, the higher laws governing all reality. It also relates to moral commitments; the ends and means of political

---

[13] Georges Canguilhem, *The Normal and the Pathological* (New York: Zone Books, 1989).
[14] Immanuel Kant, *Religion within the Limits of Reason Alone* (New York: Harper, 1960), 25–26.

action; the nature of such values as justice, freedom, and equality; and the role these values should play in constructing a program of political action.

Leaving the moral domain aside, the two terms that are linked in the expression "ideological perversion" are thus derived, at least in normal usage, from two distinct theoretical spaces, psychology (or psychopathology) and political theory. It would seem possible to understand this metaphor as referring to the psychologization of the political or the politicization of the psychic – that is, as something reductive. The first type of reduction rests on a conviction that political phenomena can be explained using terms borrowed from psychology, such as unresolved neuroses or other mental malfunctions. The second type of reduction is based on the opposite view, that certain psychopathologies have political causes. A well-known example that combines these two types of reduction is to be found in the theories of Erich Fromm and the Frankfurt school (especially Adorno) about the authoritarian personality, which is characteristic of people living under totalitarian regimes. This theory is sometimes expanded to assert that the conditions of modern societies in general appear to foster a certain personality type, which, in turn, leads to the behavior patterns typical of people living in totalitarian states (or, in the view of others, all states): absolute obedience to authority, even to the point of carrying out the most terrible and criminal of orders, as well as an ability or need to impose absolute obedience on one's underlings and treat them with great cruelty.

There may be some truth in both these kinds of reduction, but they do not convey the meaning of "ideological perversion" in our context. The assumption underlying our use of this expression is that the political realm is autonomous, sui generis, and cannot be understood by means of one form of reduction or another or a borrowing from other frames of reference. This irreducibility is conceptual or, if you like, phenomenological. It belongs to the conceptual world of the political. The latter can, and should, be extracted, distilled, or abstracted, so to speak, from concrete reality – always something infinitely complex and multifaceted – if that reality is to be comprehended theoretically. When we speak of the "political," we are speaking of the public realm, of sovereignty and the relations between ruler and ruled; of the form, structure, and organization of the common life, and the institutions that, consciously or not, give concrete form to the principles by which the common life is organized; of the ways in which security, freedom, and equality, and the relations among them, are preserved; of the ways in which a human population creates a space for common endeavor and the means human societies acquire in order to achieve change in the present and build a shared future.

All aspects of the thematic, conceptual realm denoted by the term "political," both those we have mentioned here and others we have not, but especially the last-mentioned aspect (the fashioning of the future), also have a normative meaning. But it is a normativity immanent in the conceptual world of the political, something sui generis that cannot, or should not, be comprehended in terms of the norms and principles of other realms, be they psychological, legal, or moral. One could maintain, for example, that the principles of the separation of powers and of checks and balances are internal and original to the political realm. They cannot be justified by either moral or legal arguments. (They even contradict to some degree the principle of the "rule of law," which is sometimes understood as a demand for the law's supremacy, which might, in extreme cases, take over the entire public realm and become a dictatorship of the law.) One might say that forms of government in which these principles are not protected, in which power is too concentrated, or too diluted, are perversions of the political. They are what we call a tyrannical or dictatorial regime, or an anarchic lack of it. Utopian or messianic thinking is also sometimes a perversion of the political, especially when abstract or imaginary ideals of the perfect order become the basis of a concrete political program.

Similarly, we can speak of the perversion of ideology. Just as certain forces in a society can monopolize political power, something similar can happen in the realm of political thought, the realm of ideology, even the realm of values: when a single idea, principle, or value comes to dominate all thought, becoming the sole basis of all political understanding of the world and its workings, the result is a perversion. This is what happened, for example, to Kleist's Michael Kohlhaas, who laid waste the land in order to avenge an insult and claim restitution for a wrong, palpable enough, that had been done him. For him, it was the principle of justice (a legal principle, but one that also has political significance) that took control of the whole field of action. In the same way, other principles, such as that of equality or that of the need to combat exploitation and slavery, can become enshrined above all other considerations. These are all valid and necessary principles of political life; slavery, exploitation, an unjust distribution of wealth – all are political evils that must be fought unceasingly. When these principles fade, fascism, for example, or unbridled liberalism is born. And yet, when the principle of struggle against exploitation is taken to such an extreme of purism that injustice is countenanced, we have a serious perversion of the political – both political awareness and political action. When peace and the prevention of war become dogmatic principles and an exclusive goal, not only is the concrete outcome of the action likely to prove worse than all the alternatives it was meant to prevent, but also one's ability to see and understand the concrete reality may be damaged beyond repair.

One can accept or reject this theoretical outline. But beyond the general questions, which we could go on debating indefinitely, the term "ideological perversion" has one important advantage that is worth stressing. It allows us to combine two elements that are sometimes regarded as incompatible: on the one hand, the extreme implausibility and non-normativity ("perversion") of ideological and intellectual pacts made with political evil, Holocaust denial being a prime example; and, on the other hand, the full responsibility of the ideologues and intellectuals who make such pacts. Kant saw "perversity of the heart" as belonging to the realm of freedom rather than of nature. Such perversity does not, in his view, exempt one from moral responsibility, nor is there any basis for indulging it. The same is true of ideological perversion. It is not, as a rule, a matter of "error" and certainly not one of insanity that would exempt one from responsibility for his actions. Pierre Guillaume, for example, is a relatively well-educated man who has all the relevant information and research material at his disposal. He is also a man who works for a living, who has (or had) a wife and a child or children (when we met, he spoke about his wife and about the baby they were raising at the time, and in his still-existing Web site one can read about him riding his car and going to visit his daughter), as well as friends. On that occasion in Paris, he was willing to help a stranger like myself without any mention of recompense. In short, he is a perfectly sane, normal person. Psychologically, legally, and even morally, he is both normal and "normative." But in terms of political behavior and the ideology guiding his actions, he is utterly perverted. This perversion does not, again, absolve him or his comrades of full responsibility for their actions or the views they espouse and disseminate. Nor does it make these actions or views any less mad.

An interesting attempt to unravel the inner logic of Rassinier's perversion and draw some general conclusion from it has been made in a book by the French intellectual Alain Finkielkraut, *The Future of a Negation: Reflections on the Question of Genocide*.[15] The attempt was, of course, somewhat speculative, but it also yielded interesting, illuminating insights. Finkielkraut pays relatively little attention to Rassinier's anarcho-pacifist background and sees in his life story and conversion to Holocaust denial the

---

[15] A. Finkielkraut *L'avenir d'une négation. Réflexions sur la question du génocide* (Paris: Seuil, Fiction & Cie, 1982); translated as *The Future of a Negation: Reflexions on the Question of Genocide*, trans. M. B. Kelly (Lincoln: University of Nebraska Press, 1998). References are to the French original.

manifestation – extreme and perverted, of course, but also coherent – of a mentality and, in fact, a kind of political behavior and ideology characteristic of some significant parts of the left in general. According to Finkielkraut, the Rassinier phenomenon is just one expression of something more general that can be called the "Liebknecht syndrome." Here he is referring to the fact that large segments of the European left joined the attack on Dreyfus, or at least failed to rally to the defense of the Jewish officer at the time of the "affair" that bears his name. Finkielkraut quotes (on pp. 24–28) Wilhelm Liebknecht (Karl's father and a Social Democrat leader in his own right), who, in a series of articles, explained why Dreyfus could not be innocent. One could argue with Finkielkraut's reading of Liebknecht, but he is right to point to a tendency of the ideological, and especially the revolutionary, left to divide the world into exploiters and exploited in a way that sometimes leaves no room for other victims. This tendency also makes it possible to remain indifferent to injustice that is apparently not accounted for by class conflict or any other all-encompassing explanatory principle, such as the struggle against colonialism. The proletariat has only one enemy, and that is the class to which Dreyfus belongs, the exploiting class. There is only one just struggle, the struggle against exploitation. Internal rivalries within this class do not interest the working masses, and their revolutionary energies should not be squandered on marginal, unimportant questions about injustices that may or may not have been committed against a member of the exploiting class. Both in Rassinier and in his faithful followers on the radical French left one can find this syndrome: one must not allow the crime that was committed at Auschwitz, as it were, to blind us to the main thing, which is the suffering of those who are truly exploited – the workers, people of the Third World, the Palestinians. What happened at Auschwitz was, in the last analysis, just another instance, among many, of the true source of all crimes: colonialism, imperialism, capitalism, and Zionism. Since the ceaseless concern with Auschwitz distracts us from all these things, we have to get rid of it. Thus, one cannot avoid the conclusion that nothing unique happened at Auschwitz. Its uniqueness can be negated by the claim that there was no systematic, planned extermination of Jews or, alternatively, by the claim that systematic, planned extermination, real or symbolic, is what the Israelis are doing to the Palestinians.

Although Rassinier found his place among people of the extreme right, and although there are close ties among the various groups of deniers, whose obsessions have brought them together in a single International of Denial, this does not mean the left and the right can be lumped together. Although they use the same arguments, and although with the passage of time the differences between them have blurred, one must distinguish between the tradition begun by Rassinier – "left-wing" Holocaust denial – and the denial practiced by the neofascist right. Finkielkraut, who himself comes from left-wing Parisian intellectual circles, stresses the proletarian messianism of revolutionary ideology as being at the root of the radical-left denial of the Holocaust. Although he talks about the centrality for these Holocaust deniers of their anti-Zionist and anti-Israeli obsession, he seems not to recognize it fully. Perhaps this is because his book was written in the early 1980s; perhaps it is because he himself came from the student left of 1968, and he had his own accounts to settle with that period and its aftermath; or perhaps it is because he was not lucky enough to have had the kind of eye-opening conversation with Guillaume that I did. For all these reasons, he was not sufficiently aware of the anti-Zionist and anti-Israeli element in the form of denial he practiced and the key role these ideas play in his particular ideology of denial.[16] Indeed, the victimhood claimed by those who perished at Auschwitz or who speak in their name disturbs the complacency of the dialectical theodicy of the revolution: not only do we have before us a victim that the theory cannot account for, but his victimization is radically meaningless. The extermination of the Jews is not the kind of evil that brings good in its wake, as the bondage of the working masses leads necessarily to the revolution. Thus, this event does not and cannot offer revolutionary solace. All this is interesting and perhaps even correct, but it does not explain the power and uniqueness of the kind of concern with the Jewish catastrophe we find on the left. More particularly, none of this explains the use of denial as a weapon directed almost exclusively against Israel. No less than a revolutionary perversion, what we have here is a specifically anti-Zionist and anti-Israeli perversion. The force of this denial of the Holocaust is directed at Israel no less and perhaps even more than at the advancement of the revolution.

SCHOLARSHIP IN THE SERVICE OF DENIAL AND DENIAL IN
THE SERVICE OF THE REVOLUTION: ROBERT FAURISSON AND
PIERRE GUILLAUME

The anti-Israeli, anti-Zionist bases of denial were exposed with fresh clarity in the generation following Rassinier, particularly after the Eichmann trial

---

[16] Nearly twenty years later, Finkielkraut recognized that the intellectual left classified Israel and Zionism (together with United States, especially of late) as its principal enemy. This emerges in his short book *Au nom de l'autre: Réflexions sur l'antisémitisme qui vient* (Paris: Gallimard, 2003).

and the Six-Day War (Rassinier himself died about a month after the war). They have been reinforced by each new round of violence in the Middle East. Rassinier's principal heir is Robert Faurisson, who first appeared on the denial scene in the mid-1970s. With Guillaume's valuable help, Faurisson became the leading Holocaust denier in France and one of the leaders of the Denial International. He is still active in this field today, although during the 1980s and 1990s he acquired a number of disciples and accomplices who were equally effective. Faurisson himself is not a man of the left, but he has never identified with the right either. In fact, he does not espouse any political ideology, at least not explicitly, and claims to have no commitment other than to historical and scholarly truth. Unlike Rassinier, Faurisson does not present himself as an eyewitness but bases his claims on scholarly research. It turns out that scholarship, too, can serve as a source, and certainly as an excuse and a cover, for perversion. Faurisson taught French literature at the Sorbonne and at the University of Lyon, and the scholarly authority he invokes for refuting the story of the killing of human beings with gas and the systematic, premeditated slaughter of Jews during the Second World War is that of the text scholar. That is, it is the authority of an expert in uncovering the precise meaning of texts and the errors that arise from misunderstanding them. So, for example, he gave his students in Lyon an exercise in literary analysis in which they were asked to answer the question, Is the diary of Anne Frank authentic? Applying this method of text analysis to the story of Anne Frank, like applying it to the story of the Holocaust as a whole, reveals the story to be without foundation. Faurisson also purports to employ the methods of a historian and has even dabbled in chemistry. He takes pride in having made two or three study trips to the archive at Auschwitz, on which many of his scholarly research findings are based. At any rate, it is as scholarly "findings" or "conclusions" that the well-known linguist and political critic Noam Chomsky – recently crowned "the most influential intellectual of the twentieth century" – treats Faurisson's claims that the Jews were not killed with gas nor was there any systematic extermination of them during the Second World War. Chomsky played a major role in turning Faurisson into an internationally known personality and the denial of the Holocaust into a legitimate position. But more about that later.

As we have pointed out, Faurisson does not belong to the left, and his perversion is not quite the same as that of Rassinier or Guillaume. Faurisson's theory is based on two empirical claims and one other claim that is more general and interpretive. The first of the concrete, factual claims, which could, ostensibly, be refuted and which call for objective investigation, is that Hitler never ordered the killing of Jews, or anyone else, because of their race or religion ("Fortunately, the number of Jews exterminated by Hitler comes to … zero," Faurisson states in one of his pamphlets).[17] And the second is that no one was ever killed with gas. Faurisson tries to turn Rassinier's general thesis, with all its symbolic freight, into the focus of a scientific theory and empirical research. He has studied the technical details of the use of Zyklon B gas and come to the conclusion that it could not have been used for killing. Rassinier's argument is cunning, if primitive: he does not deny the existence of the gas chambers, only that they were used for the killing of human beings. On the basis of this distinction, the denial community began to use the expression *"chambers à gaz homicides"* (homicidal gas chambers). The "scientific" question, as it were, became whether such chambers existed. That they did not is proved by Faurisson's "findings" concerning the effects of the gas. He discovered that these effects lasted more than twenty-four hours. Because the bodies piled up in the chambers, as it were, could not have been removed and the chambers readied for more killing in this twenty-four-hour period, it is implausible that extermination was carried out on the scale claimed by those who disseminate lies about the extermination.[18]

The other claim, the hermeneutical or deconstructive one, if you will, probes the deeper motivation underlying the story of the Holocaust, exposing it as a lie by exposing those who would profit from telling it. As in every good detective story, after it is proved that no murder has been committed, a motive must be found for the charge that one has. The genocide of the Jews is a Zionist invention with political and financial consequences, and the prime beneficiary of this lie is the State of Israel. The lie's victims, on the other hand, are the Germans and the Palestinians. This analysis of the motivations

---

[17] Faurisson uses here, in a seemingly clever but in fact crude, primitive way, the well-known difficulty of determining the exact source, character, and timing of the decision to systematically exterminate the Jews. The deliberate attempt to conceal the extermination, the intent behind it, and those responsible for it was simultaneous with the extermination itself and, in fact, a part of it. We can thus say that the denial came into being with the extermination. This fact enables us to place in proper perspective the criticism originating in various circles, and not only among the deniers, of Jewish and Zionist overuse of the Holocaust. From the very outset, an important aspect of the Jewish insistence on speaking about the Holocaust and reminding the whole world of it has been to counter denial and the various attempts to conceal or obliterate from memory the act of extermination.

[18] One of the more interesting figures in this affair was Jean-Claude Pressac, a pharmacist by profession, who joined the ranks of the deniers as a leading disciple of Faurisson. Taking the latter's "findings" quite seriously – indeed, too seriously, as it turns out – he undertook to investigate the matter of the gassing and to disprove it conclusively. He discovered instead that, indeed, many Jews and others had been killed by gas. The result of his investigation is the most comprehensive work on this subject, his *Les crematories d'Auschwitz: La machinerie du meurtre de mass* (Paris: Editions CNRS, 1993).

of the disseminators of the extermination story and the identification of those who benefit from it are the hermeneutic keys to understanding the true nature of the story: it is a tool of blackmail – emotional, moral, political, and economic – employed against Europe and the whole international community. It is this blackmail that gave legitimacy to the State of Israel, that made it possible to establish it on the ruins of Palestinian society, and that makes it possible for Israel to carry on with its policy of occupation and oppression, of which the Palestinians are the victims. The international community goes along with these criminal acts because it is prepared to forgive those who present themselves as the ultimate victims.

In the mid-1970s, Faurisson's writings created a journalistic, political, and legal stir known as the Faurisson affair. The commotion brought back to life the group of revolutionaries *sans* revolution who had gathered around Pierre Guillaume and La Vieille Taupe and made Holocaust denial the focus of their struggle. Aside from the Vieille Taupe group and with some affinity to it, there were another half dozen or more groups of revolutionaries who joined the denial cause. But the public influence of Guillaume and his circle was greater than all of them put together, and it was this circle that played the major role in disseminating Faurisson's doctrines and placing Holocaust denial in the public eye. Of late, Pierre Guillaume and his comrades seem to have lost the momentum they enjoyed in the eighties and early nineties. But La Vieille Taupe has had a phoenix-like revival from time to time, for example, in the wake of the Garaudy affair in 1995; but the revolutionary energy that sustained Guillaume and his comrades seems to have waned somewhat. There are several reasons for this: the revolutionaries of La Vieille Taupe have probably lost some of their youthful fervor, and they may also have had felt the need to provide for their families. The fact that a law has been passed in France making Holocaust denial a crime – the Gayssot Law, put through in 1990 by the socialist government and named for the communist deputy who proposed it – may have played a role. The background for this law was an expansion of the activities of the deniers as well as the rise of Jean-Marie Le Pen's extreme-right-wing National Front Party, its racist campaign against immigration and the African immigrants, and the support of many in its ranks for the cause of denial.[19] But evidently the law has not been successful in stopping the activities of the deniers altogether.[20]

---

[19] In 1987 Le Pen said, in a well-known interview on Europe 1, that the gas chambers were "a detail in the history of the Second World War."

[20] This, at any rate, is what Robert Kahn claims in a study of legislation against Holocaust denial in a number of European countries. There is a running controversy over such

Not only has denial not disappeared and is unlikely to do so in the foreseeable future, but it is flourishing today as never before. The Internet, for example, is a highly effective means of spreading the message. The main center of Holocaust-denial activity is now in the Arab and Muslim world. This fact is closely connected with a possible additional reason for Pierre Guillaume's near disappearance from the public arena. In many respects, his work can be said to have succeeded, and he can take considerable satisfaction from it: the question of the legitimacy of the State of Israel is now open to debate. It is now possible to assert in normative company that the creation of the state was a historic mistake and to suggest, more or less explicitly, that it should be eliminated. The flowering of denial literature in the Arab world, the close ties between the radical left in Europe and Arab anti-Zionism, and the strongly similar views these two camps hold concerning the connection between Israel and the Holocaust – all this only further confirms that the main (and sometimes only) concrete concern of left-wing Holocaust denial is the negation of Zionism and the State of Israel. In Europe, the negation of Israel no longer requires the heavy weaponry of direct denial of the Holocaust, although many of the deniers' claims have been accepted, in a more or less softened, more or less subtle version, by large numbers of other people. Along with the banalization of the idea of destroying the State of Israel, or at least the questioning of its morality and right to exist, there has been a banalization of the denial of the Holocaust. Critics of Zionism and Israel no longer need to speak the language of the anti-Semitic, neofascist right wing, and they no longer require such crude arguments as the claim that the gas chambers never existed (the exaggerated importance attributed to this matter being, after all, just a result of Jewish-Zionist historiography and propaganda, as they never tire of informing us), in order to say what Pierre Guillaume said to me at that meeting in Paris: both the *basis* of the existence of the State of Israel (i.e., the story of the Holocaust) and the *fact* of its existence (i.e., the use of that story to justify its crimes) are a scandal.

It is tempting to conclude that what Rassinier, Guillaume, and their associates represent is nothing but a further grotesque example of the eternal proximity of the radical political extremes: when they despaired of the world proletarian revolution, Guillaume and his friends took shelter in the bosom of

---

legislation, and the dilemmas it raises are not easily resolved, as Kahn ably shows. See R. A. Kahn, *Holocaust Denial and the Law: A Comparative Study* (New York: Palgrave Macmillan, 2004). Very recently, as a result of the uproar over anti-Muslim cartoons, the debate over the value of such laws has arisen anew; those defending Muslim reactions often cite these laws as justifying a limitation on the freedom of speech.

the neo-Nazi right. But that is not the case. True, an unholy alliance between the neofascist right and these retired revolutionaries of the radical left does exist; it is no accident that this alliance is based on Holocaust denial, anti-Zionism, and Judeophobia. Nonetheless, the Holocaust denial of La Vieille Taupe is different. Its devotees have always seen themselves as faithful to the historic – and true – path of the left. Holocaust deniers of Guillaume's stripe are not seeking the rehabilitation of Nazi Germany, Vichy France, or those who collaborated with the German occupation. They are also not interested in defending neo-Nazi ideas or movements, racism, hatred of democracy, or anti-Semitism, to which right-wing deniers have been trying to restore the respectability taken away by the "narrative" (as current jargon has it) of the Holocaust.[21] I have already referred to Guillaume's affirmation of total loyalty to the ideology of the left and the fact that he never changed his political commitments. But, alongside his revolutionary ideology, another major theme can be heard: when I asked him repeatedly to explain what sick imagination could have invented the monstrous lie that men, women, and children were killed with gas, and for what reason it was invented, his reply was the same as Faurisson's. It could not be simpler, and there is nothing difficult or mysterious about it: the lie was invented by the Zionists in order to justify the establishment of the State of Israel and Zionism's other crimes against the Palestinians. In the end – or such, at least, was the impression our meeting left with me – Guillaume's perversion was centered on Israel and Zionism. The real scandal in the whole story of the Holocaust is, in his view, the lie invented by the Jews and the Zionists and then the use they have made of it to justify their criminal acts against the Palestinians, on the other. Guillaume's perversion is driven by a total negation, metaphysical or theological, if you will, of Zionism and the State of Israel, no less than by a revolutionary logic gone mad, of which we have spoken earlier. In fact, this negation is an essential component of his ideological profile and revolutionary fervor, or at least their main concrete expression.

The claim that the fabrication of the gas chambers was meant to facilitate Zionist blackmail – moral, emotional, political, and financial – of the whole world and especially of Europe is one of the central assertions of the deniers. But as a rule it is made as part of a broader moral claim concerning

---

[21] See Yisrael Gutman, *Denying the Holocaust* (Jerusalem: Hebrew University Institute of Contemporary Jewry, Vidal Sassoon International Center for the Study of Antisemitism, and Shazar Library, 1985). Gutman does not deal at all with denial on the left, apart from one sentence about the USSR. Deborah Lipstadt sees it mainly as "a tool of the radical right." See her *Denying the Holocaust*, esp. 101–121. She does mention Guillaume, his activities, and his affiliation with the radical left but does not expand on this.

a world Jewish conspiracy, Jewish control of the media, Jewish political and economic power, and so forth. What makes Guillaume's position different is that it lacks this kind of anti-Semitism. The real evil, he maintains, is not Jews, the Jewish people, or Judaism as such, but Zionism and the State of Israel. Even if there is collaboration or a conspiracy among some or all the Jews in the various countries where they live, their goal is not world domination, for whatever vague purpose, but the conquest of Palestine, the seizure of its land and the subjugation of its people. While the overall ideological context of the charge of Zionist blackmail is the theory that capitalism in general, and American capitalism in particular, have tried to conceal their crimes by blaming Germany and the ideology of radical nationalism, nevertheless the main result of this diversionary tactic is the crime being committed against the Palestinian people. The death of the Jews during the Second World War was not a unique or absolute evil, as Jews claim. There have been other evils of similar magnitude. The real, radical evil, in the last analysis, is in the dubious attempt to distinguish the killing of the Jews from other historical instances of mass killing – and especially in the use of this distinctiveness to justify the killing of Palestinians.

Guillaume's ideology is not identical with Rassinier's. He is neither a pacifist nor an anarchist. His real, absolute enemies are capitalism and imperialism. His theoretical framework for thinking about the Holocaust is also better defined than Rassinier's. The theoretical stance of Guillaume and the left-wing groups that share his struggle is a dialectical one: alongside their seemingly obvious antifascism, they also espouse a radical anti-antifascism, that is, opposition to antifascism as such. It is true that antifascism has, at least since the 1930s, been an important element in the ideology and political activity of the French left. But during the Second World War, the radical left, or at least the more perceptive parts of it, discovered that the war of capitalism and imperialism against fascism was no better than fascism itself. Some radical factions of the left that were particularly perceptive politically understood during the course of the war who their real enemy was. The Trotskyites, for example, had their own resistance movement. But they did not oppose the Vichy regime or the German occupation; rather, they were preparing themselves for a revolution in which they would take up arms against the sole enemy of the working class, namely capitalism in all its forms: fascism on the one side, antifascism on the other.

After the war, there was no longer any disputing the criminal nature of fascism, and so antifascism – insofar as it served as a means of manipulation and of concealing the other crimes of imperialism, colonialism, and capitalism – became a more dangerous and cunning foe than fascism itself.

"Auschwitz, or the Great Alibi" was the title of an article of great importance to the revolutionaries of La Vieille Taupe that appeared in 1960 in the journal *Programme Communiste* and was reprinted by La Vieille Taupe in 1970.[22] The article states, among other things, that capitalism alone is responsible for the killing of the Jews. War is capitalism's way of extricating itself from the crises it regularly inflicts on the masses, and the fate of the Jews must be understood as a part of the reality of war imposed by capitalism. The source of this dreadful fate was not anti-Semitism or any other element unique to Jewish history but cold calculations of profit. What is more, capitalism was not only the cause of the murder of the Jews; as soon as the war ended, it began to exploit the slaughter for its own needs. All the misdeeds of capitalism pale, as it were, in comparison with the murder of the Jews, and capitalism uses this fact to justify its crimes, beginning with Hiroshima and ending with the alienation of labor. The Holocaust is thus the alibi of antifascism. The story, or narrative, of the Holocaust provides antifascism with its main documentary evidence and justification, and so the role this story plays, and the lies based on it, must be exposed. It is not because of fascist leanings – on the contrary, fascism must still be fought – but because the tale of the Holocaust is the means antifascism uses to falsify revolutionary theory. It must therefore be rejected and fought in the same way that fascism itself is.

Auschwitz, then, is the great alibi. It is, to be sure, an alibi with global implications. But what remains, in the end, beyond all dialectics, beyond theory and mere talk, is the concrete evil that must actually be fought: Zionism. With ironclad logic, Israel appears as the incarnation of absolute evil. Auschwitz is, as we have said, the alibi of imperialism and capitalism. The main beneficiaries of Auschwitz and the main disseminators of the story of Auschwitz are Israel and Zionism. Israel is thus the ultimate embodiment of imperialism and capitalism. And so the revolutionary struggle must be, first and foremost, against Zionism. The real victim in this whole affair is the victim of those who invented the lie of the Holocaust, that is, the Palestinians, whose land the Zionists took in the name of an imaginary crime committed against the Jews. The United States, too, is a concrete enemy, especially since the Second Gulf War. But there is a big difference between Israel and the United States: the great power and the cowboy who leads it can

[22] This journal was published by French followers of the Italian communist Amadeo Bordiga (1889–1970), a one-time comrade of Mussolini and Gramsci who exercised great influence on generations of revolutionaries. At the core of his ideology was the notion that the world is essentially evil and that this evil can only be resisted by complete negation. See Becker and Cander, *Histoire des gauches en France*, 128–131.

be condemned, but not much more. By contrast, real, effective pressure can be brought against Israel, and one can even think seriously of eliminating it altogether or at least expunging its "Zionist" character. For example, one can call for boycotts of Israeli universities, but it is hard to imagine anyone banning contact with Harvard or Princeton or, following British participation in the conquest of Iraq, with Cambridge or Oxford.

It would be a mistake to dismiss Pierre Guillaume's work as just another instance of traditional anti-Semitism, not only because Guillaume himself condemns the latter (as we shall see) and has had associates who were Jews.[23] It is obvious that the perversion he and his comrades suffer from is anti-Semitism. It is anti-Semitism because its object is the object of Jew-hatred, or Judeophobia, in all its forms, and because it includes structural elements that recur in all the varied manifestations of the rejection of Judaism, throughout history. But this is anti-Semitism of a special kind that has quickly become as virulent and conspicuous as any of the more familiar varieties that preceded it. While traditional anti-Semitism was essentially a religious, theological negation of Judaism, modern anti-Semitism is distinguished by its racist element, which makes possible the negation not only of Judaism but also of Jews as individuals. But alongside racial anti-Semitism, there is another, equally modern variety, more ideological in character than the racial kind. Like religious anti-Semitism, it seems not to negate Jews as individuals. It recognizes the possibility of changing one's religion or political identity and is prepared to embrace those Jews, even those Israelis, who are non-Zionists or ex-Zionists. What is negated is some sort of shared identity: Jewish nationhood. This identity is sometimes described as "imaginary" and at other times treated as a metaphysical entity. In any case, the Judeophobic fervor of this ideology – which we call "left-wing" – is expressed mainly in the negation of Jewish nationhood and the political expression of that nationhood, the State of Israel.

As we have already pointed out, Pierre Guillaume, an industrious man devoted unwaveringly to the cause of revolution, did not hesitate and ran out to get me various books and documents produced by La Vieille Taupe. Among other things I was fortunate enough to receive on that occasion was

---

[23] The best known is Gabriel Cohn-Bendit, brother of the notorious Danny the Red. The former, himself a Holocaust survivor, defended Faurisson's right to speak out, arguing that his claims should be taken seriously. Eventually Cohn-Bendit distanced himself from Guillaume, although the latter continued to make use of Cohn-Bendit's name and his writings in defense of Faurisson's freedom of speech. Cohn-Bendit's position and statements are quite reminiscent of Chomsky's, both in terms of the use Guillaume made of them and in terms of their effect in giving Faurisson legitimacy.

a book by one Serge Thion, *Vérité historique ou vérité politique? Le dossier de l'affaire Faurisson: La question des chambres à gaz* (Historical Truth or Political Truth? The Faurisson Affair: The Question of the Gas Chambers),[24] as well as some photocopied pages. The pages included exchanges of letters between Guillaume and the French historian Pierre Vidal-Naquet concerning the publication by La Vieille Taupe of the writings of none other than Bernard Lazare. The whole matter is grotesque, writes Vidal-Naquet, a respected classical historian who recently passed away, a very harsh critic of Israel, and a leading opponent of the deniers. But, perhaps because of this, it is of some interest. Two of Lazare's works do, indeed, appear among those published or distributed by La Vieille Taupe.[25]

The two volumes also include introductions by the editor of the series, our friend Pierre Guillaume, who, in the introduction to the first volume, for example, posits that Lazare's analysis of anti-Semitism is still the most important and interesting ever written. One could dispute this judgment without questioning the pioneering importance of the work or the uniqueness of its author. The path he took, in his short life, from assimilation to Zionism; his critical stance within the Zionist movement; the role he played in the Dreyfus affair (he was one of the first to maintain that Dreyfus had been treated unjustly); and the deeply moral character of his personal and political commitments – all this makes Lazare one of the most fascinating and stirring figures of French Jewry in particular and modern Jewry in general. His first book has provided ammunition to more than a few anti-Semites, because it contains criticism, sometimes harsh, of the Jews themselves, to the point of repeating certain traditional anti-Semitic stereotypes.

---

[24] Serge Thion, *Historical Truth or Political Truth? The Faurisson Affair, the Question of the Gas Chambers* (translation of *Vérité historique ou vérité politique? Le dossier de l'affaire Faurisson: La question des chambres à gaz* [Paris: La Vieille Taupe, 1980]), accessed at http://vho.org/aaargh/, the Web site of the Association des Anciens Amateurs de Récits de Guerres et d'Holocaustes.

[25] These books, like several of Chomsky's, were published as part of the series Le puits et la pendule, directed by Pierre Guillaume for the publisher La Différence. Among Chomsky's works included were one he wrote with Edward S. Herman, *The Political Economy of Human Rights* (Boston: South End Press, 1979), and one, *Réponses inédites*, written especially for Guillaume's own publishing house. See B. Lazare, *L'antisémitisme: Son histoire et ses causes* (Paris: La Différence, 1981; published in English as *Anti-Semitism: Its History and Causes*), and *Contre l'antisémitisme: Histoire d'une polémique* (Paris: La Différence, 1983), which includes two short, later essays by Lazare as well as other documents. On Bernard Lazare, see Nelly Wilson, *Bernard Lazare: Antisemitism and the Problem of Jewish Identity in Late 19th-Century France* (Cambridge: Cambridge University Press, 1978). In the French edition (pp. 154–157), Wilson deals with the Guillaume's use of Lazare.

Lazare later retracted many of the things he had written in this book. He became an active Zionist and even served as a delegate to the Zionist Congress. Afterward, he became a severe critic of Herzl and of some of the main policies of the Zionist movement during its first years. But none of this should distract us from the main point, which is that Lazare provides a clear example of the uniqueness of Jewish experience and its national character. He also gives explicit expression to the lessons he learned, as a socialist and a man of the left, from this experience: he objected to the revolutionaries' reduction of anti-Semitism, on the one hand, and of Jewish nationhood, on the other. In other words, Lazare opposes attempts by left-wing ideology to present both anti-Semitism and Jewish existence as mere instances of universal, historical laws, phenomena that will disappear once a new, just, socialist world order is established. Here is the source of Lazare's Zionism: more than an acceptance of the Herzlian (i.e., political and territorial) solution to the Jewish question, it is a recognition of the uniqueness, specificity, and irreducibility (not incomparability, as critics of the Zionist claim of uniqueness charge) of Jewish historical experience and Jewish existence, that is, of Jewish nationhood. Guillaume, at any rate, was pleased by Lazare's critique, as it appears mainly in the first volume, and mined it for all it was worth, presenting a completely distorted picture of this interesting personality.

It is unclear by what authority or on the basis of what expertise in the history of anti-Semitism Guillaume hands out marks to Lazare's or any other work on the subject. In any case, precisely because of his presumed ignorance in this area, the very fact that he saw fit to publish some of Lazare's writings, all the more so his writings on anti-Semitism, is undoubtedly significant. One could speculate about his motives, but it might be better simply to look at the introductions he wrote to the volumes he published. For the first volume, *L'antisémitisme: Son histoire et ses causes*, Guillaume penned a very short preface. It has one main message: anti-Semitism, the editor informs us, is not "theoretically consistent" and it is morally invalid. From this we can at least conclude that Guillaume is not an avowed anti-Semite.

In his longer introduction to the second volume,[26] Guillaume writes, among other things: "The whole life and work of Bernard Lazare demonstrate that

---

[26] The first chapter of Lazare's history of anti-Semitism deals with its economic causes. He saw Jewish homelessness as the reason for the ubiquity of Jew-hatred: "Everywhere, down to our own day, the Jew has been an unsocial creature [*être insociable*]. Why unsocial? Because he has kept himself apart." In his will, Lazare asked that in subsequent editions it be stated at the beginning that he had changed his mind – a request Guillaume did not take the trouble to honor, of course – and it was about this that he and Vidal-Naquet corresponded. In any case, Guillaume makes dialectical use of classic anti-Semitic

the struggle against anti-Semitism is inseparable from criticism of the Jews' own exclusiveness and judeocentricity" (p. 12). The internationalist hope of Lazare's Zionism was not fulfilled "because real Zionism never succeeded in becoming more than a caricature of all [kinds of] nationalism." This hope of Lazare's "became, in fact, a ruse on the part of the left-wing Zionists and certain [other] Jews, whose 'internationalism' went only so far as to criticize the nationalism of others" (p. 15). Or: "As early as 1902, Bernard Lazare (and many others) figured out the inner logic of Zionism and its inevitable future. The deconstruction of Leninist fantasies [by Trotsky] and of Zionist ones [by Lazare] was done in a similar fashion, and the zealots [in both camps] tend to distort or conceal those texts that reveal not only that they have become stick figures but that the script was written in advance" (p. 16). I suspect that some Israeli and non-Israeli Jewish anti-Zionists (see the Postscript) would adhere to much of it: like Guillaume, they are not anti-Semite. Aside from the complete misrepresentation of Lazare's character, thinking, and life experience, what is noteworthy in the latter's anti-anti-Semitism is the use of Lazare's own words about anti-Semitism – a use that is not only inherently scandalous but also silly and anachronistic – in order to negate Israel and Zionism and, indirectly but unavoidably, to justify the denial of the Holocaust.

The charge of concealment, incidentally, alludes to a question that had come up in the correspondence with Vidal-Naquet: Guillaume was accused of ignoring Lazare's will, which stipulated that any future edition of his book on anti-Semitism would have to state at the outset that the author had modified his views considerably since the book was originally written. Guillaume had presented the project of publishing Lazare's writings on anti-Semitism as the rescue of material Lazare's heirs had tried to hide. There is no point in wearying the reader here with the absurdities and pseudoarguments Guillaume employs in his "debate" with Vidal-Naquet. What is important is the claim that the texts the Zionist zealots are trying to hide are the very ones Guillaume is about to publish, among them Lazare's writings on anti-Semitism. The principal message of these writings, he believes, is not about anti-Semitism but about Zionism: that it is a caricature of nationalism. And if nationalism per se is something reprehensible, Zionism is doubly so.

Thus, anti-Semitism is both illogical and immoral. This is Guillaume's opinion. Whatever we think of his views, there is no doubt that at least they demonstrate something distinctive about the Holocaust denial that

arguments in a preposterous campaign against the allegedly incoherent character of anti-Semitism.

originates on the radical left. It is not an expression of anti-Semitism in
the classical sense, for one thing because it is based on the assumption that
anti-Semitism is not logically respectable. Guillaume's ideology, unlike that
of the radical right, is not one of hate. The European left, in many of its
varieties, has always been tainted with anti-Semitism, although there are
different views about the pervasiveness of Jew-hatred on the left in general
and the revolutionary left in particular, about the nature of this hatred, and
about its sources.[27] Left-wing anti-Semitism has been expressed in different ways. Sometimes the expression has been emotional – in which case the
traditional, religious origins of European anti-Semitism are apparent – and
sometimes more ideological and original. The ideological left is frequently
prepared to make political use of the instinctive anti-Semitism of the revolutionary "masses" (e.g., the way the Narodnaya Volya, in which there were
many Jews, related to the pogroms). But, for the most part, it has not been
anti-Semitic in the sense of hating Jews or the Jewish people as such or as the
bearers of some sort of antigospel or eternal curse.

This is, of course, not the place for a discourse on the history or historiography of anti-Semitism. But we can say that anti-Semitism, that is, the hatred
of the Jewish people and the negation of Judaism, is a significant and permanent feature of European culture. While expressions of hostility toward the
Jews and criticism of them are to be found in classical Greek and Hellenistic
literature (as Lazare notes, by the way), the main source of European anti-
Semitism is Christian religious hostility toward Judaism, which took various
forms until it emerged as modern racism. The left, on the other hand, was
never a great devotee of Christian theology, and as for racism, it saw it as
reactionary, even outrageous. If the final form of the negation of Judaism in
European culture is genocidal racism and a kind of nihilistic apotheosis of
anti-Jewish violence (ultimately to be directed at other groups as well), what
is termed "the anti-Semitism of the left" is a different phenomenon. Violence
is not, for the left, a "way of life," nor, as a rule – with exceptions like Georges
Sorrel – is it an ideology. The "direct action" advocated by certain groups of
the radical left has always been given a "dialectical" justification, not only as
a way of achieving political ends but also as a political means of circumvent-
ing representative democracy and avoiding the parliamentary "game." Even

[27] See, e.g., Edmund Silberner, *Hasotzializm hama'aravi ushe'elat hayehudim: Mehkar betoldot
hamahshava hasotzialistit bame'a hetesha-esre* (Western Socialism and the Jewish Question:
A Study in the History of Nineteenth-Century Socialist Thought) (Jerusalem: Mossad Bialik,
1955); and Robert S. Wistrich, *Revolutionary Jews from Marx to Trotsky* (London: Harrap,
1976). On Marx's attitude toward Judaism, see Shlomo Avineri, *The Social and Political
Thought of Karl Marx* (Cambridge: Cambridge University Press, 1968).

the urban terrorism of the seventies and eighties, which was a way of life for certain marginal groups, was not directed against Jews or other "foreign" ethnic groups, but against capitalism, imperialism, and their lackeys, that is, against the state and its institutions. This terrorism was sometimes directed against Israel and Jews because of the alliance between the radical left and the "progressive" Palestinian national movement and because Israel and the Jews were perceived as "lackeys of imperialism," but not out of Jew-hatred of the traditional stripe. Furthermore – and this phenomenological distinction is perhaps the most important of all – the violence of the left is not an explicit or instinctive expression of nihilism but rather of a sense of moral and intellectual superiority.

What most distinguishes the kind of anti-Semitism we find on the left, is, perhaps, its negation of Jewish nationalism, especially Zionism. This negation has always characterized the left. It is true that many European Social Democrats have changed their thinking about this over time, but the revolutionary left has been consistently anti-Zionist. Although one could maintain that the total negation of Jewish national aspirations is a kind of anti-Semitism, one must take into account that for revolutionary ideology the enemy is not the Jews as such but Jewish nationalism, that is, Zionism (as well as movements like the Bund, at certain stages) and Israel. The large number of Jews among the theoreticians, ideologues, and leaders of the socialist, internationalist, and revolutionary movements is no doubt one of the main factors behind the left's criticism of nationalism in general and, in a more specific and complex way, its ideological rivalry with Jewish nationalism. This rivalry has persisted as long as these two revolutionary movements have been around, and at times there has been real hostility toward Zionism. From the beginning, and especially after Zionism's success in realizing its main aim of establishing a Jewish state, Zionism and Israel have been seen by some of the ideologues of the world proletarian revolution as rivals whose importance was inversely proportional to the size of the Jewish people. The landlessness of the Jewish people, the Jews' stubborn insistence on preserving their distinctiveness and giving it political expression, and especially the rise of a Jewish national movement that demanded self-determination and the establishment of a Jewish nation-state – all threatened the picture the Marxists, anarchists, pacifists, and other internationalists had of the world. For a part of the radical left, this threat had an almost preternatural symbolic significance for its revolutionary worldview.

Thus, what is called "the anti-Semitism of the left" is a distinct phenomenon, something specific and irreducible that cannot be understood in a simple, linear way as part of the homogeneous universality of eternal Jew-hatred.

The two are not unconnected, of course, but left-wing anti-Israelism and anti-Zionism must be seen as a particular variety, with its own characteristics, of the general phenomenon of deep, rather irrational animosity directed against Jews or against one form or another of collective manifestations of Jewishness. Its origins probably lie in the antiparticularism of the Enlightenment and especially in the negation of Jewish distinctiveness that came with the French Revolution. Over time, other factors came to play a role: anticolonialism, "Third World–ism," and the like.[28] The upshot was a negation of the idea of Jewish nationhood and, in particular, of the right of the Jewish people to self-determination and self-rule in their own nation-state. This negation has sometimes been no less "annihilationist" than classical anti-Semitism, because, at least potentially, it serves to justify the elimination of the State of Israel. But if one is prepared to draw a distinction between the Jewish state and the Jewish people – that is, if one refuses to see Zionism as the national movement of the entire Jewish people, or the elimination of the State of Israel or its Jewish character as a real or symbolic elimination of the Jews – one could then say that this kind of animosity toward Israel is not directed at the Jewish people or Judaism as such. One way or the other, it has to be admitted that this is an emancipatory ideology: Jews, too, can take part in it on equal terms with the international forces of progress. It allows them to shed their Jewish particularism and exclusivity, or their Israeli cultural and intellectual provincialism, for example, and to become, simply, human beings.

HOLOCAUST DENIAL AND THE STRUGGLE AGAINST ZIONIST IMPERIALISM: SERGE THION AND NOAM CHOMSKY

We have mentioned a book by Serge Thion, who has been one of Guillaume's most important, longtime associates. In many ways, the case of Thion is more significant and instructive than those of Guillaume himself and his revolutionary comrades. His importance stems not only from what he has done and written but also from the fact that he is in every respect an academician, not a member of the intimate, self-contained Vieille Taupe circle. Vidal-Naquet, for example, saw him as the most dangerous of the deniers, because he was the most intelligent of them all. Thion was, until he was expelled for his Holocaust-denial activities, a respected scholar at the Centre

---

[28] The *tiers monde* (Third World). Alain Finkielkraut, in *Au nom de l'autre*, deals mainly with this variety of anti-Israelism.

National de la Recherche Scientifique,[29] an expert on the Third World (he has written about South Africa and Cambodia, among other things), and someone who could be viewed by strictly establishment scholars as a legitimate interlocutor. Like all self-respecting academics, he used to take part in scholarly conferences, and he is also known outside of France. Thion does not align himself politically – he is not committed to Marxist, Trotskyite, or any other ideology – nor was he clearly a marginal figure like Guillaume, either. The left that he represents is that of the postcolonialist sort that bases itself, above all, on a commitment to human and civil rights. This is ostensibly a much saner left, much less eccentric, much more respectable. Its worldview is shared by, among others, Israeli intellectuals who are not ideologues of the revolutionary left. In this respect, Thion serves the cause of anti-Zionism much more effectively than Guillaume and his comrades, in that he represents a much more widespread and respectable anti-Zionism than the revolutionary ideological perversion we have considered up to now. The fact that he joined Guillaume, La Vieille Taupe, and the Holocaust deniers has to be understood in terms not of a revolutionary ideology but of a much more pragmatic, scholarly, and sane anti-Zionism, as it were.

Thion's book presents itself as a strictly factual account of the Faurisson affair.[30] It claims scholarly neutrality and does not presume to take sides regarding "controversial" questions of fact: whether there were gas chambers; whether people were killed in them, and if so, how many and out of what motives; how many Jews were killed in the war, and whether to view their killing as systematic mass murder or their death as a "holocaust." In his view, such questions should be left to experts, and eventually, it is to be hoped, precise answers to them will be found. There is, by the way, a great similarity between this view, expressed by Thion in the first chapter of his book, and what Noam Chomsky writes about Faurisson: neither denies the Holocaust explicitly, but scholarly modesty and honesty prevent them from making hasty, unqualified judgments concerning the questions Faurisson raises or the "findings" of his research. Thion, at least, assumes there is more truth to what Faurisson says than he is generally given credit for and that the questions he raises merit serious scholarly attention. According to Thion, the accepted view about the question of extermination has all the earmarks

---

[29] The Centre National de Recherche Scientifique (CNRS) is the main scientific-research institution in France. It is a government body that encompasses thousands of researchers in every branch of science, working in hundreds of different research centers and laboratories.

[30] See Thion, *Historical Truth or Political Truth?*

of a universal religious belief. It has astonishing weaknesses, and it leaves too many questions unanswered for anyone who approaches the matter dispassionately to accept it as ultimate truth. Were there gas chambers? I cannot answer this question, he replies humbly. In other words, he cannot say unequivocally that there were *no* gas chambers. It could be that, here and there, Jews were killed with gas. That is certainly possible, but we already know that these things could not have been done in the way the historians tell us they were. (Note: Faurisson's "finding," as Chomsky calls it, is that it was scientifically impossible for Zyklon B to have been used in the way described in the familiar testimony, all of it dubious.) No, there was no industrial-scale killing with gas, but Jews were probably gassed on a smaller scale, in a "workmanlike" way (i.e. – how to put it? – manually). And so on.

A few nuggets from this wide-ranging work (350 pages, half devoted to "documents" of the affair)[31] are sufficient to give a whiff of its particular aroma. Because Thion, like the others who contributed to the volume, were interested only in providing a readable account of the facts behind the Faurisson affair as they came to light, much of it is devoted to a detailed description of the way it unfolded. The affair began, Thion writes, in 1974, with the publication of a letter Faurisson wrote to hundreds of experts and Holocaust survivors. He sent one copy to a "Dr. Kubovy," described as "Director of the Jewish Documentation Center, Tel Aviv." (Dr. Aryeh Kubovy had previously been the director of Yad Vashem, the Holocaust memorial and research center in Jerusalem, and, he had died several years before Faurisson sent the letter.) "Someone,"[32] Thion writes, took the

---

[31] The "documents" Thion cites include a journalist's interview with Faurisson; Faurisson's article "Le journal d'Anne Frank est-il authentique?" (in the English edition, "Is the Anne Frank Journal Authentic?"); and three texts written by Jews (one of them the aforementioned Gabriel Cohn-Bendit), which repeat what Thion calls "good news for humanity," that there were no gas chambers. The most macabre and grotesque of all the "documents" is a description, complete with photographs, of the gas chamber of a prison in Baltimore.

[32] The "someone" who brought this letter to the attention of Israeli readers was Haim Gouri, who, on the eve of Shavuot, 5734 (May 26, 1974), published a long article under the title "Hehayeta o halamti halom?" (Did it Happen, or Was I Dreaming?), which includes a photocopy of Faurisson's letter, together with a full translation, and responds to the letter at considerable length, mainly with wonderment and frustration. Faurisson was then relatively unknown and, in Israel, not known at all. It seems clear from the article that, more than ten years after the Eichmann trial, Gouri remained unaware, until receiving the letter, of the existence of the phenomenon of Holocaust denial. But he then immediately captured the impossibility of confronting it with words or perhaps by any other means. Gouri writes briefly about this episode in the introduction to the new edition of his book on the trial, published in Hebrew by Hakibbutz Hame'uhad in 2001, and in English as *Facing the Glass Booth: The Jerusalem Trial of Adolf Eichmann* (Detroit: Wayne State University Press, 2004).

trouble to publish the letter in the Israeli daily *Yediot Aharonot*. From there, the affair got underway: following its publication, the letter was also quoted in French papers, and steps were taken against Faurisson by the Sorbonne (where he was then teaching) and by the academicians' union of which he was a member. Thion's account of the sequence of events, insofar as I have been able to clarify it, is mostly correct. Thion also cites the previously mentioned letter from Faurisson: "Permit me to ask your personal opinion," he writes, "concerning an especially delicate matter of contemporary history: Do you think the Hitlerian gas chambers are a myth, or were they real?" He goes on to ask more detailed questions of a technical nature, as it were, such as: "Has your opinion about these chambers changed since 1945, or has it remained unchanged over these twenty-nine years? I have so far not been able to find photographs of gas chambers with any assurance of authenticity. ... Do you, for your part, know of any photographs that could be added to the existing documentation of this matter? Thanking you in advance, etc."

One can only imagine the reactions of the Holocaust survivors who received this letter. Thion, at any rate, presents it as being matter-of-fact and polite, which in fact it was, as the attentive reader can undoubtedly see for himself. He does describe the storm that arose when it was published but does not endorse the use of Faurisson's words to rehabilitate Hitler (an undertaking no different, in his view, from the memorial tributes some peoples accord departed tyrants, such as Napoleon). He stresses that it is not the defense of Hitler that is at issue. Such attempts should not distract us from the main point, Thion says: the extraordinarily energetic and dedicated scholarly work Faurisson is carrying on despite all the difficulties. He must be enabled to continue, untrammeled by limitations on his freedom of speech; and all the false accusations, threats, silencings, and harassments to which Faurisson has been subject since the affair began must be exposed – and combated.

Concluding his chronicle, Thion asserts that the real question is not about Faurisson but about what actually happened in the Nazi concentration camps. Rassinier's name should be cleared, he says, and he should be recognized as the first to show that the extermination story, as related by Raul Hilberg, for example, is largely unfounded. But Rassinier was ahead of his time. Is Faurisson, too? Perhaps not, because the taboo surrounding the subject of the Holocaust and the extermination has finally been broken. "Another element in the ongoing breakdown of the taboo on this question is undoubtedly Israel's attitude toward the Palestinian question." Israel's stiff-neckedness, its militarism, the extremism of its policies, the bombing of civilians, the political assassinations – all these have led to a situation where Israel is no longer necessarily seen as compensation for Auschwitz. That being the case, there is now the possibility of creating a public space for discussion of the actions of the Nazis.

Thion continued his denial activities even after La Vieille Taupe began to fall apart (but not for good, it seems). He has written and published articles and even an entire book centered on the subject of the gas chambers. Recently he has, together with Guillaume, been running a Web site that offers an abundance of literary productions by Holocaust deniers.[33] His opposition to Zionist imperialism has, incidentally, not declined with the years either. Thus, for example, in an article he published in October 2000, after the failure of the "peace process" (quotation marks his), he suggests a "very simple" solution (quotation marks mine) to the Israeli-Palestinian conflict: the Jews should leave Palestine, return to the countries they came from or others willing to accept them, and give the country back to its rightful owners. Like Joan of Arc, the Palestinians will accept no other solution, and they are right. It is their country, and they have been expelled from it and from their homes by force. The massive Jewish immigration to Palestine came in the wake of the Balfour Declaration, that is, it is a colonialist crime. The Jews never had, do not have, and never will have a right to settle in Palestine. They learned their methods of oppression from the Gestapo and the NKVD (the conjunction of the two is noteworthy, a matter of central importance, as we have seen, in the anti-antifascism of the deniers), but they have outdone their teachers. "The terrible net result of the violations of human rights, war crimes, and crimes against humanity committed daily for over fifty years now by the Israeli system of oppression, is too great to be able to speak [about peace between Israel and the Palestinians]." In other words, the Jews have never had any right to this country, and if they have, they have lost it as a result of their cruelty, which is worse than any the twentieth century has known. There is thus no room for negotiation and no point in talking about "peace." Now, at long last, the Palestinians are fighting for their rights, and the Jews must realize that they will never let them live in peace in this country. They must recognize this now, while it is still possible to leave. The violence against the Jews in France is not anti-Semitic; it is action taken against the local collaborators of the Jewish criminals in Palestine. The Israeli neo-Nazis have been at war

[33] Curious readers will find the following Web site instructive: http://www.abbc.com/aaargh/fran. It is devoted to two subjects: denial of the Holocaust and criticism of Israel. One can download free the writings of Faurisson, for example, or Maurice Bardache, as well as Uri Avnery, Israel Shahak, and others.

since 1948, and they have been victorious in all the major outbreaks of fighting. In order to maintain a strong army, Israel has had to develop an ability to muster resources on an international scale; hence the "Holocaust industry."[34] The Holocaust, incidentally, is alluded to in three different contexts in this program for the simple solution of the Israeli-Palestinian conflict: it is the pretext used successfully by the Jews to gather the resources needed for their war with the Arabs; the Israelis are the real Nazis; and if they do not leave while they can, who knows what will become of them?

Thion is important for us because his anti-Zionist, anti-Israel obsession is not based on any revolutionary theory or ideological hatred of the state as such or of nationalism. In this sense, he is, as we have said, a good representative of the anti-Israelism now widespread among the European and American intelligentsia. He also represents well the perverted, obsessive character to which this anti-Israelism is prone and the way it can lead to active denial of the Holocaust. He is important, too, because his stature as a respected academician has enabled him to play a key role in the process of turning denial into a legitimate point of view and making it a central public issue in France and elsewhere. The well-known linguist Noam Chomsky has also played a special role in this process. The distance between Chomsky and the subject of Israel is, as we know, quite short and the links between them many. It was apparently Thion who put Guillaume and Chomsky in touch with each other, at a conference on Cambodia held in Paris in 1979 – itself a painful chapter in Chomsky's career. It was after this meeting that Chomsky signed a petition on behalf of Faurisson's freedom of speech.

Some readers may find Chomsky's contribution to the Faurisson affair of interest. Guillaume relates that during his meeting with Chomsky the question of the existence of the gas chambers came up. Chomsky, in Guillaume's words, "asked me three questions to see how sincere I was in my commitment

---

[34] The article can be accessed at the previously mentioned Web site. The link "Holocaust industry" leads to a discussion of Norman Finkelstein's *The Holocaust Industry: Reflections on the Exploitation of Jewish Suffering* (New York: Verso, 2000). This book, which caused an uproar in the Jewish world, especially in the United States, deals with the ways Jews and the Jewish establishment manipulate the international community, particularly the Swiss banks, to extort money in the name of victims of the Nazi regime. Thion, incidentally, is not the only Holocaust denier to quote Finkelstein's book with relish, which of course does not prove that his many critics – or supporters – are right. It may be relevant to point out that Finkelstein is responsible for another controversial book, published not long ago, that includes criticism of Israel for "the corruption of scholarship on the Israeli-Palestinian conflict" and for automatically accusing all its critics of being anti-Semites: *Beyond Chutzpa: On the Misuse of Anti-Semitism and the Abuse of History* (Berkeley: University of California Press, 2005). Even more recently, Finkelstein justified the Hizbullah attacks on Israel.

[to Faurisson], and he promised to do his best to defend Faurisson's freedom of speech and his rights." After returning to the United States, Chomsky kept his promise, signing the previously mentioned petition. The publication of the petition raised a storm, in which Chomsky was attacked directly by, among others, Pierre Vidal-Naquet. The latter refused to see the petition as merely an innocent defense of Faurisson's freedom of speech. Like others, he read in the wording of the petition a subtle attempt to bestow scholarly respectability, as it were, upon Faurisson's claims and not just to defend his right to say whatever he wanted. Thus, for example, the petition says that "Dr. Robert Faurisson has served as a respected professor of twentieth-century French literature and document criticism [*sic*] for over four years at the University of Lyon-2 in France. Since 1974 he has been conducting extensive independent historical research into the 'Holocaust question.' Since he began making his findings public, Professor Faurisson has been subject to a vicious campaign of harassment, intimidation, slander, and physical violence in a crude attempt to silence him." The wrath of the critics was provoked mainly by the treatment of Faurisson's activities as "research" and the reference to his published conclusions – for example, the claim that the Germans never exterminated Jews or anyone else with gas – as "findings."

Chomsky responded to his attackers with a short, derisive essay entitled "Some Elementary Comments on the Rights of Freedom of Expression." (He charges, among other things, that Vidal-Naquet did not have sufficient command of English to realize that "findings" is nothing more than a neutral term for conclusions. One might question the innocence of this assertion, and it is not clear what difference it makes anyway.) In 1980, when Guillaume published Faurisson's summary volume,[35] he appended to it Chomsky's essay. It is not entirely clear whether Chomsky agreed to have his article published by Guillaume and Faurisson, but there is no doubt about the great service it performed for the cause of the deniers. In fact, Chomsky's intervention on Faurisson's behalf and the clever way Guillaume harnessed Chomsky to his chariot were what turned what had up until then been a matter of limited interest into "the Faurisson affair" – that is, a major scandal that brought the subject of Holocaust denial even to the furthest reaches of French public awareness.

It is interesting to examine the contents of the essay, which is supposed to be a radical defense of the right of free speech. Chomsky naturally presents a kind of modern version of Voltaire's well-known statement that he was willing to die for the freedom of speech of his worst enemies. As it happens, Chomsky

[35] Robert Faurisson, *Mémoire en defense: Contre ceux qui m'accuse de falsifier l'histoire: La question des chambers à gaz* (Paris: La Vieille Taupe, 1980).

compares himself explicitly to Voltaire on other occasions, in connection with his role in the Faurisson affair. Be that as it may, he is not actually willing, here, to sacrifice his life or reputation for Faurisson. Nor, apparently, does he see him as an enemy in any sense. As we know, Chomsky generally reserves a different sort of treatment for his enemies. The renowned linguist, too, is unwilling to take a stand on the validity of what Faurisson has written, and he expresses this in much the same language as Thion. He does not say there were no gas chambers or that human beings were not killed in them. But he is also not quick to state the opposite. Caution and lack of prejudice, like the principle of free speech, are, after all, the conditions of true scholarly inquiry and scientific integrity. On the other hand, Chomsky has taken other opportunities to make clear that he knows Jews were, in fact, exterminated during the Second World War. This is some consolation, perhaps. Yet this assertion is a bit surprising, given the fact that he avoids making it in his introduction to Faurisson's book and given the almost friendly tone of that introduction.

Be that as it may, Chomsky's critics generally insist on citing certain lines from "Some Elementary Comments." For example, "I am concerned here solely with a narrow and specific topic, namely, the right of free expression of ideas, conclusions and beliefs. I have nothing to say here about the work of Robert Faurisson or his critics, of which I know very little, or about the topics they address, concerning which I have no special knowledge." Chomsky, the most knowledgeable person on all matters of politics and modern political history, knows "very little" about the matter of the gas chambers? Oddly enough, some critics think this is a curious way to relate to the claim that people were never systematically killed in the gas chambers. And there might actually be good reason to wonder at the precise meaning and deep structure (psychological or, here, ideological) of Chomsky's statement that he does not have "special knowledge" about the gassing of the Jews or the existence of the gas chambers. Near the end of the article, he writes: "Let me add a final remark about Faurisson's alleged anti-Semitism.... Is it true that Faurisson is an anti-Semite or a neo-Nazi? As noted earlier, I do not know his work very well. But from what I have read ... I find no evidence to support either conclusion.... As far as I can determine, he is a relatively apolitical liberal of some sort." Although there are insufficient grounds for Chomsky to take a stand on the quality of Faurisson's scholarly findings, the grounds are sufficient to pronounce him a "liberal." In any case, the notion that a Holocaust denier can be described not only as not an anti-Semite but as a "liberal" to boot strikes some readers as odd.

Aside from the passages from Chomsky that I have quoted and that are quoted endlessly by his critics, the following lines may also be of interest.

"I have," he writes, "frequently signed petitions – indeed, gone to far greater lengths – on behalf of Russian dissidents whose views are absolutely horrendous.... No one has ever raised an objection." On the other hand, he explains, the opposition to the petition for Faurisson stems from the fact that while "in the case of the Russian dissidents, the state (our state) approves of supporting them, for its own reasons, ... [i]n the case of Faurisson ... defense of his civil rights is not officially approved doctrine." In other words, Chomsky does not see any real difference between the nationalistic, even anti-Semitic, views of opponents of the Soviet regime and denial of the Holocaust. Both are matters of opinion. Furthermore, the scandal aroused by the Faurisson petition did not grow out of legitimate opposition to his views or even anger (excessive or otherwise) at his statement that there had been no gas chambers, but from the fact that he was a "dissident" (against what? against whom?), whose rights "the state" was not committed, as a matter of "doctrine," to defending. As usual, there is a conspiracy behind the opposition to Faurisson and the attacks on those who would defend his elementary rights; and the intellectuals, such as Vidal-Naquet, who opposed the petition in his defense, are tools of "the state."

I feel I owe an explanation to the English-speaking reader: I have quoted Chomsky at some length because he has many admirers – as well as quite a few loyal disciples – in Israel, because the Faurisson-Chomsky affair had only weak reverberations in Israel, and because there may be good reason to see this side of him as well. Aside from some experts and Francophones, very few people have taken an interest in it. One could surmise that a hidden hand, perhaps someone who does not want Chomsky's name besmirched, has kept the matter quiet. But the truth is almost certainly simpler: public opinion in Israel has a healthy tendency to be bored with the perversion of denial. Those who have heard of Chomsky's introduction to Faurisson's book generally dismiss it as a "mistake." And, indeed, who among us does not make mistakes? Chomsky himself, though, has never, as far as I can tell, thought it a mistake on his part. He has defended himself on a variety of occasions, done a bit of fancy footwork over the tacit consent he gave or did not give to having his letter published as the introduction to Faurisson's book, and let it be known that he sees the destruction of European Jewry as a terrible crime; but he has not criticized Holocaust denial or expressed misgivings about the role he has played in giving it, or Faurisson, legitimacy. Evidently he maintained, and perhaps still maintains, quite correct relations with the Holocaust denier from Lyon.

Despite the boredom this affair has generated, there may, nonetheless, be good reason to discuss it, if only because it provides an opportunity for us to understand Chomsky's political thinking more fully. A number of his Israeli disciples, some of whom have international reputations in their own fields, go to great lengths to publicize his political positions, his ideas on world affairs, and his critical views regarding the great wrongs committed in that arena. But somehow this affair has escaped their notice. In Israel, Chomsky's most prominent disciples who are politically active are professors Tanya Reinhardt (who recently died) and Yosef Grodzinsky, formerly of Tel Aviv University. The former, before leaving Israel, was teaching, beside courses on computational linguistics, also a course devoted to Chomsky's political criticism. In January 2000 the latter published in the daily newspaper *Haaretz* a review of the Hebrew edition of Chomsky's book *Powers and Prospects: Reflections on Human Nature and the Social Order*, which provides an opportunity to get to know the essentials of his thought in his many different fields of activity. "The intellectual responsibility of the writer, or any decent person, is to tell the truth," Grodzinsky paraphrases him as saying in the book. And a little further on, "Anyone who is willing to confront his own opinions is likely to reach painful conclusions." True words, no less beautiful for their similarity to something Pierre Guillaume prints on the covers of the books he publishes: "The worst thing about the pursuit of truth is finding it." At any rate, the truth about Chomsky's involvement in the Faurisson affair is something Grodzinsky has not taken the trouble to confront. Although he has appointed himself a spokesman for survivors of the Holocaust and those who, in their name, have accounts to settle with Zionism (see Chapter 2), he apparently does not think this truth is of the sort there is any moral or intellectual value in confronting. With an almost religious awe, Grodzinsky lays out for us Chomsky's critique of American policy, mentioning the sharp controversy that arose over Chomsky's remarks about the slaughter in Cambodia and, of course, his criticism of Israel. He even notes that American support for Israel is an "interesting" departure from the Chomskyan schema. But there is no reference whatsoever to the Faurisson affair. It may not be possible (as, e.g., Alan Dershowitz claims) to separate the Faurisson affair from Chomsky's campaign to get American universities to divest funds from companies doing business with Israel, or to separate the affair from Chomsky's sharp criticism of Israel in general. Everyone will have to judge for himself. But the fact that Chomsky aligned himself, however briefly, with the denial crowd is perhaps not as innocent as he wants us to think and maybe not be entirely unrelated to his anti-Israelism.[36]

---

[36] An extremely detailed, critical review of Chomsky's contribution to the Faurisson affair can be found in Werner Cohn, *Partners in Hate: Noam Chomsky and the Holocaust Deniers* (Cambridge: Avuka, 1995). This pamphlet is polemical, demonstratively unobjective, and

HOLOCAUST DENIAL AND ISLAMIST HUMANISM

Probably the clearest embodiment of this kind of denial perversion is Roger Garaudy. He was born in 1913, and his outlook was shaped by the two world wars and the period between them. He was a philosopher, a Marxist, and a Communist Party activist, serving, among other things, as one of its delegates to the French National Assembly. In the years following the Second World War, he was one of the party's main in-house intellectuals. He served as one of its principal spokesmen in dialogues with intellectuals, artists, and scientists, many of whom, as we know, were party members or fellow travelers. Among other things, Garaudy played an important role in the party's ongoing confrontation with Sartre, whose relations with it ran hot and cold. Within the party, at a later stage, he took a humanistic stand against Louis Althusser and his antihumanistic Marxism. Yet he was always a loyal party spokesman, faithfully and effectively presenting its Stalinist line. At the height of the Cold War, Garaudy helped direct the party's "thought police," as the historian Michel Winock has put it.[37] He wrote dozens of books and articles of a philosophical, ideological, and political nature. Some of his books have been translated into other languages, and in the 1950s and 1960s he was quite prominent in the political and intellectual community in France and elsewhere.

In the late sixties, Garaudy began to distance himself from the communist line, and in 1970 he was expelled from the party. For some years after that, as the party itself grew weaker, he disappeared from the public arena. He reappeared in the early eighties and became known primarily as a critic of Israel. During Israel's first Lebanon war, his attacks against Israel were particularly sharp, systematic, and relentless. He published several full-page ads in *Le Monde*. He may have had supporters of one sort or another, but it was he who signed the ads. A little while before the war he had converted to Islam – there was a story with a woman involved – and, along the way there from Marxist dogmatism, went through a phase of Catholic piety as well. Beginning with Israel's first Lebanon war, the struggle against Israel and Zionism became his main public activity. In what seems like a real obsession, he published a whole series of works attacking Israel during those years.

hostile to Chomsky. Yet it contains quite a bit of interesting information. Among other things, the author insists on Chomsky's importance for the Vieille Taupe circle and on the extent and closeness of his relationship with it.

37 Michel Winock, *Le siècle des intellectuals* (Paris: Seuil, 1997), 451. A very detailed biography of Garaudy has recently appeared in France: Michaël Prazan and Adrien Minard, *Roger Garaudy: Itinéraire d'une negation* (Paris: Calmann-Lévy, 2007).

One of Garaudy's later books, the one that caused an uproar known as "the Garaudy affair," bears the meaningful title *Les myths fondateurs d'Isräel* (Israel's Founding Myths).[38] This book was the last in a trilogy, or "triptych" as he called it, concerned with the struggle against various kinds of *"intégrisme"* (roughly, fundamentalism), which he describes as "the terminal illness of our time." Having been expelled from the Communist Party for claiming that the Soviet Union was not a socialist state, he employs a similar logic in this book: the Vatican, he says, is not truly Christian, Islamism is not Muslim, and political Zionism is not Jewish *"prophétisme"* (prophetic Judaism). In the first book in the trilogy, called *Grandeur et décadences de l'Islam* (The Greatness and Decline of Islam), Garaudy attacks Saudi Arabia and its late King Fahd as collaborators with the "American invasion," as political prostitutes, a hotbed of fundamentalism, and a disease in the body of Islam. Then there is a two-part work devoted to Catholic fundamentalism, one part entitled *Avons-nous besoin de Dieu?* (Do We Need God?) and the other, in which he attacks "marketplace monotheism," called *Vers une guerre de religion? Débat du siècle* (Toward a Religious War? The Debate of the Century).

The third book, on "Israel's founding myths," tries to show that the fundamentalist entity called the State of Israel represents, in fact, a betrayal of the ideals and values of the prophets of Israel. Once again, then, Garaudy is apparently not an anti-Semite, at least not in the usual sense. As usual, the book relies on innumerable quotations, ranging from Lord Balfour to the Hebrew newspaper *Haaretz*. For dessert, the author serves up an inspiring appendix, a little sampling of the writings of those few Israelis who, he says, remain faithful to the Jewish prophets, none other than "the New Historians

---

[38] Roger Garaudy, *The Founding Myths of Modern Israel* (Newport Beach, Calif.: Institute for Historical Review, 2000), 35. This book was first published by La Vieille Taupe. In 1966 Garaudy himself published a revised edition. The cover bears the colophon "Samizdat Roger Garaudy." The Russian term *samizdat* means literally "self-publication." During the period of communist rule, it signified the forbidden works of dissidents that were, as a rule, typewritten and passed from hand to hand in the underground. Garaudy's book has been translated into many languages, among them Arabic, and has been a best seller in a number of Arab countries. The author has become a kind of culture hero in those countries, and most of the sales of the book are there. On this, see Meir Litvak and Esther Webman, *Yitzug hasho'a ba'olam ha'aravi: Gorem mesaye'a o mikhshol betahalikh hashalom?* (The Representation of the Holocaust in the Arab World: Aid or Obstacle to the Peace Process?) (Tel Aviv: Tami Steinmetz Institute of Peace Studies, 2006). Prazan and Minard, *Roger Garaudy,* describe in detail Garaudy's frequent changes of belief and ideological alignment, leading to what the authors see as the climax of a tortuous career, his denial of the Holocaust. One point worth mentioning is the authors' insistence on Garaudy's leading role in disseminating the denial thesis in the Arab world.

of the Hebrew University" and some other devotees of a just peace who have
called attention to the true nature of the Zionist myths. Garaudy quotes – how
could he not? – Jerusalem professors Moshe Zimmerman and the late Baruch
Kimmerling and adds a paragraph by the late journalist Aryeh Caspi. At least
in regard to the latter quote, he admits that it is taken "out of context."

A glance at the table of contents will give the reader an idea of the nature
of the book. (It might also point up a certain similarity to statements made
now and then by some of the Israeli heroes of the second part of the present
book.) The "founding myths" are divided into two categories: theological
myths and twentieth-century myths. Among the former, the French Muslim
scholar lists the myth of the Promised Land: is it promised or conquered?
he asks. He goes on to discuss the myth of the Chosen People, and finally
that of the book of Joshua, "ethnic cleansing." The contemporary myths
Garaudy enumerates include those of Jewish antifascism,[39] the Nuremberg
trials (where, he claims, it was not justice but the opposite that was done), the
Six Million, and "a land without a people for a people without a land." The
last part of the book deals with the political uses of these myths, especially
by the Zionist-Israeli lobby in the United States and France and the myth of
the "Israeli miracle" that covers up the truth of "foreign financing."

In order to dispel the myth of "justice at Nuremberg," the author points
to a number of flaws in the indictments considered at the trial. Thus, for
example, according to Garaudy, one of the worst lies, one that is still causing
unparalleled damage today, more than half a century after the events, is the
myth of the six million Jewish victims, a myth used to justify and even sanctify all Israel's crimes. But no one has ever proved that six million Jews died,
just as no one ever heard Hitler order the Jews exterminated. What is more,
up until 1994 the sign at the entrance to Birkenau said that four million
people had been killed there, but recently it was changed to just a million
and a half.[40] Later in the book, Garaudy considers the testimony of Rudolph

---

[39] Here Garaudy speaks of the alliance that Lehi – he mentions Yitzhak Shamir in particular –
wanted, as it were, to make with the Nazi regime and more broadly about the cooperation
of part of the Zionist movement with that regime. This does not prevent him from pointing
out, over and over, that two days after Britain and France declared war, in September 1939,
Weizmann declared that the Jews would fight alongside the Allies, which was "a real declaration of war by the Jewish world against Germany" and created "the problem of the detention of the Jews in the concentration camps as citizens of an enemy country," much like the
detention of Japanese Americans by the U.S. government (*Founding Myths*, 32). In general,
the only thing that was important to the Zionists, he claims – on this Yosef Grodzinsky
concurs – was the establishment of a strong state and not the fate of the Jews of Europe.

[40] During the period of communist rule, when Auschwitz was depicted as a killing-ground
of the Polish people and the fate of the Jews concealed, it was claimed that some 4 million

Hess, commandant of Auschwitz, that three million were killed in the camp he oversaw; he tries to prove that this testimony is highly unreliable, among other reasons because Hess had been tortured. He also cites Faurisson's claim about the technical impossibility of the use of Zyklon B gas for killing, in order to show how weak the case of the prosecution against Nazi Germany's leaders was.

In a way typical of Garaudy's approach throughout the book, the chapter about the myth of the Six Million begins with some illuminating quotes. One is taken from the French translation of Israeli journalist Tom Segev's book *The Seventh Million*: Segev's statement that the Holocaust, much like the biblical promise, served as an ideological justification for the establishment of the State of Israel. Incidentally, Garaudy often quotes two kinds of Israeli and Jewish writers: those who exemplify the true character of Zionism and Israel, and those who share his critique of the latter. Segev apparently belongs to the second category.

Like other members of the denial community, Garaudy offers the reader learned conceptual analyses, insisting on rigorously precise definitions. In discussions of the fate of the Jews in the Second World War, he says three terms are generally employed: "genocide," "holocaust," and "Shoah" (the Hebrew term for holocaust, meaning, literally, "disaster" or "great calamity"). Can "genocide" in its exact denotation really be said to have taken place? In his view, the answer is no. Real genocide was, in fact, perpetrated in Canaan by Joshua, the son of Nun – not in Auschwitz, that is, but in Jericho. Or take "holocaust." That term, which has a religious origin, is simply a way of turning the death of the Jews in the war into something holy and justifying the establishment of the State of Israel on religious grounds. A few pages later, Garaudy admits that Hitler did want to expel the Jews from the Reich and that he sent them to concentration camps. Their fate there was a bitter one: not only did they perform slave labor there for the benefit of German industry, and not only were their living conditions bad,

---

human beings were murdered there. It was only in the beginning of the 1990s, more or less parallel to the recognition and more accurate depiction of the role of the Jews among the victims of Auschwitz, that studies were published estimating the number killed as only 1,100,000, among them nearly a million Jews, 70,000 Poles, 21,000 Gypsies, 15,000 Soviet prisoners of war, and 10,000 to 15,000 nationals of other countries. These figures are drawn from Yisrael Gutman, "Auschwitz: An Overview," in Yisrael Gutman and Michael Berenbaum, eds., *Anatomy of the Auschwitz Death Camp* (Bloomington: Indiana University Press, in association with the United States Holocaust Memorial Museum, 1994), 5–31. See also Franciszek Piper, "The Number of Victims," in ibid., 61–80. Garaudy repeats endlessly the story of the change in the estimate of the number killed at Auschwitz. This, he thinks, is conclusive proof of Zionist mendacity and manipulation.

but many of them also died of disease, particularly, alas, from typhus. Is this not bad enough? asks the author. "Do we really have to invoke other methods to explain the high mortality rate in the camps or to exaggerate the numbers to boot?" (*Les myths fondateurs*, 87). And he continues in this vein, on and on, for dozens of pages, arriving finally at this conclusion: the Israeli myths have to be exploded once and for all. The Israeli reading of the historical books of the Bible; the tribal, particularistic attitude to the notion of chosenness; the misuse of the death of many Jews in the war in order to justify the establishment of Israel, the conquest of the territories, and the subjugation of the Palestinians – all this needs to be questioned. We must also refute the intolerable exaggerations of the number of Jewish victims in the war, the claims about a policy of deliberate extermination that was never implemented, and the talk about killing with gas.

In 1996 Garaudy was prosecuted and convicted under the Gayssot Law. As might have been expected, the trial brought his book the kind of public attention it had never had in the year since it had been published. What gained it even more attention, however, was the intervention of a priest known in France as Abbé Pierre, whose philanthropic work, over many years, had made him one of the country's most admired figures.[41] The latter wrote a letter in support of Garaudy that raised a huge hue and cry. In the end, Father Pierre partially retracted what he had written; but, again, what is important here is that he was motivated mainly by anti-Israeli and anti-Zionist sentiments that had grown stronger, as they had for many other Frenchmen, during the eighties and especially after the first Lebanon war.

Garaudy's book about Israeli myths has become very popular in the Arab world. Denial of the Holocaust has become a central topic in Arabic literature and the Arabic press, where we find all the same claims we have encountered among the European deniers: direct denial of the extermination; the claim that it has been used as a political, ideological, and propagandistic justification for the creation of Israel and the injuries done to the Arabs; the comparison between Nazi crimes and those of the Zionists, who are, in fact, the real Nazis; and the idea that the Oslo Agreement was no different from that between Hitler and Marshall Petain.[42] The latest media event of the chorus of denial, in which Garaudy's voice was heard

---

[41] For a very detailed description of the affair, see Prazan and Minard, *Roger Garaudy*, 17–38.

[42] See Goetz Nordbruch, *The Socio-Historical Background of Holocaust Denial in Arab Countries: Arab Reactions to Roger Garaudy's* The Founding Myths, ACTA publication 17 (Jerusalem: Vidal Sassoon International Center for the Study of Antisemitism at the Hebrew University, 2001).

loud and clear, was in 2000–2001, when the Institute for Historical Review set about organizing a Fourteenth Revisionist Congress in Beirut. This institute, located in California, is one of the deniers' power bases, and it conducts a variety of more-or-less-regular activities centered on Holocaust denial. It has an active Web site, and it has for years been organizing international conferences in which members of the denial community from North America, Europe, and elsewhere take part. Garaudy was to have been one of the main participants in the Beirut gathering, as were Faurisson and many others. When the institute announced its intention to hold the congress, there was a great outcry involving a number of Arab intellectuals, and in the end the Lebanese government did not allow the congress to be held. Some months later, in May 2003, the Jordanian writers' union, which opposes normalization with Israel, held its own conference on "What Happened to the Revisionist Congress in Beirut?" The conference condemned the fourteen Arab intellectuals who had opposed the Beirut meeting and resolved to set up an Arab committee on historical revisionism. The recent convention called by the Iranian president to discuss the veracity of the Holocaust story was very much inspired by Garaudy's writings. This initiative cannot be described as anti-Semitic either; after all, among the distinguished participants were a number of Jews – of the Neturei Karta (extreme, anti-Zionist ultra-Orthodox) variety, that is.

THE COMMUNITY AND THE OPPROBRIUM

Guillaume is at the center of a community of opprobrium. Despite the various odd alliances members of this group have made with, for example, the extreme right or Islamic fundamentalism, and despite the fact that the boundaries between the various ideologies of denial are sometimes blurry, there is a distinct group here that is generally referred to as "leftist." It is a community with a distinctive political culture, intellectual style, and ethos. Its members share a systematic rejection and radical criticism of injustice, social evil, inequality, exploitation, and political avarice. They also share a commitment to human rights and minority rights. They fight economic, social, cultural, and political oppression and all its agents: imperialism, colonialism, and the state itself. The denial of the Holocaust voiced by some of these groups – together with the negation of Zionism and Israel that are based upon it – purports to be an authentic expression of left-wing political culture. As such, and despite its bizarre character, this denial is of great interest. It is true that Pierre Guillaume and La Vieille Taupe, as well as the other Faurissonist groupings of the radical left, were a marginal phenomenon. Yet they made their voices heard quite effectively in the media and among the intelligentsia. Chomsky's involvement contributed greatly to this, as we have pointed out. In the small group of revolutionaries, Trotskyites, socialists, and the like that Guillaume gathered around him, not all were in complete agreement with his ideas. Not surprisingly, the group was riven repeatedly by weighty ideological disagreements. Despite this, and despite the group's marginality, it managed not only to place itself and its message in the public eye and stir up public controversy around it; it also won legitimacy for its cause. For the banalization of the Holocaust and the questioning of its uniqueness, on the one hand, and the depiction of Israel as the main, even sole beneficiary of unceasing Holocaust-related activity, on the other, came to be widely accepted. There is no longer any embarrassment about expressing such views aloud. Of course, Guillaume did not do all this single-handedly. But he was well aware of where the wind was blowing. In fact, his case represents a much wider and more important phenomenon. This is why one should not take lightly the connection between Guillaume's group and the radical anti-Israelism of much of the left-leaning European intelligentsia today.

An important fact that emerges strongly from any consideration of the denial phenomenon is the intellectual poverty and utter lack of sophistication of the deniers' writings. The claims they make are weak and easily refuted, and their mode of argument is pompous and vacuous. The whole enterprise is simply grotesque. Yet their overall message, especially the part involving the delegitimation of Israel by means of the Holocaust, turns out to have struck a responsive chord. It is common, even in the universities, to treat even the denial thesis itself seriously, not only in the sophistical, disingenuous way in which Chomsky gave Faurisson legitimacy by ostensibly defending his freedom of speech, but also in a way that relates directly and substantively to Faurisson's views. How to account for this? To say that foolishness and wickedness always go hand in hand is only a partial explanation. More to the point is that in this case much of public opinion, especially among the Western intelligentsia, seems to have a strange desire to listen to these kinds of nonsense. This would seem to be the real importance of the phenomenon of Holocaust denial on the left: it is, in the end, just an extreme manifestation of a general cultural and ideological perversion. At its core there is a principled negation of Israel, of Jewish nationhood per se and its political embodiment. The perversity of this negation is evident in the outrageous glibness with which it lapses into a negation of the Holocaust and, more generally, in the varied uses it makes of the Holocaust in order to demonize and delegitimize Zionism and Israel. Among saner intellectuals, including Israelis and other Jews, there are quite a few devotees of this view, and the fact that there are (still?) no outright deniers of the Holocaust in Israel should not obscure the affinity between these Israeli intellectuals, on the one hand, and the deniers and their fellow travelers, on the other.

The primitive Holocaust denial of Guillaume and La Vieille Taupe is more than an episode, and not only because of its widespread effects. It represents, as we have said, the boundary of a thematic space where Holocaust denial and the negation of Israel come together. This connection has received its ripest, most complete expression on Guillaume's and Thion's Web site, which we have already mentioned. For reasons related to current events, such as the violent conflict between Israel and the Palestinians, or perhaps because of the nature of the medium, the message comes across there without qualification or inhibition. And what emerges most clearly is how much the two negations – of the Holocaust and of Israel – have been fused into a single thesis in which the denial reinforces the delegitimation and vice versa. The power of this symbolic connection between the Holocaust and Israel, between the denial of the one and the delegitimation of the other, is expressed in an instructive way, not only by the left-wing deniers but also by those on the right. It is well known that quite a few people on the radical right in France (and elsewhere) have supported Israel. This was the case during the war in Algeria, but also much later, when Israel was seen as a bastion of the West and a front-line position in the struggle against communism. In such right-wing publications as *Rivarol*, one finds support for Israel along with classical anti-Semitism. In many cases, even extreme right-wing anti-Semitism could not overcome hatred for Islam and the Arabs or admiration for the nationalism and militarism that Israel was seen as symbolizing. At the same time, in those instances where denial of the Holocaust was expressed and legitimized, support for Israel vanished, to be replaced by a negation of it and a questioning of its right to exist. Even the most vigorous opponents of Holocaust denial are not entirely immune to this perversion, and the need some of them have to attack Israel with the weapon of the Holocaust appears to be an uncontrollable disorder.

Thus, for example, Vidal-Naquet, in his "Un Eichmann de papier,"[43] undoubtedly one of the most important documents in the debate with the

---

[43] P. Vidal-Naquet, "Un Eichmann de papier. Anatomie d'un mensonge," in *Les Juifs, la mémoire et le present* (Paris: Maspero, 1981), 193–272; translated as "A Paper Eichmann (1980) – Anatomy of a Lie," in *Assassins of Memory* (New York: Columbia University Press, 1992). Later, revised, version in *Les assassins de la mémoire* (Paris: La découverte, 1987; Seuil-Points, 1995). References are to the 1981 French version.

"revisionists" (as the Holocaust deniers like to call themselves), could not refrain from expressing his anti-Israel views, although the whole point of the article is to refute the claims of the deniers. Vidal-Naquet accepts the argument that the history of the Second World War should not be written only from the vantage point of the victors and that, therefore, Auschwitz and Treblinka should be seen in the context of all the horrors of the twentieth century. One should be mindful of Dresden, for example, and the destruction of Hiroshima and Nagasaki. But, as he sees it, the comparison must be done fairly. There can be no comparison, for example, between the Nazi camps and the wartime camps set up in the United States for citizens of Japanese ancestry. There may, at times, be similarities between Nazi actions and the actions of others; but, in fact, Vidal-Naquet finds such similarities only in Israeli actions. The Nazi deportations were not the same as the expulsion of the Palestinians, but "one can compare, more or less, the massacre perpetrated by the Irgun and the Stern Gang at Deir Yassin with Oradour" (p. 215). Not with Auschwitz, he stresses, but with Oradour. The village of Oradour-sur-Glane, it may be recalled, was destroyed and 642 of its inhabitants killed by the German army on the June 10, 1944. It is not completely clear why this was done. The name Oradour, however, is engraved in French national memory as a major symbol of Nazi cruelty and murderousness.

The combination of denial and negation has a sociological and a thematic aspect. One can speak of a community of opprobrium that is united around several issues. The boundaries of that community are not congruent with those of the denial community, and this is what makes denial, and the interest in it, important: through it, one can understand the larger phenomenon better. It is precisely the extreme implausibility, the perversity, the utter intellectual shallowness that blare from every page of the writings of the deniers, and the Gordian knot tying denial to the negation of Israel, that can illuminate the whole, this ideological and intellectual subculture of opprobrium. For the denial of the Holocaust, especially on the left, is a borderline instance of a much wider phenomenon, the center of which is the systematic use of the Holocaust – not necessarily its denial – in an ideological struggle against Zionism and Israel. This use of the Holocaust has many aspects, and at times they seem diametrically opposed to one another. Nevertheless, there emerge here, in the end, a curious consistency and perverse logic. Though there is no single guiding hand, no organization or conspiracy behind all this, there is one single result: the Holocaust becomes one of the most effective, widely used arguments in the ideological struggle against Israel. Like many perversions, this one has a logic to it: the full weight of the Holocaust must be brought to bear on the matter, because the conclusion that is being drawn is a total one, with an almost theological import. In other words, the Holocaust has given rise to a theology of guilt. Israel's very nature – that of Zionism and of the state – is to be a bearer of guilt. Whether there was no Holocaust, and Israel and Zionism invented a monstrous lie, which they exploit in a monstrous way, no less, to justify something truly monstrous, the crimes committed against the Palestinian people; or whether there was a Holocaust, but Israel has betrayed its mission of bearing witness to it and saving the survivors; or whether Israel is behaving in a Nazi-like manner and committing real or symbolic genocide – one way or another, Israel is evil, be its evil radical or banal. It is, in any case, unforgivable. As Hannah Arendt said so forcefully, one must never get used to, accept, or forgive either form of evil. We must fight them without compromise, not resting until they and their sources are expunged from the world. That is what the conjoining of the Holocaust with Israel shows with great clarity: the establishment of the State of Israel was from the outset illegitimate and the product of two sins that are really one – the sin of the lie that the Jews were exterminated, and the sin of expelling and killing the Arabs. That sin has continued until now, and Israel's criminal, demonic nature is demonstrated in the Nazi policies it pursues and the crimes it commits. The conclusion is clear: it has no right to exist.

The strength of the negation is explained by the strength of the evil being negated. The strength of Israel's evil is demonstrated by a systematic use of what has, since the Second World War, been perceived in Western culture as the ultimate evil: the Holocaust. Anti-Zionism in general, including that of the left, can potentially lead to an annihilationist position. This potential is realized in the Holocaust denial of Pierre Guillaume and his comrades. The use of the Holocaust to deny Israel's right to exist stems from the assumption that destruction can be justified only by extremely weighty arguments; and when one speaks of the Holocaust, one is speaking of destruction. Those who deny the Holocaust dispute its factuality while at the same time making use of the symbolic power of the term "holocaust" to advance the idea of destroying Israel. According to the deniers, it was not the Germans who did the destroying and not the Jews who were destroyed. The real victims of the Holocaust, Faurisson and others have said, were the Germans and, especially, the Palestinians. To refute the ultimate justification used, as it were, by the Zionists to justify the establishment of the State of Israel is essentially to demonize the Zionist project: there was no extermination, and the Jews are not victims. Certainly, they are not victims entitled to compensation. Nazi Germany was not absolutely evil, and thus the true evil is the fabrication of the extermination and that which the fabrication justifies. This demonization is a radical one because it applies to the very essence of the Zionist idea; if Zionism is based on a monstrous lie like that about the gas chambers, it is truly, itself, a monstrosity. There was no Holocaust, and the word is meaningless; yet, at the same time, a holocaust is happening right now, and if you want to understand the meaning of the word, just watch El-Jezira.

What characterizes this community of opprobrium? The following is an incomplete, unsystematic list of its features: sociological, stylistic, structural, formal, and thematic.

The Holocaust as a Justification for the Establishment of Israel and for Its Actions. The main thematic element on which this community of opprobrium is built is a sort of "master postulate" shared by all the critics of Israel in the name of the Holocaust: the latter, they maintain, is the principal justification or excuse for the establishment of the State of Israel, its ongoing existence, and the policies it pursues. Pierre Guillaume and his fellow deniers at one pole of the community of opprobrium and, at the other, those for whom denial is scandalous, and even those who speak in the name of the Holocaust or of the survivors, at the opposite pole, all share, explicitly or implicitly, the idea that the Holocaust is the main rationale for the Zionist claim to Jewish self-determination in a sovereign state in the Land of Israel. This claim has two sides to it, the objective and the subjective. On the one hand, the Holocaust is the one thing that can give moral legitimacy to the establishment of a Jewish state; on the other hand, they often say, the Holocaust and its memory provide Israelis with a psychological basis for behaving as they do, the foundation of the Israeli ethos and especially its more murderous aspects. The uses of this claim, in its various forms, are many and seemingly contradictory. There is the categorical denial of legitimacy to the State of Israel, based on a denial of the Holocaust. There is the charge that the Zionist movement collaborated with the Nazis or that its policies are Nazi-like, making its claims invalid. There are the various efforts to suppress the memory of the Shoah, to limit or circumscribe its presence in the Israeli (and wider Jewish) public sphere, in order to avoid encouraging the Israelis in their criminal actions against the Arabs or supplying a rationale for them. And there is the charge that Israel betrayed the victims of the Holocaust, the survivors, and the immigrants who came from the hell of Europe, that it even exploited them, thus failing to fulfill the very purpose for which it was established and which alone could justify its creation. All these claims have a similar structure and a similar conclusion: Israel has no justification other than the Holocaust; this justification is not valid; ergo, Israel is not a legitimate entity.

Blackmail, Misuse, and Manipulation. The Holocaust gives both Zionist and non-Zionist Jews a basis for blackmail. The collective guilt feelings aroused by the Holocaust in the West are, of course, used to extort political and financial support. Whether they are lying about the Holocaust, or whether they are exaggerating it, the Jews/Zionists/Israelis are misusing it to manipulate Western public opinion. There is also domestic manipulation: the establishment – always the establishment – uses awareness of the Holocaust, endless talk about it and commemoration of it, to rally Jews in general and Israelis in particular to its political purposes. The Jews/Zionists/Israelis instrumentalize it, exploiting it for their own purposes – in regard to European public opinion, of course, but also in regard to public opinion in Israel and in the Jewish world in general. In the end, the question of "historical truth" disappears, and the Holocaust becomes a colossal instrument of manipulation.

Responsibility. A regular concern of denial literature is the Jews' responsibility for the war. According to the neofascist, right-wing deniers, not only was there no systematic extermination of Jews but what killing did take place was justifiable retribution, for it was the Jews who had instigated the war to begin with. Nazi propaganda had, as we know, always depicted it as a "Jewish war" – before it began, while it was underway, and after it ended – and quite a few of the deniers pick up this image and run with it. As we have seen, Rassinier made this claim repeatedly and forcefully. It was also he, if I am not mistaken, who coined the well-known saying, frequently cited by his followers, that it was the Jews who invented their own death. This charge can be understood as a subtle, metaphorical version of the claim that the Jews were responsible for the war and for their own mass destruction. The idea comes back in even more complex form in the attribution of Nazi-like behavior to the Jews. When the Portuguese writer José Saramago visited the Palestinian town of Ramallah during the height of the Palestinian suicide-bombing campaign, he talked about the Jews having done to the Palestinians what the Germans had done to *them*. What right, then, did they have to complain about their current suffering? They themselves were responsible, in the last analysis, for the human bombs exploding in buses on the streets of Israeli cities. The same charge has recurred in certain other instances where the behavior of the Jewish leaders was criticized and they were held responsible for the holocaust of their own people – for example, by Hannah Arendt.

The Victim. The Jews have thus misappropriated the role of absolute victim. Not only do they not deserve it, but it serves them as a justification for abusing the real victim. Whether the Holocaust is a lie or really took place, it is the Palestinians who are paying the price. To be sure, according to this logic no one can claim to be the absolute victim, because there is no such thing as absolute victimhood; nevertheless, the Palestinians are the absolute victim.

Uniqueness. The Jews maintain that the Holocaust was unique, but of course they were not the only people to perish in the war. Even if there was mass killing, even if there was extermination, the victims were not only Jews. More than this, the Holocaust is not unique in the annals of crimes committed down through history or even in the twentieth century.[44] The Nazi concentration camps did not differ from the Stalinist gulag, and if we are to achieve a correct theoretical understanding of modernity we cannot consider the Nazis in isolation but must look at the global phenomenon of concentration camps and other forms of mass confinement. Democracy, too, has had its share in this phenomenon.

The Scholarly Pretense. One important component of the image projected by the community of opprobrium and denial is that of academic respectability. Many of the writings of the deniers appear to be academic works, with numerous footnotes and bibliographical references, indexes, and long lists of sources. Many of the writers have spent days on end in archives and, on occasion, unearthed little-known documents. Faurisson often speaks of his visits to Auschwitz and the time (a few weeks, perhaps less) that he has spent in the archive there. A place of honor is accorded in this community to establishment academics like Serge Thion, and the patronage of well-known scholars like Chomsky is worth its weight in gold to them. The same applies in cases where the exploitation of the Holocaust does not involve a full-fledged denial of it: there is a "theory," a jargon, a canonical literature. It is no accident that most of the work of harnessing the Holocaust to the ideological struggle against Israel is done by academicians claiming scholarly standing for their arguments.

---

[44] In one of the pamphlets written by members of the Vieille Taupe group, we find: "What is the difference between a child burned by napalm in Vietnam and a Jewish child imprisoned at Auschwitz? ... What is the difference between one tortured in Buenos Aires and one tortured by the Gestapo? ... For us, the very existence of the German camps or any others, wherever they may be, justifies the struggle. For us, it is not a matter of accusing Nazism of more crimes than it actually committed. The all-too-real and more-than-sufficient atrocities of the war and the deportation interest us more than an imaginary Nazism. Never again, we say. Of course. ... These excessive reminders, have they prevented anything? This religion of death, has it made it possible for people to live a better life? ... Whatever happens, we say, nothing can be worse than Auschwitz. ... And so, many suffer and die, and is the suffering and death of all of them not the same?" Etc., etc. Quoted in Igounet, *Histoire du négationionisme en France*, 257.

The Official Historiography. Despite the reliance on "scholarship" and the talk of objective historical research, one of the main enemies of the denial community (as well as other communities of *resentiment*, including the Israeli, with whom it sometimes finds common cause) is the scholarly establishment. Like the political establishment, the state, and the media, the academy maintains a "hegemonic discourse" and has an interest in concealing the truth. These "other" scholars – the establishment scholars, the Zionist or Jewish ones – are participants in different campaigns of manipulation, obfuscation, and the dissemination of a slanted version of historical events. One must therefore distinguish between the partisan historians and the official historiography, on the one hand, and, on the other, those few, generally persecuted theoreticians who have managed to free themselves from the clutches of the "hegemonic narrative" and its disseminators within and outside the academy.

Theory and Criticism. The deniers on the "left" are the bearers of a special truth that enables them to escape manipulation. Revolutionary theory is somewhat esoteric, but it provides a key to a critical grasp of reality as well as to political action aimed at changing it. This theory makes possible not only knowledge and understanding but also membership in a kind of secret order of the initiated, those who have privileged access to the truth, to a common theoretical and methodological framework within which innovative, revisionist research can be done and new, more plausible interpretations of reality proposed. Various communities of opprobrium adopt different substitutes for the *Communist Manifesto*; they work to disseminate them and use them to define their intellectual and scholarly identity. Today there is a new "theory" that, in various ways, not all of them entirely explicit, overlaps with the old theories. Its chief heroes are, for example, Carl Schmitt, Giorgio Agamben, Hannah Arendt, and also, in Israel, certain theorists both within and on the margins of the academic world.

The Fraternity of the Persecuted and Those Ahead of Their Time. Rassinier, Serge Thion said, was ahead of his time. Obviously, Thion himself and the rest of the fraternity of denial are ahead of their time as well. The wider public and especially the establishment, the state, and their systems of control are not yet ripe for the new message. That is why they try by various means to harm those who would disseminate it; they shut them up, passing laws that limit their freedoms of speech and inquiry. In short, they persecute them.

Alone against All. Complementing the notion of the fraternity of the persecuted is another distinguishing notion: the deniers and their fellow travelers are certain that their enemies are all alike, despite the apparent contrasts between them, and that they themselves are quite alone in their understanding of the truth. As we have seen, the fascists and antifascists are all, in the last analysis, of the same stripe.

The Alibi. One of the deniers' entry cards to the public sphere is the appearance of respectability. Guillaume's interest in Bernard Lazare is an example: Lazare could not be accused of anti-Semitism. A newsletter circulated in 1988 by La Vieille Taupe maintained, among other things, that criticism of "National Zionism" and a refusal to get caught up in the war fever it was trying to foist on humankind had nothing to do with anti-Semitism. The participation of Jews in the denial campaign provides another sort of alibi.

The Dilemma of Responding. A final point concerns the strategic dilemma of how to respond. Everyone who tries to debate the deniers runs into it. On the one hand, the public sphere cannot simply be abandoned to them. As experience shows, their claims eventually gain a real foothold not only in the popular culture but also in the most respected media and eventually even in the academic world. Mere condemnation, let alone suppression, of them is ineffective and even dangerous, for it grants them a presence and visibility and can evoke reactions like Chomsky's, which make victims of them, people whose rights are being threatened. Such reactions give the deniers additional arguments, based not only on rights but also on the scholarly nature, as it were, of their work. On the other hand, a measured response that seems to take their claims and "findings" seriously also gives the deniers visibility and respectability, which are exactly what they are looking for and what best serves their purposes. For, in any case, what is really at stake is never the validity of the "findings" they publish, and disproving them strengthens the deniers' hand no less than substantiating them.

The Denial Community and Its Supporters. All these elements add up to a phenomenon that can be described with some precision. If not from the outset, at least after the fact, a community of deniers is formed, in effect a subculture, a bio- or ecosystem of denial. It assumes different forms and manifests different measures of intensity. It is, to be sure, an amorphous community, but it has real character and even a sociopolitical structure. Participation in this community is based on loose agreement concerning the denial of the Holocaust and particularly the theoretical and ideological implications of such denial. Despite their ideological identity, its members find it easy to ally themselves with deniers on the extreme right. The boundaries of the community are vague and meandering. There is a hard core, and there is a wide periphery of supporters, devotees, fellow travelers, and those who simply indulge them. One way or another – and whatever excuse they give for this support – the fellow travelers are always strongly anti-Israeli (and usually anti-American too). It is an international community, based on shared codes and a shared language or, at times, jargon, consensus about a basic credo, a feeling of victimhood, and shared secrets. The community has logistical centers and centers of activity, such as La Vieille Taupe publishing house and bookstore. It holds international conventions, publishes periodicals, and has recognized leaders, disciples, and leaders-in-training.

As we have said, the boundaries of this community of opprobrium are not obvious. In the foregoing discussion, an apparently strange connection began to emerge: Faurisson-Guillaume-Thion-Chomsky-Grodzinsky. It is not an accidental connection, nor is the conjoining of these names arbitrary or merely provocative. They allow us to locate the boundaries of a whole, coherent thematic space, to locate the community of opprobrium and sketch its portrait. Just as with the outright deniers, so here too, at the center of this space are two subjects that are indisputably linked: the Holocaust, on the one hand, and Zionism and Israel on the other. What characterizes this community of opprobrium and is shared by its two opposite extremes is a reliance on the Holocaust as the basis for placing blame on Israel. Guillaume, on the one extreme, and Grodzinsky, on the other, make use of the Holocaust to attack the legitimacy of the State of Israel and undermine the moral basis of its existence. Ostensibly, Grodzinsky is Guillaume's polar opposite: he voices the outcry of the dead whom Zionism and the organized Jewish community in Palestine failed to rescue, and he takes up the anguished cause of the survivors whose plight was exploited by the state. He is certainly not a denier of the Holocaust; in a polemical article attacking the present book after its publication in Israel, he describes himself as a Shoah "emphasizer" rather than denier (*madgish Shoah*, not *makkhish Shoah*). He is right, and in all likelihood Guillaume and Faurisson are people with whom he would not want to be associated. And yet, he shares with them more than he is willing to acknowledge: the instrumentalization of the Holocaust in the service of a delegitimation of the *essence* of Zionism and the State of Israel. Because he is close to Chomsky, and Chomsky is (or was) close to Thion, it is a bit more difficult to guess what Grodzinsky would say about Thion. We have already mentioned Grodzinsky's silence over the fact that Chomsky took Faurisson's side. This, however, is not the only factor linking him with that crowd, a community built on a general agreement concerning, on the one hand, the profound immorality of the ideological foundations on which the State of Israel was built and of the ethos underlying its unacceptable conduct, and, on the other, the legitimacy of invoking the Holocaust as an effective weapon in the ideological, political, and moral struggle against Israel.

Because this community exists, and because it is intensely active, we have to talk about it, even if it means stooping to the gutter. It is the interest of the deniers, the very essence of what they are about, to succeed in provoking outrage. This is how they keep themselves going and how they make the intolerable a part of public discourse. The present essay expresses a way of resolving the dilemma of response and the need to take a stand; it is also, to some extent, a trudge through the gutter. For even here in Israel, and among Jews outside it, such a gutter culture is emerging unhindered.

2

The Holocaust and the Good Israelis

FIND THE DIFFERENCES

Consider this:

No, Israel has no right to exist, although, let it be said, the same applies to every state and nation. Every attempt to criticize Israel is fended off by a single weapon: the religion of the "Holocaust" and the "genocide." The fuller, more shocking formula used to silence argument is: the six million Jews who were "exterminated" during the war by the Nazis. Why six million? The truth is, this number is much more effective than the (more realistic) figure of one million (although, at bottom, from a human point of view, there is no difference!). Indeed, it is a number that has acquired a religious significance. It is enough to mention "the six million" to put an end to any criticism of Israel or Zionism, just as holding up a cross or a bulb of garlic stops a vampire.

It is unlikely that the saga of the slain Jewish people will be one of flood, war, or *akeda* [sacrificial killing, as in the Binding of Isaac]. More likely it will be a story of revelation. It is the absolute, the divine, that is the source of the evil. Until absolute evil came along, no one believed there was a hidden law governing all manifestations of evil in the world. Until then, no one put his trust in a unique, transcendent, absolute evil, the meaning of our life and death, the logic of our finitude and suffering, the rock of our destruction, the promise of our perdition. Those in Israel who insist on the uniqueness of the Holocaust cling tenaciously to an unbridgeable gap between the catastrophe that befell the Jewish people and the disasters that have befallen other peoples. They see themselves as the heirs of the victims and even as virtual victims themselves, their memories preventing them from seeing the real victims of their own power in the recent past and in the present.

In fact, it does not take especially keen insight to distinguish between the two statements. The first appeared in 1980 in one of the periodicals of the revolutionary Holocaust deniers. The second is a collection of quotes from a volume by the Israeli writer Adi Ophir, *Avodat hahoveh: Masot al tarbut yisraelit ba'et hazot* (The Worship of the Present: Essays on an Israeli Culture for Our Time).[1] Despite the differences, there is, however, a similarity: both use the same metaphor: the theologization, as it were, of the Holocaust and our relationship to it. Both see this theologization as removing the killing of the Jews from the realm of rational discourse, and both oppose the "religion of uniqueness" (*emunat hayihud*) – as Ophir calls it, with heavy irony – which they see as characterizing the Jewish and Zionist relationship to the Holocaust. Similarly, both regard this way of relating to it as a defense against criticism, a source of moral blindness, and, in fact, the origin, or at least the rationale, of Israel's policies in the conflict with the Palestinians, policies that have brought catastrophe upon the latter. Just as the deniers claim that what the Jews and Zionists refer to by the magical term "the six million" is no different from other historical instances of mass murder, Ophir thinks a "conceptual continuum" needs to be established between the catastrophe Jews suffered and the one they have themselves wrought. The conclusions drawn by the Holocaust deniers and by Ophir are ultimately the same: they both link their claims to a more or less radical delegitimation of Zionism and Israel and a denial of the right of a Jewish people to self-determination.

Is it just a surface similarity? Is there any real similarity at all? After all, it has never occurred to Ophir to claim that Jews were not killed with gas or that the Jewish holocaust in Europe is a lie. On occasion he has even spoken out clearly and adamantly (if briefly) against Holocaust denial. Can there be any validity in trying to lump a serious philosopher and ethicist like Adi Ophir together with an ignorant, upstart, Left Bank revolutionary who represents nothing more than a grotesque ideological perversion? Is the comparison we have just made between the two texts not demagogic, scandalous, perhaps even paranoid? Or might they both be right, in fact, that the disaster of European Jewry has taken on an inverted sanctity and become the underpinning, cause, and excuse for a great, new, terrible evil of Israel's own doing? Could Zionism have managed to fuse the Holocaust and Israel into a single indissoluble entity, in which the sanctity conferred on the one justifies or conceals the crimes of the other?

Such contentions always have some measure of truth to them. Even what the Holocaust deniers say has a grain of truth. It is true, for example, that no documentary evidence has yet been found of Hitler ordering the extermination of the Jews,[2] and the whole subject of the crystallization of the

[1] Tel Aviv: Ha'Kibutz ha'Meuhad, 2001.
[2] See, e.g., Leni Yaḥil, "Some Remarks about Hitler's Impact on the Nazis' Jewish Policy," *Yad Vashem Studies* 23 (1993): 281–294. See also below.

Final Solution policy is still being debated by historians of the mass murder. Reality is complex, we know. The Holocaust and its consequences, the reactions to it, the way the memory of it has been handled – all are certainly endlessly complicated. Of course, this complexity cannot be used as an excuse for immoral behavior on the part of Jews or Israel. There is no question that the Holocaust has played a formative role in modern Jewish consciousness and the Israeli ethos; and we cannot ignore the fact that some people misuse it. But it is also true that this very complexity can be easily manipulated to serve more questionable purposes. The fact is, the misuse of the Holocaust is done not only to defend Israel's misdeeds; sometimes, perhaps even more blatantly, it is done to batter and defame Israel.

An important part of the complexity of the subject of the Holocaust and the way the Jews treat it is the connection, or set of connections, between it and Israel.[3] In this tangled, painful, sometimes questionable interrelationship, it can be quite difficult to discern what is true and false, honorable and reprehensible. But looming above this whole, immense, complicated subject is a phenomenon that stands out in its absolute clarity: denial. The great advantage of the denial phenomenon, its "theoretical edge," if you will, is its absolute mendacity and wickedness. Not sharing Chomsky's scientific modesty in this matter, I will state categorically that this is beyond doubt. The deniers, generally in quite a primitive way, make use of certain clichés that contain a grain of truth. But the latter cannot conceal the complete falsity of their main arguments. It is because of this that Holocaust denial offers us an opportunity to see what political perversion, in its pure form, looks like. But, more controversially, denial also reveals the perversity of the linkage between the Holocaust and Israel that is made by Guillaume and his fellow deniers on the left. Most important, denial allows us to see the utter moral bankruptcy of turning this linkage into a broad-scale indictment of Israel and Zionism, the moral outrage of using the link as evidence in an extended public trial that finds them guilty, with no possibility of appeal.

Because of the simplistic, immediate, direct, and exclusive connection between the Holocaust and the moral condemnation of Israel, we can, indeed, make the case that the similarity between Adi Ophir's position and that of La Vieille Taupe is neither coincidental nor superficial. Both have made the Holocaust their central concern, along with criticism, condemnation, and even negation of Israel and Zionism. In both cases, what we are dealing with is not merely the uncovering, as it were, of a similarity (between the actions

---

[3] See, e.g., Yosef Gorny, *Between Auschwitz and Jerusalem* (Portland: Vallentine Mitchell, 2003).

of the Nazis and the Israelis) but, more than this, a kind of argument: both link the Holocaust and Israel in a questionable moral syllogism. The latter, a product of rational thought and of logic, can be seen, with a little effort, as a sort of transshipment mechanism. What it transfers is the thing, the attribute, we call truth. If the syllogism is properly constructed, if it is valid, as the logicians say, the conclusion acquires the veracity of the initial assumption, that on which the syllogism is built. In our case, the syllogism common to the deniers and Ophir– "Ophir" representing here the whole community of opprobrium; one could put in his stead, for example, "Tony Judt" – is a vehicle for transferring blame and negation. It is assumed that the Holocaust represents absolute evil, limitless guilt, and suffering; then, in one way or another, these things are transferred to Israel and Zionism. Whatever Ophir can say in his own defense, his argument belongs to the same thematic, ideological, political, and even stylistic sphere as La Vieille Taupe. The boundaries of this sphere are determined by the use of similar rhetorical devices, such as the charge that the Holocaust has been made the object of religious veneration; or the claim that the Palestinians are the true victims of the Holocaust, or the victims of its victims; or the comparison of the misdeeds of Israel with what the Germans did to the Jews; or the essential linkage of the Holocaust to the criticism, delegitimation, and even demonization of Israel; or the priority given to "criticism" (i.e., the criticism of Israel), whenever the subject of the Holocaust comes up, to the point of treating any discussion of that subject, especially in public, as illegitimate. But the boundaries of the sphere are also determined by the dubiousness, complete or partial, and certainly the blatant one-sidedness of the factual claims made about Israel, Israeli society, the conflict, and the occupation. This is the very purpose of the Holocaust syllogism and the displacement of guilt that it entails: they relieve the accusers of the need to think about Israel historically or politically.

There is certainly room to question whether the picture Ophir gives of Israeli society in his various writings is an accurate one, whether presenting Israel as a machine of evil, completely blind to the suffering of its victims, is true to the facts. At the very least, the factual basis he offers for his critique of Israel is open to dispute. For Ophir ignores the "Zionist" scholars more or less systematically, casting suspicion on "establishment" research just the way the Vieille Taupe crowd does. As for the literature he does rely on, one can dispute both its empirical accuracy and its methodological validity. And, given its ideological commitments, it is not clear how much room is left in it for scholarly integrity. The writers to whom Ophir accords unimpeachable authority generally belong to the local community of grumblers, of *resentiment*; and what is important is not so much that they are grumblers but that they constitute a community.[4] These scholars quote one another, and they have a canonical literature that provides a theoretical basis, as it were, for their campaign of vilification. At one time, it was Marx and Trotsky; today the canon includes, for example, the works of Foucault, Hannah Arendt, Carl Schmitt, and Giorgio Agamben. The esoteric wisdom of these writings and the culture of mutual citation prevailing in this community not only supply the members with a comfortable sense of togetherness and in-group collegiality; they also produce a kind of intellectual autism that effectively insulates the community against contrary views. Because Ophir is a philosopher (probably the reigning philosopher of this school of thought) and not a sociologist or a historian, his work does not, for the most part, involve the painstaking collection of data or even relating data analytically to theory. His job is to *understand*, that is, to offer an interpretation of the facts or illuminate the empirical data with concepts. At the very least, one might expect that his cultural and political criticism would not be at the expense of careful conceptualization. But a close reading of his essays, as well as his main philosophical work, reveals that this is sometimes indeed the case.

To take one example, Ophir attributes great importance to the "religion of the Holocaust" that has, as it were, developed in Israel, and he sees it as a great danger. But it is really not clear that the Holocaust is being treated in a religious manner. If the claim of the "theologization" of the Holocaust is to be taken seriously, the terms "religion" and "theology" need to be defined, and we need to know what makes preserving the memory of the Holocaust – through memorial ceremonies, teaching the Holocaust in the schools, educational trips to the death camps, monuments, museums, and research institutes – into a religion, or discussion of the subject into theology. The author of the Vieille Taupe pamphlet does not take the trouble to explain to us what he means when he speaks of the Holocaust as a religion. It is unlikely that he would be able to enlighten us very much on the nature of religion or theology, aside from some pat phrases drawn from the rhetoric of revolution. Nor would he be likely to know a thing about the extensive theological consideration that has been given to the Holocaust, particularly in English, not to mention Hebrew. But what might, in some sense, be forgivable coming from Pierre Guillaume and his ilk – what, after all, can be expected of them? – is much graver, more reprehensible, and more dangerous coming from the pen of an Adi Ophir. The pseudotheoretical jargon

---

[4] Adi Ophir draws on the work of Tom Segev, Idith Zertal, and Moshe Zuckerman, who, in turn, generally use each other's work and that of Ophir to substantiate similar arguments. He hardly mentions any other sources.

of the La Vieille Taupe group does not hide the utter vapidity of what they say; Ophir's theoretical presumption is harder to penetrate, his "discourse" harder to deconstruct. But a critical effort should show that, here, too, language has been used – admittedly rather eloquently in this case – to express things that are only partly true and to articulate an ideological message that is quite well developed but quite disgraceful.

Ophir uses the concept of "civil religion" to describe the way the Holocaust is dealt with in Israel. Here we have a small but typical instance of the effort to give theoretical respectability to the notion of the theologization and "religionization," if you will, of the Holocaust. He quotes the work of Eliezer Don-Yihya and Charles Liebman,[5] repeating their contention that Holocaust-related activity in Israel is a part of the country's civil religion. The latter concept, long used by political scientists and sociologists, has had a strange and convoluted career. It made its first appearance in the writings of Jean Jacques Rousseau, in the penultimate chapter of *The Social Contract*. There, Rousseau speaks of a kind of faith, consciousness, ethics, and the like that have a religious character – that is, that flow from a relationship to God or the sacred and that tie the individual to the state and its laws, and to his fellow citizens, in a bond of civil loyalty enjoying some kind of vague transcendent foundation. Nevertheless, there are some grounds for thinking that the modern idea of the political, historical, and this-worldly character of religion, the modern "theological-political" problem," had a slightly earlier philosophical origin, more specifically in Spinoza's critique of religion.[6] Spinoza's *Theological-Political Treatise* was written against the background of the transformation of the problem of the relation between state and religion, or between this-worldly and otherworldly authority, into a modern problem. He also suggests a radical solution: religion is fundamentally a political phenomenon, and the state should use it to secure the

---

[5] Charles Liebman and Eliezer Don-Yehiya, *Civil Religion in Israel: Traditional Judaism and Political Culture in the Jewish State* (Berkeley: University of California Press, 1983). Ophir is not alone in this; the treatment of Holocaust commemoration and discourse as a "religion" has become quite fashionable.

[6] The English historian Jonathan Israel sees Spinoza as the leading figure of a "radical philosophy" that gave rise to the cultural, political, and social phenomenon known as the Enlightenment. See his *Radical Enlightenment: Philosophy and the Making of Modernity, 1650–1750* (Oxford: Oxford University Press, 2001). Spinoza's radical secularism found expression, among other places, in his philosophical attempt to make religion completely subordinate to the state; at the same time, he recognized the great political utility of religious sentiment and ritual and of organized religion. However, it should be pointed out that a critique of religion as a natural, psychological, or quasi-political phenomenon is already to be found in, for example, Epicurus and the Epicureans. For a comprehensive history, see Georges Minois, *Histoire de l'athéisme* (Paris: Fayard, 1998).

obedience of its citizens. Rousseau broadens the scope of the question a bit, but at bottom he stands within the critical tradition represented by Spinoza: alongside "natural religion" (mainly a personal matter) and historical religion (something dangerous), there is also "civil religion," which is the basis of the solidarity and social bonds without which no civic community (state) can survive.

Emile Durkheim and Alexis de Tocqueville are more recent sources for the sociological discourse about civil religion. Durkheim sees the essence of religion as social, and the transcendent – the main concern of religion and the central element in the formation of religious consciousness – as simply the way we conceptualize the basic relationship between the individual and the society in which he lives, that is, the transcendence of society over the individual. This is also the basis of society's claim on the individuals who make it up, a claim that is sometimes total. Tocqueville, too, in his classic description of American democracy, points up the important role played by religion in crystallizing the American political and civic ethos. But neither of these writers questions the unique role, sui generis, played by religion in relation to other significant human phenomena. The same is true of Robert Bellah, the important American sociologist, who, in his studies of the role played in American political culture by religion, religious sentiment, and religious attitudes toward law and the state, introduced the term "civil religion" into the sociological literature. But the original meaning (or meanings) of this term in Spinoza, Rousseau, Durkheim, Tocqueville, and even Bellah are completely dissolved in the work of Adi Ophir.[7]

Liebman and Don-Yihya operate within a scholarly paradigm in which the concept "religion" – especially as it functions in the term "civil religion" – has lost all specific meaning. They distinguish "traditional religion" from "civil religion," but it is not at all clear how they can justify applying the term "religion" to phenomena in both these categories. In the last analysis, the concept of civil religion becomes so general as to have no concrete definition – and thus also ceases to be theoretically fruitful. By the same logic, the term could be applied to *all* phenomena in the public and political spheres. It is hard,

---

[7] The specificity of "civil religion" is linked, in Bellah's view, to a position that regards itself as being above the law and standing in judgment of it. He (and his disciples, especially Robert Wuthnow) apply this concept to America after the Vietnam War. Their point of view is clearly a religious (Protestant) one. The importation of the concept to Israel and its application to Holocaust discourse here not only reflect ignorance, it would seem, but are also ironical; Ophir is a much firmer believer in civil religion that those he criticizes; he is convinced that his theory allows him to interpret, criticize, and reject not only this or that law or policy but the whole idea of the state, the sovereign, etc.

for example, to see why Liebman's and Don-Yihya's definitions could not be applied to alternative Holocaust commemoration ceremonies, or to gatherings conducted by Israeli conscientious objectors and opponents of the occupation (before conscientious objection became a program of the religious right), so as to classify those phenomena, too, as "religious." One could also call the permanent presence of the checkpoint-watch women at army roadblocks in the territories a kind of rite or ritual; and the same could be said – why not? – of the various public activities Adi Ophir himself organizes or takes part in.[8] Those who participate in such activities would undoubtedly object to being described as "religious," and they would be right. But the same logic applies to what Liebman and Don-Yihya, followed by Ophir, term "civil religion": first of all, the commemoration of the Holocaust, both organized and private; writing about the Holocaust; and research into the subject. This is because, among other things, there is important, extensive inquiry of a theological, religious nature into the matter of the Holocaust, and blurring the boundaries between such inquiry and other forms of Holocaust-related public activity is really an intellectual affront.

In a little over a page of their *Civil Religion in Israel* (pp. 10–11), Liebman and Don-Yihya suggest ways of recognizing the phenomena of civil religion. They admit that "at this stage" they do not have clear answers and are going on intuition. They have such an intuition, for example, regarding the Israeli national Holocaust memorial institution Yad Vashem. Its museum, research center, and monuments constitute, in their view, a "shrine" (p. 101). But in fact, aside from this word, it is hard to find any other argument in their work that would justify calling Yad Vashem a religious institution or, for that matter, describing any of the commemorative events, some of them now established traditions, as components of a civil religion. They describe the circumstances under which Yad Vashem was established and its modus operandi; but description is not the same as explanation or argumentation, and the intuitions on which they rely could be matched by contrary ones. It is hard to shake the feeling that the expression "civil religion" is just a label or code name for phenomena to which one wants to give a certain ideological coloring.

With Adi Ophir, there is no need for intuition to ascertain that what we are speaking of is ideology. The highly charged title of his collection of essays

---

[8] Especially during the First Intifada (Palestinian uprising), Ophir was quite active in, indeed a leader of, various dissident groups that organized demonstrations against the Israeli occupation of the West Bank and Gaza Strip and against the conduct of the Israeli army and government during this conflict. Once or twice he was even briefly arrested.

Avodat hahoveh (The Worship of the Present) points almost explicitly to what the book spells out in detail: we must stop worshiping the past, for the worship of the past, and especially of Auschwitz, prevents us from paying obeisance to the present, that is, the suffering of the Palestinians under the yoke of occupation. Ophir makes extensive use of religious and theological metaphors. And, quite unlike the Vieille Taupe crowd, he is also familiar with the theological literature of the Holocaust, even mentioning some works and authors in that genre. He knows, or should know, the difference between theology and collective memory. He also knows, or should know, that there is very little consensus among theologians of the Holocaust. There are even some who hold views quite close to his own.[9]

Although he knows, or should know, these things, Ophir takes the liberty of informing his readers, some of whom are not as familiar as he is with the theological literature of the Holocaust, that the theologians are all (!) "seeking a dimension of sanctity among the ruins" (from *The Order of Evils*, p. 666). This phrase appears in a footnote illustrating the claim that Auschwitz has been made into a kind of "upside-down Sinai," "a new focus of revelation that turns all the other sacred places into altars of idolatry" (p. 528). Here in Israel, "a new 'religion' emerges, with its centers of priesthood, knowledge and belief, with its practice of rituals and pilgrimage, with the economic and political capital invested in nurturing religious institutions and spreading faith" (ibid.). It is hard to argue with these sociological insights, which speak of an entity that is more or less abstract or, in any event, hard to locate. (Is it in Israeli society? Popular culture? World Jewry?) But insofar as his talk about "seeking a dimension of sanctity among the ruins" is aimed at a well-defined target – *all* the Jewish and non-Jewish theologians who write about the Holocaust – we can say with certainty that there is not a shred of truth to it.

---

[9] See Adi Ophir, *Avodat hahoveh: Massot al tarbut yisra'elit ba'et hazot* (The Worship of the Present: Essays on Contemporary Israeli Culture) (Tel Aviv: Hakibbutz Hameuhad, 2001). A revised version of the essay "Sofiuto shel hapittaron ve'einsofiuto shel ha'ovdan" (The Finality of the Solution and the Endlessness of the Loss) is to be found in Dan Michman, ed., *Hashoah bahistoria hayehudit: Historiografia, toda'a, ufarshanut* (The Holocaust in Jewish History: Historiography, Consciousness, and Interpretation) (Jerusalem: Yad Vashem, 5765 [2005]), 637–681. In this "revised version," which came to my attention long after the present book was written, Ophir appears to be relating to several studies on the Holocaust and the ultra-Orthodox. It turns out he has discovered that the theologians are not all of one mind, but he ignores the Zionist Orthodox (among others) and, in fact, does not depart one whit from his basic positions or arguments. A brief but more balanced survey of Jewish theological literature on the Holocaust is to be found in the aforementioned book, *Between Auschwitz and Jerusalem,* by Yosef Gorny and in Eliezer Schweid, *Wrestling until Day-Break: Searching for Meaning in the Thinking on the Holocaust* (Lanham, Md.: University Press of America; Jerusalem: Jerusalem Center for Public Affairs, 1994).

Take Emil Fackenheim, for example. For Ophir, he expresses most systematically the notion that Auschwitz is the basis of a new religion. Indeed, Fackenheim is probably *the* theologian of the Holocaust. He sees the destruction of European Jewry as an event of unique importance, posing an unparalleled challenge to theology and moral philosophy. Fackenheim belonged to more or less the same political and cultural set – the German Jewish intellectuals who grew up between the wars and escaped when Hitler came to power – as did the philosophers of the Frankfurt School, or Hannah Arendt, for example, for whose philosophical thought the Holocaust came to play a pivotal, formative role. Fackenheim goes even further than they do in the importance he assigns to it; he regards the Holocaust as a "philosophical event." I, for one, would not subscribe to such a position. I would add, however, that what mainly distinguishes him from the other thinkers just mentioned is that he thinks about the Holocaust not only *because* he is a Jew but also *as* a Jew.

At any rate, not only does Fackenheim not seek a sacred dimension to Auschwitz; he sees it as just the opposite. At Auschwitz, he says, divine revelation was for the first time called into question, historically and empirically. Auschwitz made not only plausible but concrete something that no believing Jew in history ever thought possible: that historical reality could triumph over faith. At Auschwitz, the concept of holiness was emptied of all content and became a nonconcept. Ophir sometimes seems to take seriously his jibe that Auschwitz has become an upside-down monotheism, with theologians looking for a sacred dimension to it; but Fackenheim's idea – that, at Auschwitz, history defeated revelation – is just the opposite. For Fackenheim, Auschwitz is a proof – unanswered by theology or philosophy – that Jews should give up Judaism. If we undertake, after Auschwitz, despite Auschwitz, a systematic theology, it is because "life," not thought, has compelled us to do so, in the form of what he calls the 614th Commandment: it is forbidden to let Hitler win. The historic decision of the Jews, a nontheological, even antitheological decision, to go on living as Jews, is the fulfillment of this commandment. It is not a theoretical, theological, or philosophical consideration that leads them to this but rather the active determination, even after Hitler's demise, to safeguard the physical and spiritual existence of the Jewish people. *Despite* Auschwitz, not because of it. It is a moral and political decision of which the State of Israel is the most authentic and important expression. As with any moral or political decision, one can agree or disagree with Fackenheim's position. Ophir disagrees; he finds in the ruins of Palestinian society the opposite commandment. But Fackenheim is not looking for a "dimension of sanctity" in Auschwitz any more than Ophir is looking for one in Deir Yassin or Rafah. To portray Fackenheim's moral and theological decision as a positive response to Auschwitz is, at best, a matter of incomprehension and ignorance.

Or take Rabbi Teitelbaum, for example, "Our Master Yoel Teitelbaum, may the memory of a holy, righteous man be a blessing for life in the world to come," as he is referred to on the title page of the compilation *Al hage'ula ve'al hatemura* (On Redemption and its supplement) and his earlier work *Vayo'el moshe* (Moses Consented [Ex 2:21], a play on the name Yoel).[10] In these two works, the leader of the Satmar Hasidim draws up a balance sheet of the Holocaust and the establishment of the State of Israel. This Hungarian Jew, who fled for his life on a train arranged by the Labor Zionist Israel Kasztner, leaving his flock behind, bemoans the destruction that has befallen the Jewish people, "unprecedented since it first became a people." As Jews down through the ages have always done, he seeks to know "what this means and wherefore, what sin brought this about." In his view, this time "we need not hunt high and low for the transgression that brought this disaster upon us," for it is clear as day that the Jews have violated "the oaths not to ascend the wall [i.e., to return to the land of their own accord] or to force the End [i.e., the ultimate redemption]." Secularization in general, and Zionism, leading to the establishment of the State of Israel, in particular, are the great sins that brought down upon the Jews the worst catastrophe in their history. There is much theology in Teitelbaum's writing, but it can hardly be claimed that he sought a "sacred dimension" in the destruction of Hungarian and European Jewry. Nor is there anything holy about Israel's victories. The compilation *Al hage'ula ve'al hatemura*, written after the Six-Day War of 1967, tried to put a damper on the messianic fever that gripped even many ultra-Orthodox Jews. It is clear, the rabbi says, that "there was nothing miraculous about [the Zionists'] victory in the war; rather it was a natural occurrence. For the Arabs are not a martial people, and they tend to flee from the sword of war." The Zionists "say the opposite in order to blind us and magnify their victory, their false, imaginary miracles" (p. 36).

There was nothing holy about the destruction, but there was in the rescue of the few who survived. Those saved from the wicked Germans, curse them, were saved by nothing short of a miracle. "[They] are brands plucked from that terrible fire, and each and every one of them was saved miraculously and through wondrous divine intervention." What is more, "it is well known that some Jews were saved with the help of the wicked Germans,

---

[10] Both books are edited by the Yerushalaim publishing house of Brookline; the first was originally published in 1967, the earlier in 1961. Both are available online.

curse them, by means of bribes, but no sensible person would think of
praising [the latter] as rescuers. ... And wicked Zionists, our own people,
were involved in this rescue too, yet no one in the whole world would think
of praising them as rescuers or giving them credit, for everyone knows they
did not rescue but rather did even more harm and caused the deaths of tens
of thousands of Jews" (p. 73). The Satmar Rebbe's theology is a kind of
theodicy, that is, a justification of God and of the catastrophe. But what is
especially striking here is not the attempt to exonerate God but the depiction of secularism, and Zionism as its ultimate expression, as a great sin, so
great that the Holocaust is a fitting punishment. Fackenheim's theology, by
contrast, is not a theodicy at all. He does not pose the theological question
of the Holocaust as a question about the goodness of God, how to reconcile
His goodness, wisdom, and omnipotence with, let us say, the murder of a
million and a half of the children of His chosen people. In Fackenheim's
view, such reconciliation is not possible. This difference is but one of the
reasons the two thinkers, Teitelbaum and Fackenheim, cannot be lumped
together under the heading "all the theologians." If Ophir finds a common
language with one of them in terms of Zionism, he is closer to the other
from the point of view of theodicy. For he is philosophically opposed, in the
strongest terms, to any effort to justify God's ways. And for good reason.
It is understandable that Ophir, a self-proclaimed secular thinker (despite
the fact that his writings are filled with religious jargon), is not particularly
interested in theology. But one might expect him to treat it fairly. Not only is
his turn of phrase concerning the quest for a "sacred dimension" completely
off base, but one cannot speak of all the theologians of the Holocaust in
the same breath. Philosophers also have to admit that it was theologians,
or at least some of them, who first understood the importance of thinking
about Auschwitz (or dared to do so). At least in some cases, and I believe
Fackenheim is one, the theological approach to the question of Auschwitz is
an acknowledgment of how seriously it is taken. And seriousness is in short
supply.

   The claim that theologians preceded philosophers in taking the Holocaust
seriously is, of course, a sweeping generalization and not an entirely accurate
one. Many intellectuals have written about the Holocaust in ways that can
be defined as philosophical – thinkers of the Frankfurt school, for example, especially Horkheimer and Adorno (the value of whose reflections on
the subject is debatable), but also other German Jews of that generation:
Hannah Arendt, Hans Jonas, Erich Fromm. Jean Amery should also be
mentioned here. But systematic philosophical grappling with the subject
of the Holocaust is rather uncommon. A rare exception is the writing of

the Jewish American philosopher Berel Lang.[11] Lang discusses at length a number of the issues raised by the Nazi destruction of the Jews; and much of what is said here is quite close to his thinking.

At any rate, some Jewish theologians have *not* recognized the theological significance of the Holocaust or the seriousness of the theological difficulties it raises. Ophir mentions a few of these, without the contempt he reserves for the Zionist state's religion of the Holocaust. He refers to Yeshayahu Leibowitz, for example, who thought the Holocaust had no theological import. And, in fact, Leibowitz never said anything philosophically interesting or valuable about the German murder of the Jews. Among ultra-Orthodox thinkers, Teitelbaum was probably unusual in the intensity of his hatred for the Jewish state; but the non-Zionist, ultra-Orthodox theology of the Holocaust generally views the death of the Jews at the hands of the Germans as punishment for the sins of the Jewish people, especially the sins of secularism and Zionism. Other Jewish theologians do find religious meaning in the Holocaust, but it is not, in their view, unique. This is the perspective of the religious-Zionist thinkers, especially those who are more messianically inclined. Like Ophir, they have drawn a conceptual continuum on which Auschwitz can be located. Their continuum parallels Ophir's, but it has the opposite purpose: while the latter describes a range of human atrocities, the former describes a range of divine acts of redemption. Whereas Ophir builds an economy of evil on his continuum, the messianic theologians build an economy of salvation on theirs. Neither of them, at any rate, recognizes the essential uniqueness of the Holocaust. And neither is prepared to accept the State of Israel for what it really is: a man-made, political, historical artifact. Not perfect, of course, but also not monstrous.[12]

---

[11] I mention Lang's Jewishness because he does so himself. He even tries to explain the inescapable uniqueness, for him as a philosopher, of his Jewish point of view. See Berel Lang, *Act and Idea in the Nazi Genocide* (Chicago: University of Chicago Press, 1990). A later work is *Post-Holocaust: Interpretation, Misinterpretation, and the Claims of History* (Bloomington: Indiana University Press, 2005). In an afterword to the latter, entitled "Philosophy and/of the Holocaust," Lang speaks of the marginality of philosophy in the literature of the Holocaust.

[12] In an article on the Holocaust theology of the late Rabbi Tzvi Yehuda Kook, spiritual leader of the Bloc of the Faithful, Yishai Rosen-Tzvi tries to show that, for Kook, the Holocaust served mainly to confirm his doctrine of the redemption (*ge'ula*) of the Land of Israel. Kook does not speak of a Jewish state but, first of all, of the land itself. In any case, the Holocaust has no status of its own for him but is only a stage in the salvation-history of the Jewish people, dependent entirely on the cosmic or universal logic of redemption. See Yishai Rosen-Tzvi, "Haholeh hamedumeh: Tzidduk hashoa bemishnat harav Tzvi Yehuda Kook vehugo" (The Imaginary Invalid: The Theodicy of the Holocaust in the Teaching of Rabbi Tzvi Yehuda Kook and His Circle), in *Tarbut Demokratit* (Democratic Culture)

No doubt the question Ophir raises about the relationship between the Holocaust and religion is a serious, complex, and multifaceted one. Nazism's combination of extreme nihilistic and quasi-religious elements has led some scholars to try to comprehend it under the heading of "political theology" or as a "secular religion."[13] On the other hand, there are those who speak about reactions to the Holocaust on the part of the survivors, their families and descendants, as well as people unrelated to them – and especially of the public commemoration in Israel and the Jewish world at large – as phenomena of a religious character. Theological discussion of the Holocaust, by Jews and non-Jews alike, is, as we have said, widespread. These questions are only a part of the larger subject of the relation between the Holocaust and religion, or, to borrow Ophir's favorite expression, between Auschwitz and God. But to speak, as he does, about the "apotheosis" of the Holocaust or to describe a concern with it as upside-down theology does not constitute real discussion of this question. In the final analysis, it is just rhetoric. Rhetoric, as Aristotle teaches us, is the use of less-than-rigorous arguments – that is, arguments of limited or, as we say now, "soft" rationality – to persuade or influence people. This mode of argumentation is not necessarily invalid. There are cases where arguments cannot be substantiated in the manner of, for example, mathematical proofs. But rhetoric can also sometimes be indecent. It is apparently now in favor to use semireligious terminology to talk about attitudes to the Holocaust, and some see in it a sort of scholarly sophistication.

---

6   (5762/2002): 165–209. Much has been written in recent years about both Orthodox Zionism and Orthodox anti-Zionism. This literature – for example, the writings of Eliezer Schweid, Aviezer Ravitzky, Dov Schwartz, and, most recently, Hava Eshkoli-Wagman (*Bein hatzala uge'ula: Hatzionut hadatit be'eretz yisrael lenokhah hashoa* [Between Rescue and Redemption: Orthodox Zionism in the Land of Israel in the Face of the Holocaust] [Jerusalem: Yad Vashem, 5764/2004]) – presents quite a complex picture of the treatment of the Holocaust in Jewish theology, far more complex, at any rate, than Ophir's.

13 The term "political theology" is no less problematical than the concept of "civil religion." For example, Uriel Tal, who uses the former extensively in his historical interpretation of Nazism, seeks to analyze and clarify the term, both historically and conceptually. See his *Teologia politit veharaikh hashelishi* (Political Theology and the Third Reich) (Tel Aviv: Sifriat Poalim and Tel Aviv University, 1991). The opposite approach, interpreting Nazism as an antireligion or negation of religion (and morality) is taken by Hermann Rauschning, for example. See his *Germany's Revolution of Destruction*, trans. E. W. Dickes (London: William Heinemann, 1939). The term "secular religion" is widely used in political science literature. It usually refers to the great ideologies of the twentieth century, such as fascism, Nazism, or communism. One also finds it in linguistic combinations such as "the religion of progress" or, lately, the "human rights religion." These, and other such uses, usually convey a critical sense, and point to the allegedly irrational nature of the phenomena in question. Apart from this it is not very clear if this terminology adds much to the attempt to understand them.

What is important, and what is common to the Vieille Taupe people and Adi Ophir, is their use of such rhetoric to underline a direct connection between the Holocaust and Israeli evildoing, reinforcing a single basic message: the demonization and delegitimation of Israel.

Ophir, too, allows ideology to interfere with his scientific rigor. Not only is he an ideologue, and not only has ideology taken over his presentation of reality, but, if we judge from *The Worship of the Present*, his ideological agenda bears a considerable resemblance to that of La Vieille Taupe. What began merely as criticism of the theologization, as it were, of the Holocaust ends up with this two-hundred-page collection of post-Zionist essays. The first one actually offers the reader a pleasant surprise: it adds a touch of captivating irony to Ophir's otherwise deadpan writing style. Entitled "Zero Hour," it gives a short history of the founding of the State of Israel. To summarize briefly, it recalls the opposition, on the part of both Jews and non-Jews, to Zionism and the establishment of Jewish sovereignty in Palestine. The objective is not only to preserve the memory of this opposition but to bring it, alive and kicking, into the current debate. In other words, to "worship the present" by worshiping the past after all. In any case, it is "worship" in the cause of questioning the moral and practical validity of the idea that there needs to be a Jewish state. The recollection of the past that needs to be avoided is that which justifies the establishment of a Jewish state; that which undermines it is permissible.

The last essay, "Post-Zionism," lays everything out explicitly. Ophir teaches us to distinguish among Zionism, plain anti-Zionism, and post-Zionist criticism. The latter "denies Israeli Jews the ability to enjoy the self-image of eternal victim, innocent and passive" (p. 274). Definitive as this statement may be, it is not at all clear that Israeli Jews ever enjoyed such a self-image. One can only marvel at Ophir's powers of contemplation, which lay bare to him the depths of the Israeli Jewish soul and find *enjoyment* there, not the anxiety observed by others. But leave that aside. Post-Zionist criticism, with which Ophir says he does not fully identify, also prevents Israeli Jews (i.e., all of us) from ignoring the wrongs that their presumed victimhood has caused them to inflict on others. The real distinction of post-Zionism, he adds, is in its scholarly rigor and the place it has now earned in Israeli "discourse," that is, in the academy. We have already considered the pretense of scholarly rigor; as a rule, it is just the obverse side of the license these critics take to ignore whatever scholarly research they dislike, to dismiss it and treat it contemptuously. The main point, however, is that post-Zionist criticism sketches for us a profile of Zionism's victims – primarily Arabs, but also Middle Eastern Jews and, no doubt, a long list of others – and what we see in the sketch is the end of the Zionist era. This end is both desirable and inevitable. According to post-Zionism, the contemporary Zionist reality is full of contradictions. Of course, thinks Ophir from the high moral and intellectual ground he occupies, the post-Zionism discourse is itself, in the last analysis, a part of this contradictory reality and perhaps even a dialectical means of preserving it and putting off the explosion that threatens to destroy it from within. But

> this situation cannot last long. In a few years, a decade or two at the most, Zionism will be a relic of a vanished world, of concern only to museums, archives, and university history departments. Post-Zionism will then be remembered as a name given to the moment in which Israeli Jews became fully aware of the end of the Zionist era in Jewish history. This will have been the moment when Israeli Jews began to allow non-Jews to assume the mantle of victimhood and dared to take responsibility for those "other" victims of the Zionist project. (p. 280)

What will that era following the disappearance of Zionism be like? Ophir doesn't know, or, at any rate, he isn't letting us in on it. We can only guess.

Be that as it may, the central and longest part of the essay is devoted to the concept of the victim, how the Israeli Jews took on this identity, and how it made it possible for them to transform the Palestinians into victims in turn. The Jews' presumed victimhood is, of course, based on Auschwitz. Ophir cites at length the French philosopher Jean-François Lyotard and his discussion of the concept of the victim. This discussion is Lyotard's contribution to the dispute with Faurisson and the Holocaust deniers. Ophir knows this – in his book on evil he even expands on it a bit – but he is not true to Lyotard's spirit. In a kind of dialectical pirouette, he turns a harsh attack on the Holocaust deniers – a philosophical condemnation of the political and ideological purpose of their denial (the delegitimation of the Jewish state in Palestine) – into a basis for conclusions much like those the deniers themselves draw: it was inappropriate to create a Jewish state to begin with; the victims, or those who assumed the mantle of victimhood and presumed to speak in the victims' name, became the executioners; the Palestinians are the main victims (if not the only ones) of the upheaval caused by Zionism. Like Pierre Guillaume, Roger Garaudy, and Serge Thion, Ophir depicts a Gordian knot of compound, unmitigated evil binding the Holocaust up with the establishment of the State of Israel and its insane cruelties. The Holocaust becomes the central tenet in an ideological struggle – ostensibly merely critical but in fact abusive and destructive – against Zionism and Israel. This is because Ophir, like Thion, for example, singles out the Holocaust and its "representations" as the main rationale used by Zionism to justify the establishment of Israel. He describes the appropriation of victimhood as the root of Israel's criminality, the psychological, political, and cultural explanation for its exceptional ability to do wrong, cause suffering, and remain indifferent to its victims' plight. The Holocaust is the most effective means Israel has to garner international support, to ensure the world's silence in the face of the evil it commits, and to get the Jews to accept its rule over their lives.[14]

Ophir has high regard for contemporary French philosophy.[15] He also takes Lyotard very seriously, and with good reason. But the need to marshal all available resources for the "worship of the present" sometimes prevents him from seeing certain truths. For example, Lyotard's statements do not jibe with those of one of his other sources: Idith Zertal. The latter sees the Eichmann trial as a sort of minor catastrophe. She describes it as a historic turning point that changed not only the way Israelis related to the Holocaust but also, as a result, the face of Israeli society and the whole course of Israeli history. The trial, according to Zertal, was the cause of almost everything that happened to Israel afterward, especially the bad things: the Six-Day War, the occupation and settlement of the territories, the atomic bomb, and God knows what else. Ophir buys into this line of argument, lock, stock, and

---

[14] Ophir's description of Israeli society is not only tendentious and ideologically biased but basically false. As usual, it contains some elements of truth, of course. How could it be otherwise with something so complex and painful – above all, painful – as the memory of the Holocaust? The Israeli culture of self-victimization is a myth. The opposite is much closer to the truth; at least this is what emerges from many studies of the ways Israelis see themselves and their country. Which does not prevent many writers from referring to the myth repeatedly, ad nauseam, as if it were fact. A recent, grotesque and preposterous, psychoanalytic portrayal of the Israeli society can be found in Jacqueline Rose, *The Question of Zion* (Princeton: Princeton University Press, 2005). Another recent book built entirely around this idea and no less preposterous is Esther Benbassa's *La soufrance comme identité* (Suffering as Identity) (Paris: Fayard, 2007).

[15] Actually, only for certain schools that are ultimately more or less peripheral. The centrality and importance Ophir attributes to the French thinkers he quotes so extensively is more typical of the way they have been received in some American academic quarters than of the way they are seen in France, either within or outside the academy. The uncritical dogmatism with which thinkers like Lyotard and Derrida are accepted is more characteristic of the United States than of France. Gadi Taub is right to describe Israeli post-modernism (a subculture to which Ophir belongs, though he may resent being linked to it) as more an American than a French import. See his "Post-tzionut: Hakesher ha tzarfati-amerikai-yisra'eli" (Post-Zionism: The French-American-Israeli Connection), in *Teshuva le'amit post-tzioni* (Answer to a Post-Zionist Colleague), ed. Tuvia Frilling (Tel Aviv: Yediot Ahronot, 2003), 224–242. In a compelling, often amusing book, a French cultural historian shows how certain French philosophers – who are important but by no means unique or even central in their native land – have come to be seen as proponents of a "French theory" that is, essentially, the invention of literature, sociology, and anthropology departments on several American campuses. See François Cusset, *French Theory: Foucault, Derrida, Deleuze & Cie et les mutations de la vie intelletuelle aux Etats-Unis* (Paris: La Découvete, 2003).

barrel, although it lacks even the slightest academic seriousness or historical truth.[16] The Eichmann trial was, indeed, a very important event, but to deny the legitimacy of conducting it or of the way it was conducted, and to use this delegitimation in order to lambaste Israel and its policies, in fact to question their fundamental morality, is highly questionable. It is no less dubious than the way Rassinier acknowledged the great importance of the trial and then tried to rescue the "true Eichmann trial" from the myths and manipulations with which Zionist propagandists surrounded it. For Rassinier, as for Eyal Sivan, Zertal, and Ophir (a partial list, of course), the trial, with all its historic and emotional freight, becomes an important symbolic tool in a campaign to delegitimize Israel, the policies of its government, and the ethos of its people. Hannah Arendt's book *Eichmann in Jerusalem* is a major source of this campaign.

Invoking Lyotard in support of such criticism of the Eichmann trial, that is, in order to delegitimate it, is especially interesting. It is interesting because it is symptomatic and because it turns the French philosopher's views on end, not only in general, philosophical terms but also in terms of Lyotard's specific views on the subject of Israel and the Eichmann trial. In fact, Lyotard sees the trial as one of the most important expressions of Israel's moral legitimacy as a state, and he certainly does see the existence of a Jewish state as morally legitimate. The extermination of the Jews and the denial of that extermination – Auschwitz and Faurisson – are his points of departure. This leads him to what might be described as a postmodern attempt to overcome relativism. Lyotard is a postmodern pluralist who recognizes the limits of would-be universal assertions of truth but also the need, at times, to make choices, moral and otherwise, and he refuses to forgo the possibility of making such choices. He employs the concept of *différend*, which is also the title of a well-known book of his.[17] This, by the way, is a perfectly good French

[16] And he is not alone. In the preface to the Hebrew translation of her book, *The Question of Zion,* Jacqueline Rose refers to Zertal's work– and only to it – as an authoritative confirmation of the correctness of her views and as a source of consolation after the attacks her book evoked. So does Tony Judt in a much discussed article he published in the *New York Review of Books* in 2003. We shall come back to it in the Postscript. It is nothing short of amazing that a respected scholar like Judt can speak with such seriousness about a work of this ilk. More than anything else, it is symptomatic of how, when it comes to the question of Israel, especially in its relation to the Holocaust, elementary critical ability, sane judgment, and, in fact, plain common sense seem to disappear.

[17] See Jean-François Lyotard, *The* Différend: *Phrases in Dispute* (Minneapolis: University of Minnesota Press, 1988). The book was published when deniers, especially on the left, were flourishing and when – in the wake of the Faurisson affair and thanks to Chomsky's aforementioned assistance – they were able to capture the French public eye. One of Lyotard's main reasons for writing this book was to take issue with them.

word meaning controversy or disagreement. Lyotard uses the word mainly metaphorically, and he does not try to turn it into a philosophical term with a life of its own – which it is not, in French philosophical language – in contrast to the way Ophir uses the term or the way it is used in a certain provincial literature.

Différend is a legal metaphor. Lyotard defines it as a confrontation in which there are no clear rules that could be applied fairly to the claims of the disputants so as to adjudicate between them. In such cases, language, the ability to give verbal expression, is one means of overcoming the difficulty of deciding the case. But the model for applying rules of adjudication is, first and foremost, the court and the legal hearing. The prime example Lyotard uses to construct his theory is how to decide between the claims of the Holocaust deniers and those of the victims. The Eichmann trial provides a paradigm for such a decision: doing justice on behalf of those who would otherwise remain unheard. Since French philosophy, too, has already gotten past the "linguistic turning point" and freed itself from the need to base all deliberation on metaphorical language, we can perhaps also extract from Lyotard's statements some more user-friendly meaning. Language is important in that it gives voice to what would otherwise remain unheard. The same is true of the tribunal where the litigants make their pleas. If the tribunal did not, through its procedural rules, provide the possibility of setting forth these pleas, they would remain unheard. Language, and the trial itself, are thus conditions for the expression – of necessity public – of what can be called a "unique point of view." This is how we should understand Lyotard's discussion of the Eichmann trial. It was this trial that gave voice at last to the Jewish *différend*, to the viewpoint of the victims. Although Lyotard never says so explicitly, he implies that allowing the Jewish point of view to emerge from its silence and, in particular, making it possible to adjudicate the *différend* between the victims and the deniers depend on the victims and their heirs being able to set up a tribunal, that is, to bring Eichmann to Jerusalem and try him there.[18]

Since Adi Ophir is not party to the postmodern culture of "narratives" and does not recognize the right to ignore objective truth, and since it is hard to believe that he does not understand Lyotard's writings or has overlooked something in them, there is no escaping the melancholy conclusion that in his case, too, ideology has gotten the better of thought, triumphing over critical

---

[18] Lyotard returned to such questions, and more explicitly to the role played by the Jews in the treatment they received, in a later book, *Heidegger and "The Jews"* (Minneapolis: University of Minnesota Press, 1990).

probity and intellectual honesty. In his case, too, a familiar perversity has tied the Holocaust together with Zionism and Israel in a single bundle of unredeemed evil that is intolerable and will, it is hoped, disappear. Ophir's case is particularly interesting, and not only because of the undeniable disparity between his intellectual ability and the grotesque shallowness of the deniers. Ophir is not an ideologue in the same sense as Guillaume. He is a moral philosopher, and he looks at the world from a moral point of view. In his case, it seems, it is not ideology that has gone mad but morality.

Criticism of Israel and Zionism is, of course, legitimate. But one must distinguish between criticism of Israeli policies or various aspects of Zionist ideology, on the one hand, and criticism of Israel and Zionism as such, on the other – that is, questioning the Jewish state's right to exist and the legitimacy of Zionism as a program for the establishment of such a state in the Land of Israel. The theological metaphor serves to validate the statement made in the pamphlet published by La Vieille Taupe cited earlier: Israel has no right to exist. Of course, neither does France or Australia, for example. But, in fact, only the challenge to Israel's right to exist has any relevance or significance. Perhaps it is because neither France nor Australia is harmful in the way Israel is; perhaps because it is only in relation to the Zionist state that the rhetoric can be translated into a political platform and a concrete plan of action; and perhaps because only Israel has enemies who speak seriously of its destruction – and act accordingly – and the idea of wiping it off the map is one that is still current. For certain Iranians, for example. And for Adi Ophir. He is also critical of the notion of sovereignty in general. But for him, too, the only practical consequence of the general theory is the desire to see Israel eliminated as a Jewish or Zionist state and to take determined, consistent action toward that end. He, too, connects this stance firmly with the Holocaust, the wrongs done to the Palestinians, and the theological or religious character of the rationale Israelis give, to themselves and others, for their crimes.

Ophir is not alone in his battle. Although he is rightly opposed to the accepted Zionist labels, it seems to me there is good reason to identify him with the group we call post- or anti-Zionists, especially those (not few in number) who have turned the Holocaust into one of their principal weapons for delegitimating the Jewish national state. What Ophir says is typical of a whole community of opprobrium and the systematic exploitation of the Holocaust to reinforce that opprobrium. One example, of a different character, was the focus of a relatively recent brouhaha. It was connected with Eyal Sivan, an Israeli film maker who now lives in Paris. On various occasions, Sivan has described himself publicly as an anti-Zionist, and not long ago he and a Palestinian colleague made a film entitled *Highway 181: Parts of a*

Journey in Israel-Palestine, which describes the reality along the partition line, that is, the line that, according to the United Nations General Assembly resolution of 1947, was to have divided Palestine into Jewish and Arab states.

The film raised a storm in France because of what critics saw as numerous hints at a similarity between Israeli actions and those of the Nazis. One scene, in particular, aroused viewers' wrath: a Palestinian Arab barber, at work, tells of the expulsion of the Arabs from Lydda (Lod). He speaks of a massacre of the Arab inhabitants of the town, of rape and other cruelties, at the time it was captured by Israeli forces in 1948.[19] The scene concludes with a shot of railroad tracks. Many viewers saw this scene as an allusion to a well-known one in Claude Lanzmann's film *Shoah* in which Abraham Bomba, a Jewish barber now living in the Israeli city of Holon (if I recall correctly), tells of his experience working at Treblinka. He and sixteen others were assigned the task of shearing women's hair before they were sent to the gas chambers. Sivan explains (in the Hebrew daily *Haaretz*, March 18, 2004) that, to him, Lanzmann's barber and the Arab barber from Lydda "are two sides of a single trauma," even though, he adds, there is obviously a difference between the desire to annihilate the Jews and the "ethnic cleansing" that took place in Palestine. There is no comparison – but one can hint at a similarity. Sivan's film was made in Paris, Guillaume's home town. The audience to which he addressed himself was Guillaume's audience. The film's message is simple: true, the publications of La Vieille Taupe contain many exaggerations, particularly about that gas chamber business. There were gas chambers. But what was done with them is like what the Jews did to that Arab barber in Lydda. They are two sides of a single coin. Or a single trauma. Ultimately, some Parisian viewers will draw the conclusion that there is something to what the Vieille Taupe people say; there are even Israelis saying it: *the real Nazis are the Israelis*. Or at least one can compare

---

[19] Between July 10 and 12, Ramla and Lydda were captured by Israeli troops. There were in these cities some 10,000 and 40,000 Arab civilians respectively, many of them refugees from Jaffa and the surrounding villages. During the heavy fighting, some of them fled, and many others were expelled. Only a few hundred remained after the battle. The "new historian" Benny Morris cites Lydda as proof that there was, at the time, a policy of expelling the Arab population; Yoav Gelbert, another prominent historian of the war, disputes this thesis. Among other things, he cites an explicit order by Ben-Gurion to stop the expulsion of women, children, the elderly, and sick. But commanders in the field did not always obey. The fighting in Lydda was among the bloodiest of the war: Palestinian authorities estimated some 340 Arabs died; the Israeli army estimated 250. Rumors among the Arabs spoke of 3,000.

what the Nazis did with what the Israelis are doing now to the Palestinians; one can suggest that there is no real difference between them.

The juxtaposition of the "two sides of a single trauma" comes across not only in the film about Israel-Palestine but also in Sivan's more general cinematic interest in the two questions. An earlier film of his dealt with the Eichmann trial. It is just a simplistic piece of manipulation based on filmed excerpts from the trial. Sivan is not interested in describing this important event to the viewer. Rather, he has a blatant ideological aim: to demonstrate Eichmann's "banality," following the famous definition Hannah Arendt set forth in her controversial book on the trial. It is not a documentary film but a propagandistic one, made entirely to serve the director's ideological agenda. The film clips it uses were chosen with unconcealed tendentiousness and not even much subtlety. There is not much to say about this film except that, on the one hand, what Sivan means by Eichmann's "banality" is not very clear, and, on the other, Eichmann himself hardly comes across in the film as a banal figure, whatever that term might mean.[20]

Adi Ophir and Eyal Sivan provide two examples of Israeli artists and writers who make the same connection we see in Guillaume between the Holocaust and anti-Zionism. And they are not alone. Another Israeli, Ran Hacohen, published an article on the Web site antiwar.com in March 2004, following the assassination of Sheikh Ahmed Yassin, the charismatic founder and leader of the Islamist Hamas movement. The title was "Who Won the Second World War?" The true victor in that war, Hacohen tells us, was Hitler. The proof: the assassination of Yassin. That act was in violation of the Geneva Convention, for, as the Nuremburg Tribunal ruled, the partisans who fought the Nazis in the ghettos and elsewhere were not terrorists and deserved protection against execution without trial. Yassin should be seen as a "partisan," whatever reservations we may have about the terrorist acts he perpetrated. Israel, on the other hand, has now violated all the relevant clauses of the Geneva Convention, it is furthering the barbarization of humanity, and if the international community does not take

---

[20] In the beginning of 2005, this film (*The Specialist: Portrait of a Modern Criminal*) was accused of being fraudulent. A newspaper article, "Hanadon: Ziyyuf kit'ei seratim mimishpat Eichmann" (The Point in Question: The Fabrication of Film Clips from the Eichmann Trial) (*Haaretz*, January 31, 2005), which, incidentally, presents the film as "one of the most important documentaries on the ... trial," describes some of the "artistic" devices it employs. Sivan (*Haaretz*, February 14, 2005) does not really answer the accusations leveled against him but defends his right to film "a political essay about obedience to the law and the concept of responsibility," in the spirit of Hannah Arendt. The pretension and ignorance betrayed by this remark are equaled only by the worthlessness of the film.

action, the moment of Yassin's assassination will become a historic turning point in which Hitler's concept of war will have triumphed. Two weeks later, Hacohen published another article on the same Web site. This time he responds to letters from readers of his first column. Of all the things he said there, he tells us, only one drew angry reactions: he had attributed a barbaric conception of war to the Germans alone. And also to the Israelis, of course. But, several readers thundered, the Americans, too, had been barbaric. They too had committed atrocities. These angry readers cited a book – another one of those books – that blamed Dwight Eisenhower for starving a million German prisoners of war to death after the war and for causing what they called a "second Holocaust." Hacohen, who describes himself as a child of Holocaust survivors, is extremely sensitive to Holocaust denial, picking up its odor from a great distance. In his great sensitivity, he immediately noticed the affinity between those letter writers who spoke of a "second Holocaust" and those who would deny that the (first) Holocaust ever happened. It is merely an affinity in this case, but it calls for a sharp retort nevertheless. So far, Hacohen. On the face of it, what could be simpler? Hacohen criticizes Israel, claiming that it has waged war in Hitler's barbaric fashion. But he also opposes Holocaust denial. What is not so simple, however, is the fact that the deniers chose to react to what Hacohen said. Could they, or their relatives, have understood that they and Hacohen shared common ground, that they had little reason to argue with him? If Israel is a Nazi state, their point has already been proved: Hitler was not unique, and in the crime against the Jews he had collaborators. How did George Bernard Shaw put it to that lady? We agree in principle; now all we have to do is set the price: just Israel, or the Americans, too? Just Sharon, or Eisenhower as well?

Hacohen's dispute with the Holocaust deniers is, in the end, a family quarrel. Their response to him is a kind of hug. Just as he can smell the deniers from afar, so, evidently, can they. He and the other Israelis who harness the Holocaust to their war of words may fend off, no doubt quite sincerely, the embrace of the deniers. They may even resent that embrace – presumably, Jerusalem professors Moshe Zimmerman and Baruch Kimmerling would utterly reject Garaudy's co-optation of them – or my attempt to show an essential partnership, not just a superficial similarity, between them. But the truth is that there is a real affinity between them and Guillaume and his friends. It may not be coincidental that my being an Israeli did not surprise Guillaume in the least; he even informed me that, now that Israel's criminality was widely known, Jews, too, and occasionally even Israelis, had begun to think he was right. For what Guillaume did was to take anti-Zionism and anti-Israelism to its logical conclusion, exposing, however grotesquely, the perversity they concealed. The use some Israelis make of the Holocaust to further their war of words masks a very similar perversity.

There is collusion and affinity between Holocaust denial, as it appears among certain radical left-wing circles in Europe, and the way certain Israeli scholars and intellectuals, generally on the left too, connect the Holocaust with their radical critique of Israel: its policies, the ethos underlying its cultural and political identity, the way its existence as a Jewish nation-state is justified. This connection is made in different, sometimes contradictory ways. For the time being, the Israeli community of *resentiment* does not include anyone who denies that the Holocaust took place. Not only do none of them deny the existence of the gas chambers or their use for mass killing, but they do not even question the official Jewish narrative according to which the Germans conducted a deliberate campaign of extermination against the Jews of Europe. (It is not clear why, but even Ilan Pappe refuses to see Holocaust denial as a legitimate narrative!) On the contrary, some of them even think the Shoah of European Jewry was the greatest moral calamity ever to take place, that the genocide committed by the Nazis and their henchmen was the worst crime in human history. How, then, can they be associated with the deniers of the Holocaust? After all, some of them feel the pain of the victims and the survivors, feel their pain and speak for them. They probably consider themselves to be, as Ophir put it, virtual victims. It is not hard to imagine how the subjects of this little essay will react to these words, if they ever read them. It will probably seem to them like just another instance of Israeli-Zionist paranoia – or propaganda – that immediately brands all criticism as anti-Semitism.

But it isn't so. The sad truth is that these local grumblers do belong to the ideological space created by Holocaust denial. Unfortunately, some Israelis who criticize their country and its ideological underpinnings are closely bound up with people like Guillaume and Thion, not to mention Chomsky, of course. The way the Holocaust figures in quite a number of essays, articles, and books written in Hebrew, the way it is used as a central tenet in scathing criticisms of Israel's conduct in the occupied territories or of the moral and historical justification given for the establishment of a Jewish state – all this reflects a perversion quite similar, if not identical, to that of which Holocaust denial (particularly the radical left-wing version) is the most extreme symptom. Though the revulsion expressed toward Holocaust deniers is often sincere, though some who use the Holocaust to attack Israel certainly believe deep down that to accuse them of affinity with the likes of Pierre Guillaume is a moral and intellectual outrage – one can nonetheless find in their writings the main outlines of the perversion I tried to sketch in the preceding chapter. This is so, first of all, because for both the Parisian deniers and the Israeli grumblers the question of the Holocaust is hostage to their (negative) attitude toward Israel.

Adi Ophir's volume of essays, which we discussed earlier, is a good example. We find there, expressed quite openly, the central feature of this perversion, which is the essential, exclusive, and mostly false connection drawn between the Holocaust and Israel. Israel is what gives the Holocaust meaning, and the Holocaust is the chief explanation for the wrongs Israel commits. This is true of Guillaume and his circle, as I have tried to show; and it is equally true of the group of local grumblers here who deal with the Holocaust. None of them has written about the Holocaust or its conse-quences as a subject of inquiry in its own right, only in terms of its ideologi-cal effects in general, and on Israel and in the Israeli context in particular; and all of them see the Holocaust as the ultimate test of Israel's right to exist as a Jewish state and as the grounds for negating that right.

As we have pointed out, there is certainly a close, integral connection between the Holocaust and Israel. There cannot be any doubt that the two most important events in modern Jewish history have been the destruction of one-third of the Jewish people and the establishment of Israel. These two events have had enormous ramifications in many spheres, even if one is opposed to their theologization and mystification. But the systematic, simplistic, tendentious, and utterly baseless way the Holocaust is used to lambaste Israel is also a kind of mystification. It is based on two principles that are shared by all the theoreticians or pseudotheoreticians of the Israeli community of *resentiment*: the Holocaust led to the establishment of the state; and there is no other basis for its right to exist. Both historically and morally, the Holocaust is the sine qua non of the existence of the state and of its policies. It is also the main factor contributing to the culture of anxi-ety so characteristic of Israelis; the bedrock of the Israeli ethos, collective consciousness, collective memory; and the source of the ideological and psy-chological rationales Israelis give for their country's political behavior. In particular, Holocaust consciousness shapes the more violent and aggressive aspects of Israeli life. The destruction of European Jewry was the *historical* cause and *moral* justification of the state's establishment, but it is also the *phenomenological* or *psychological* basis of Israeli reality.

Along with these basic ideas, we find the following notions, shared to different degrees and with different emphases: The guilt feelings aroused in the people of the world, and especially in Europe, by the destruction of European Jewry drove them to support the establishment of the Jewish state. The Holocaust is, indeed, the only argument in favor of the Zionism program: the Jews are not a nation deserving of self-determination, Zionism is a colonialist phenomenon, and the State of Israel was erected on the ruins of another people's homes, following a long series of crimes Zionism committed against them. Consequently, the Jews living in the piece of land called Israel do not have a "natural" right to self-determination or a state. They obviously have no "historic rights" to the land either. The world consented to the wrong done to the Palestinians as atonement for not having prevented the wrong the Germans did to the Jews. For various reasons, either weakness or a desire to be rid of the "Jewish question," but in any case without justification, the international community agreed to regard the Zionist movement as the legitimate representative of the Jewish people, its spokesman and the voice of its suffering. But the Palestinians were never consulted about this, and they have never agreed that Europe's crimes should be expiated at their expense. The State of Israel thus persists on moral credit given by the world at the Palestinians' expense. Even if this credit had originally been understandable, it was squandered by Israeli policies, at least since 1967, but in fact ever since its founding, by the conquest and abuse of the Palestinians. In fact, there is an almost exact similarity between the actions of the Nazis and the Israelis. The Holocaust is also the main basis for Israel's claim to represent the Jewish people as a whole. But the non-Zionist Jews, never mind the victims of the Holocaust, were never consulted about this either, and many of them never agreed that Israel should represent their suffering, that of their forebears, or that of the victims.

Several conclusions can be drawn from all this. If, for example, Zionism and the State of Israel are not the legitimate representatives of the Jews who suffered in the Holocaust or their offspring, the state's legitimacy is called into question. If it conducts itself immorally (especially toward the Palestinians), its moral credit gets used up and, along with it, its right to exist. This is quite aside from the fact that the Palestinians' refusal to pay the price can no longer be covered up. Similarly, if the way the Israelis relate to the rest of the world, to themselves, and, above all, to the Palestinians is distorted by its memory of the Holocaust, if, in other words, the Holocaust is not just a reason and a justification but an *excuse*, then a new basis for Israeli life, in fact a whole new identity, must be sought.

Aside from the ultimate aim and principal concern of Holocaust denial, which is the delegitimation and demonization of Israel, we must be attentive to the content and structure of its claims, its rhetoric and polemical strategies, and its sociocultural characteristics – that is, a whole set of factors and ingredients. Some or all of these can be found in the writings of the denial community Guillaume created around La Vieille Taupe. But they can also be found in the discourse (to use the current term) that, in Israel, brings the Holocaust and criticism of the country together in one way or another, more or less explicitly, in order to call its very existence into question.

EXCURSUS I: IDEOLOGY AND HISTORICAL TRUTH

Even if the use of the Holocaust in anti-Zionist discourse in Israel is symptomatic of a perversion, and even if what we have called the Israeli "community of *resentiment*" does belong in some degree to the same ideological culture as La Vieille Taupe, it is still possible that what the members of this group are saying about the Holocaust and Israel is true. If "truth" is something we attribute to the *substance* of claims – as opposed to the way the claims are made, the source from which they are drawn, and the mentality that gives rise to them – then these claims are certainly worthy of consideration. Or more precisely, what we have said so far is not enough to dismiss them. Even if what motivates the advocates of these views is not truthfulness or even an interest in truth, that does not discredit the views themselves. Even if everything we have said here about these people is correct, they may still *have* something. Hence, we need to comment, albeit briefly, on the accuracy of their factual claims concerning the Holocaust, which play such an important role in their broad-scale indictment of Israel.

I will not comment here on the comparisons between Israeli treatment of the Palestinians and Nazi behavior, or on the notion that Israel, or one or another aspect of its society, has a Nazi, or quasi-Nazi, or potentially Nazi character. It seems to me that anyone who is even slightly familiar with the character of the Nazi regime and what it called the "Final Solution" and who manages to retain some measure of intellectual honesty, even when Israeli actions infuriate him, knows there is not much truth to such comparisons. I also have no intention here of entering into the argument over the nature of historical knowledge or of various kinds of narratives, be they metanarratives or any other kind. As often happens, there is a real question here, but it is obscured by mountains of verbiage, full of fashionable jargon but of little theoretical interest. The fact that there is a large, practically unbridgeable gap between human reality and the theoretical tools we, as historians or social scientists, employ to understand it is obvious and trivial. Slightly less trivial is the fact that all such efforts at understanding are made in the particular situation in which the historian or social scientist finds himself, that every scholar looks at the reality he is investigating from a specific point of view. But this does not necessarily mean that historiography should, once and for all, dispense with the category known as "objective knowledge." On the contrary (as we shall elaborate later on), the very fact that there is a point of view that imposes itself both on the observer and on the facts observed is a prerequisite for the objective knowledge of those facts.

There would appear to be a single, central thesis or cluster of theses shared by the deniers and the Israelis we are speaking of here that can be subjected to a more or less reasonable test of historical truth. What they share is a two-sided idea about the essential role of the Holocaust in giving rise to the phenomenon known as Israel and in shaping its behavior and outstanding capacity for causing suffering and wrong. Like the mythical Janus, one side of this thesis faces outward, toward the international community, which agreed to the establishment of the State of Israel and condones its ongoing actions. The other side concerns the way the Holocaust has shaped the character of the people of Israel or been used to shape it. The Holocaust, it turns out, is the reason for the creation both of Israel itself and of its political culture, which is one of force and violence. As we have seen, the Holocaust is said to be a necessary and perhaps also sufficient cause both of the state's existence and of the policies it pursues. This general thesis divides into a number of more concrete factual claims concerning:

- The role of the Holocaust in persuading the international community to support the 1947 UN resolution to partition Palestine, which was the principal legal basis for the establishment of Israel
- The role of the Holocaust in garnering the international support that Israel needed to set up and equip its army and achieve military superiority over its enemies, but especially to abuse and inflict cruelty upon them
- The key role assigned to the Holocaust in Israeli diplomacy
- The role of Holocaust awareness in Israel, particularly organized, public commemoration, in the development of the country's ethos, its militarism, and moral blindness

For accuracy's sake, certain facts should probably be pointed out. The years immediately following the Second World War were difficult ones for the Zionist movement, perhaps the most difficult in the entire history of the "Zionist project." Beginning in the mid-1930s, shortly after the 1933 accession of the Nazis to power in Germany and the outbreak in 1936 of the three-year Arab "revolt" (in which some five thousand Arabs were killed by British and Arabs alike) in Palestine, Britain reneged on its promise to establish a Jewish national home there. With the war looming in Europe, Britain sought to win the Arab world over to its side. It rejected the Peel Commission's 1937 recommendation to partition the country, and its opposition, expressed in the prewar 1939 White Paper, continued throughout the war, even after the scope and barbarity of the destruction of European Jewry came to light, and after the war ended, when the scale of the disaster was clear to all. Strategic considerations during the war and imperial ones afterward caused the Labor Party, traditionally supportive of Zionism in its main goals, to adopt, once it came to power in 1945, a policy opposing the establishment of a Jewish state in even a part of Palestine. Even with hundreds of thousands of Jewish "displaced persons" (as the homeless Jewish survivors were called) crowded into transit camps across Europe and no one else willing to take them in, Britain refused to allow significant numbers of Jews into Palestine. In 1945 a mere 13,100 Jews were given entry permits.[21]

At the Yalta Conference after the war, the fate of Palestine was never brought up; Roosevelt, for example, was not affected by the plight of the European Jews when he sat down with Stalin and Churchill to decide on a postwar world order. Even Truman's support for Jewish sovereignty, achieved with great effort, stemmed more from an appreciation of Zionist pragmatism and willingness to compromise than from guilt over the wrong done to the Jews. Incidentally, Truman's decisive support for the General Assembly's partition resolution was strongly opposed within his own administration, particularly by the State Department.[22]

If we examine the deliberations of the various United Nations bodies during the long months leading up to the vote on November 29, 1947, especially the report of the Special Commission on Palestine (UNSCOP), we see that a number of reasons were offered for the establishment of a Jewish state in Palestine alongside an Arab state there, but that the killing of the European Jews was not prominent among them. True, there was a desire to rectify a historic injustice against the Jewish people and to find a solution to the problem of the Jewish displaced persons in Europe, but the main arguments advanced were historical (the age-old connection of the Jewish people to the Land of Israel) and legal (Britain's promise, in the Balfour Declaration, to establish a Jewish national home and the international recognition that promise had been given in the mandate it received for Palestine after World War I). France's support for partition, for example, was not secured even by persistent American pressure but only when Leon Blum, pressed by Weizmann, intervened with the French prime minister.[23] We should also

[21] According to Martin Gilbert, *Exile and Return: The Struggle for a Jewish Homeland* (Philadelphia: Lippincott, 1978), 274.
[22] See Sasson Sofer, *Zionism and the Foundations of Israeli Diplomacy* (Cambridge: Cambridge University Press, 1998), 40–53.
[23] See Ilan Greilsammer, *Blum* (Paris: Flammarion, 1996) (in French), 522–523.

note the support of the Soviet Union for the establishment of a Jewish state, support that certainly did not, indeed could not, stem from guilt feelings over the Holocaust. A much more important consideration was undoubtedly the desire to acquire a foothold in the Middle East.[24]

In the last analysis, the stance taken by the various countries toward the establishment of Israel was determined, as such things always are, by their perception of their own interests. Soviet support for Israel was short-lived, as we know, and the famous French love affair with Israel, which came to an abrupt end with De Gaulle's remarks about the Jews being a "self-confident and domineering people," was based primarily on France's view of Israel as an ally in the struggle to hold onto its colonies in North Africa. The massive support of the United States for Israel came much later, of course, and here, too, it can hardly be assumed that guilt feelings were the main motive.

In recent years "Zionist" historians have been divided over the role of the Holocaust in the establishment of the State of Israel. Evyatar Friesel, for example, in a series of articles, maintains that the destruction of European Jewry was actually a major hindrance to the Zionist cause, disrupting in a fundamental way the original plan to gain access to a Jewish national home in the Land of Israel and then gradually develop there a society that could sustain a well-run state. What disrupted this plan was the fact that the main reservoir of human, cultural, and political material for such a project was destroyed in the Holocaust. Other historians, Yehuda Bauer and Hagit Lavsky being good examples, see the plight of the Jews – even before the Holocaust but especially after it – as an important, perhaps necessary, condition for the establishment of the state.[25] But Lavsky, for one, has not forgotten that, even before the Holocaust, the Zionist movement set the establishment of a Jewish state in the Land of Israel as its main goal and that

---

[24] A detailed discussion of this issue can be found in Alexander Yacobson and Amnon Rubinstein, *Yisrael umishpahat ha'amim: Medinat le'om yehudit uzekhuyot ha'adam* (Israel and the Family of Nations: A Jewish Nation-State and Human Rights) (Jerusalem: Schocken, 5763 [2003]), 19–79. English edition: *Israel and the Family of Nations* (London: Tayler and Francis, 2008).

[25] See Hagit Lavsky, "She'erit hapeleita vehakamat hamedina: Hizdamnut asher nutzla" (The Saving Remnant and the Establishment of the State: An Opportunity Seized), *Katedra* 55 (1990): 175–181. Lavsky, who surveys the outlines of the aforementioned debate briefly in this article, rejects Frilling's unequivocal judgment that the State of Israel was not established *thanks to* the Holocaust but *despite* it, but neither does she see the Holocaust as a necessary and sufficient condition for its establishment. A summary of this debate can be found in Dan Michman, "The Causal Relationship between the Holocaust and the Birth of Israel: Historiography between Myth and Reality," in Michman, *Holocaust Historiography: A Jewish Perspective; Conceptualizations, Terminology, Approaches, and Fundamental Issues* (London: Vallentine Mitchell, 2003), 303–328.

the foundations for the realization of the Zionist program were laid long before the Holocaust even became a possibility.

The issue of the role of Holocaust consciousness in shaping Israel's political culture and ethos is a more complicated one. The claim that the Holocaust is the root of Israeli wickedness is not necessarily more truthful than any of the other claims we have been considering, but the tools needed to test its veracity are harder to come by. But that is precisely the point. There is a more general difficulty here, one that applies to all those who claim to have exclusive access to the conflicted, violent, dangerous soul of the Israeli people.[26] Even if we assume there is such a thing as an Israeli "Holocaust discourse," something that is also doubtful, for both methodological and substantive reasons; even if we accept some of the all-too-similar descriptions offered by the various psychologists of the national soul; and even if we agree – and there are good reasons not to – that the term "discourse" has some conceptual content, methodological validity, or real theoretical value, one question remains unanswered: do the texts offered in evidence in these analyses of the nation's soul have any concrete, practical effect on Israeli public policy, for example, in relation to the conflict with the Palestinians, or even on the behavior of individual Israelis toward their friends and enemies? Most studies of decision making – wise or misguided – by Israel's leadership indicate rather clearly that the Holocaust does not figure as a significant factor. No one has seriously investigated the influence of Holocaust consciousness, of experiences such as the March of the Living in Poland, on the behavior of Israeli soldiers – some of them Druze, Beduin, and Circassians (i.e., non-Jews) – at army checkpoints or in Palestinian residential areas, behavior that is constantly brought up in all kinds of recriminations against Israel.

We have only scratched the surface of this subject, of course, but it seems to me it is enough to call into question the definitiveness of the claim that the State of Israel was established because of the Holocaust and can be understood only in light of it, the claim, that is, that the Holocaust is the necessary and sufficient explanation for the wickedness of Israeli society,

[26] Daniel Gutwein has surveyed the academic and semiacademic study of the Holocaust and claims that since the 1980s an approach he calls "the privatization of the Holocaust" has been predominant. What this means is that the Holocaust is being used to call Israeli collective identity into question. In his view, this is part of a general process of sectoral-ization and privatization in Israeli society. See his article "Hafratat hashoa: Politika, zikkaron, vehistoriografia" (The Privatization of the Holocaust: Politics, Memory, and Historiography), *Dappim leheker tekufat hashoa* (Holocaust-Era Studies) 15 (1998): 52–57. The interested reader can find here a rich, comprehensive bibliography of academic and semiacademic literature dealing with the role of the Holocaust in Israeli culture.

the aggressive policies of Israel's government, and the evil character of the Jewish state. There is no doubt, of course (and it could not be otherwise) that the Holocaust, the Second World War, and the order – or disorder – established in its wake were significant factors that eventually made it possible to establish a Jewish state in the Land of Israel. There is also no doubt that, in different ways, the Holocaust played an important role in shaping the way that state was treated, its image in the eyes of the world and especially of Europe, and even the policies of various other governments toward Israel. Nor can there be any doubt that the Holocaust and the various ways its memory has been shaped in Israel have been a key factor in the formation of the Israeli ethos and, in fact, Israeli identity. But the Holocaust was not the *main* reason, and certainly not the only reason, Israel was established, and it is foolish to think that Israel's foreign relations can be explained as hinging on blackmail or a willingness to give in to that blackmail on the part of the international community. Even less plausible is the effort to explain the Jewish settlement movement in Judea and Samaria, or the brutality (real or imagined) of the occupation in terms of Holocaust consciousness. The same is true even of such problematical episodes in the history of the Israel-Arab conflict as Golda Meir's rejection of peace feelers on the eve of the Yom Kippur War, Moshe Dayan's blindness to the potential consequences of his decisions, or Yigal Allon's obsession with security. If there has ever been an Israeli leader whose perception of the world and of Israel was shaped in an essential way by the Holocaust, it was Menahem Begin, the Israeli prime minister who returned the Sinai Peninsula to Egypt down to the last grain of sand (as Sadat had demanded) and made peace with that country.

There is some truth in these claims. It is the exact mirror image of the truth – and there is some – to be found in the claims of the Holocaust deniers. Despite the big lie they are trying to foist on the world, a certain veracity echoes in their words. But it is never truth per se that they are after. The kernels of truth they recognize are always just a means to be employed in an ideological struggle. That is why they do not investigate the truth but rather make use of it. They use the little historical truth they accept in order to distort the larger truth, to turn it on its head, and to bolster their ideological message. The Israelis we are speaking of here are not, of course, party to the lie or the denial; but for them, too, the historical truth about the Holocaust is not something to be sought for its own sake. For them, too, it is a means to an end. They manipulate and instrumentalize it. For them, too – just as for the deniers – discussion of the Holocaust serves to prevent rational, even critical, consideration of the various complex claims and demands made by the spokesmen of the Zionist movement and Israel. Contrary to what these

Israelis say about themselves, their rhetoric is not a contribution to public debate over the difficult questions on Israel's political and cultural agenda; rather, it is an attempt to stifle this debate. This is done by casting over Israel's public forum the shadow of an intellectual threat that, a priori, calls into question the legitimacy of the Zionist point of view. It is no different from the way the Holocaust serves the left-wing deniers merely as a means of delegitimating Zionism and Israel.

THE HOLOCAUST AS AN ALIBI

The ideological use of the Holocaust against Israel is a kind of paradox. One part of this paradox is that the Holocaust provides an alibi for expressing radically anti-Israeli views. We have spoken about Pierre Guillaume and his use of Bernard Lazare's name. Another example, different – but not entirely so – is the way the moral stature of the Israeli journalist Amira Hass, who now enjoys an international standing, is enhanced by her personal connection to the Holocaust. Hass seems to have won more prizes than any other Israeli journalist. No doubt she is deserving. But there is also no doubt that along with the professional caliber of her work there are political and ideological reasons for the adulation she enjoys. I do not know what role her Holocaust connection plays outside Israel, but here it has great bearing on her image. At any rate, Hass herself certainly attaches great significance to the fact that she is a child of Holocaust survivors, and she presents herself to her readers not only as being courageous, dedicated, and highly sensitive to the suffering of the Palestinians, but also as someone with special links to the Holocaust. The fact that the memory of the Holocaust and her family's involvement in it play a central role in her identity is something that is brought up whenever a profile of her is presented in the press or her life story is told. It is always cited as explaining her deep moral commitment to the Palestinian cause, her identification with Palestinian suffering, and the strength of her dedication to the self-imposed mission of informing Israeli readers of the horrors of the occupation. Hass is a recognized international authority on Palestinian affairs, but she does not write only about the Palestinians or the occupation. From time to time she contributes a piece on other matters as well, always connected to the Holocaust. Whether reviewing a film or a book or writing about anti-Semitism in Europe, she is an expert on Holocaust-related matters. She thus wears two hats, as a self-appointed spokesman of the Palestinians and of the Holocaust, and whether she intends it or not (I am not convinced she does not), her authority on everything having to do with Palestinian suffering derives from her authority on matters of Jewish suffering. Hass, too, has made her modest contribution to the drawing of a link between Auschwitz and the Arab refugee camps. And although she protested when the Portuguese writer José Saramago compared Israeli and Nazi actions, she herself has not always avoided such comparisons, albeit usually only implied.

All these ingredients are fully and explicitly woven together in a small autobiographical piece published in the eighth issue of *Mita'am: A Review for Literature and Radical Thought*, the editor in chief of which is a prominent member of the community of opprobrium, Yitzhak Laor. The piece tells the story of Hass's parents, and it bears the pregnant title "'Eifo hakhi tov lekha?' omrim lo, vehu oneh, 'Baderekh'" ("Where is it best for you?" they ask him, and he answers, "On the way.")

Hass tells the story of her parents' last years and death. They were both Holocaust survivors, communists, trying after the war, in their private abyss, to find comradeship, as she puts it, in an inner circle of communist dogmatism reluctant to recognize this abyss and a "Zionist outer circle pretending, in its arrogance, to be the revival [after] the destruction" (p. 134). The truth is, it is a rather banal story. If there is one thing Israel does not lack, it is Holocaust survivors. And the ideological idiosyncrasies of old party members have long since ceased to be of interest, even for those who once took an interest in them. The story is also told with a bizarre mix of sentimentality, verging sometimes on exhibitionism, and ideology.

"Stop merchandizing the Holocaust," wrote the Hasses and their comrades in a tract they distributed when Begin, during the first Lebanon war, compared Arafat to Hitler. But, admits Hass, there were other comparisons coming from the left, and there was a family consensus that these comparisons were not fair and did not serve the Palestinian cause. Yet – and given this reservation, the statement supposedly carries greater weight – during the First Intifada, Mr. Hass once said to his daughter that he no longer knew which was worse. "We, it is true, were deported and murdered, but this went on for just six years, and then it ended. But there is no end in sight to the suffering we [*sic*] inflict on the Palestinians" (p. 140). And during the time of the "Oslo peace" (quotation marks in the original), he said that "if the ghetto had been sealed up like the [Gaza] Strip, we would not have survived." Maybe he did not know that Israel was then providing, and still provides, livelihoods to many Palestinians in Gaza. And, to complete the comparison, the Jews of the ghetto would also have had to be doing something to the Germans that was comparable to the Qassam rockets fired from Gaza at Israeli towns and villages.

Hass's mother – to take just one more point – was forced by post-Holocaust anti-Semitism out of Yugoslavia, which she apparently regarded as her homeland and which her daughter still considers to be her homeland. So she came to Israel, and she lived here in full freedom, security, and even, perhaps, some comfort, albeit always reluctantly, a fact that apparently did not arouse in her – or her daughter – even a flicker of gratitude. They – father, mother, and daughter – have only complaints about this country and a good deal of compassion for the Palestinians. No wonder, then, that when she refers to the first Israeli-Arab war, Hass uses neither the usual Israeli name "War of Independence" nor the neutral "1948 War" but, unhesitatingly, the conventional Palestinian name *Naqba* (disaster). In an earlier article, written during one of her periods of residence in Gaza during the First Intifada, she tells how she joined her Palestinian hosts in throwing stones at Israeli troops. Her father, as we now know, was always "on the way"; his daughter has apparently come home at last, indeed, has long since arrived.

Or take Azmi Bishara, a former member of the Knesset and an intellectual. Bishara makes much of the fact that he, an Arab, often speaks about the Holocaust and does not deny that it took place. That is one of his trademarks. Several years ago (if I may be permitted another personal anecdote), I was present at a meeting between Bishara and a group of army officers. The meeting took place at the Van Leer Institute, a liberal think tank in Jerusalem where Bishara had worked and done research before being elected to the Knesset. Admittedly, though the discussion was civil, it was not especially pleasant. But what was interesting about it, and what surprised even me, was that Bishara began his remarks by saying that he was the first Arab intellectual to take a serious interest in the Holocaust, that he did not deny its having occurred, and that he understood its scope and significance. (He went on to say other things that were less surprising, that we have become accustomed to hearing, about "a state for all its citizens," and so on).

All the participants in the meeting had the distinct feeling that the Holocaust was being acknowledged and discussed as a tactic of the kind I have described as an "alibi," a certificate of legitimacy and admission ticket to the realm of civilized discourse and to the common ground Jews and Israelis share. For Bishara, it could head off any possible accusations of anti-Semitism or of the illegitimacy of his main point, that the Jewish people had no right to a state of its own. It was as if anyone who was not guilty of the most shameful, radical, farfetched anti-Jewish or anti-Zionist views was "kosher." This is a typical ploy in the use of the Holocaust, turning the usual way of using it upside down. Because denial – along with religious and racial Jew-hatred and the crudest, most explicitly liquidationist forms of anti-Zionism and anti-Israelism – is not acceptable in enlightened circles,[27] Bishara makes a point of distancing himself from it. Coming from an Arab intellectual, this distancing is, apparently, doubly effective; by giving the speaker legitimacy it also gives his anti-Zionism a new respectability.

This anti-Zionism is not necessarily any milder than that of the Holocaust deniers. In a long article he published several years ago ("The Arabs and the Holocaust: An Analysis of the Problematics of a Conjunction" [in Hebrew], *Zemanim* 53, 1995, 54–71) and then in a retort to a critique of this article by Dan Michman (*Zemanim* 54, 1995, 117–119), Bishara not only deals with the question of the Arabs and the Holocaust but also gives real meaning to the "conjunction" between the two terms; that is, he negates the conjunction "in order to negate the negation, to turn the conjunction into a mediating factor and thus something with substantial content" (*Zemanim* 55, 1996, 102105). This subtle dialectic, and the content that fills the "conjunction" as a result of negating the negation, can be described more simply: there was, indeed, a catastrophe; it had victims; but it is not those who caused the catastrophe who are paying the price; it is, rather, *other* victims. The dialectical aspect of this, it seems, is the fact that the first victims, that is, the Jews, died "there," whereas the *Aufhebung*[28] of their death is taking place "here": "The scene of the catastrophe ... was Europe, both theoretically [*sic*] and historically. But the 'reparations' for it are being made ... in the Middle East." No, Bishara is not referring to the fact that German reparations money goes to Israel; rather, in making this fine point he can claim just what Faurisson and his friends repeat endlessly, that the true victims of the Holocaust are the Palestinians. To Bishara's credit, at least he does not claim that the Germans, too, are their victims' victims.

In responding to Michman, Bishara tries to show, first of all, that the professor, who is, of course, a Jew, "doesn't know how to swallow Arab critical thinking or the development of an enlightened Arab position on the Holocaust." Second, he tries to show how enlightened his own position in fact is. He says he speaks out unambiguously "against the denial of the

[27] As an intellectual and a scholar, Bishara has devoted considerable attention to the question of the Enlightenment. See, e.g., Azmi Bishara, ed., *The Enlightenment: An Unfinished Project? Six Essays on Enlightenment and Modernism* (Tel Aviv: Hakibbutz Hame'uhad, 1997).

[28] A Hegelian concept meaning, roughly, a negation or cancellation that preserves the element negated and thus reveals rich, hidden content that constitutes a higher truth. This principle, which Hegel calls "dialectical," underlies the construction, by reason, of logical connections between concepts, as well as the pattern of all historical development. If I am not mistaken, Bishara is an expert on Hegel. He wrote his doctorate on Hegelian philosophy in East Berlin before the fall of the wall.

Holocaust, against its relativization or minimization or any comparison between it and the suffering of the Palestinians. ... The Arabs must relate to the Holocaust and understand what it did to the Jews, *to us, and to the world*" (emphasis added). But this claim is precisely the one he uses to lend respectability to the claim that the Holocaust was "[the] central factor in the establishment of the State of Israel." Perhaps without being fully aware of it, he lets us in on the meaning this typical claim has for him when he says that Hagit Lavsky,[29] "though a Zionist," attributes a pivotal role to the Holocaust in Israel's creation. It is as if there were some contradiction between Zionism and the notion that the Holocaust made an important contribution to the establishment of the state. Why should these be contradictory? Because "one must distinguish between Zionism and the unbroken connection, as it were, between the Jews and the 'Land of Israel' in Jewish history." The operative logic here is apparently this: Zionism is a result of the Holocaust; but the Holocaust, which happened *there*, cannot really justify what happened *here;* so Zionism tries to find another, more comprehensive and universal justification, and it invents the tale of the historical connection; then, to shore up this contention, it denies that the Holocaust was the reason and sole justification for establishing the state – hence, the surprising observation about Hagit Lavsky. Bishara is "ready to admit that after the Holocaust the notion of Palestine as a refuge for the Jewish people became plausible" – not a national home or a state but only a refuge, by the good graces of the country's legitimate inhabitants, to be sure, and under the patronage (following the prestate pattern in the Islamic countries) of enlightened Arab intellectuals like him who took an interest in the Holocaust and did not deny it had taken place.[30] Bishara is unwilling to accept "the connection of the people of Israel to

[29] In the aforementioned article, which Bishara quotes selectively and tendentiously, quite out of context.

[30] Incidentally, Bishara is not alone in this campaign. A number of other Arab intellectuals have opposed the denial of the Holocaust. Nor do they even necessarily connect this with the idea of turning the Jews into a *dhimmi* (subject) group in Palestine. Thus, in the lead-up to the conference of Holocaust deniers in Lebanon (which never took place), fourteen Arab intellectuals published a statement voicing anger at what they termed an "anti-Semitic undertaking." Among the signatories were the Lebanese poet Adonis, Mahmoud Darwish, and the late Edward Said. Other examples could be cited, but not many. (This information is taken from the Web site of MEMRI, the Middle East Media Research Institute). In recent years a group of Israeli Arabs, both Christian and Moslem, among them clergymen, intellectuals, political activists, and teachers, have taken an interest in the Holocaust. At the initiative of Father Emile Shofani, of Nazareth, a joint Arab-Jewish study delegation visited the death camps in Poland. Yad Vashem now has a full display in Arabic on its Web site. A real change appears to have taken place in this respect, at least among Arabs living in Israel.

the Land of Israel since the time of Joshua and Yehuda Halevi." Joshua, incidentally, is cited as "the perpetrator of the first genocide in history." Sure enough, the Bible should not serve as the basis for claiming a historic right to the land; it is nonetheless a reliable source for some anti-Semitic innuendo. As we have seen, Garaudy, too, reads the book of Joshua this way, as do quite a few Israeli writers. But be that as it may, there is no other reason, historical or not, for having established the state or, for that matter, having gathered a certain number of Jews together in the place they call "the Land of Israel." What we have here is the very assumption that underlies the political agenda of the deniers: that the Holocaust was the only possible justification, and the principal excuse, for establishing the Jewish state, and the calamity of the Palestinians is its final outcome.

Bishara's answer to Michman is a caricature. But that in itself is not so important. His ostensibly historiographical argument is meant only as a cover for the ideological thrust of his position, which is to instrumentalize the Holocaust in the service of the Palestinian critique of Israel and of an interpretation of Zionism that refuses to take its main assertions seriously. Another voice has made itself heard in this dispute: Moshe Zuckerman has taken sides with Bishara and sharply criticized Michman (*Zemanim* 55). He has typical doubts about Michman's reading of history – the latter "uses" scholarly research, and his choice of what to use is in itself "an integral part of a distinctly ideological act." We have already seen that the systematic relativization of historiography, especially of the "official," "establishment" variety, is a staple of the Holocaust deniers. But this is not the only similarity between their argument and Zuckerman's: the rejection of historiography does not imply a repudiation of coherence, and Michman, who supposedly disconnects the establishment of the state from the Holocaust (he does not quite do this, but never mind) might well have been surprised that "it was precisely the State of Israel that monopolized the institutional memory of the Holocaust in all its dimensions, including the prosecution of Eichmann and the acceptance of material reparations on a massive scale."

There is, then, a connection between Israel and the Holocaust, and it should not surprise us, because "objectively," and all the more so from the (subjective? – only Zuckerman can say) point of view of the Palestinians, it can be argued that "the price of the Holocaust was paid in *Palestine* by the Palestinians" (emphasis in the original). Zuckerman is extraordinarily generous here, being willing to assume, in the name of all other Israelis, the whole responsibility for the Palestinian disaster. There is not a word about the possibility that the price the Palestinians have paid might be a result, at least to some extent, of their own policies; but from a critical Arab voice like Bishara's one might have expected to hear something about this. In typical fashion, both of them use the Holocaust to make the familiar arguments about Israel being, in principle, the guilty party in the conflict with the Palestinians. "Objectively," in Zuckerman's words, the Holocaust was the reason for the Palestinian catastrophe. But, on the other hand, the Holocaust does not justify the actions of the Zionists, their use of it as an explanation being a "monopolization" of its memory, what amounts to a usurpation. What is important here – and this is something Bishara and Zuckerman share not only with each other but also with Guillaume and Faurisson – is that the price of the Holocaust was paid *here*. The question of whether there actually was a Holocaust becomes secondary, if not trivial, in light of this new iniquity, that is, the payment that was collected here for what happened there. If the establishment of Israel was really the repayment of a debt created by the Holocaust, they – Bishara and Zuckerman, Guillaume and Faurisson – are right, and there are no moral grounds for asking the Palestinians to pay the price of what was or was not done by the Germans to the Jews of Europe.

THE HOLOCAUST AND THE COLLECTIVE PATHOLOGY OF THE ISRAELIS

Zuckerman considers himself a nonreligious Jew, and, like Bishara (as well as Garaudy), he is critical of Zionist mythmaking and reliance on the "archaic dimension of the attachment of the Jews to the land." He believes that "the life of a group of people in ancient times does not bestow any rights upon a contemporary civil grouping" and that "we must guard against the ideological and political reification of various collective mental attachments and the fetishization of 'longings.'" "The real justification" for establishing the state in which the Jews have been gathered is, in his view, the ideology of the negation of the Diaspora, on the one hand, and, on the other, a deep existential anxiety derived from the memory of the Holocaust, as Yehuda Elkana put it in a frequently quoted article.[31] By "real," Zuckerman evidently means the motives and emotions that prompted the Zionists to act as they did. The use of the word "justification" (*tzidduk*) could be confusing, because it usually connotes something that makes a thing or an action right. It depends on the validity of arguments (e.g., regarding the right of the Jewish people to self-determination in its historic homeland) rather than on interpretations or subjective feelings. For Zuckerman, "justification" is

---

[31] Yehuda Elkana, "Bizekhut hashikheha" (In Praise of Forgetting), *Haaretz*, March 2, 1988.

evidently that which explains and rationalizes. The Holocaust is thus also, and primarily, an excuse, at best a rationalization, for the policy of oppressing the Palestinians. As we have said, the latter, too, have been victims of the Holocaust.

Again, according to Zuckerman both the establishment of the state and the oppressive policies it now pursues are rationalized by this well-known Israeli-Jewish anxiety. Can we conclude from this that both are to be judged the same way? Should we hope for the liquidation of the state the same way we hope for the end of the occupation? Is this what should happen when, as we would wish, the rationale disappears, that is, when we forget the Holocaust (as Elkana, for example, recommends in the article to which we have referred) and overcome our collective neurosis, our "existential anxiety"? Zuckerman is not clear about this, which is unfortunate, for this question, of the legitimacy of a Jewish state, is being asked today as never before. It is "objectively" on the public agenda, even if Zuckerman and some of his colleagues avoid posing it directly, for the simple reason that people today are asking it, and they have been asking it quite openly for some time. The questioning is going on not only in certain circles – such as those of the deniers and their fellow travelers, or Azmi Bishara and his ilk – but also in polite society. Whoever has truck with intellectuals, academicians, or journalists today, especially in Europe but also on the other side of the Atlantic, knows how the guilt feelings there over the establishment of Israel and the hope of rectifying that misdeed by giving the Palestinians the "right of return" and abolishing the Jewish state have grown.[32]

In his various articles and in a book he wrote after the First Gulf War, Zuckerman recycles one central idea prevalent in the literature critical of Israel. There seem to be certain quasi-canonical works from which the community of instrumentalizers of the Holocaust derive their critical tools for attacking and negating Israel and Zionism. One such work is a long, programmatic article by Boaz Evron, the dramatic title of which, "The Holocaust: A Danger to the People" (*Iton 77*, 21 [May–June 1980]), is not, despite appearances, at all anachronistic. According to Evron, the Holocaust is a danger here and now. The article begins like this:

Two terrible things have happened to the Jewish people in this century: the Holocaust, and the conclusions that were drawn from it. The false, unhistorical interpretations, either intentional or ignorant, given to the Holocaust and the instrumental exploitation of it in relation to the non-Jewish world and the Jewish diaspora, on the one

---

[32] See Judt's article "Israel: The Alternative," *New York Review of Books*, October 23, 2003.

hand, and the Israeli people, on the other, have become a danger to both the Jewish people and the state.

No more and no less, the Holocaust, in which six million Jews were intentionally and systematically exterminated, is equivalent in its awfulness, Evron maintains, to the interpretations given to it and the inferences drawn from it. These interpretations are unhistorical and unscientific and therefore not only harbor terrible danger but are already, now, themselves "terrible." Of course, the author goes on to offer us the outlines of a rational, historical interpretation that is "unmythical" and well considered.

What is unhistorical about the way the Holocaust has been interpreted? First of all, of course, the contention that it is unique. The Germans killed not only Jews but also Gypsies, Poles, and others. From Hannah Arendt, for example, Evron learns that, had the war gone on, the Germans would have turned the machinery of extermination on the Slavic peoples. He sees this as a historical, even empirical observation – perhaps because there is no way to prove or disprove it. How can anything valuable be said about what the Germans would have done had they won the war? At any rate, the claim made by Jews that the Holocaust was unique is no different from the Nazi claim that the Jews are unique, that is, the contention that they are subhuman and need to be eliminated. The Nazis, for their part, and the Jewish nationalists, for theirs – that is, both those who think the German extermination of the Jews was different from other genocides and those who did the exterminating – accomplish just one thing: both distinguish the Jewish people from the rest of humanity.[33] Evron sees a danger in Jewish and Israeli "monopolization" of the Holocaust. The danger is that it can lead to the indulgence of neo-Nazism (the claim of uniqueness conceals the danger they represent) but also to Jewish paranoia, to the separation of the Jews from the human race and their transformation, in the end, when they have the power, into Nazis themselves.

What is more, the Holocaust as a uniquely Jewish event is a story the Zionists (for understandable reasons) concocted, but so did the Germans, who thought it would help them obtain the world's forgiveness if they presented the extermination as an isolated act of madness, directed only at foreigners (Jews and Gypsies). The Allies had a similar interest, hoping that

---

[33] As the saying goes, great minds think alike. The French philosopher Alain Badiou recently published a book entitled *Portées du mot "juif"* (Paris: Lignes, 2005), translated as *The Uses of the Word "Jew,"* http://www.lacan.com/badword.htm, accessed September 9, 2007. Badiou sees the meaning Hitler gave the word "Jew" and the meaning it has had for Jews themselves since the war as identical: "Jew" has become a Nazi predicate. When Israel defines itself as a "Jewish state," it is merely following in Hitler's footsteps.

this very claim of the uniqueness of the event and the recognition that the killing did not indicate a fixed German character trait would make it possible to include the Germans in the anti-Soviet alliance created in Europe after the war. The description of the Holocaust as a uniquely Jewish story was thus, in essence, a worldwide conspiracy.

Another element contributing to the ongoing negative effect of the Holocaust is the Zionist claim that the State of Israel and its army guarantee that another holocaust will not occur. According to Evron, this is a false claim. Why? For two reasons that reflect, however unintentionally, quite an original logic: (1) Had the Nazis succeeded in annihilating the Russians as well, as they intended to do, for example, it would have proved that military power is no guarantee against extermination. Well, the Germans did not actually succeed in doing this and, in fact, were beaten back by the Red Army, but in this case the "as if" seems to be stronger than reality, for this argument is still supposed to be persuasive to the reader. (2) Zionism did not save even the Jews of Palestine. They were saved only because the Germans were defeated at El-Alamein and Stalingrad. However, Evron's claim proves, once again, just the opposite: that it was military power, nevertheless, that saved the Jews from total destruction. Of course, it was not Jewish military power but Soviet and British, but that is military power too. In the last analysis, Stalingrad and El-Alamein were purely military victories. The fact that the armies that were victorious in those battles were not Zionist does not prove decisively that the Jews do not need to acquire military power of their own.

So this is the sort of logic Evron uses. Another matter that he raises but that can also be found, recycled, and refurbished, in the anti-Zionist literature of the Holocaust is that of Adolf Eichmann. Holocaust consciousness in Israel was, he says, "on the wane" until the Eichmann trial. Of course, this is completely untrue, but obviously what is important here is not historical truth but ideology. What interests the writer about this trial is not its historical significance or even the legal reasons for conducting it (with which he, in fact, agrees) but the political considerations that led to the decision to conduct it: the political and economic profit to be derived from stirring up the German sense of guilt. But, Evron teaches us, the special status Israel achieved by basing its relations with the rest of the world on guilt is harmful, first and foremost, to the country itself. Its diplomacy and economy are cut off from the political and economic realities of the world at large. Meanwhile, twenty-some years after these prophetic words were written, they seem, if anything, too optimistic, especially in view of the development of the local high-technology industry and Israel's place in the globalization process. Be that as it may, according to Evron the ongoing effects of the Eichmann trial have also prevented Israeli Jewish life from being normalized. Moral blackmail has turned Israel into a Diaspora Jew; while Jews in the West live as equal citizens, Israel "has sunk to the level of a perpetual mendicant, a burden to the world, surviving, not by its own efforts ... but on the 'credit of the six million,' on baring our wounds and travails to the rest of the world, on the past, rather than on the present and future." But despite Evron's powers of prediction, his fears concerning Israel's standing in the world appear to have been somewhat excessive.

What is most original in Evron's argument is his introduction of the anxiety narrative, the neurosis that is the source of Israeli moral blindness. I do not know if he was the first to make this discovery; but the anxiety narrative is probably the local *resentiment*'s most innovative contribution to the standard arguments of the Holocaust deniers and more generally to the literature that uses the Holocaust to indict Israel. To the extent that this line of thinking appears elsewhere, it is apparently imported from Israel itself. What typifies Evron's writing and distinguishes it (and, later on, the writings of other Israeli grumblers as well) from things published elsewhere is that his demonization of Israel, his depiction of it as the main or sole source of all evil in the Middle East, is based on a psychological, political, and cultural portrait of Israel society drawn *from within*. A picture based on intimate knowledge of the country would seem to be more empathetic than the usual one of Israeli manipulativeness, cynicism, and wickedness. The picture has two or three fixed components: a blurring of all political differences – between left and right, for example, or religious and secular – when analyzing the Israeli ethos of anxiety; the charge that this collective anxiety neurosis is the product of intentional manipulation by the Zionist regime, no less, and perhaps more, than of the Holocaust itself; an infantilization of the political thinking and political culture of the Israeli public, making the latter out to be helpless in the face of manipulation on a global scale, to which the rest of the world is also prone. This leads to the conclusion that the struggle of the Arabs against the Jews is essentially a rational one, for the Jews, aside from being the victims of wholesale manipulation, are trapped "in a world of monsters and myths" and do not live in "the real world."

Zuckerman, too, was quite interested in Israeli fears and particularly their destructive effects. A book he wrote and published following the First Gulf War, *Sho'a baheder ha'atum*,[34] made him an active and well-known

---

[34] Moshe Zuckerman, *Sho'a baheder ha'atum: Hashoah ba'itonut hayisra'elit bitekufat milhemet hamifratz* (A Holocaust in the Sealed Room: The "Holocaust" in the Israeli Press during the [First] Gulf War) (Tel Aviv: published by the author, 1993).

participant in his own right in the discourse about the Holocaust. The book is partly a scholarly one but also, to borrow one of the author's own phrases, "a distinctly ideological act." In other words, it is a book that sets out to use the Holocaust, its aftereffects, and its commemoration for ideological purposes. Zuckerman is troubled by the possibility "that the victim might become the murderer" (p. 30). He thinks, too, that every "irregular" action in Gaza and every oppressive act resulting from the occupation distances the Zionist collective [*sic*] "from the ethical, humane identity it inherited, with the attendant moral obligations, from the victims of the Holocaust and brings it ever closer to the mentality represented by the identity of the murderers." It might be a bit difficult to decipher this language – the translation does scant justice to the magnificently awkward Hebrew of the original – but what Zuckerman seems to be saying here is not only that he knows what obligations the victims imposed on us but also that he is perceptive enough to discern in us a Nazi mentality.

Ostensibly, he means to rescue the Holocaust from being cheapened and to protest against its instrumentalization, its use for evil purposes; but he himself is using it. He describes, analyzes, and criticizes the phenomenon of Holocaust fear that seized the people of Israel when the country was attacked by Iraqi Scud missiles during the First Gulf War. In particular, he surveys the references to Germany and the gas chambers that appeared at that time in the great flood of verbiage produced by the Israeli press. According to his analysis, these were signs of a national neurosis with many dangerous political ramifications. Others, including the author of the present book, who lived through that period and read the press, are convinced that, despite its highly surrealist nature, it was a time when Israeli society proved its resilience and basic sanity. But, of course, we do not belong to the enlightened minority. Be that as it may, while the psychoanalysis of the "Zionist collective" offered in this book is based on evidence from a particular historical episode, the book is quite wide-ranging in its theoretical sweep, including much more than just a survey of the Israeli media. It even contains some brief foreplay, in the form of a methodological discussion of the nature of empirical research, that is, the theoretical significance of the dozens, or perhaps hundreds of quotes with which the book is laden. Zuckerman then offers his readers a veritable bounty of information, studded with quotes, names, and jargon. Among other things, he provides a survey of the German press, a description of how Germany comes to terms with the memory of the Holocaust, and, in particular, a defense of the German New Left, its pacifism and its stance toward Israel in the First Gulf War. In this connection, he castigates renegades from his camp like Wolf Biermann, a protest singer and well-known left-wing activist, who dared to criticize the left's opposition "to the capitalist war of the United States and its partners" (p. 165). Zuckerman rebukes Biermann for calling names. The most recent of these, incidentally, does not appear in Zuckerman's book: in the buildup to the Second Gulf War, Biermann called Zuckerman's friends on the German left "national-pacifists."

For all his defense of the German left, Zuckerman does not give the Israeli left high marks. He accuses left-wing Israeli intellectuals of contributing "objectively" to the official instrumentalization of the "Holocaust code." He shoots in all directions and, as usual, lumps together left and right, religious fascism and secular Zionism, Kahanist racism and Yossi Sarid, national-ist and security-minded annexationism and A. B. Yehoshua.[35] The "Zionist left," a crybaby that will, of course, "never depart from the Zionist consensus," is no different from the population-transfer camp of Rehav'am Ze'evi, and the slogan "two states for two peoples" is only a cover for the ideology of "blood mendicancy," or plain fascism and the like, which the reflexive "activation" of the "Holocaust code" exposes again and again.

To me, the most interesting chapter of this strange book is the last one. Here, Zuckerman discusses writer Yoram Kaniuk's report on a television confrontation he had with Günter Grass during a visit to Germany right after the First Gulf War. Kaniuk expressed anger at the German left's treat-ment of Israel during the war. Grass, on the other hand, and as part of his ongoing struggle against fascism, war, and arms sales, rejected any claim for a "special attitude" toward Israel – for example, on the issue of providing German submarines to the Israeli navy. I must admit that, while reading this chapter, maintaining the distance, irony, and sense of humor I needed to get through all the material I had to read to write this book proved extremely difficult. There was a gulf here, difficult to bear, between Kaniuk's anger and frustration, his certainty of his inevitable defeat, his knowledge that the German-Israeli "dialogue" would prove futile (which reminded me, perhaps unjustifiably, of the well-known "German Jewish dialogue" that ended at Auschwitz – a point undoubtedly in favor of Zuckerman's thesis), and his powerlessness in the face of the Germans' talent at turning themselves into universalists when so many particularistic murderers of Jews were still living among them, on the one hand, and Zuckerman's self-satisfaction, arrogance,

---

[35] A typical quote from a pamphlet of one of the radical-left-wing groups that supported Faurisson: "The fiction about the 'gas chambers' was officially endorsed by the Nuremberg tribunal, where the Nazis were tried by the victors. Its first function was to permit the Stalino-democratic camp …," etc., etc. Cited by Valérie Igounet, *Histoire du négationion-isme en France* (Paris: Seuil, 2000), 283.

condescension, self-righteousness, and, above all, provincial self-abasement, so typical of his like, on the other.[36]

Only a person suffering from an advanced case of moral blindness – maybe not a terminal illness of the moral sense like the one the Holocaust has brought on ordinary Israelis, but a certain moral disability all the same – can acquire such an ability to identify with the children of executioners. Yet it must be admitted that Zuckerman is right. Kaniuk evidently had a kind of mental Tay-Sachs syndrome, a congenital Israeli-Jewish defect that prevents its carriers from conducting normal relations with Germany or Germans. This faulty gene causes those suffering from it to feel that any truck they have with Germans – even the best, most progressive, most Judeophilic among them – is bound to be rather complicated. They think, alas, that only rarely, if at all, can there be such an interchange without the children and grandchildren of the victims suppressing, wholly or in part, their own point of view, without their giving up what Zuckerman, with his characteristic obtuseness, arrogance, and off-putting heavyhandedness, calls "Jewish particularism."

By the way, Kaniuk is not the only one to suffer from this defect. We also find traces of it in Fanya Oz-Salzburger's book *Israelis, Berlin,*[37] about a year she spent in that city recording the experiences of other Israelis living there. Or take Jean Amery. He, too, was a carrier of this particularism.[38] Although he was an intellectual with the cultural identity and political leanings of what we call "the left," although he did not really consider himself a Jew, and although Jewish particularism was forced upon him in a death camp – Amery was unwilling to give it up. Like other carriers of this accursed gene, he never adjusted to the normalcy of German life after the war or the rapidity with which it was achieved. He also never overcame his astonishment, perhaps even revulsion, at the German Jewish intellectuals who flocked back

---

[36] Shortly after this was written, Yoram Kaniuk's book *Haberlina'i ha'aharon* (The Last Berliner) (Tel Aviv: Yediot Aharonot, 2004) was published. This wise, funny, sad book tells of Kaniuk's experiences in Germany and his hopeless dialogue with the Germans. It was hopeless not only because of the Germans' obtuseness and arrogance but also, and perhaps mainly, because of his own personal madness. In any event, the present writer, perhaps because he is an unreconstructed devotee of Jewish particularism, prefers Kaniuk's madness to what Zuckerman, in his intellectual narcissism, attributes to himself as "universalism."

[37] Jerusalem: Keter, 2001.

[38] Five of Jean Améry's essays are collected in *At the Mind's Limits: Contemplations by a Survivor on Auschwitz and Its Realities* (New York: Schocken, 1986). For example, he says he could not help feeling some unpleasantness at not being able to forgive the Germans, even when they told him, ever so politely, that, unlike him, they harbored no grudge against the Jews (p. 67).

after the war to what they insisted on regarding as their homeland, to teach philosophy or sociology and to bemoan the fact that, after Auschwitz, it was impossible to write poetry. Of course, Zuckerman has respect only for this crowd. Amery was a real, not an imagined, Holocaust survivor. He recoiled from the sympathy that was showered upon him and railed against the desire of those who had not been there, in the world of the camps, to exploit – or appropriate, as we say today – his private experiences for their various and sundry needs. He was right, of course. But, as it turns out, even if we leave Amery himself alone and just read what he wrote (this, after all, was what he wrote it for), there are still some Israelis and Jews here and there, not all of them survivors, who suffer, perhaps because of stories like Amery's, from a curious discomfort when they listen to Zuckerman's chatter – even when he is quoting Adorno. Amery, as we know, committed suicide in the end, as did Primo Levi and Paul Celan, among others – all of them carriers of particu-laristic Auschwitz defects.

One way or another, Zuckerman is renouncing "Jewish particularism" not, as he thinks, in favor of some imaginary "universalism" but rather in favor of another particularism, that of the children and grandchildren of the executioners. It might be appropriate to mention here that the Nazis, especially Hitler himself, also had a supremely universalistic worldview. They were out to eradicate the Jews from the face of the earth, not only in Germany or for the sake of the German *Volk*. Hitler, sure enough, went to war against world Jewry for the good of the Aryan race but also to save all of humanity – not only to liberate his own people from the yoke of the alien Jew and not only out of a narrow, particularistic consideration of German inter-ests but out of a desire to change the course of human history. That is why he was not content with the ethnic cleansing of the German fatherland or the securing of *Lebensraum* for Germans in Eastern Europe but imported Jews to the camps from all over Europe and even North Africa. He even thought that in his war against the Jews he was doing God's work. What could be more universalistic? This universalism, or at least the universal support the Nazi regime enjoyed until its dying day in Germany, certainly explains in some measure why, as early as the 1950s and more emphatically and with less shame later on, many Germans called for "closing the books," that is, burying the subject of their Nazi past.[39] Other Germans (not too many, it seems) settled, or are still settling, their account with Nazism, but it is their account. We – the victims and their offspring – only get in the way of their

---

[39] See inter alia the articles by Saul Friedländer collected in *Memory, History, and the Extermination of the Jews of Europe* (Bloomington: Indiana University Press, 1993).

settling accounts with themselves. It occurs perhaps not always, but often enough, especially in the case of what Zuckerman calls "the German left."

But even if they are not seeking to turn the page on Nazism, the great darkness from which the German left looks out on the world and tries to understand it is not the darkness of the Jewish catastrophe but of the crime their own parents committed. They do not understand how the Holocaust happened to *them*. Not to us, the Jews, but to them, the Germans. How did Hitler and his generation manage to inflict on their children what they did? How could they have made them the heirs of a nation of murderers? That is the question, or the experience, that informs Günter Grass's point of view, the place from which he looks out on the world. It is the point of departure of his debate with Kaniuk. When the Hebrew version of this book was going to press, in August 2006, Grass revealed, in a well-known interview, that he had been a soldier in the Waffen-SS. He even served as a tank gunner in one of the famous Panzer divisions during the very last stages of the war. As the public uproar that this revelation stirred shows, what most upset Grass's critics was not so much his military role as the fact that he had managed to hide it from the world for some sixty years. All this is now history, and no one, including myself, has ever claimed that Grass was a Nazi or an apologist for the Nazis. He seems, though, to share the special talent that Germans, of all people, sometimes seem to have, for pontification, the belief that their unique experience gives them access to some universal wisdom, some special knowledge, which the victims, or their children, do not share, about the horrors of fascism and nationalism; it is a moral advantage that allows them to instruct everyone else, particularly Americans and Israelis. Zuckerman may not realize it (and I doubt if he knows any better now), but there was, not only because of the Waffen-SS episode, a certain irony in Grass's refusal to recognize the claim of the victims, or those who speak in their name, to a special moral standing: it has never prevented him, belonging as he does to the executioners' children's generation, from making, explicitly or implicitly, a very similar claim to moral and intellectual superiority himself.

The new German left refuses to recognize the special status of the Jewish catastrophe and those who actually speak in its name. This is because Israel today is a criminal state. But it is also because of the moralistic arrogance and presumption of those who, unlike us Israelis, have been wise enough to recognize the universal lessons of their parents' disaster. But the claim that there is too much talk of the Holocaust, or the Jewish aspect of the Nazis' crimes, and that this excess prevents the Germans from understanding their past and coming to terms with it – this argument is heard in other quarters as well, including among respected historians whose main concern is the Nazis, their history and crimes. One of these was the late Martin Broszat, whom no one suspects of apologetic revisionism in regard to Nazism. In the 1980s he called for a "historicalization" of the Nazi period.[40] What he meant by this was, roughly, making the period between 1933 and 1945 the subject of rational historical inquiry and the application to it of the usual methods of historical research; in other words, placing the Nazi period in the context of the German history that preceded and followed it. This would not be the place to consider the question Broszat raises or other questions that have arisen in the debates among the historians; what matters for our purposes is that these questions reflect a need, at least in terms of German history, to be free of the more or less exclusive identification of this period with the *crimes* of the Nazi regime, particularly the destruction of the Jews. A full understanding of those years, Broszat maintains, requires seeing elements of continuity in Germany stretching back before 1933 and forward past 1945.

Broszat is afraid of the trap set by various taboos and blocks – mainly connected with the destruction of the Jews, of course – that can make the historiography of Nazism and modern Germany didactic and the public commemoration "monumental," that is, centered on monuments, museums, ceremonies, and the like. The historian Saul Friedländer, who disagrees with him in general, seems to share some of his concern on this point. This concern is also sometimes directed at commemorative activities in Israel as well, as we have pointed out. But unlike the German case, for reasons that are not altogether clear, I dare say such concerns, in regard to the Israeli public are exaggerated, if not mistaken altogether. Even the famous March of the Living program that takes Israeli youngsters to Poland, a program that is certainly a didactic, "monumental" form of public commemoration, is not so harmful as to justify real concern, either for the health of Israel's collective memory or for the soundness of historical research. Contrary to the impression that many of Israel's critics try to give, there has been, in Israel, a serious, protracted debate about these excursions to the death camps. And without going any further into the issue, it may be of interest that, according

---

[40] Following this call – *plädoyer* is the term Broszat uses in the article – a well-publicized exchange developed between him and Friedländer. In several of the latter's essays in *Memory, History*, he makes reference to this exchange. The letters were published in Peter Baldwin, ed., *Reworking the Past: Hitler, the Holocaust, and the Historians' Debate* (Boston: Beacon, 1990). See also Otto Dov Kulka, "Major Trends and Tendencies in German Historiography on National Socialism and the 'Jewish Question,'" in Yisrael Gutman and Gideon Greif, eds., *The Historiography of the Holocaust Period: Proceedings of the Fifth Yad Vashem International Historical Conference, Jerusalem, March 1983* (Jerusalem: Yad Vashem, 1988), 1–52, esp. 30ff. Kulka seems more critical of Broszat than Friedländer does.

to at least some of the many studies of this matter, the visits to Auschwitz do not change the basic opinions and attitudes, political or otherwise, of the young people who take part in them.

In any event, the question that arises in Zuckerman's discussion of the German left is a weighty one: should Germans not be allowed to express opinions about what goes on elsewhere or to criticize, even harshly, the actions of others, including Israelis? That claim would, of course, be very hard to argue against. But still, their defective gene leads many – not all – Israelis and Jews to expect, or at least hope, that the Germans might display some modesty, some of that hard-to-define quality known as tact, some patience, and wait a generation or two before preaching to us. Zuckerman admires the universalistic wisdom of those Germans who are impatient and in a hurry. He is not the only Israeli to share the enthusiasm with which many on the German left beat *Israeli* breasts for the sins of their own parents, atoning for those sins with a purely universalistic concern for the suffering of the victims of violent Jewish nationalism. Nor is he the only one to think this Jewish expectation of the Germans is just emotional blackmail and the manipulation of collective guilt feelings.

The discomfort aroused by the German left's criticism of Israel reflects a German dilemma no less than a Jewish-Israeli neurosis. (We shall leave the charge of manipulation to those who treat what is marginal as central.) In the last analysis, this dilemma turns on the question of guilt and collective responsibility. A comprehensive, systematic – and courageous – theoretical treatment of this question was undertaken right after the war by Karl Jaspers, one of the few German philosophers who did not collaborate more or less enthusiastically with the Nazi regime. In a book he published at that time, *The Question of German Guilt*,[41] he draws several interesting distinctions, on the basis of which he maintains that all Germans, even those who personally did nothing wrong, bear political responsibility for the crimes committed by the German state during the war. Thus, in his view, they have no choice, as German citizens and members of the German people, but to pay the price of those crimes.

Perhaps because the book was written immediately after the war, it does not take up the question of historic responsibility; for example, the question of whether the Israeli claim to "special treatment" (such as giving Israel German submarines) is justified, as is the tendency of many Germans to accept and respond to that claim. Some of the latter have rather instrumental,

---

[41] Karl Jaspers, *The Question of German Guilt,* 2nd ed., rev. ed. (New York: Fordham University Press, 2001).

even cynical motives in doing so. Others – the German foreign minister at the time of this writing, Joschka Fischer, seems to be one of them – think Germany has a special responsibility to Israel and the Jews. Guilt and collective responsibility, especially when they are passed on from one generation to the next, are not only hard to live with but also theoretically subtle and complex. It is not at all clear how blaming the children or grandchildren of murderers for what their forebears did can be justified or how any claim can be made on this basis. However, a claim could be made on the basis of what Jaspers, for one, writes, a confirmation of the moral validity of the biblical saying, "The fathers eat sour grapes, and the children's teeth are set on edge."

Without pretending to exhaust this complicated subject, one or two comments are in order. Germans who were too young to take part in the war or who were born afterward bear no guilt or responsibility for what their parents or grandparents did. But one cannot overlook the fact that for more than a generation thousands, perhaps tens of thousands of people who were party, directly or indirectly, to those crimes went on living, peacefully and contentedly, in Germany. Many held prominent positions in government, the academy, cultural institutions, the press, and other spheres. It has also become clearer and clearer that, in fact, all Germans knew, more or less, what was being done to the Jews, and the vast majority not only failed to oppose these actions but accepted them and perhaps even supported them. Many profited from them as well, particularly from the despoiling of Jewish property. Quite a few of that generation are still alive, and it is in their name that the German government has tried to atone for Nazi crimes, among other things by giving Israel "special treatment." Furthermore, economic and financial institutions, organizations, industrial concerns, and public and political bodies generally maintain some continuity of identity, over and above the identities of the individuals of which they are composed. In Germany, it is known that during the war big, rich manufacturers employed many thousands of slave laborers – often Jews – and that they continued to operate and prosper without interruption after the war was over. That is but one example. To the extent that such institutions form an important part of German society, they perpetuate the institutional, cultural, and political responsibility of Germany as a whole. But that responsibility remains abstract and takes on concrete meaning only in the actions, feelings, and lives of individual people living in Germany today. Here, it would be well to refer again to a citation of Jürgen Habermas that appears in Zuckerman's book. The lives of contemporary Germans, Habermas says, are "connected with the form of existence of our parents and grandparents by a mesh of family, local, political and intellectual traditions which is difficult to untangle – by an historical milieu, therefore, which in the first instance has made us what we are and who we are today" (p. 46).

Zuckerman quotes these words when describing the "debate of the historians." This famous controversy stirred up not only historians but also intellectuals and public opinion in general in Germany in the late 1980s. It was provoked by a statement of the well-known historian Ernst Nolte to the effect that the character of Nazism should be investigated historically, in the context of the wider European phenomenon of fascism, and that the murderousness of the Nazi regime should be seen as a reaction to Stalinism. Even the Third Reich's war against the Jews should, according to Nolte, be understood as a response, not altogether unintelligible or illegitimate, to, among other things, Zionist leader Chaim Weizmann's famous 1939 "declaration of war," promising that the Jews would fight Nazi Germany with all their might. Incidentally, the deniers of the Holocaust, long before Nolte, used this statement to pin on the Jews responsibility for the war and their own destruction.[42]

Nolte denied the uniqueness of Nazism and the so-called special path, that is, the uniqueness of German history in relation to those of the other Western democracies. So it turns out that the Germans, too, are preoccupied with questions of uniqueness. Indeed, for several decades now a debate, in fact a whole series of debates and controversies, has raged in Germany over the question of its uniqueness, the uniqueness of the Nazi regime, the uniqueness of the German destruction of the Jews and the character of the "Final Solution," and other such issues. In the end, all these questions are connected, either directly and explicitly or indirectly and implicitly, with the question of collective responsibility for German crimes. What mainly motivated Nolte, for example – and infuriated Habermas – was his firm rejection of the real or imagined demand made of him and Germans in general to acknowledge guilt or take responsibility for the Nazi crimes.

It is true that, like us, Israelis and Jews in general, the Germans are trapped in the memory of the Holocaust, with no escape. As we have said, feelings of guilt and collective responsibility are a complicated business and a heavy burden to bear. Often, the source of the guilt is quite near at hand – the guilt of parents, uncles, other relatives, or teachers. Nevertheless, the German trap seems easier to deal with than the Jewish and Israeli one. For one thing, for

---

[42] The principal documents related to *Historikerstreit* are available in English translation in James Knowlton, ed., *Forever in the Shadow of Hitler* (Atlantic Highlands, N.J.: Humanities Press, 1993). See also the references in note 40.

Germans the memory of the Holocaust has not gotten tangled up inextricably with the question of wrongs (real or imagined) done to the Palestinians. But, in addition, pangs of conscience can often be a kind of self-love, as those who take up the cudgels against the culture of Jewish and Israeli victimhood know very well. Incidentally, Habermas, too, comments (in the passage cited by Zuckerman) on the narcissistic character of the debate over the nature of Nazism. The Germans, or at least some of them (most are not interested in the past or are weary of dealing with it), have the best of both worlds: pangs of conscience and soul-searching on the one hand, and a highly developed sense of victimhood on the other. After all, not only the Jews suffered in the war; innocent Germans, too, were killed. The tens of thousands who died in Dresden, for example, or the thousands of civilians, mostly children, who fled westward out of fear of the Red Army, crowded onto the decks of the *Wilhelm Gustloff*, and died in the frozen seas when the ship was sunk by a Soviet submarine.[43]

Still, to be fair, many Germans are honestly trying to come to grips with this burden, and the collective expression of German responsibility toward the Jews – which, after all, is what matters – cannot be ignored. In addition, Israel has enjoyed, and to a great extent still enjoys, a special status and special treatment in Germany. Not only has it received large amounts of money, in the form of reparations and other payments, from the German government, but it has also enjoyed and continues to enjoy fairly consistent German political support. Germany is, as they say, Israel's best friend in Europe. Nor can one ignore the close cultural and scientific cooperation between the two countries, which, among other things, means that a lot of German money goes into bringing Israeli scholars, artists, writers, students, and intellectuals of one sort or another to Germany. Among them are more than a few who speak Zuckerman's language.

More interesting, and sometimes quite moving, is the serious, fair-minded manner in which German historians have, for a generation now, been dealing

---

[43] The sinking of the *Wilhelm Gustloff* is said to have been the greatest maritime disaster in history. Günter Grass, perhaps Germany's leading living writer, has published a novel, *Crabwalk* (Orlando: Harcourt, 2002), that tells the story of the ship and its demise. In this brilliant, quasi-fictional work, Grass alludes artfully to the anguish of contemporary German historical memory, its contradictions, and the dangers it carries – but also the need for it. Much of the novel is likely to cause some discomfort, let us say, to the Jewish and Israeli reader who has not yet freed himself of the personal and collective dilemmas raised by the memory of the Holocaust. Since the publication of the book, we have also learned that Grass did not tell the whole truth – either in the debate with Kaniuk or on other occasions. As mentioned before, he has only very recently owned up to the fact that he was a member of the SS.

with the destruction of the Jews. Although there were historians and others who dealt seriously with the "Final Solution" even earlier, for a long time most German academic treatment of this subject was highly problematical, to put it mildly. Following the historians' debate, there seems to have been a slow, gradual change in the way German historians treated the Holocaust. At least that is the impression one gets as an outside observer not sufficiently well versed in the enormous body of research that has been done by scholars in general on the Holocaust or by German scholars in particular.[44] At any rate, the latter have undoubtedly made major contributions to the awareness and understanding of the Nazi genocide.

The scope of the research – by historians, sociologists, and political scientists – is so broad, the mass of publications so great, the differences of opinion so deep, and the implications so complex that the scholarly literature of the Holocaust has itself become a subject of scholarly inquiry. In fact, one can discern the emergence today of a new subdiscipline, that of the historiography of the Holocaust: its development, methods, and internal controversies. Many important historians of the Holocaust are now concerning themselves at the same time with its historiography: Lucy Dawidowicz, Leni Yahil, Saul Friedländer, Yehuda Bauer, Omer Bartov, and a number of other worthy scholars, including Jews, Germans, and others. Along with the growing discussion of this subject, there are other, more general debates with a variety of theoretical aspects and often an ideological and political side to them as well. Thus, for example, books have been written on the relation between historiography and memory, and on the different ways the Holocaust can or cannot be "represented." Can it be represented artistically? Can it only be spoken about or also shown? How can we speak about it, and what is the role of survivor testimony in the understanding of what happened? These

---

[44] Readers of Hebrew can get a sense of this development from the testimony of German and Israeli historians, as collected, for example, in Moshe Zimmerman, ed., *Darka hameyuhedet shel germania bahistoria* (Germany's Unique Historical Path) (Jerusalem: Magnes, 5749 [1989]), which contains a number of articles on this issue. Kulka, "Major Trends and Tendencies," is also of particular interest. A more up-to-date survey is to be found in the Ulrich Herbert, "Extermination Policy: New Answers and Questions about the History of the 'Holocaust' in German Historiography," in Herbert, ed., *National Socialist Extermination Policies: Contemporary German Perspectives and Controversies* (New York: Berghahn, 2000), 1–52. See also Henry Wassermann, ed., *Hahistoria hagermanit-yehudit sheyarashnu: Germanim tze'irim kotvim historia yehudit* (Our Inherited German-Jewish History: Young Germans Write Jewish History) (Jerusalem: Leo Baeck Institute and Magnes Press, 2004). Wassermann points out in his introduction that about a decade had passed since primacy in the study of German Jewish history, at least from a quantitative point of view, passed to the Germans. One of the articles in the book deals with the Holocaust.

are some of the questions being asked about "representation," a term that plays a central role in contemporary intellectual discourse.

Several conclusions can be drawn from this body of literature. It turns out that most of the general descriptions of the Holocaust have been written by Jewish scholars.[45] In recent years, several German and other historians have contributed comprehensive studies of the subject and a larger number of more limited studies, but in the nature of things they have, without exception (based on an outsider's impressions, again) dealt with the destruction of the Jews and not with the Holocaust. The two are quite different things. Scholars of the destruction of the Jews customarily divide the subject into three interrelated aspects, a division first suggested, if I am not mistaken, by Raul Hilberg: the perpetrators, the bystanders, and the victims. It turns out that the study of the subject in terms of the victims, and specifically the Jewish victims – where the term Holocaust acquires its full meaning – was a relatively late development, undertaken almost exclusively by Jewish scholars.[46] This was not the result of an artificial or ideologically driven "division of labor," nor did it stem from a desire to give the victims – that is, the *Jewish* victims – some preferential status. Nor has there been an attempt to hide the fact that there were other victims, contrary to what is sometimes claimed.

This tripartite division has become so firmly entrenched in historical discourse that it is sometimes forgotten that it is merely schematic, general, methodological, even metahistoriographical. Though the terms are similar, there is a distinction between the "aspects" of the Holocaust (the subject of the historiographical research), on the one hand, and the points of view of the historians, on the other. The work of historians has always been problematic in many ways, but today they face systematic skepticism about the scientific character of their profession. One of the discoveries of "postmodernism" has been the obvious and ultimately trivial fact that the historian always operates in the context of a certain time and place, language and culture, and personal and collective memory and experience. The same is true of historians of Nazism, the destruction of the Jews, and the Holocaust – especially the

---

[45] See Dan Michman, "The Holocaust in the Eyes of Historians: The Problem of Conceptionalization, Periodization, and Explanation," in Michman, *Holocaust Historiography*, 9–40. Michman discusses, among others, books by Léon Poliakov, Gerald Reitlinger, Raul Hilberg, Lucy Dawidowich, Leni Yahil, Daniel Jonah Goldhagen, Yehuda Bauer, and Saul Friedländer. We might also mention the more recent book of Robert Wistrich, *Hitler and the Holocaust: How and Why the Holocaust Happened* (London: Phoenix, 2001).

[46] See Yehuda Bauer, *Rethinking the Holocaust* (New Haven: Yale University Press, 2001), 68ff.

Jews among them. For when it comes to these events, history and memory are
still intertwined – as Saul Friedländer, for example, often points out. Many
of those who study the history of these events experienced them in their own
flesh. As we have said, this does not give them a particular advantage, but
neither does it cast doubt on their "objectivity."

Saul Friedländer himself is a good example. As a historian, he works, to a
large extent, in the context of the German historiography of the Holocaust.
He is in contact with the leading German historians and takes an active part
in their debates. Thus, for example, he was one of Nolte's chief critics in the
"historians' controversy," and his correspondence with Martin Broszat is no
less important. Much of his work concerns the same questions that preoc-
cupy the German historians – German society in its relation to the destruction of the Jews – and emerges from dialogue of one sort or another with
them. He is also well aware of the inevitability of having a specific point of
view, that is, the inescapable fact that he and other Jewish historians look at
the Holocaust through Jewish eyes. We see this in the collection of articles,
the introduction to which we have just quoted (n. 39), and, especially, in
his book *Nazi Germany and the Jews: The Years of Persecution, 1933–39,*
which is the first part of what is likely to be – in fact, already is – one of the
most interesting and, in the view of knowledgeable critics, most important
works yet on the Final Solution.[47] But it seems to have taken a historian with
a point of view like Friedländer's, that is, a Jewish point of view, to write this
book. This may not be an a priori or mathematical necessity, but experience
teaches that it is the case.

The fact that German scholars are concerned mainly with the nature and
history of the Nazi regime; with how the Final Solution came about, how
the decision, or series of decisions, that led to it came to be made; and with
how individual Germans and German institutions carried out the destruction is a function of their perspective as Germans. So too is the fact that they
deal with the Holocaust much less. It is not that they are uninterested in it.
On the contrary, it interests them very much. But "the Holocaust" is the
name of the Jews' catastrophe, the destruction as the Jews experienced it
and remember it, as only they can document it, study it, and write its history.
The Germans deal with Nazism and its crimes, the Second World War, and
the destruction of the Jews. The Jews deal with these questions, too, but in
a different way. The pioneering work of Raul Hilberg, which deals with the

---

[47] Since the publication of the Hebrew edition of the present book, and long after these lines
were written, the second volume came out: *The Years of Extermination: Nazi Germany
and the Jews, 1939–1945* (New York: HarperCollins, 2007).

way the destruction of the European Jews was carried out by the German extermination machine, that is, the Holocaust from the point of view of the perpetrators, is a good example. He also wanted to know and understand the catastrophe of the Jews of Europe, and focusing on the perpetrators was based on the assumption that this would be the proper way to do so. But, despite this focus on the perpetrators, his was an unmistakably Jewish perspective. In the last analysis, it is only the Jews, or mostly the Jews, who deal with the Holocaust as such.

Zuckerman cannot accept the fact that there is a specific (or particular, as he likes to call it) point of view from which Jews are bound, rather than choose, to see the Holocaust. They cannot get around it except at the price of violence, which frequently, as in Zuckerman's case, is violence committed by Jews against Jews. He also fails to grasp that this inescapable viewpoint has various peculiar consequences. This failure explains statements like the following: "It would be hard to say which possibility was worse, denial of the Holocaust because of ignorance or denial of it based on an ideological instrumentalization of it" (p. 298). This could hardly be stated more bitingly, although other possibilities can be imagined, such as denial of the Holocaust out of malice despite full knowledge of the facts.

But note what he is actually saying: the instrumentalization of the Holocaust is its denial. This, despite the fact that, in a halfhearted attempt at self-criticism, Zuckerman acknowledges somewhere that he, too, uses the Holocaust for ideological purposes. And he is not alone. We do not need Zuckerman to recognize that the public space in Israel, and to a considerable extent in the world at large, is permeated with the subject of the Holocaust. More or less explicit comparisons with Nazism, Germany of the World War II era, and Auschwitz abound, on both the left and the right. For every example there is a counterexample. It is true that Menahem Begin, for instance, did not hesitate to make demagogic, populistic use of the Holocaust. As I write these lines, settlers displaced by the Israeli withdrawal from the Gaza Strip are going about with numbers on their arms. Some wear orange Stars of David, like the yellow ones the Nazis required, on their chests, and they call Ariel Sharon another Hitler. Then too, there are abundant examples coming from the other side of the political map. Thus, when the editor of a literary journal recently commented on television on the plan of a certain deputy minister to remove from the school curriculum the works of writers who had demanded the investigation of those responsible for targeted assassinations of Arab terrorist leaders, the analogy he used was not, of course, that of McCarthy but of the Nazi book burnings. Or when a certain literary critic and author of thrillers expressed disgust at the way Israeli border policemen treated an elderly Arab arrested in the streets of Jerusalem, it was not the abuses committed by the generals in Argentina or the handling of blacks by the Los Angeles police that she referred to but the way Jews were treated in Nazi Germany. Or when a sociology professor sought to enlighten newspaper readers in Belgium (of all places) about the horror of the assassination of Palestinian terrorist leader Sheikh Yassin, he charged Israel with waging a campaign of symbolic genocide against the Palestinians, and when asked to explain this statement, he said that the Holocaust had blinded Israelis to the terrible suffering of the Palestinians. Or take another example: when the former Israeli army chief of staff spoke about the use of a powerful bomb to assassinate a Palestinian terrorist, causing the deaths of many innocent people, some of them children, a leading Hebrew poet suggested that he take up the study of German.

Zuckerman does not deny this, but he is quick to explain (*Haaretz*, November 28, 1995) that there is no symmetry here between right and left. When iconoclastic professor Yeshayahu Leibowitz, for example, called the Jewish settlers (or maybe it was soldiers carrying out orders; I cannot recall) "Judeo-Nazis," there was, in Zuckerman's Teutonic Hebrew, something emancipatory about it. One can only wonder whether he would apply the same label to his own use of the Holocaust. Too bad he did not tell us what he thought of the expression "Ashke-Nazis." In any event, it is only others, in his view, who instrumentalize the Holocaust in a way that is not emancipatory, these others being all who do not use the Holocaust to crush Israel, to criticize it, to slander it – in short, all who belong, if not to the right, then at best to a left that has lost "the last shred of it critical function," a left that, alas, in Israel, had never been a "revolutionary political and social force" to begin with (p. 256).

EXCURSUS 2: WHAT IS WRONG WITH INSTRUMENTALIZING THE HOLOCAUST?

Zuckerman is partly right: there is no symmetry here between the left and the right, or, in fact, between the Zionists and their detractors. But he is also partly wrong: the direction of the asymmetry is just the reverse of what he thinks; the instrumentalization of the Holocaust by the radical left is much more immoral, more significant, and, as it turns out, more effective than Zionism's. It also seems much more widespread. Zionist blackmail appears to have run its course. But the negation of Zionism and of the Jews' right to a state of their own is no longer taboo, and the horror of Auschwitz no longer haunts those who would cast doubt on this right. According to the opinion polls, support for Israel in Europe is minimal, only about one-fourth the percentage enjoyed by the Palestinians. Opposition to Zionism has won the day among large parts of the public in many places, particularly in Europe and to some extent in the United States as well. The trend appears even among Jews, and even in Israel. And just as the denial of the Holocaust has played a certain role – not quantifiable, of course – in the process of delegitimizing Israel, the use of the Holocaust by the Israeli *resentiment* community has contributed significantly to the domestic post-Zionist movement as well as to the worldwide anti-Israel campaign.

Zuckerman is one of those who speak about the anxiety narrative. Citing several anecdotes about the fears Israelis felt during the First Gulf War, he complains about what he sees as the irrational linkage made between the fear of attack by chemically armed Iraqi missiles (manufactured with the help of German scientists, as rumor had it) and the memory of the Nazi gas chambers. On the basis of these findings, he makes a general observation about Israeli culture: it is one of neurotic anxiety, and of course it is this anxiety that gives rise to fear and hatred of the Arabs. The cliché about anxiety is, as we have pointed out, a recurrent theme in the writings of Zuckerman and his comrades. They are out to educate the Israeli public to forsake memorialization of the anxiety-provoking kind. Some of them even posture as defenders of the authentic memories or as spokesmen for the victims or the survivors. It is they, as it were, who stand fast against the manipulation and trivialization of the memory of the Holocaust by the political, educational, Jewish, Zionist, Israeli, and other "establishments." It is they who warn against its commercialization, its misuse, its destructive effect on our collective neuroses, and on and on.

Of course, these phenomena do exist, to one degree or another. One can, and sometimes must, criticize them. Yet they are all inevitable to some extent, and the damage they do is generally less than the critics claim. In most cases, it is very hard, in the great, complex, multifaceted totality of Israel's culture of commemoration, to distinguish what is legitimate, respectable, and correct from what is despicable, ridiculous, or obscene. Most dubious is the explicit or implicit charge that Holocaust consciousness and its manipulation play a key, or even central, role in shaping the Israeli culture of power, the policy of expansion and occupation, and other aspects of public conduct. Not only is there no evidence whatsoever to back up this charge, but it has also been called into question by historical research into the determinants of Israeli public policy. The trouble is that, according to Zuckerman, such research is usually done by official, establishment historians whose findings must be taken with a very big grain of salt – in fact, disregarded altogether.

The claim that the Holocaust has given rise to an Israeli culture of power is also disproved by the fact that the Holocaust feeds no less, and perhaps even more, into a culture of criticism of and alienation from power, not only in the case of the *resentiment* community but also among loyal Zionists.

There is indeed a big difference, a moral difference, between the Zionist and the anti-Zionist instrumentalization of the Holocaust. The use Zuckerman and his friends make of the Holocaust is immoral, in stark contrast to the sort of use he rails against. It is immoral not only, or even primarily, because it gives a one-sided, superficial, and tendentious, if not altogether distorted picture of Israeli society, but because it tries to suppress memory, which in this instance can only mean eliminating identity. For many Israelis, associations with Nazism and the Holocaust are immediate and understandable. They arise at every turn and serve every need. There is, in fact, no real harm in this. At worst, the excessive use of imagery and metaphors based on the memory of the Holocaust is a sign of bad taste and an impoverished imagination.[48] Perhaps invoking the Holocaust, directly or metaphorically, is unavoidable. Any attempt to suppress it is doomed to failure; but, more than this, such attempts do violence, not only to the obligation to remember – which is certainly debatable – but, above all, to the legitimacy of a uniquely Jewish-Israeli perspective on the Holocaust and, in effect, to the foundations of the personal and collective identity of many Israelis.

On the face of it, Zuckerman and at least some of his fellow travelers do not aim their criticism at personal memories of the Holocaust. He is quite willing to recognize the legitimacy of personal pain. But the notion that one can separate private and public, even national, memory is not just questionable (for such a distinction is impossible); it is obscene. Though death is always something personal, Jews did not die in Europe merely as individuals but rather as Jews and only because they were Jews. Therefore, those who feel the pain of their individual deaths or the individual suffering of the survivors cannot rest content with private commemoration. Nor do they want to. Historical commemoration must be public, and the literature of the Holocaust, however personal and individual, confirms this. Many survivors never speak about the Holocaust, and others despise the public rituals of commemoration. But the systematic, reasoned attempt to suppress such commemoration in all its forms is liquidationist: it cannot be done

---

[48] In the "Weekend" supplement to *Ma'ariv*, May 6, 2005, Rubik Rosenthal provides readers with a brief, one-page, practical glossary of common Hebrew usages drawn from the Holocaust. From the Internet, he quotes the line, "What a motherf—king Gestapo teacher! She has a computer that sees what everybody's doing."

without wiping out the "Zionist entity" altogether. And like all programs of liquidation, it is immoral.

In fact, completely contrary to what Zuckerman and people like him claim, most Israelis, precisely because of the seriousness of their memories of the Holocaust, are fairly immune to rhetoric and demagoguery that overuse those memories. One confirmation of this can be found in the negative way they reacted to the hysterical Holocaust rhetoric of the opposition to evacuating Jewish settlements from the Gaza Strip. In any case, their immunity is greater than that of the people who take the jargon of Zuckerman & Co. seriously. But the obsession of the latter with the memory of the Holocaust, their consistent obliviousness to, or contempt for, the need for, and difficulty of, commemoration, and, above all, the fierceness of their criticism – all these lead one to suspect that their real motives are not merely theoretical, not merely a concern for the health of Israeli discourse about the Holocaust, but something else.

The sad truth is that Zuckerman and his friends have imported to Israel the perversion of Guillaume and his circle. This is almost explicit in the case of those who advocate forgetting about the Holocaust. With others, such as Zuckerman, the picture would seem to be more complicated, more dialectical, if you will. They speak as if they represent the "right" way of remembering the Holocaust, or as if representing the victims; but what this kind of talk conceals is precisely, or almost precisely, what motivates Holocaust denial on the part of the radical left, namely, the negation of Zionism. The negation can be direct and explicit, as in the case of Serge Thion, or more subtle and nuanced. Zuckerman and his friends generally accept the views of these left-wing circles – the revolutionary, *tiers-mondiste*, postcolonial left – on the subject of Israeli policy and responsibility for the situation in the Middle East. Even when their criticism pretends to confine itself to certain aspects of Israeli life or Israeli government policies, the very fact that the Holocaust is invoked as an argument or rhetorical ploy places that criticism in Guillaume's universe of discourse. That discourse, as we have seen, is based on the double assumption that the Holocaust and its memory are the main, if not the sole, explanation for the reality of Israel and its moral intolerability. Zuckerman is a good example, because he does not content himself with an "objective" analysis of the presence of the Holocaust in the sealed rooms Israelis have had to build for defense against unconventional attack – an analysis that is, no doubt, legitimate, if trivial – but goes on from there to a sweeping criticism of the Israeli government, the Israeli left, and in fact the whole Israeli ethos and reality. What exactly he thinks about Israel's right to exist as a Jewish state remains, as we have said, somewhat unclear, but evidently, even if he does not oppose Jewish sovereignty, he is annoyed by most of its manifestations.

However, even if one were to conceal his political and ideological agenda more cleverly, and even if one were not committed to a radical anti-Zionist ideology, the use of the Holocaust as a basis for ideological criticism would have clear implications of a liquidationist nature. Sweeping condemnation of the "Holocaust mentality" of Israeli society and the Israeli establishment can often obscure the simple, if politically incorrect fact that Jews, Israelis, and Zionists have a moral right to speak of the Holocaust whenever and however they wish. We also have a moral right (though not an obligation, of course) to instrumentalize the Holocaust, even when it is unaesthetic or damaging to do so. But the Zuckermans of the world do not have this right. Zuckerman's recognition of the right of individuals alone to remember their loss is a gross impertinence, as is his foolish attempt to delegitimate our collective memory in all its diverse forms, be they more or less pleasant or aesthetic. For in his case, quite unlike the cases he criticizes, the instrumentalization of the Holocaust is tantamount to its denial. As the death of the Jews in the Holocaust was not aesthetic, the memory of it is also not always pleasing to the eye. It does not always suit the refined, universalistic sensibility of the Zuckerman variety. But the real outrage is not this memory, in its various manifestations, but the perverse, self-righteous, condescending attempts to suppress it, to educate it and preach to it.

There is another phenomenon that distinguishes the perverted discourse of those who use the Holocaust to attack Zionism, including their Israeli contingent, from the culture of excessive commemoration, be it on the left or on the right. As opposed to the popular, organized, or academic memorialization of the Holocaust; as opposed to the instinctive use of Holocaust metaphors at nearly every opportunity; as opposed to the use of the Holocaust for any and all purposes; as opposed to the demagogic Holocaust rhetoric of such leaders as Menahem Begin; and as opposed to the artistic uses made of the Holocaust in Israel, particularly in theater and literature – as opposed to all these, the use of the Holocaust made by Guillaume, on the one hand, and Ophir and Zuckerman, on the other, is systematic and purportedly theoretically based. Here, too, there is a lack of symmetry, for there is no parallel "theory" on the other side. There are apologetics concerning the right and need to remember, but there is no ideological or theoretical community, well defined or otherwise, no community whose intellectual identity is defined by the use of the Holocaust. On the one side, as we have already seen in the case of the Holocaust-denial community and in the Israeli case as well, an entity has come into being that has a describable structure. First of all, it has an ideological focus: radical criticism of Zionism, of Israel as a Jewish state, and of key aspects of its cultural and political identity. In addition, it uses a similar academic style of writing and, most of the time, a set jargon; it relies on the same theoretical sources; and it pretends to be scientific. One can see here a systematic effort to develop a kind of theory aimed at undermining Zionist thought and the political, cultural, and ideological self-confidence of Zionism and Israel. Here too, the pretense at theory has no real basis; the data on which Zuckerman relies are taken mainly from the daily press. But it takes more than some newspaper clippings,[49] a few quasi-theoretical terms, and a semisarcastic tone to come up with a serious analysis of the Israeli collective consciousness and to claim that all this determines, or even influences, Israel's political behavior.

The sad, simple truth is that, in the last analysis, remembering the Holocaust amounts to fighting a battle where there can be no victory and where defeat is assured from the outset, making the memorialization easy to attack, as Zuckerman does. For "there are two kinds of Jews left, the dead and those who are a bit crazy." This line is spoken in George Steiner's novel *The Portage to San Cristobal of A. H.* by one of Hitler's Israeli captors, in the Brazilian rain forest, after he has explained to a colleague that the death or humiliation of a small child can never be avenged.[50] And, indeed, mental hospitals in Israel are filled with people driven mad by the Holocaust, and even now, nearly sixty years after the end of the war, the Holocaust is still claiming its victims. Not among the Germans (as Faurisson thinks) or among the Palestinians (as Bishara and Zuckerman think), but among the Jews, those who were children or adolescents when the catastrophe befell them and who were robbed by it of their childhood, as well as the children and even grandchildren of the survivors. In light of this reality, the things Zuckerman says, and the various reckonings given by others of what they call

[49] See Dan Michman, ed., *"Post-tzionut" vesho'a: Hapulmus hatzibburi hayisra'eli benose ha-"post-tzionut" bashanim 1993–1996 umekoma shel sugiat hasho'a bo* ("Post-Zionism" and the Holocaust: The Israeli Public Debate over "Post-Zionism" in 1993–1996 and the Role of the Holocaust in It) (Ramat Gan: Bar-Ilan University, 1997). This is an illuminating collection of articles and polemical pieces that appeared during these years in the Israeli press. It is not clear how much Zuckerman's analysis adds to what can be read in these sources themselves. They show not only the intensity of public debate in Israel on the questions that occupy us here but also how widespread is the ideological linkage of the Holocaust with incriminating criticism of Israel. (A second volume, covering the period from the beginning of 1997 until July 1998 – that is, shortly after the fiftieth anniversary of Israel's independence, as some of us still call it – has appeared recently. I have not yet seen it as of this writing.)

[50] George Steiner, *The Portage to San Cristobal of A. H.* (New York: Simon & Schuster, 1981), 63.

the "Holocaustism" (*shoanut*) of the Israelis and the Zionists are exposed in their full intellectual and moral nakedness.

Zuckerman is against particularism and in favor of universalism. Steiner is the paragon of the universal Jewish intellectual. He is also a great defender of this universalism and, especially, of the moral superiority of not belonging to or being politically involved in anything, a superiority that Israel and Israelis forfeit, of course, as a result of the very logic of the existence of a Jewish state. The last chapter of his fictional work includes Hitler's speech in his own defense, at the time of the field trial his captors arrange for him when their mission comes to an end. Hitler's third and last point, with which the book concludes, deals with Herzl, Zionism, and Israel. Don't fool yourselves, Hitler says to the Israelis. Without the Holocaust, that is, without me, the world – the Americans, the Soviets – would never have given you Palestine for your state. "It was the Holocaust that gave you the courage of injustice, that made you drive the Arab out of his home, out of his field, because he was lice-eaten and without resource, because he was in your divinely-ordered way" (p. 169). This is but one more expression, ostensibly literary, of the phenomenon of which Holocaust denial is one aspect and the demonization of Israel the other.

THE ACCUSATION OF ABANDONMENT, BETRAYAL, AND EXPLOITATION

The so-called new historians and other "post-Zionist" writers often use the categories "hegemonic discourse," "Zionist historiography," and "official historiography." They also speak of intellectuals who do the bidding of the state and collaborate with the establishment. This is, of course, an effective way of dismissing a priori anyone whose views differ from theirs. One of those who use such terminology is Yosef Grodzinsky, a professor of psychology (psycholinguistics), whom we have met before. In recent years, he has published a book and a number of reviews dealing with different aspects of the complex and painful question of the relations between the Yishuv (the prestate Palestinian Jewish community) and the State of Israel and its leaders, on the one hand, and the victims of the Holocaust, on the other. He is, of course, not a denier of the Holocaust; on the contrary, he sees himself as speaking in the name of its victims and demands an accounting for the wrongs done to them. Although it is not German but Zionist crimes that he enumerates, his indictment of the Zionists is validated by the suffering of the Jews in Europe at the hands of the Nazis and the scope of the crime committed against them, as well as the weight of the moral burden the Holocaust imposed on those who survived.

Grodzinsky's so-called research and his criticism of hegemonic historiography were the two methods he employed in his recent minicampaign against Israel's dominant ideology, Zionism. (In the meantime, he has disappeared from the public eye in Israel, perhaps because he moved to some North American university.) Thematically, too, his offensive had a dual objective. It was based on two more or less well-known episodes, one the efforts of the Yishuv to rescue Jews in Europe during the Second World War, the second the way the Yishuv and its political and military leadership related to the displaced persons (the Holocaust survivors who were temporarily housed in camps all around Europe, mainly in Germany) after the war. On the basis of these two episodes Grodzinsky mounts a double indictment against Zionism: quasi-criminal negligence and abandonment of the Jews in Europe to their death; and cynical exploitation of the survivors for the needs of the Yishuv once the war was over.

Needless to say, Grodzinsky is not a denier. Quite the opposite. He considers himself to be talking in the name of the victims and the survivors and to be pleading their case. During the debates that followed the publication of the Hebrew original of the present book, he expressed a deep indignation at being accused, he thought, of Holocaust denial. Not only am I not a denier, he said, but, on the contrary, I am a "Shoah emphasizer." (In Hebrew it sounds more natural: *madgish sho'a* and not *makkhish sh'oa*). In fact, this is precisely what the book said: Grodzinsky is not and has never been a Holocaust denier. Yet there are very good reasons to consider him in this context. Grodzinsky, in fact, speaks in the name of the victims of the Holocaust, the dead and the survivors alike. He pleads their case. Only he mounts this case not against the Germans but against the Zionists and Israelis. Although there is no reason to doubt the grief he feels for Jewish suffering during those terrible years, like the other members of the community of opprobrium, he is not, at least in his writings, really interested in the Holocaust but in the indictment of Zionism and Israel that can be built on the basis of the Holocaust. The enormity of the calamity only serves to strengthen the accusation. In this respect, Grodzinsky does belong to the same crowd as Guillaume and Thion, not to speak of Zuckerman, Ophir, or a number of others we shall mention later on. Like them all, he bases his case on the master postulate, even if in doing so he seems to proceed in the opposite direction: the Shoah is the only possible justification for the establishment and existence of the State of Israel; it also imposes an absolute moral obligation upon the Jews; however, the Zionists did not respect this obligation; ergo … .

Many of Grodzinsky's reviews, as well as the critical responses to them and his responses to the critics, appear in the collection *Post-tzionut veshoa*

(Post-Zionism and the Holocaust). The Hebrew reader can thus easily acquaint himself with his positions. Their general tenor can be seen, for example, in a review he wrote of Ra'ya Cohen's book *Bein sham lekan: Sippuram shel edim lashoa velahurban: Shvaitz 1939–1942* (Between There and Here: Stories of Eyewitnesses to the Holocaust and the Destruction: Switzerland, 1939–1942).[51] The review appeared in *Haaretz* early in 2000. After describing the book and giving it a little criticism and praise, he explains the historical conclusion to which the book leads: if the Zionist movement was meant to concern itself with the well-being of Jews everywhere, "then the record of [its] rescue efforts during the Holocaust proves it was a dismal failure." Indeed, a moral failure. The Holocaust thus provides a reason to question the legitimacy of the Zionist movement and, implicitly, of the Zionist idea as well.

In fact, he maintains, Zionism's failure has been immense. It is not that the Zionists miscalculated or misunderstood the situation; they effectively betrayed the exterminated Jews of Europe. On the occasion of the publication of several studies of the Hatzalah (the Yishuv's rescue campaign), Grodzinsky cites the case of Rabbi Weissmandel. Michael Dov Weissmandel (1903–1956), an Orthodox rabbi in Slovakia, was a member of the so-called Working Group that had been engaged in all sorts of rescue efforts during the years of the extermination. In close collaboration with Gisi Fleischmann, a Zionist activist, Weissmandel had proved himself courageous, resourceful, and dedicated. Fleishmann, also an exceptional woman, later gave herself up to the Germans, so that numerous Jews would be spared the fate the Germans usually reserved for their hostages. She was deported to Auschwitz and murdered there.

In 1942 the Working Group paid Dieter Wisliceny, Eichmann's representative in Slovakia, the sum of $50,000 to stop the deportation of Jews from Slovakia. They also paid some Slovakian functionaries. The deportations were in fact stopped for two years. Although there were other reasons for this, Weissmandel was convinced that it was the bribe given to Wisliceny that was responsible. He approached the Zionists – and it is noteworthy that he addressed them and not the Orthodox leadership – for more money, but they were rather skeptical about the possibility of buying more Jewish lives, and recent research shows that they were probably right.[52] After what

---

[51] Tel Aviv: Am Oved, 1999.

[52] Shlomo Aronson has recently shown, on the basis of Slovak and German documents, that not only had the reason for stopping (temporarily) the deportations not been the bribe given to Wisliceny, but also that the latter had actually wanted to continue the deportations. See Sh.

he took to be his first success, Weissmandel proposed an ambitious plan, known as the Europe Plan, which envisaged buying the lives of Jews still living in other parts of Europe. He did not manage to get more money, but it is in any case unlikely that the Germans were seriously considering sparing any more Jews, even in very small numbers. Weissmandel himself was later deported to Auschwitz. He managed to jump off the train, leaving his wife and children behind, and they were murdered at Auschwitz. After the war he moved to the United States. In a posthumous volume containing his letters, he tells his story and the story of the rescue efforts in which he was engaged. He also criticizes the Jewish leaders, notably the Zionists, for not saving Europe's Jews during the years of extermination.

There is some controversy about the authenticity of some of Weissmandel's letters, which he, or rather the anti-Zionist Orthodox editors of the volume, claim were never answered by the Zionist activists to whom they had been sent. Grodzinsky has no doubts that the letters were sent or that the Zionists did not answer, out of what the editors of the book describe as criminal negligence. He repeats Weissmandel's accusations to the effect that the Zionists had abandoned him – along with the whole Orthodox population and, in fact, the rest of European Jewry as well. Grodzinsky refuses to consider the arguments of "Zionist" historians, whom he mentions only as opponents to be refuted, never as sources of reliable knowledge.

Accusations of betrayal, abandonment, indifference, or –worst of all – selective rescue were leveled against the leadership of the Yishuv while the war was still on. They later served as propaganda in the political and ideological struggle against the hegemony of the labor parties in the Zionist movement, in the Yishuv and in Israel in the first years after the creation of the state. The most important party in the socialist camp, Mapai, and its leader Ben-Gurion, were particular targets of these attacks. On one side, the anti-Zionists – the left-wing bundists and communists, as well as the Orthodox and ultra-Orthodox – and on the other side, the nationalist right in Israel and in some Jewish communities abroad, notably in the

Aronson, *Hitler, the Allies, and the Jews* (Cambridge: Cambridge University Press, 2004), 170–180; Y. Bauer, *Jews for Sale?* (New Haven: Yale University Press, 1994); D. Porat, *Hanhaga bemilkud: Hayishuv nokhah hashoa, 1942–1945* (Tel Aviv: Am Oved, 1986), 328–346, translated as *The Blue and the Yellow Stars of David: The Zionist Leadership in Palestine and the Holocaust, 1939–1945* (Cambridge, Mass.: Harvard University Press, 1990); Leny Yahil, *Ha'Shoah. Goral yehudei Eiropa, 1932–1945* (The Shoah: The Fate of Europe's Jews, 1932–1945) (Jerusalem and Tel Aviv: Schocken and Yad Va'Shem, 1987), vol. 2, esp. p. 651; Saul Friedländer, *Nazi Germany and the Jews, 1939–1945*, vol. 2: *The Years of Extermination* (New York: Harper, 2007), 372–374.

United States, accused Mapai of betraying and abandoning their brethren in Europe. The best-known chapter in this sad story is the Kasztner affair in 1954–1955. Kasztner was a Zionist active in rescue efforts in Hungary. He became known for his long and rather risky negotiations with Eichmann, which resulted in a train with 1,684 Jews aboard being allowed to leave Hungary. After the war and his immigration to Israel, he was accused of trafficking with the Germans. He lost a libel suit and was said by the judge to have sold his soul to the devil. He was assassinated immediately afterward but posthumously exonerated by the High Court.[53]

A similar strain of thinking is to be found in Grodzinsky's book *In the Shadow of the Holocaust: The Struggle between Jews and Zionists in the Aftermath of World War II*, his main historiographical work.[54] The book is a clear example of the phenomenon with which we are concerned here, both because, as historiography, its only value is in the minor scandal it caused, and because its scholarly veneer disguises none too successfully what is merely a political tract. Although it is the work of a respected academic, indeed a scholar of international standing, it does not, in fact, measure up to the most basic requirements of historical writing. The tiresome repetition of the same quotes and references is only one expression of the thinness of the material, as is the tedious proliferation of minor details. The author makes up for the lack of real historical analysis with semiliterary descriptions in which much that is imaginary is combined with bits of factual information, mostly well known and, in any case, mostly trivial; and when his writing is not blatantly amateurish, it hardly amounts to more than rummaging through archives. In the end, the main contribution of this pseudoscholarly work is its discussion of a single episode in 1948, lasting several months, in which a partially successful attempt was made to recruit to the Zionist cause young Jews living in the displaced-persons camps in Germany. The notion

---

[53] There exists a vast literature on this subject, among other things a number of studies by Yehiam Weitz, that Grodzinsky criticizes on several occasions. The principal source of information for the non-Hebrew reader seems to be Tom Segev's *The Seventh Million: The Israelis and the Holocaust*, trans. H. Watzman (New York: Hill and Wang, 1993). This is unfortunate because Segev's book is anything but an objective study. For a general view, see Anna Porter, *Kasztner's Train* (New York: Walker, 2007). The interested reader will find a comprehensive survey of literature on this subject in Tuvia Frilling, "David Ben-Gurion vehashoa: Shorashav vegilgulav shel stereotip shelili" (David Ben-Gurion and the Holocaust: The Origin and Development of a Negative Stereotype), in Frilling, ed., *Teshuva le'amit post-tzioni* (Reply to a Post-Zionist Colleague) (Tel Aviv: Yediot Aharonot, 2003), 418–456.

[54] Yosef Grodzinsky, *In the Shadow of the Holocaust: The Struggle between Jews and Zionists in the Aftermath of World War II* (Monroe, Maine: Common Courage Press, 2004).

that some of these people could be forced, even by threat of violence, to go to Palestine and fight, perhaps even die, seems doubtful to me, though various kinds of pressure, perhaps even heavy pressure, were probably brought to bear on them to join up.

Reactions to the book by those subjected to this "forced" conscription, reactions Grodzinsky has questioned as not grounded in objective scholarship, make clear that his description is at least exaggerated and definitely one-sided. Grodzinsky, like many in his circle, believes in the unlimited, godlike ability of government, overtly or covertly, to manipulate (all except him, of course) and coerce. As usual, the truth is more complicated. A regime's ability to move people to action, even to coerce them, always depends on some sort of acceptance of its legitimacy. Only a totalitarian regime can act without such recognition, and not always. That is because, by employing unrestrained violence, it destroys the moral character and spontaneity that are essential to individuality – as Hannah Arendt, for one, explains it. Arendt, as we know, thought there were two totalitarian systems in the twentieth century, Nazism and Stalinism, that they were unprecedented and completely different from anything known before. Is Grodzinsky hinting that the use of the survivors was an expression of the totalitarian, that is, criminal, nature of Israel too? It should also be borne in mind that the coercion of the camp residents was exerted by a few emissaries sent by a regime that was just being organized and was fighting for its life in a distant land. Even Hitler and Stalin could not have sustained their coercive rule under such conditions.

What makes the whole argument at once ridiculous and outrageous is the use of this episode to delegitimize Zionism and Israel wholesale. Let us assume that Grodzinsky is right about Hagana operatives recruiting forcibly in the DP camps. Let us even assume that those who refused to go were shot (which they were not). Let us assume that such recruitment is illegitimate, perhaps even outrageous. What do these assertions have to do with the historiosophical conclusions he draws from these supposed facts? Clearly, there was a prior assumption, and the study was done merely to confirm it.

Grodzinsky's conclusions are the only thing worth quoting from his book, not because they are of any inherent intellectual interest, but because they exemplify the phenomenon we are considering here. Our interest in them stems not from the existence of a scholarly or even quasi-scholarly attempt to give the reader as accurate a picture as possible of any historical incident. They interest us only as a symptom. The last chapter in the book, the "epilogue," consists of nine pages of metapolitical ruminations. The Zionists, he avers, needed manpower to set up their state. They found this resource after the war primarily among the weak, the stateless, and the displaced. But even here, the Zionists were looking only for "good material" – as the book's original Hebrew title *Homer tzioni tov* (good Zionist material) puts it – those who could make a real contribution in the coming war. Both during the Second World War, when the question of rescue came up, and afterward, when thousands of displaced persons were gathered in the camps, the policy of the Zionist leadership was always "Palestinocentric," that is, one that saw "Zionist history [as] the necessary, hence sole, continuation of Jewish history." Furthermore, Grodzinsky adds, "The irony in this ... is hard to miss: the very movement that was created to bring deliverance to the Jews now took possession of ... Jewish identity and in its name expropriated the rights of the people, so that its own needs could be served" (p. 230).

This appropriation, and particularly the "Zionization" of the Holocaust, is a kind of theft. After all, the Jewish people are, as always, characterized by "a multiplicity of alternative fates" (p. 191 in the Hebrew edition only). We must, Grodzinsky says, free ourselves of "the grip of [Israeli] ideology," and then we shall be able to see this here in Israel as well. It's a tempest in a teapot, as if we didn't know. This multiplicity of fates is, in fact, just two: to live in Israel or to live elsewhere. Beyond this, we are talking about lifestyles, communal loyalties, and more or less successful ways of living as Jews in the various countries where Jews live, but not about "fates." Grodzinsky has no other alternatives to offer or meanings to give to his term "fate." In other words, it is simply the old argument between Zionism in its various forms and what is called "Diasporism," between Zionism's demand that it be recognized as the Jewish national movement and the rejection of this demand. Such rejection is tantamount to rejection of the State of Israel as the state of the Jewish people and thus a denial of its legitimacy. Even factoring the Holocaust into this argument is nothing new; it has been done by both sides, of course. What makes Grodzinsky's argument original is its dialectical quality: he speaks in the name of the victims and the displaced and thus uses their suffering and death to revive an old claim in an old dispute and to undermine Israel's claim to being the state of the Jewish people. For, as we have seen, the Holocaust is, as it were, the main reason the State of Israel was established, and this justification can be based only on the responsibility Zionism and the state assume for the Jews, "wherever they may be," on harnessing all available resources to rescue them. But as we see, the Zionist movement not only did not do this; it did the opposite: it exploited the distress and neediness of the survivors of the Holocaust. In effect, this made it an accomplice in the catastrophe of European Jewry.

The title "The Yishuv and the Shoah" covers a number of topics, including the Hatzalah (rescue), Aliyah Bet (the smuggling of the DPs out of Europe), and the reception accorded the survivors in Israel. All these matters occupy an important place in Israeli historiography; in fact, research in these domains is done mainly by Israeli historians and writers. This is also one of the reasons why it is so easy to spread all kinds of myths about them. As expected, the picture that emerges from the scholarly research is very complex and ambiguous. This is understandable, if we give serious thought to what was at stake at the time, both historically and morally. Regarding the nature of Jewish solidarity during world war, what was known and when, what was actually done as opposed to what could and should have been done to limit the scope of the catastrophe – to such questions there can be no simple answer. These are not only complicated, serious questions; they are also quite painful. This is clear, for example, from things said by survivors like Antek Zuckerman and Chaike Grossman (both active in resistance to the Nazis in Poland) after living in Israel for many years. No doubt there is much to be said about these questions on both sides. What is more doubtful is whether they can be used to draw up a historical indictment of Zionism, assigning to it a guilt of metaphysical, theological proportions, that is, whether the matter of rescue or nonrescue can be used to delegitimate Zionism as such. It is no accident – and we have already called attention to the seemingly odd coalition created by radical anti-Zionism – that in this matter Grodzinsky should find himself in league not only with Weissmandel (against whom there can be no complaints, unlike those who would make use of his pain and loss) and the ultra-Orthodox, but also with the more hysterical elements in the Zionist camp. For example, with revisionists like Shmuel Tamir, the lawyer who represented Malkiel Grunwald in the Kasztner trial, or Judge Binyamin Halevi, who, in his well-known verdict, said that Kasztner (a Mapai man, of course) had "sold his soul to the devil."

The charge of "betrayal" has come up repeatedly over the years since the catastrophe in Europe as one of the main arguments in the ideological struggle against Zionism (and also, more specifically, against Ben-Gurion and Mapai). It has been one of the most effective ways of using the Holocaust in this struggle. Tom Segev, for example, touches on this question in his well-known book *The Seventh Million*. Let it be said right away that Segev does not, as far as one can judge, have an explicitly anti-Zionist agenda. The canvas he paints in this book is much wider than Grodzinsky's; he tries, in fact, to present the entire history of prestate Palestinian Jewry (from 1930 on) and the State of Israel (until the First Gulf War) in terms of how they related to the Holocaust in all its dimensions: the arrival and integration of the Jews who escaped from Hitler's Germany before the war, life in Palestine during the war and the question of rescue, the treatment of the survivors, the smuggling of Jews into Palestine in 1945–1948, the German reparations payments, the Kasztner and Eichmann trials, Israel's wars, and the effects of the Holocaust on Israel's culture and policies – in short, virtually everything. If truth be told, Segev achieves only modest success in the gigantic task he has taken upon himself. He is not, as we have said, an anti-Zionist in the same sense as Ophir, for example, or Grodzinsky; but a fashionably negative, critical attitude toward "Israeliness" in general and Israeli attitudes toward the Holocaust in particular pervades the book (as it does other books of his, at least those I have read). It is no accident that this book is often quoted by Israel's harshest critics, some of them anti-Zionists, both in Israel and elsewhere. Segev repeats the familiar arguments about the role played by "official" historians in shaping the way the Holocaust figures in Israeli life and about the way it is used to justify Israel's use of force and its conquests, as well as other clichés that have already achieved mythic status – that is, they no longer need proof and serve to define a certain ideological and cultural identity – among the various myth busters and narrative deconstructors in our midst. As often happens, this genre of writing is well received. Alternating between journalism and partly scholarly chronicle, lacking any real depth or originality, and easy to digest, it has made Segev a best-selling author, widely translated and quoted. What this book usually leaves behind in the reader's memory, and what is most quoted, is that aspect of it that creates the atmosphere, so to speak, of betrayal or near betrayal by the State of Israel and Israeli society of the responsibilities placed upon them by the Holocaust.

This impression, however, is mistaken. There was no betrayal, no abandonment. As Dinah Porat – to take just one example – has put it, the Yishuv's leadership was completely trapped. The dilemmas these men and women had to confront were insurmountable: the ever-more-violent refusal of the Arabs to accept any compromise, their absolute rejection of the idea of a Jewish national home in Palestine and especially of any Jewish immigration;[55] the British volte-face concerning the Balfour Declaration and, consequently,

---

[55] One of the known affairs in the sad story of the rescue attempts is that of the Byalistok children. The British government proposed to the Germans to transfer five thousand Jewish children to Palestine. One thousand children were brought from Byalistok to Theresienstadt with the intention of exchanging them with German prisoners of war. The Germans informed their ally the Grand Mufti of Jerusalem, Haj Amin el Husseini, about the negotiations. Following his request, the deal was cancelled, and the children were deported to Auschwitz, where they were killed. See Aronson, *Hitler, the Allies, and the*

the draconian limitation of Jewish immigration into Palestine; the war in Europe. Above all, they were completely helpless in the face of the dimensions of the catastrophe and the reluctance of the Allies to do anything to rescue, or even help rescue, the Jews in Europe. When all was said and done, the saving of any significant number of Jews was never a real possibility. Porat is not the only one to deal with this subject, and the picture she and others paint is quite complex. Nevertheless, whatever criticisms can be leveled at one or another aspect of the conduct of the Yishuv's leaders, there can be no reasonable doubt that Grodzinsky's allegations are baseless and false.[56]

Neither Segev nor Grodzinsky takes Porat's work, or that of others like her, into consideration. Indeed, it is a wonder that Segev has come to be considered such an authority on Israeli society and, in particular, the question of Israel and the Shoah. His writing does have certain qualities that appeal to a broad readership. But it also lacks qualities that would give it real scientific value. It is tendentious, whether for ideological reasons or for the sake of popular appeal. Probably both. His allegations – some of them explicit, some only insinuated – of betrayal, cynicism, and indifference; of preferential treatment for personal or political associates; of exploiting the survivors for the needs of the Zionist enterprise – are false and slanderous. It is true, on the other hand, that the attitude of Israelis, or of what is called "Israeli society," toward the survivors who appeared so suddenly, en masse, during and after the War of Independence remains, in the memory of those newcomers, an open wound. But when one probes a bit into what was happening elsewhere – and it is only in recent years that this topic has begun to get more attention – it seems that, in this matter, too, Israeli society comes off rather well.

Like the other topics in this section, the question of the reception of the survivors has inspired a rich and multifaceted body of research, academic and otherwise. Many recent studies show a picture very different, or at least much more complex and less one-sided, from the one Segev draws. Others follow his line of thinking. One of the characteristics of the latter – that may help to explain why books like *The Seventh Million* are taken as authoritative while others are ignored – is the glibness, parading as scholarly knowledge, with which highly complex issues are treated. (Does the fact that the deportations from Slovakia were stopped for two years really show that

Jews, 170–172; Bauer, *Jews for Sale?*, 88–89 ; Sara Bender, *Facing Death: The Jews in Bialistok, 1939–1943* (Tel Aviv: Am Oved, 1997) (in Hebrew).
[56] See Porat, *Hanhaga bemilkud*.

an opportunity was missed because there was no more money to give to Wisliceny?) The judgmental pose is also appealing.

The rules of the game here are clear: whoever says otherwise can be dismissed as "official historians"; "hegemonic voices"; or producers or propagators of mini-, meta-, or supernarratives that serve the interests of the regime, the ruling elite, or other interest groups. They do not merit anything but scornful disregard. The truth, however, is that there exists in Israel a body of very rich, varied, and serious historiographical work on all these topics. It is also far from being "hegemonic," given the massive presence of so-called post-Zionists in the history, sociology, and political science departments of Israel's universities. But for the self-appointed revisionists (like Faurisson), new historians, and critical theorists, everyone else belongs to a single homogeneous crowd.

From the point of view of the history of the Shoah, let alone that of the war in general, the whole question of rescue – what was done, what should have been done, what could have been done but was not – is completely ridiculous. The parachutists sent from Eretz Yisrael to occupied Europe could not have made much of a difference even if there had been a hundred Hannah Szeneses. (Actually, there were some 250 volunteers from the Yishuv, but the British agreed to parachute only a dozen, and even this, only very late.) But this question is very important for Israelis, not because they have to defend themselves against the kinds of allegations Grodzinsky or Segev makes, but because, contrary to those allegations, the attitude of the Zionists, of the Yishuv, and of the Israeli government has always been one of deep concern, complete solidarity, and absolute moral commitment to Jews elsewhere. As the Tel Aviv historian Yaacov Shavit said concerning one of Grodzinsky's writings, the allegedly apologetic tone of works such as Dinah Porat's (written well before Grodzinsky embarked on his anti-Zionist offensive) is not merely polemical but grows out of a deep sense of responsibility, a permanent soul-searching, shared by many Israelis, which has, in turn, led professional historians like her to painful and honest investigation into the behavior of the Yishuv and the Zionist movement in general during the catastrophe in Europe. But it is precisely this great vulnerability that makes Dinah Porat and her like an easy prey for the derision and mockery of the opprobrium community. Indeed, this vulnerability plays a role in all Shoah-related criticism in Israel, as well as in the anti-Zionist literature that uses the Shoah as a weapon.

The gravest of all the accusations brought against the Yishuv leaders is that they abandoned the non-Zionist European Jews – the Orthodox, notably, but others as well – and even members of Zionist movements other than the ruling

Labor Zionists. It is a false and abject accusation. This particular polemic has, nevertheless, played an important role (notably in the Kasztner affair) in the evolution of Israeli society and the Israeli ethos. In order to understand a bit better what is at stake here, the kinds of choices and dilemmas that confronted the leaders of the Yishuv and the binds in which they found themselves, it should be remembered that radical, vicious, dishonest anti-Zionism is not a recent invention. It did not take Tony Judt, Jacqueline Rose, Judith Butler, or Daniel Boyarin – to mention just a few names – to inform us that Zionism was a demonic and/or pathological phenomenon. What Orthodox, ultra-Orthodox, Marxist, communist, and Bundist Jews said long ago about the Zionist movement was not very different, in principle or in tone, from what is said by today's anti-Zionists. A little mental exercise might give us a better insight into what Grodzinsky was talking about. If, *per impossibile*, a great calamity were to befall American Jewry; if, as happened in the 1940s, it would be only the one politically organized Jewish community, Israel, that could take concrete action to help; if, as happened then, it were possible to save only a few individuals – in such a case, would the Israelis, the Zionist entity or regime, have the same kind of moral obligation to try to save, say, Judt, Butler, or Boyarin as it would to save supporters of Israel who planned to make their homes here? In more general terms – does one have the same moral obligation of solidarity toward those who reciprocate that solidarity as toward those who do not? A difficult question. But because this is not an essay in moral theory, it is enough to note that, in the last analysis, and despite what is too often said, most Zionists – be they members of Mapai or not – have never had any doubt: as difficult as it is, one has to try as hard to save the Judts as to save the others.

THE INTERNATIONAL

We have already encountered the most prominent, articulate spokesman of the culture of negation and *resentiment* in Israel, Adi Ophir. In his anthologies and articles, in his public activity, and of course in his major work, he is not only blunt, articulate, and harshly critical but also emerges as one of the leading theoreticians and ideologues of Israeli anti-Zionism. His writings present a real challenge to apologists of the Zionist idea. Because, to my knowledge, no one has yet come to grips with the theoretical, philosophical, and other bases of Ophir's radical delegitimation of Zionism and of Israel as the state of the Jewish people, I would like to suggest here, for the interested reader, some possible points of contention. I have no choice, then, but to undertake a somewhat wearisome examination of the philosophical aspects of his work, in other words, to apply to his writing the sort of deconstruction that he, in turn, does with considerable acumen to the standard Zionist texts.[57]

Ophir's writing is nothing if not up-to-date. He follows closely what is being said and written in the most avant-garde philosophical circles (particularly in Europe) and is one of the main importers of their "discourse" (to use one of his favorite expressions) to Israel. Although he defines his own theoretical framework as that of post-structuralism (especially the French variety), one consequence of his being so up-to-date is a considerable eclecticism. His writing belongs to a more or less distinct kind of "discourse," but from within that intellectual, ideological, and political culture, he draws upon many different, constantly changing sources. There is nothing wrong with eclecticism, of course. But when one is in such a rush to be up-to-date, there is not much time for critical consideration of the sources one is drawing upon, the difficulties and contradictions inherent in them are not always noticed, and the result can be somewhat problematical.

In issue 22 (Spring 2003) of *Teoria uvikoret* (Theory and Criticism), a journal Ophir founded and edited for several years, he has a long article of his own entitled "Technologiot musariot: Nihul ha'ason vehafkarat hahayyim" (Moral Technologies: The Management of Catastrophe and Disregard for the Living). As stated in its introduction, the article deals with a juxtaposition of "two cardinal questions: how can morality survive in contemporary culture[, and] what is the role of catastrophe ... in the processes of globalization?" The question about the survival of morality has, of course, been around since people started asking questions. The question of the relationship between catastrophe, globalization, and morality, on the other hand, is a truly contemporary one. Ophir's article is not so much a learned as a programmatic one, focusing on something he sees as being of great philosophical importance: the nature of nongovernmental activity in times of disaster, whether natural disasters like famine and earthquake or humanly caused ones like mass murder or expulsion. This affords him an opportunity to clarify theoretically the weighty question of the relationship between morality and the state.

An overall conceptual framework that should make it possible to consider these two questions together, the ancient one about morality and the new one about catastrophe, is provided by Michel Foucault and the

[57] The following paragraphs constitute the first part of such an attempt, and later on the interested reader will find the second part. This discussion can be skipped without missing the main point.

contemporary Italian philosopher Giorgio Agamben. From Foucault, Ophir takes the term "management technologies," transposing it from the context of hospitalization and imprisonment, discipline and disciplining, to that of catastrophe. Ophir also uses the dual concept of knowledge-power (based on a connection recognized earlier by Francis Bacon that "knowledge is power"), though probably not in Foucault's original sense. Foucault knew how to employ surprising, thought-provoking turns of phrase, usually semirhetorical devices, that brought his reflections on modernity and on key social and political phenomena to a high art. He had brilliant ways, often original and unexpected, sometimes provocative and unsettling, always stimulating, of illuminating various aspects of hegemony and power, madness and sexuality. The empirical and theoretical basis on which his work is built is sometimes somewhat shaky, but this does not necessarily detract from his unique, important contribution to modern thought. This is because his real aim was not to be a theoretician but a critic or, as he put it on several key occasions, an archaeologist. More than giving positive descriptions or explanations of various phenomena, he tried to trace and decipher the accepted ways of looking at them. His aim, incidentally, was not necessarily to dispute these views. Generally speaking, the main theoretical purpose of the terms he coined can be described (as he himself does) as the "problematization" of important parts of social and political reality and the basic concepts with which we relate to them. More exactly, Foucault tried to show systematically that things not usually regarded as needing clarification – for example, the objective existence of the phenomenon of madness – are, in fact, not obvious. Most of the expressions he used to make problematical what seems obvious are not presented in a rigorous fashion, that is, capable of replacing the concepts, terms, or theories he is criticizing. At times this is intentional, but at other times he could not carry it off even if he tried. Such is the case with the concept of "episteme" or the methodological principle he calls "the archeology of knowledge." It is also true of his use of the expression "technology" to describe social and political institutions, as well as the concepts of "power" and "knowledge" and his analysis of the relation between them. This methodological and critical aspect of his work is frequently absent from the discourse of the *au courant* intellectuals, political scientists, sociologists, legal scholars, and others who consider themselves his disciples.

The same is true of the expression *biopolitique* (biopolitics) or *biopouvoir* (roughly, biopower), which figures in a number of Foucault's writings but first appears in a lecture he gave at the University of Rio de Janeiro, in

1974, as part of a course on medicine as a social institution.[58] Although (or perhaps because) Foucault never really discussed this term, Agamben has made it the linchpin of a theory of "the political," and it has become part of the currently fashionable discourse. Recently (in late 2004), notes from Foucault's 1978–1979 lectures at the Collège de France were published. The course bore the title "The Birth of Biopolitics," and the result is actually not one of Foucault's best works.[59] The lectures form part of an analysis of what Foucault calls "the art [i.e., technique] of ruling," and they deal mainly with American and German liberalism. The "archeology" of liberalism, or the analysis of the intellectual tool – political economy – that is the source of its reasoning, shows, according to Foucault, that the principle of liberalism is one of limited rule, "not ruling too much," the well-known idea of laissez faire. He begins with what the title indicates, an analysis of the liberal state as an expression of "biopolitics"; but he ends up speaking at great length about German liberalism, and not much is left of "biopolitics" other than the programmatic principle according to which an important attribute of the liberal state is the politicization of life itself, especially in the sociological sense. The liberal state treats its citizens as a "population" to be managed. This idea is not new, by the way, as Foucault and most of his audience at the Collège de France were well aware. It appears in the Jacobin thought of the French Revolution and in a more organized way in the developing sociological thought of the nineteenth century.

The concept of the "biopolitical" thus belongs to an oral tradition, and as often happens in such cases, Foucault's disciples, and more often his epigones, permit themselves to use the term in ways that would probably not have thrilled him. This is the case with Agamben, who makes the concept one of the terminological foci of an ambitious, virtually all-embracing attempt at a general theory of "the political," an attempt to uncover (as did La Vieille Taupe and Adi Ophir) the universal principle underlying all states and regimes, wherever they may be. It is worth mentioning here that in one of his lectures at the Collège de France (March 7, 1979; see note 59) Foucault explains that he has not been able to explore the concept of the "biopolitical" as fully as he had hoped, partly for reasons of "critical morality." It was a moral need that induced him to criticize the current intellectual climate: a kind of "state-phobia," a fear of the state's inherent tendency to extend its reach, which leads it to dominate completely "that which is at one and

---

[58] *Dits et écrits* (Paris: Gallimard, 2001), 1:210.
[59] *Naisssance de la biopolitique: Cours au Collège de France 1978–1979* (Paris: l'École des Hautes Etudes, Gallimard, and Seuil, 2004).

the same time its own, its externality, its purpose and object, namely civil society" (pp. 192–193). A permanent feature of this phobia is the contention that "there is an affinity, a kind of genetic or evolutionary continuity, between different forms of the state: the administrative state, the welfare state [*état-providence*], the bureaucratic state, the fascist state, the totalitarian state" (p. 193). This view, in which everything loses its specificity and the welfare system (and the administrative apparatus that supports it) is like a concentration camp, represents, for Foucault, a kind of critical inflation. It is an inflation that allows for "a sweeping criticism (or negation) using the worst case [*disqualification générale par le pire*]; for whatever the object of the analysis, … to the extent that it can be linked, in the name of the inner dynamics of the state and the latest forms those dynamics have, for better or worse, assumed, the lesser can be negated by the greater, the better by the worse" (ibid). In other words, it allows one to criticize, and in effect to negate, liberal democracy or secular Zionism, for example, by linking them in a "conceptual continuum" (as Ophir calls it) with the ultimate purpose, as it were, of all forms of hegemony, that to which they all aspire as a matter of teleological necessity: the gulag and Auschwitz. Another element in this state phobia is a general, sweeping, a priori suspicion of the state that makes it inherently culpable, thus relieving its accusers of the need to give real thought to their actual situation and that of the society in which they live – for example, the fact that the real problem today is not the growth of the state (internal or external) but the diminution of its ability to rule (p. 197). This school of criticism is also very good at not criticizing itself. Had I not known that Foucault died shortly after giving this course, I would think he had read Ophir and Agamben.

Agamben thus uses a term borrowed from Foucault (biopower) to further a theoretical program that is very un-Foucaultian. In a way that is not only eclectic but actually absurd, he takes, in addition to Foucault (and such other thinkers as Arendt and Heidegger), another source of inspiration that is utterly anti-Foucaultian, the German thinker Carl Schmitt. He relies broadly on two or three of Schmitt's writings, and it is from him that he borrows his all-inclusive idea of "the political," which takes precedence even over the metaphysical. But if Foucault, undoubtedly one of the most important thinkers of the second half of the twentieth century, is first and foremost a philosopher of freedom, Schmitt – who not only belonged to the Nazi Party but was also an ideologue of the "strong state," an apologist for the Nazi regime, and, lest we forget, the one who supplied the main theoretical rationale for the Nuremberg Laws – was the exact opposite. And it was his theory of "the political" or of "sovereignty" that Agamben and Ophir adopted.

As befits an up-to-date philosopher, Ophir has devoted a lot of time lately to Agamben. In his article on catastrophe,[60] he embraces the latter's main theoretical assumptions. But he has reservations about some of Agamben's conclusions, especially his implied criticism of "global humanitarianism," his claim that the nongovernmental humanitarian organizations represent "a possible form of biopolitical alignment of the modern nation-state that in principle can serve democratic and totalitarian regimes equally well" (p. 68). It is not the lumping together of democracy and totalitarianism that bothers Ophir; the attempt to conceptualize "the modern state" and, in fact, "the political" all through Western history, in a way that embraces all regimes and forms of government, is one of the hallmarks of Agamben's theory, as it is, apparently, of Ophir's. This approach may not be very original, but it is certainly close to that of the theory of the state (if one may call it that) of the Vieille Taupe circle.

A little further on in the article, which is devoted entirely to Agamben, Ophir repeats and expands upon some things he said in the first article. He even has a few critical things to say about the Italian philosopher. The article is meant to acquaint the Hebrew reader with the first volume of *Homo Sacer I*, Agamben's major work – major at least in the sense that it made him a celebrity in certain precincts of the academic left. The article is a fluent, intelligent, knowledgeable review; unfortunately, it is also largely a wasted effort. First of all, by the time it was published, the energetic Agamben had already added two more volumes to the work, in which, especially in the last (to date),[61] his perspective has changed. He seems to have revised his thinking about the conceptual sequence that clarifies the nature of "the political." In light of this new exposition, Ophir's review seems somewhat outdated.

But Ophir's efforts might have been wasted for other reasons as well. Though one may well take seriously, even very seriously, what to others seems like a pseudotheory devoid of any real intellectual value, one cannot

---

[60] Adi Ophir, "Bein kiddush hahayim lehafkaratam: Bimkom mavo le-*Homo Sacer*" (To Sanctify Life or Abandon It: An Alternative Introduction to *Homo Sacer*), in Shai Lavi, ed., *Tekhnologiot shel tzedek: Mishpat, mada, vehevra* (Technologies of Justice: Law, Science, and Society) (Tel Aviv: Ramot Press, University of Tel Aviv, 5763 [2003]), 353–394. This volume, ostensibly devoted to more or less technical discussions of legal issues related to society and technology, also includes a translation of sections of *Homo Sacer I*. Only the editor knows what the article on Agamben has to do with the legal issues.

[61] This book, *Homo Sacer: Sovereign Power and Bare Life* (Stanford: Stanford University Press, 1998), which was published almost simultaneously in the original Italian and in French, actually preceded by three years, in the *Homo Sacer* series, a volume devoted to Auschwitz entitled, in the English translation, *State of Exception*. The latter is a legal concept Karl Schmitt thought could shed light on the "essence" of the political.

ignore the fact that Agamben works efficiently and that his virtuosity has some clear advantages: he produces books with astonishing rapidity, and his books are quite short, and highly readable and accessible. The intelligent reader does not seem to need help reading him. His work is actually a kind of intellectual parasitism, with little effort invested, as a rule, in research, either historical or empirical – for example, the history of law or of nationalities – or in the analytical interpretation of texts and thinkers. Most of the sources he quotes are secondary, written by scholars who did invest effort in research.[62] He adopts several concepts from the literature of general philosophy, political philosophy, and law (e.g., sovereignty, biopolitics, the state of emergency); gets bogged down in marginal details and oddities (like the term *homo sacer*, drawn from Roman law, or, later, *muselmann*); and lifts terms out of their historical and theoretical context, even giving them a completely new meaning. He goes on to provide a bit of linguistic, historical, or etymological clarification (mostly questionable or secondhand) of some fundamental concepts in legal and political theory, and on this basis he develops his comprehensive view of "the essence of the political." His arguments and the historical or empirical bases for them generally lack substance, and the power of his writing apparently stems from its simplicity and rhetorical suggestiveness. Then too, in the last analysis, it answers the need of a certain academic culture for a seemingly esoteric focus on identity or a prophet-of-the-month. In this instance, the prophet is, under the surface, the controversial German thinker Carl Schmitt, and Agamben is one of the most important of Schmitt's disciples and spokesmen.

At the heart of *Homo Sacer I*[63] is Schmitt's definition of sovereignty, or at least one aspect of it. In his view, the essence of the political, or of sovereignty, is revealed in the decision to declare a state of emergency, that is, to suspend the law. In fact, even for Schmitt himself the story is much

---

[62] Aside from some aspects of his early work on madness and institutions for the insane, Foucault, for example, did not do empirical research either, although he regarded his work as scientific. But he spent many long hours in libraries, especially the National Library in Paris, and his "archeology" is based on a close acquaintance with the literature of early modernity (especially the part that has been forgotten with the passage of time). Agamben apparently has not gone to this trouble, and he draws his nourishment from predigested food. Israeli and other customers of his supermarket who do not read the original languages thus enjoy fare that has already been digested twice or more.

[63] The book was first published in Italy in 1995. Its full title translates roughly as "Homo Sacer I: Sovereign Power and Naked Life." The latter phrase is generally translated by Ophir and other Hebrew readers of Agamben as "Life Exposed." The origin of the expression *homo sacer* is in an obscure Roman law, where it refers, more or less, to someone who has been banned, that is, excluded from society, from the community, but who may not be harmed.

more complicated, but leave that aside. What is important is that Agamben simplifies Schmitt's definition and uses it to go beyond legal theory, political science, and even political theology, to what Ophir calls "ontology," that is, something that turns out to be mythology. In fact, Agamben turns Schmitt on his head. For the latter, the ability to suspend the rule of law and declare a state of emergency is the highest expression of sovereignty but not its definition. For Agamben, the opposite is the case: declaring a state of emergency is not merely the exclusive prerogative of the sovereign but the essence of his status. The sovereign is not the one whose prerogative is to suspend the law (though he is not obligated to do so); he *is* the suspension of the law. The sovereign really comes into being only when the law is suspended and a state of emergency is declared; hence, sovereignty is nothing but an indefinite suspension of the law and a perpetual state of emergency, even when we are told we are living in a constitutional state. The suspension of law, or the ability to suspend it, is not the result – desirable, as Schmitt sees it – of what we call sovereignty, with all its inner contradictions, but its essence. Thus, according to Agamben, the term "state of emergency" does not describe a contingency but an essence. This reversal of definitions is important, because it shows we are not dealing with the history or sociology of governance – as Foucault, for example, thought – but, in fact, with a kind of pseudo-ontology or, perhaps, false theology.

What exactly is the essence that is revealed by the state of emergency? The suspension of the rule of law creates a direct relationship, unmediated by law, between the sovereign and his subjects. Sovereignty is thus left untrammeled – its perennial nature finally revealed – while the status of subject takes on a new form, or rather is stripped of all form. Life stands naked before the sovereign. He is sovereign, but his subjects, in this situation, are no longer "citizens," legal entities, but mere human beings outside the law, mere animals, in fact. Because, in this situation, the sovereign remains sovereign, one can speak of a special structure that can be discerned in the state of emergency, when the true nature of "the political" becomes clear. Agamben describes the latter in terms of a kind of dialectic of inclusion and exclusion: the sovereign who suspends the rule of law or excludes certain individuals or groups from its jurisdiction is, by that very action, extending his authority over them. In this way, a category of existence is created that is excluded, by law, from the rule of law, a "naked existence" that must confront the sovereign directly, without the law as an intermediary. Agamben finds a paradigm for this state of being in an obscure corner of Roman law, in the semilegal, semireligious concept of the "holy man," the *homo sacer*, who is denied the protection of the law but, at the same time, may not be sacrificed to the gods.

Here, he thinks, is where the true, perennial essence of sovereignty and of the political is revealed.

The "camp" is the modern form of this perennial category of existence, the modern locus of this inside-outside phenomenon. It is where the highest and deepest essence of "the political" in general has always been found, but especially since the emergence of the modern nation-state. From Agamben's presentation – and the way his Israeli disciples swallow this drivel whole – we can see why it is of interest to speak about him here and why Ophir chose to make him an intellectual celebrity in Israel. As we have seen in the case of other thinkers, Agamben does not distinguish between the totalitarian and the democratic state. It is in the "camp" that the nature of sovereignty becomes clear: putting in while taking out, enclosing while disclosing, applying a legal norm while suspending it, or some such thing. The *Lager* and the gulag, like the lockups for illegal foreign workers in Israel; the Vélodrome d'Hiver, where the Vichy regime interned its Jews before shipping them off to Auschwitz, quite like the Hôtel Arcade (three stars, if I'm not mistaken) near Paris's Charles de Gaulle Airport, where the immigration authorities used to detain illegal immigrants until their status was determined – all these are "camps." They are places where "living things" stand "naked" before "sovereignty," without the intervention or protection of the law, and this, "the production of bare life as originary [*sic*] political element and as threshold of articulation between nature and culture,"[64] is the true concern of sovereignty and its perennial essence; this, not justice (as Aristotle thought), civil rights, the rule of law, legislative authority (as Bodin thought), public order (as Hobbes thought), or freedom (as Spinoza thought). But the high point of this way of thinking is yet to come: the clearest example of this universal kind of sovereignty, the clearest example of a "camp," is – what else? – Auschwitz. The latter is the symbol, the model, and the quintessence of "the political," that is, of the modern state as such. Yes, of course, at Auschwitz they killed Jews, Gypsies, Poles, Russians, and many others, and that was really terrible; but the main thing, what is really important, is its universal theoretical meaning, not the extermination, the killing, the humiliation and torture.

Let us not cast suspicion on the innocent: Agamben is not a denier of the Holocaust. On the contrary, he has devoted an entire book to Auschwitz. *Homo Sacer II* (self-published in 1998) bears the subtitle *Remnants of Auschwitz: The Witness and the Archive*, and this indicates the kind of thinking on which the book is based: "Auschwitz" is merely an opportunity for theory building. "Auschwitz," by the way, for both Agamben and

---

[64] *Homo Sacer*, 181.

Ophir, is not only a particular camp but a generic term for what others call the Holocaust. Agamben rejects such familiar expressions on the basis of a pseudo-etymology of them. Hence, Auschwitz.

But as it turns out, Auschwitz also – not coincidentally – provides an opportunity to hone this intellectual parasitism to perfection. Thus, for example, at the very beginning of the book, Agamben informs us, from his exalted perch of scholarly authority, that, thanks mainly to Raul Hilberg's book, "the problem of the historical, material, technical, bureaucratic, and legal circumstances in which the extermination of the Jews took place has been sufficiently clarified" (p. 11). So that's that. Now the research institutes, documentation centers, and university departments of Holocaust studies can be closed, and, in any event, there is no need to read the great outpouring of publications and studies that are still trying to come to grips with what happened. Such reading, not to mention the effort needed to do the actual historical research, would be onerous. We can now dispense with this labor and concentrate on more important tasks that are admittedly also more pleasant. Now what we have to do is think. The theoretical objective still to be attained is clarifying "the ethical and political significance of the extermination, ... a human understanding of what happened there – that is, ... its contemporary relevance" (ibid.).[65] In other words (and these are also the words of Zuckerman, Ophir, et al.), what is really interesting and important is not the historicity of Auschwitz, and certainly not its "particularism" – the particularistic suffering and destruction of the Jews (and others), for example – but the universal theory that can be extracted from it, and especially the "worship of the present" that can be based upon it.

And, in fact, that is just what Agamben does in the two hundred pages of his book: he mainly tells the terrible story of the *Muselmänner*, those half-dead camp inmates who the witnesses he cites – first and foremost Primo Levi – were not sure were still human. "Telling," in his case, means quoting at length from, or paraphrasing, various testimonies (and a little scholarly literature), and in this respect the book is, indeed, horribly fascinating. But the story of the *Muselmänner* in and of itself does not interest Agamben; or, to be precise, the story – the "testimony" – could be interesting, but the *Muselmänner* themselves are not. What is really important is the "meaning," that is, the "theory" that explains the essence of *Muselmann* existence; the concept, or rather word, that enables us to see what was universal about it. Note: not the extermination, but the phenomenon of the *Muselmänner*. So it's really quite simple. Nazism is the embodiment of "biopolitics"; the Nazis

---

[65] *Remnants of Auschwitz: The Witness and the Archive* (New York: Zone Books, 2002), 11.

turned "the people," a political entity, into "the population," a biological one; racism enabled them to divide the population, that is, the biological sphere, into superior and inferior "races."[66] The conclusion is worth quoting: "It is then possible to understand the decisive function of the camps in the system of Nazi biopolitics. They are not merely the place of death and extermination; they are also, and *above all*, the site of the production of the *Muselmann*, the final biopolitical substance to be isolated in the biological continuum" (p. 85, emphasis added). The *Muselmann* condition is that very state in which life is "exposed" or stripped down almost to the vanishing point, or, to be exact, until the human being is gone and all that is left is life in all the glory, or shame, of its nakedness. The *Muselmann*, then, provides the perfect opportunity to theorize "the political."

After explaining to us the ultimate paradigm of the political (the "camp"), and after discussing the ultimate example of a camp (Auschwitz) and teaching us its significance (the production of the *Muselmann*), Agamben returns to the subject of the state of emergency, that is, to the conceptual essence of "the political."[67] Here, however, there is a certain surprise in store for his readers: after turning on its head the concept of the "sovereign" that he has learned from Schmitt, and after the ontological deepening he accomplishes with this reversal, he invites us to make another reversal. Now it turns out that the dialectic of the state of emergency is not only the quintessence of "the political," but it is also, by itself, an essence opposed to "the political" and a threat to it. More than exemplifying sovereignty as such, the state of emergency exemplifies law and legal norms. More precisely, the state of emergency, which Agamben now describes as an indeterminate boundary area between law (*nomos*) and what lies outside the realm of law (anomy), is the foundation of law itself and an internal contradiction in "the political," as the latter has existed in the West since the time of the ancient Greeks. This has especially been the case since the First World War, as best exemplified by the Nazi regime, and is so prevalent today that we find ourselves in a global state of emergency. As it turns out, Agamben's intention is not to rescue law or legal norms from the blind power of sovereignty or from the state, but rather to criticize the former. He suggests establishing, in place of the quasi-Nazi global state of emergency in which we all live, a political space for pure

[66] Ibid., 84–85. Agamben is quoting and allegedly "expanding upon" Foucault, except that the latter hardly speaks of the destruction of the Jews by the Nazis, and there is a certain effrontery – not to mention utter superficiality – in the attempt to present Nazi racism as being based so unequivocally on the concept of "biopolitics."

[67] *Homo Sacer I* and *Homo Sacer II* were published in 2003. The citations that follow are from Giorgio Agamben, *State of Exception* (Chicago: University of Chicago Press, 2005).

action. That is, he wants to put "the political" before the legal, out of a kind of nostalgia for pure action that has no purpose beyond itself, very much in the spirit of Schmitt, the ideologue of the strong state. Thus, it turns out that in this book the nostalgia for Schmitt apparently goes way beyond the "critical use" of his work, even though the point of departure remains, of course, a critique of the existing order and a critical theory. It turns out – and this should not surprise us – that the radical critique of liberal democracy, the theoretical impulse to lump it together with various forms of totalitarianism, and particularly the blurring of the uniqueness of the Nazi regime and the destruction of the Jews lead the critics to a dangerous affinity with reaction and the defenders of fascism.

A theme running through all Agamben's political writings (at least those published so far), which gives an inner logic to the three volumes of *Homo Sacer*, is his idea of a characteristic structure, a dialectic of inside and outside, inclusion and exclusion, *nomos* and anomy, authoritative norms and life, that is the essence of the political (and, in the end, of the legal). The symbolic expression of all these dualities is the mythic figure of the *homo sacer*, as well as the utterly concrete figure of the *Muselmann*, drawn from the Nazi camps and the Nazi regime. As we have seen, what is interesting about these two figures, the mythic as well as the concrete, is their universal meaning, not the historical realities they represent.

We should thus not be surprised to read the following words that appear at the beginning of Agamben's book on the "state of emergency": he speaks there of the situation of the Taliban fighters being held at Guantanamo neither as prisoners of war nor as criminals. "The only [!] thing to which it could possibly be compared," says Agamben, "is the legal [!] situation of the Jews in the Nazi *Lager*, who, along with their citizenship, had lost every legal identity, but at least retained their identity as Jews" (pp. 3–4). Not everyone can take this statement with equanimity, much less find wisdom in it. Take, for example, Eric Marty, a professor of literature at one of the campuses of the University of Paris (and, it should be stated, a staunch friend of Israel), who wrote a highly detailed critique of Agamben's book.[68] It is not clear,

---

[68] Eric Marty, "Agamben et les tâches de l'intellectuel," *Les temps modernes* 626 (2003–2004): 215–233. After the beginning of the Intifada and in light of what he thought of the treatment of Israel by the French media and intelligentsia, Marty thought the decent thing would be to visit Israel at such a time and see for himself. As a result, he wrote and published a collection of essays that included impressions of his visit as well as a long essay on Jean Genet, pointing out the strong, explicit connection between that writer's admiration of Hitler and Nazism, his virulent anti-Semitism, and his love for the Palestinians. It will be recalled that Genet published a long article on his visit to the Shatila refugee camp right

Marty writes about the sentence just quoted, if Agamben is guilty here of innocence or of obscenity. The Jews "at least" kept their Jewish identity in the *Lager*? Yet the prisoners held by the Americans have not lost their identity as Taliban or as Afghans being in custody. If we look more closely at this statement, Marty adds, "we can see the depth of the chasm into which philosophical discourse can fall." True, the camp Jews "kept their Jewish identity;" but keeping this identity was the necessary and sufficient condition of their extermination – it was, as we know, only because they were Jews that they were killed. And if we look at the sentence for another moment, it turns out that it proves just the opposite of what Agamben sets out to prove – the nature of all states of emergency, or exceptional circumstances of any kind – and shows that he radically misunderstands what took place at Auschwitz. For the implication of this sentence is that the Jews, in fact, had a certain advantage over the Taliban: unlike them, the Jews "at least" succeeded in holding on to their identity as Jews, even as prisoners in the camps. It must be said to the Nazis' credit that they did not try to efface the Jews' identity as Jews: after all, they were put in the camps (and exterminated, it will be recalled) precisely because of that identity. If it had been taken away from them (and many of them believed they had long since lost it), they would not have been killed. In other words, the Jewish (and other) *Muselmänner* may have been more or less naked in the biological sense but not at all in the political, Agambenian, Ophirian sense: they were not left without any intermediary, as mere living things, before the sovereign, but were clothed, we might say, in their Jewishness.

Aside from the poor taste, ignorance, arrogance, and superficiality Agamben betrays in these remarks, beyond even the great theoretical difficulties they pose, not to say their outright falseness, what is interesting about them is the way they have been received by the international academic community and in certain quarters of the intellectual community here in Israel. His "universalism" and that of his concepts of "sovereignty" and "the political" allow him to speak about the prisoners at Guantanamo and those slaughtered at Auschwitz as if there were no difference between them. To Agamben's Israeli disciples, this universalism makes it possible to speak in the same breath of Auschwitz and the Israeli army's checkpoints in the

after the massacre there, for which he blamed Israel exclusively and in the most extreme terms. Toward the end of his life, he also wrote a book expressing in philosophical and poetic language his hatred of Jews and Israel and his support for the Palestinian *fidayun*. Unlike many Third World sympathizers, Genet did not idealize the Palestinians in the least. He stated outright that his love for them derived from his hatred of Jews and his (anti-Semitic) animosity toward the State of Israel.

administered territories, as if they were just different expressions of the same thing. Ophir, we should point out, has expressed reservations about Agamben's blurring of the differences between democracy and totalitarianism, but these reservations have not prevented him from lumping together Auschwitz and Israeli-Jewish treatment of the Arabs. Elsewhere, Agamben has had numerous critics who, at least to some extent, have managed to put his ideas in proper proportion. But here in Israel, the wide acceptance of his writings betrays only provincialism and self-abnegation. The idea that Auschwitz was the ultimate expression of sovereignty – like Ophir's idea that it was the ultimate expression of the human, to which we shall return shortly – demands some consideration, be it critical or casual, of other commentators, historians, and scholars of the Third Reich and Auschwitz for whom the Nazi regime was the embodiment of the *anti*political and of *non*-sovereignty. This is the view of Hannah Arendt, for example, whom both Agamben and his Israeli disciples seem to take quite seriously. In fact, she is to some extent just rehashing the argument of Franz Neumann in his important book *Behemoth*.[69] As the latter explains in the beginning of the book, the title is a reference to Hobbes's work of the same name. If the Leviathan symbolized for Hobbes the political community that derives its life from the fact that it has a sovereign, someone who swallows up the rights and powers of all the citizens and thus prevents a war of all against all, the Behemoth – the other biblical monster – symbolizes political chaos, that is, the civil strife that breaks out when there is no sovereign – the antipolitical. Neumann sees this as the essence of the Nazi regime, which represent the antithesis and negation of "sovereignty." Many scholars of Nazism have, in one way or another, accepted Neumann's pioneering analysis, showing in a vast number of studies how it applies to the Nazi phenomenon. But there is no mention of any of this by Agamben or his Israeli followers.

---

[69] Franz Neumann, *Behemoth: The Structure and Practice of National Socialism, 1933–1944* (New York: Harper & Row and Oxford University Press, 1944). The following quote is taken from the second edition, 1966. Ophir, it turns out, discovered Neumann only after writing what we have seen he did about Auschwitz. He had also written about it in his book on evil, to which we shall return. This is made clear in a brief marginal note in his article on Agamben, mentioned earlier ("Bein kiddush hahayim lehafkaratam," 360). Although he mentions Neumann respectfully, he is in complete disagreement with him that the Nazi regime was a unique phenomenon, totally different from other known regimes, good or bad, and especially that it was the complete opposite and absolute negation of democracy. With certain reservations, he, in fact, accepts Agamben's position concerning the continuity between democratic and totalitarian regimes. Though he seems to dispute the latter's view about the place of morality in his critique of sovereignty, he, like Agamben, takes Schmitt's side as a critic of liberal democracy and, whether intentionally or not, as an apologete for totalitarian utopia.

I am not aware of any statements made by Agamben about Israel or Zionism. During the Second Gulf War, he took an anti-American position on several occasions, only theoretical, of course, in the spirit of the anti-Americanism of the European left. Presumably he was not a great fan of Sharon's, for example. Had he been, Agamben would probably not have become the current culture hero of the Israeli branch of the community that has turned *resentiment* into an entire theory. Agamben's place in that community is interesting because, as we have already suggested, he is one of the main spokesmen of the campaign to rehabilitate Carl Schmitt. Arguments could certainly be made in favor of Schmitt's importance as a political philosopher and as a theoretician of constitutional law, though this can also be disputed. What is beyond any doubt is that his wide-ranging, multifaceted opus, and particularly his political stance and moral character, are highly problematical. We could ignore the matter of character, but in light of the political positions he took (his joining the Nazi Party in 1933, his anti-Semitism), the silence of his Israeli disciples is – how to put it? – symptomatic.[70]

No less symptomatic or characteristic is the coalition around Schmitt of the radical left and the extreme right. An example, relevant to us here: one of the better-known, more articulate and educated intellectuals of the French far right is Alain de Benoist. Not long ago, he published in *Eléments*, an extreme right-wing periodical, an article defending Schmitt. It is a long, knowledgeable article, but also harsh and full of anti-Semitic slurs and innuendo, aimed at Yves-Charles Zarka, the (Jewish) editor of a journal of social and political thought called *Cités* who had attacked Schmitt and publicized some of his anti-Semitic and Nazi pronouncements.[71] We are not concerned here with Parisian ideological wrangling, but the following detail, for example, is interesting for our purposes: the same Benoist who is an ideologue of the far right in France speaks highly of philosophy professor and left-wing intellectual Etienne Balibar, who has lately gained some international standing, and who published Schmitt's book on Hobbes – possibly the most disgraceful of all his books – and even wrote a lengthy introduction to it. This

[70] Since Franz Neumann is kosher even for Ophir, we can take the former's word regarding Karl Schmitt. In Neumann's book about the Nazi regime, *Behemoth*, Schmitt is often mentioned as having been the foremost German jurist to try to give that regime a legal foundation and justification. In recent years, mainly in Germany but also in other countries, much has been published exposing the depth and breadth of Schmitt's anti-Semitic feeling and his admiration for the Nazis. This was more than opportunism. Schmitt has been mentioned quite a bit lately in Israel; but apart from an almost indulgently raised eyebrow over his affinity for the Nazis, little attention has been paid to this aspect of his biography.
[71] See, e.g., his *Un detail Nazi dans la pensée de Carl Schmitt* (Paris: Presses Universitaires de France, 2005).

book was written during the Nazi period and contains some of Schmitt's ugliest anti-Semitic diatribes. Balibar, a close disciple of Althusser who later became an expert on Spinoza (like many left-wing Parisian intellectuals disillusioned with Marx) and who was never considered more than a mediocre member of the Parisian philosophical community,[72] has become, in recent years, one of Israel's most outspoken, vicious opponents. He was also one of the initiators of a petition calling for a boycott of Israeli universities and a suspension of European cooperation with them, a petition that some Israelis, too, are known to have signed, among them Tanya Reinhardt, whom we have mentioned previously. Nevertheless, Balibar recently visited Israel. He came to take part in a seminar organized by none other than Adi Ophir, on the subject (as I recall) of catastrophe. Balibar, this anti-Israeli, anti-Zionist professor – who is not taken very seriously by anyone, especially in his native country, except the extreme rightist Alain de Benoist, and by Adi Ophir, some lecturers and students at the Palestinian universities, and people who frequent certain American campuses – appeared at the seminar as a serious thinker on globalization and catastrophe (or some such thing). Thus does up-to-dateness turn into a pathetic provincialism.

What does all this have to do with the use of the Holocaust in the campaign against Israel? Nothing. But then again, perhaps something. Right after the Second Intifada broke out (and if I remember rightly, it was at a time when negotiations were still going on, and Barak's proposals to Arafat and what was called the "Clinton draft" were on the table), *Le Monde* published a declaration signed by a dozen or so Jewish intellectuals (eventually more than 150 joined the venture). Among them was – just to mention one signatory to whom we shall return in the Postscript – Professor Daniel Bensaïd, who supports, alongside Balibar, the appeal to boycott Israeli universities. The signatories proudly declare that *en tant que juifs*, that is "as Jews," they refuse to allow Israel to speak in their name. This, by the way, is a recurrent theme among Jewish detractors of Israel who, for some mysterious reason, feel that, though very far from this country in any sense, they are somehow implicated, probably mostly in the eyes of their non-Jewish friends, in Israel's mischiefs just because they are Jews. The appeal *en tant que juifs* is interesting in many ways: for instance, because it called for the resumption of peace talks precisely at a time when a peace process was still taking place and when Israel was saying it was ready to accept a far-reaching compromise with the Palestinians – in fact, the most far-reaching

---

[72] Marty applies to him the well-known remark of his teacher Louis Althusser: "He is known for his fame." It sounds better in French: *"connu pour sa notoriété."*

compromise ever accepted by any Israeli leadership, left or right. Yet more interesting, for us at least, in this petition is the appearance in it of the master hypotheses. It begins by a sort of an apology – we, citizens of different countries and of the planet, do not usually speak as Jews. But now we do. Why? Because we deny Israel's right to speak in our name about the Holocaust. The signatories too, being Jews, demand the right to speak for themselves, of their own suffering and that of their parents. Here again we see, this time with no excuses offered and no visible reason – neither Barak nor Sharon had brought it into the quarrel with the Palestinians – the mysterious connection between the Holocaust and the right to represent its victims, on the one hand, and the Palestinian uprising and the Israeli suppression of it, on the other. Incidentally, sometime later one of the signers of the declaration, a well-known civil-rights lawyer and activist, declared Israel to be an outlaw state (*hors la loi*), that is, an entity not protected by the law. Speakers of Agambenish could now see in Israel the *homo sacer*, or, better still, the *civitas sacra*, among the nations. On second thought, though, the comparison may be a bit too hasty: it is not at all clear that these people will grant Israel the right to live, unlike the *homo sacer* of Agamben, whom, it will be recalled, it was forbidden to sacrifice.

EXCURSUS 3: WHAT MAKES AUSCHWITZ UNIQUE
AND TO WHAT IS IT COMPARABLE?

"Martyrdom" (*kiddush hashem*), "the aura of the Holy Name," "the belief in uniqueness" (*emunat hayihud*), "the prohibition against comparing Auschwitz to other catastrophes" – such expressions and others like them are basic to Adi Ophir's discussion of the Holocaust. As with other critics of Holocaust "discourse," it is not always clear who is the target of his criticism. Is it Israeli society? The "establishment"? The educational system or other agents of manipulation? Academic research? Literature? As we have already pointed out, a close consideration of all these candidates, separately or together, shows that, at bottom, what this rhetoric is really trying to do is show the a priori irrationality, not only of the public treatment of the Holocaust, but also of the historiographical, legal, moral, theological, and philosophical treatment of it, especially among Jews and Israelis. The pseudotheological language Ophir uses to discuss this question is his way of indicating that the prevailing "discourse" about it is outside the bounds of serious thought, of casting suspicion on it as being subservient to political purposes that are inherently illegitimate and especially reprehensible in view of the present Israeli reality, the essence of which is "Occupation."

The fact that uniqueness and the prohibition against comparison are always mentioned together creates the impression that what Ophir calls "the belief in uniqueness" is simply a ban on comparing the calamity that befell the Jews at Auschwitz to other calamities. At one point, he makes the simple, quite correct claim that the expression "incomparable" is a paradox, perhaps even an oxymoron, a kind of hermeneutic circle turned upside down. How can we know Auschwitz and Jenin, for example, or, for that matter, Adi Ophir and Serge Thion, cannot be compared if we have not already compared them? Comparison is a kind of relation, a *universal* relation in fact. All things are comparable. A particular comparison may be of no interest, it can point up essential differences, or it can show a matter or an event to be relatively important or unimportant (in comparison to other matters or events). Like many other expressions that come up in discussions of the Holocaust, the statement that "it cannot be compared" is metaphorical and has a variety of uses. In the face of the phenomenon of denial, with all its offshoots – attempts to deny that the Holocaust ever happened, to suppress its memory or minimize its scope, to negate its implications, or to shake off the debt it is supposed to have imposed on its perpetrators – this statement could even be considered a defensive one. So Ophir is playing games with language and terminology. When he speaks of the prohibition against comparison, he knows very well there is no such prohibition; it would be meaningless. But rhetoric aside, what he calls "the belief in uniqueness" is not a prohibition or refusal to compare at all but an attempt to extract, from the comparison, whatever distinguishes the destruction of the Jews from other mass crimes.

But the question remains. In recent years, the public and academic debate over the uniqueness of the Holocaust has intensified. All sorts of "conceptual continuities" have been rehabilitated, invented, or simply exploited to prove that the destruction of the Jews by the Germans and their accomplices was a unique phenomenon, that the differences between it and other cases of mass murder outweigh the similarities; or, the other way around, that the murder of the Jews was not unique but is only one horror among many. This debate is, it should be pointed out, a German one (related to the "unique path"), on the one hand, and, on the other, an American one, although a few Israelis (Yehuda Bauer, in particular, appears to be one of them) have been taking part in it. Incidentally, Israelis are not entirely absent from the ranks of those who *deny* the Holocaust's uniqueness. We have already commented on the debate in Germany, and it is not difficult to see what drives it. Among the many reasons a parallel debate has developed in the United States, in particular, we could mention two. The first and most important was the creation of the Holocaust museum in Washington, D.C., and the circumstances surrounding it. Even before it was built, a controversy arose, both within and outside the Jewish community, over whether this national site should commemorate only the Jewish catastrophe or also mention others, whether it should be remembered as a Jewish catastrophe or one with a universal message. A second reason for the decidedly American tone of the debate over the uniqueness of the Holocaust is the great cultural, intellectual, and political weight exerted by the Jewish community in the United States, and perhaps also the way the Holocaust has become a central and sometimes almost exclusive component of the Jewish identity of this large community. The Holocaust has never had such centrality in Israeli life.[73]

Should we not compare, then, what was done at Auschwitz and, say, what was done in Jenin or Hebron? Or, of late – out of a strange though not coincidental similarity to the comparison of Auschwitz and "the Occupation" – should we not ask how Auschwitz and the evacuation of the Katif Bloc of Jewish settlements in the Gaza Strip resemble one another? What lesson is to be learned from comparing the destruction of the European Jews during the Second World War and the genocide carried out against the Gypsies at the same time and by similar methods, the genocide against the Armenians, the genocide against the American Indians, the ethnic cleansing that took place in the former Yugoslavia, the genocide in Rwanda, or that which is taking place right now in Darfur?[74]

One relatively new legal concept that has served as the basis for a certain "conceptual continuum," allowing for a comparison of the Holocaust with other evils, is that of genocide. The concept, introduced by the American Jewish legal scholar Raphael Lemkin, figures in the Genocide Convention

---

[73] See Gorny, *Between Auschwitz and Jerusalem*, and Peter Novick, *The Holocaust in American Life* (Boston: Houghton Mifflin, 1999). Novick's book is interesting in many respects, although he, too, belongs to the school of *resentment*, those who feel an almost aesthetic distaste for the Jewish way of relating to the Holocaust, especially that of the organized community in the United States. There is considerable similarity, and no doubt mutual influence, between Novick's critical arguments and things said in Israel by the critics of the domestic "Holocaust industry." Berel Lang criticizes Novick in a way similar to my own criticism of the Israeli *resentment*: he denies that any moral harm is caused by the centrality given the Holocaust or that the Holocaust can seriously be said to play a key role in the formation of American Jewish identity. See Lang's article "Lachrymose without Tears: Misreading the Holocaust in American Life," in Lang, *Post-Holocaust: Interpretation, Misinterpretation, and the Claims of History*, 128–136.

[74] Except for the latter two cases, this list is taken from the introduction Israel W. Charny (editor of *The Encyclopedia of Genocide* [Santa Barbara: ABC-CLIO, 1999]) wrote for Alan S. Rosenbaum, ed., *Is the Holocaust Unique? Perspectives on Comparative Genocide* (Boulder: Westview Press, 1996).

adopted by the United Nations General Assembly in December 1948.[75] Since then, and especially in recent years, the concept has come into much wider use. In fact, there is a whole new discipline, "genocide studies," and, along with it, a new genre of writing concerned with documenting cases of genocide from the legal, political, and historiographical points of view and studying – comparatively, too – the factors that have precipitated these events and made them possible. Such research has, indeed, been fruitful in documenting the horrors of the twentieth century and the various attempts to construct a theory of the phenomenon of mass murder, a typology of it, and conceptual tools for understanding it. Thus, for example, attempts have been made to create an overall category of crime of which genocide is but one example, to construct a hierarchy of severity.[76]

It is in this dual context, then – of public discussion in the United States and of genocide studies – that the intense debate over the uniqueness of the Holocaust has, of late, taken place. What is evidently the most comprehensive, ambitious attempt thus far to prove this uniqueness was undertaken by the American historian Steven Katz. In a hefty tome (almost seven hundred large-format pages), he tries to show, first in a general, programmatic way, that there is an ineluctable difference between the destruction of the Jews by the Germans and all other known instances of mass murder. This claim rests on an exhaustive, detailed comparison – not a denial of comparability – of the Holocaust with other mass crimes committed in premodern times. In

---

[75] On the circumstances of the adoption of the convention and its meaning, see, e.g., Nehemiah Robinson, *The Genocide Convention: A Commentary* (New York: Institute of Jewish Affairs, 1960).

[76] Such an attempt was made by, for example, the historian R. J. Rummel, who distinguishes among different kinds of governmental murder. The most inclusive category is "democide," the killing of entire populations. Under this heading, he subsumes genocide, politicide, and mass murder. See his *Death by Government* (New Brunswick, N.J.: Transaction Publishers, 1996). This book is one of the most comprehensive inventories of the atrocities committed in the twentieth century, but it, too, makes certain omissions. Thus, for example, Rummel does not deal with the expression "symbolic genocide," which we have already encountered. It may also be of interest that this book, like most dealing with genocide (e.g., *The Encyclopedia of Genocide*), makes no mention of crimes committed by Israel. This gap has been filled by another respected member of the Israeli community of opprobrium, the late sociologist Baruch Kimmerling, who shows, in a book published in English not long ago, that the military and political biography of Ariel Sharon can be described as a sustained, systematic campaign of politicide against the Palestinians. Of late, he has widened the application of this term, claiming that Israeli policy in general, not just that of Sharon, is one of politicide. Rummel defines this term as the murder by a government, on political grounds, of an entire population or people (p. 31). Leaving aside the case of Israel, Rummel's book shows– surprisingly? – a certain difference between democratic and nondemocratic regimes: the latter are much more murderous.

two subsequent, as-yet-unpublished volumes, Katz promises to carry on his history of horrors and to prove, in the end, on the basis of comparative historical research, that the Holocaust was unique.[77]

Katz calls his method for proving the Holocaust's historical uniqueness "phenomenology." He says he is trying to offer a phenomenological description or understanding of genocide in general, of the various known kinds of genocide, and particularly of the mass murder of the Jews during the Second World War, showing that, phenomenologically speaking, the latter instance was one of a kind. He uses the term "phenomenology" in the limited sense accepted by social scientists, which is not quite the same as the meaning philosophers give this term. What he means, in fact, is the careful description of a phenomenon and the attempt to discern its characteristic components as the main means of arriving at an understanding of it, on the one hand, and of disregard for causality as essential to theory, on the other. One way or the other, he believes the phenomenological uniqueness of the Holocaust stems from the fact that, except in this case, "no state has, as a matter of conscious principle and active policy, ever set out to destroy physically every last man, woman, and child belonging to a particular group" (p. 28).

Katz has had many critics and, of course, supporters. Those for and against the notion of the uniqueness of the Holocaust have had an opportunity to state their opinions in a collection of articles edited by Alan S. Rosenbaum. Among the wealth of essays in this volume, representing a wide range of views, I would like to mention one in particular. It is a severe critique, long and detailed, of Katz and others who make the claim of uniqueness. It is worth reading, if only for the catalog of other mass murders and crimes he cites as evidence.[78] The author, David Stannard, a professor of American studies at the University of Hawaii, provides a dry, factual description of the destruction of entire populations. In particular, he speaks of the annihilation of thousands (!) of native peoples and ethnic groups, of hundreds of millions of people, amounting to 90 to 95 percent of the population, during the colonization of the Americas. And this is but one example. While trying to show that the Holocaust was not unique, he nevertheless does not take the Jewish catastrophe lightly or try to minimize its scale or the wickedness of its perpetrators. One could dispute one or another of his contentions, but, in fact, given the scope of the disasters human beings have

[77] Steven T. Katz, *The Holocaust in Historical Context*, vol. 1: *The Holocaust and Mass Death before the Modern Age* (Oxford: Oxford University Press, 1994).
[78] David E. Stannard, "Uniqueness as Denial: The Politics of Genocide," in Rosenbaum, *Is the Holocaust Unique?*, 163–208.

inflicted on each other and the wickedness and depravity of their actions, as he describes them, it would be pedantic and pointless to argue with him. Nonetheless, something odd happens toward the end of the article. What at first seemed like an honest expression of resentment, however sharp and polemical, against the claim that the Holocaust was unique turns into something quite different. Suddenly, the meaning of the article's title, "Uniqueness as Denial," becomes clear: this claim amounts to a "denial [*sic*]" that any other holocausts have occurred.

It should be pointed out that, factually speaking, Stannard is wrong. More than this, he is unfair. His criticism is aimed mainly at Steven Katz (who also contributed an article to the volume) and Yehuda Bauer. Though, as he says, these writers have made some questionable statements, they certainly do not deny that other holocausts have taken place. Nor has Deborah Lipstadt, whose campaign against Holocaust denial he actually supports but from whose writings he quotes an incautious remark. At the same time, he cites some more problematical cases, like the statement of Rabbi Seymour Siegel, a member of the board of the United States Holocaust Memorial Museum, who opposed devoting a room in the museum to the Nazi extermination of the Gypsies (p. 195); Israel's support of the Turkish demand that it not recognize the massacre of the Armenians as a case of genocide; and the refusal of the Israeli educational system to include this massacre in the school curriculum.[79]

However one looks at it, the damage caused by the claim of uniqueness, Stannard maintains, is enormous. His argument must be read to be believed. One can well understand the psychology of this claim, he says (and here he quotes Israel W. Charny), that is, one can see it as an expression of the sense of bereavement, shock, and outrage people feel when their own kind suffer tragedy. But, he emphasizes, this is not the point. Rather, it is a question of "moral bookkeeping" originating in "a small industry of Holocaust hagiographers arguing for the uniqueness of the Jewish experience with all the energy and ingenuity of theological zealots. For that is what they are: zealots who believe literally that they and their religious fellows are, in the words of Deuteronomy 7:6, 'a special people ... above all people that are on the face of the earth'" (p. 193). Like other peoples who believe they are "chosen" – the Boers in South Africa, the Protestants in Northern Ireland, or the New England Puritans, all of whom engaged in conquest, oppression, and even

---

[79] There is no mention, however, of the fact that Israel's Open University, a recognized public institution, has a course unit devoted to the Armenian genocide. Apparently, this is one of the few academic offerings on this subject anywhere.

genocide – and especially because of the biblical imperative of racial purity (as he sees it), the ideology of the covenant (between the people Israel and its God) is only one step removed from real racism and the violent oppression of the unchosen. Indeed, "Justifications for Israel's territorial expansionism and suppression of the Palestinian people, when it has been admitted that the Palestinians *are* a people, of course, have long followed this same path of Chosen People self-righteousness. Moreover, it is a self-righteousness that is commonly yoked to the Holocaust's role as part of the founding myth of the Israeli state" (p. 194). No two people could be farther apart than Stannard and Garaudy; how is it, then, that they are so close to each other on the subject of the "founding myths"?

If Stannard is to be believed, the Jewish sense of uniqueness has a certain dialectical complexity: the uniqueness of suffering and death, on the one hand, and the uniqueness of chosenness and superiority, on the other, are one and the same. The worst part of this is that it is not just the Palestinians who are victims of the Chosen People, the people that believes itself to be chosen because it is the ultimate victim, but all the other victims of mass murder are as well. The claim that Jewish suffering in the Holocaust was unique plays an important role in a theocratic state – that is, Israel – that regards itself as being under siege. This is a fraud for which others have had to pay a heavy price. For an essential component of the notion that the Holocaust was unique is the trivialization or even outright denial of other instances of mass murder – of the Armenians, the Gypsies, the Native Americans, the Cambodians, the Rwandans, and others – they being unchosen and their deaths therefore being insignificant (ibid). The Jews, it turns out, are the Chosen People not only because they have exclusive claim on the status of victim (or the other way around) but also because the ridiculous theocracy they have set up in a small corner of the Middle East (at the expense of the Palestinians, let it be remembered) determines the morality or immorality of the entire world. Stannard goes on to make the point even more explicit: the obliviousness of the world to the genocide currently being committed, in South America, for example, is the fault of those (though, fortunately, not only those) who argue that the Holocaust was unique (p. 198).

This article is of interest not only for its content but also because it blurs the historiographical and philosophical questions about the uniqueness of the Holocaust with the moralistic fervor of its attack on those who assert this uniqueness and by the questionable character of that attack. More than what it tells us about them, about the matter of uniqueness itself, or about other cases of genocide (described in such horrifying detail), the article is informative about its own author. His righteous wrath, not only against those historians who have not done their homework but also against the idea of chosenness and, in effect, against Jewish history as a whole, against the State of Israel and its treatment of the Palestinians, and against many of the Jewish historians of the Holocaust – this wrath is symptomatic, typifying a certain category of intellectuals who have allowed their universalism to cloud their judgment.

The reference to Deborah Lipstadt, too, is symptomatic. Stannard, like Ophir, can certainly not be labeled a Holocaust denier. But the way he picks a quarrel with Lipstadt puts him in dangerous proximity to the deniers. In the end, and "objectively" speaking (to use Zuckerman's Marxist terminology), his resentment of the claim of uniqueness (like Ophir's) represents collusion with Holocaust denial. This is true regardless of how much, or how sincerely, he speaks of the evils of Auschwitz. Lipstadt's main concern is to describe the phenomenon of denial and the struggle against it. She is not particularly concerned with the question of uniqueness, except to the extent that the *denial* of uniqueness serves the denial of the *Holocaust*, and to the extent that she is trying to answer the deniers and refute their claims. Lipstadt's work is a response; if her book contains any statements at all about the Holocaust itself, about the historical truth of what can be known about it or about its scope and meaning, they are meant to be an answer, if not to the deniers, then to denial as a stance and a phenomenon. These things have to be said because the deniers have turned the obvious into a subject of debate.

It may be appropriate to repeat here something we said earlier: the phenomenon to which Lipstadt is responding goes back a long way. Long before the victims began to claim special status, Rassinier and his friends had already begun speaking about the universality of suffering and its triviality, even banality: everyone suffers; wherever there is a state, there are camps. It is true that the fate of the Jews has been bitter and unhappy, Rassinier writes at the beginning of his book *The Real Eichmann Trial*. But they are certainly not the only ones to have suffered. The denial, as we have said, goes back even further, antedating even the extermination itself.[80] And just as the extermination and its denial have gone hand in hand since the beginning, so the refusal to recognize the uniqueness of the victims' suffering goes back as far as the suffering itself, or at least to a time before any demand

---

[80] On the all-out effort of the Nazis to conceal any reference to the Final Solution and destroy systematically all evidence of their intentions and of the attendant decision-making process, see, e.g. Leni Yahil, "Some Remarks about Hitler's Impact on the Nazis' Jewish Policy," *Yad Vashem Studies* 23 (1993): 281–294. It is thus likely that, unlike Ophir, Hitler and his accomplices did see their crime as unique.

for recognition of it, much less of its uniqueness, had been made. This more precise chronological analysis could well show that the discussion of the uniqueness of the Holocaust is in its origin, and perhaps in its essence, a reaction, largely apologetic, on the part of Jews resentful of efforts to erase the memory of the crimes committed against them or their parents from the face of the earth. At bottom, and despite all its less pleasant manifestations (less in both quantity and quality than those who dispute the uniqueness claim), it could be that the claim of uniqueness, like Jewish historical research into the Holocaust in general, represents a defensive response to the attempt to deny the Jews the possibility of speaking about their catastrophe.

Although the question of the Holocaust's uniqueness is a separate one, what we have been saying is not irrelevant to a discussion of it, even when the discussion tries to be nonpolemical. It turns out to be important to read the theoretical views that have been expressed, as well as the arguments made in their favor, against the background of the overt or covert political objectives they are meant to serve. The effectiveness of Stannard and those like him derives not only from their willingness to stretch the bounds of factual accuracy here and there but also from their ability either to ignore the conceptual confusion and fogginess characteristic of the discussion of this question or to take advantage of it. The question of uniqueness is primarily a historical and historiographical one, that is, a question of facts and their interpretation; but it requires a certain amount of conceptual, perhaps even philosophical clarification. Thus, for example, if we are to know how to treat the issue, we must first determine what exactly it is we are talking about. In other words, we must first clarify what we mean by "uniqueness." The unique is not, as we have said, that which is beyond compare (there is no such thing) but that which comparison shows to be different from everything else or, more precisely, shows that all other things resemble each other much more than it differs from them.

Every historical phenomenon is unique in some ways and not others. Every crime, such as an instance of genocide, is unique, first of all from what might be called an "ontological" point of view and in terms of what is sometimes described as its "individuality." It is a one-time event. It has more or less definite boundaries in space and time, its own history, and its own distinct consequences. Its perpetrators' identity is well defined and its victims' identity even more so. This uniqueness is such a general and basic quality – everything that can be considered a *thing* is unique in this sense – that some have called it the fundamental ontological attribute, that which makes every being into a being. On the other hand, from the point of view of our concern here and from a theoretical point of view, such uniqueness is trivial and of little interest.

What is of interest is the degree of similarity between different things or phenomena. In other words, since we are concerned with "degree," that which is of interest, the similarity, is a matter of more or less. "Uniqueness," too, is thus a matter of more or less. Similarity and its degrees, or uniqueness and its degrees, can be discovered by what is called "comparison." Comparison is a mental process, that is, always, a matter of both deliberation and decision. In other words, one must not only gauge the degree of similarity or difference but also decide what parameters to consider, which differences and similarities are significant.

One example: it is well known that the Nazis exterminated not only Jews but also, as part of a dress rehearsal for the extermination of the Jews, people suffering various physical and mental handicaps (some 70,000 in the first, more or less open stage of the "euthanasia" program, as they called it). Together with the Jews, they also murdered Gypsies. According to an article by Ian Hancock, of the 16,275 Gypsies in Germany in 1938, some 85 percent were deported to the camps, and only 12 percent of these survived.[81] Nevertheless, there were important differences between the destruction of the Jews and that of the Gypsies. For example, Nazism was both a racist and an anti-Semitic ideology. The murderous hatred of the Jews was a basic component, as they say, of the Nazi racial theory (or pseudotheory). One might even say that this racism was a kind of rationalization of Nazi anti-Semitism. The latter had roots in European religious Jew-hatred, though with some significant new aspects. The Gypsies, on the other hand, were apparently never the subject of an entire theory of negation or rejection. They were hated and persecuted, but their extermination was most likely a result of the broader Nazi ideology of extermination of which anti-Semitism was, as we have said, a basic component. They hitched a ride, so to speak, on the extermination of the Jews. What opened up the possibility of killing them was the Nazis' murderous anti-Jewish racism. Some, like Yehuda Bauer, for example, think it was the hatred of the Jews that provided a basis for the broader racial ideology, and not the other way around. Furthermore, the Gypsies in certain places were a highly visible "other." In places outside

---

[81] On the systematic extermination of human beings deemed unworthy of living, the theoretical justifications given for such killing, and, in particular, the active participation of scientists and physicians (almost without exception), see Benno Müller-Hill, *Murderous Science: Elimination by Scientific Selection of Jews, Gypsies, and Others in Germany, 1933–1945* (Plainview, N.Y.: Cold Spring Harbor Laboratory Press, 1998); and Ian Hancock, "Responses to the Porrajmos: The Romani Holocaust," in Rosenbaum, *Is the Holocaust Unique?*, 39–72 . See also Gilad Margalit, *Germany and Its Gypsies: A Post-Auschwitz Ordeal* (Madison: University of Wisconsin Press, 2002), 25–56.

Germany where this was no longer the case, where they were no longer nomadic, there was no attempt to exterminate them, nor was there any sense of their still being the carriers of some invisible, ineradicable essence. The Jews, at least in Germany and other Western European countries, were an imaginary "other." A century and a half of emancipation and assimilation had not only effaced the visible differences between Jews and Germans but also turned the Jews into prominent partners in German cultural life. Their extermination was an act of cultural suicide no less than the annihilation of an alien people.

One could enumerate other differences.[82] And, no, we are not talking here about "moral bookkeeping." The continuum of comparison is not a "conceptual continuum" of entitlement to grievance and complaint. It is also not a Richter scale on which the strength of moral claims or degrees of suffering or victimhood can be gauged. Though it sometimes seems this way, and it is certainly said to be, this notion of degree is not what we are talking about. The question we are asking here is whether, to further our understanding, we can rest content with the observation that the Gypsies were murdered together with the Jews, with the same cruelty and by the same means. In terms of any moral judgment of the severity of the act, there is really no difference. But if we are seeking to understand the nature of the act, it turns out that the extermination of the Jews had certain characteristics (phenomenological ones, if you will) that distinguished it from that of the Gypsies.

But the real point lies elsewhere altogether. Ian Hancock, in the previously cited article (like David Stannard, in the first part of his article) complains about the way the extermination of the Gypsies is mentioned, or not mentioned, in the Washington Holocaust museum. The latter is an American national memorial, and in this respect we can understand, and even identify with, Hancock's complaint. But Hancock never mentions Yad Vashem (the Israeli national Holocaust memorial), for example, or the way Israel relates to the catastrophe of the Jews. As we have pointed out, the debate about the

---

[82] The literature is filled with attempts to characterize the uniqueness of the Jewish Holocaust, the differences between it and other instances of genocide. They speak of an "unprecedented" event, or, in Hannah Arendt's terminology, a "new crime," with no harbinger in all of history before the Second World War. They speak of the bureaucratization of the extermination and of the mobilization of the apparatus of a modern state and, in fact, of an entire society to carry it out. They speak about the intention to annihilate all Jews, wherever they may be, not only to eliminate them from Germany or the territories inhabited by "Aryans." They speak about humiliation and depersonalization as integral parts of the extermination process. Above all, perhaps, they speak of the utter lack of self-interest or rational purpose, however criminal, behind the desire to kill the Jews. These are some of the reasons often given to substantiate the claim of "uniqueness."

"uniqueness" of the Holocaust is primarily an American one. As imported to Israel by Adi Ophir & Co., it has a completely different meaning from what it has in the American context: instead of the attempt to deny the Holocaust's uniqueness and to criticize the way it and other catastrophes are presented in the American public eye, we have the negation of another uniqueness, that of the Jewish point of view – the Jewish *différend* – as Lyotard, whom Ophir holds in high esteem, calls it and which he thought that only Israel could express. What Ophir really means – and he says so openly – is to deny the right of the Jews, especially Israeli Jews, to treat their catastrophe and that of their parents and grandparents as something that affects them differently than other people's catastrophes do. No one even dreams of making such a demand of the Armenians, the Gypsies, or the Native Americans. Or the Palestinians, for that matter.

The problem of the "unique" point of view of the victim or of the victim's family or folk, is not a psychological one, as we have quoted Israel Charny as saying. It is not enough to recognize this point of view as a "natural" reaction to something that happened to one's relatives. Natural reactions are obvious and to some degree inevitable, and thus they are sometimes forgivable. But what we are talking about here is not a readiness to understand Jewish reactions to the Holocaust – in the paternalistic way a parent can understand a rebellious child – or the possibility of forgiving them their particularism. We do not need forgiveness for wanting to relate to the Holocaust in a distinctively Jewish way; and, as a matter of fact, if we are talking about forgiveness, it is from us that it should be asked. We are talking about something else altogether, something far more serious: our identity. We are talking about the moral right to a particularistic point of view. The right to remember and remind, to press charges against the evildoer for the evil he has done, to take steps to prevent the same thing from happening again – not only to human beings in general but, first of all, to these particular victims, the Jews. It is not the same as the right – or duty – of a bystander to bear witness or of a judge to pronounce a verdict; it is the right of the injured party, the victim, as such, insofar as he was hurt. The obligation not to hand Hitler a victory and the right to try to overcome the conditions that made possible the extermination of the Jews of Europe are not the same as the universal obligation and right to prevent murder in all times and places. Although there is no necessary contradiction between these two points of view – the particular and the universal, to use a worn-out, inaccurate formulation – or the rights and obligations they entail, it is also not easy to reconcile these points of view and respect them both. Quite a few Israeli Jews have given up on the universalistic point of view; not only the destruction itself but the world's systematic indifference to it have prompted them to adopt a pessimistic, even nihilistic moral outlook. Others have adopted a reverse nihilism: they deny any right to a particularistic point of view (usually, it must be admitted, only to Jews and Israelis). They do this in the name of a questionable, abstract, misleading universalism. It is not clear which of the two kinds of nihilism is to be preferred. Morally speaking, of course.

ON THE HUMANNESS OF AUSCHWITZ AND ISRAELI GUILT

Adi Ophir's most important contribution to Israeli culture – and it is a real contribution – is his lengthy book (close to five hundred closely spaced, large-format pages in the original), published in English as *The Order of Evils: Toward an Ontology of Morals*.[83] In many respects, this is a praiseworthy work. First of all, it is an attempt, uncommon in these parts, to develop a comprehensive philosophical theory, growing out of contemporary Israeli reality and couched in contemporary Hebrew, filling an entire volume, and not focused on historical scholarship or commentary. The book has original-ity and intellectual sweep and daring. Much of the content deserves serious philosophical consideration, be it critical or supportive. This is particularly true of the second part of the book, in which, it seems to me, the layers of jar-gon, theorization, and trendiness are pierced by what seems like an authentic philosophical and moral sensitivity. But unfortunately the book has another side to it, where it alternates between the pathetic and the obscene. If I had to sum up this impressive book in a single sentence, I would have to say that its theoretical and substantive shortcomings outweigh its virtues. I do not refer to purely philosophical issues but to something else. What is particularly troubling in the book is that apparently at least some of its philosophical faults stem from the ideological and political purposes it is meant to serve and that the author's political agenda is the source of his philosophical think-ing, not the other way around. If so, the book represents not just a missing of the mark but a defeat for the enterprise of thought. I do not, of course, intend to undertake a philosophical discussion of this book here. I will say only a few things relevant to our subject, even if, in the nature of things, it will not be possible to do so without a bit of technical philosophical analysis.

Ophir aspires to being a moral philosopher and a universalistic social and political thinker. To do so, he thinks he has to transcend Jewish and Israeli particularism. In the foreword to his book, he establishes the context in which

---

[83] Adi Ophir, *The Order of Evils: Toward an Ontology of Morals* (New York: Zone Books, 2005).

it was written. Though he gets most of his inspiration from contemporary French sources, the book is contingent on the "the Israeli situation"; and, indeed, it is what might be called a metaphysics of the (anti-)occupation no less than an "ontology of morals" (the book's subtitle).

In any event, the Israeli situation and the limitations it places on theoretical thinking have to do, first and foremost, with "the meaning of the Holocaust in Israeli culture and the status of 'Auschwitz' as a synonym of 'absolute' or 'radical' evil" (p. 22). In fact, it is not only in Israel that "Auschwitz" is a synonym for absolute evil, but Ophir is naturally interested in the limitations it imposes on Israeli thought in particular. Thus, in Israel, thinking philosophically the question of evil must get out from under the shadow cast by "the halo of the name 'Auschwitz'" (ibid.). In the Hebrew original, the wording is slightly, but significantly, different: Ophir speaks there not just of "the name" but of "*hashem hameforash* [normally the proper name of God] Auschwitz." Auschwitz gets in the way. More precisely, Auschwitz is a hindrance to philosophical thinking about evil. Not about any other matter, not even about the miserable situation of the Palestinians, but about the philosophical question of evil. True, the paths of thought are convoluted: in the (relatively) meager philosophical literature and the (richer) theological literature trying to "think Auschwitz" (as the current usage has it), there is frequent reference to the fact that in neither literature was the subject of the Holocaust dealt with directly (or, in fact, even indirectly) for twenty or thirty years after the war. With few exceptions, even philosophical works devoted to the subject of evil did not pose questions about the evil embodied in the annihilation of the Jews of Europe. There was much historiography, fiction, and poetry about it, but "thought" awakened to the subject of Auschwitz relatively late. Only many years after the war did theology and philosophy begin, rather hesitantly, to confront the subject. And it seems that Israeli philosophy was even more hesitant than the European or American. And now that an original Israeli philosophical work, ambitious and wide-ranging, has at last proposed a comprehensive theory ("ontology") of evil, it tries consciously and explicitly to resist the temptation (!) to think about Auschwitz. Or to be more exact, it does try to think, not about Auschwitz, but against it. Even Agamben, who knows everything there is to know about Auschwitz, believes the time has come to think about it. If we had the impression that Israeli philosophy had reached maturity and was finally ripe for engagement with the really difficult – philosophically difficult – questions, along comes Adi Ophir, a senior Israeli philosopher, and tries to roll back the cart.

So Auschwitz gets in the way of thinking "about other catastrophic events that may be less horrible than Auschwitz, perhaps [?], but whose call upon thought is much more urgent" (p. 23). Although Ophir is in complete agreement here with Stannard, for example, it is not, in fact, at all clear that Auschwitz really gets in the way of thinking about that other evil. Nor is it clear that it is much more urgent, philosophically or from the point of view of moral theory, to "think" the problem of the Palestinian refugees, for example, before we "think" Treblinka or the Warsaw ghetto. At most, it is more urgent to think the refugee problem from an Israeli political point of view and perhaps even from the point of view of moral action. There is indeed an "ontological" urgency to the suffering Israelis and Palestinians are causing each other: it is real suffering, here and now, that promises to extend into the future and could therefore be reduced by concrete action. There is also a need, even an obligation, to think of ways to do this. To this end, we must understand the nature and causes of the suffering, to think about "the conflict" and "the Occupation" historically and politically. Such action can no longer be taken, directly at least, in regard to the suffering at Auschwitz. But while this distinction is interesting in some ways, it is trivial and uninteresting in others; the headaches some of us suffer also have a certain ontological urgency, but this does not imply that they are of any special philosophical interest or that it is "urgent to think [of them]." Nor is the urgency of the matter of the occupation a philosophical urgency. As pressing and concrete as the need to deal with it may be, from the point of view of general moral theory, it is not necessarily of particular interest.

Turning philosophy into political flag waving is not a philosophical act; it is a betrayal of philosophy. Whether intellectuals have an obligation to get involved in politics is debatable. It is also debatable whether such involvement serves any useful purpose. Given the generally melancholy history of intellectuals' involvement in politics in the twentieth century, the claim made by some of them, including here in Israel, that their words carry extra weight is dubious. But turning philosophy into ideology, or an ontology of evil into a metaphysics of the Occupation, is not simply a matter of philosophers getting involved in politics; it is a prostitution of philosophical thought.

All philosophy, but especially the moral and the political, is anchored in the particular situation (as Sartre called it) in which it is written. It responds to that situation and takes a stand in relation to it. Frequently, perhaps always, the content and direction of philosophical inquiry are determined by prephilosophical moral commitments. Schopenhauer, for example, thought that moral philosophy could do no more than provide a meaning and a basis for that which was already beyond doubt. This could be so. The harming of innocent children is an absolute moral evil, and no philosophical reflection can make it otherwise. All that the philosopher can do is try to understand the meaning of such an affirmation and where it comes from. In any case, the fact that the philosopher always finds himself in a particular situation does not contradict the independence of strictly philosophical interests from nonphilosophical ones, be they political, ideological, or any other. This is ostensibly what Ophir, too, is saying: he tries to break free of the limitations of the Israeli situation in order to think about the problem of evil in universal terms. But he does not really succeed; his attempt to transcend Auschwitz is itself plainly an Israeli undertaking, however well it may go together with other, similar efforts. The way he presents the Israeli situation, rather than Auschwitz, as being exceptionally evil is itself distinctly Israeli, especially given the forced, provincial attempt to speak in the language of Agamben, for example. But more than a desire to be universalistic, there is here a desire to shed particularity and selfhood. The talk about overcoming Auschwitz is nothing more than an attempt to take away from Israelis – be they philosophers or not – the right to be in their true situation, which is one where Auschwitz plays a central role. Such talk thus, in effect, digs philosophy a much deeper grave than any dug previously by those on whom Ophir vents his wrath, that is, those who have never tried to get out from under the shadow of the holy name of Auschwitz.

The result of harnessing philosophy to that which is not philosophical can at times be a defeat not just of thought but also of morality. The rest of Ophir's ontology of evil provides an example: as we have seen more than once, Ophir, with his familiar stress on the theological, as it were, calls for a rejection of "the semi-religious imperative, so prevalent in Israeli culture, that forbids any comparison between Auschwitz and other sites of Evil" (p. 23). He urges us to find a way "to restore a conceptual continuum that allows for a comparison" between Auschwitz and other calamities people have inflicted on each other. But Ophir is not speaking here of some abstract, general comparison. The purpose of this reconstruction is to allow for a specific comparison, that "between the Evil that took place in Auschwitz and the Evil that the descendants of the victims and their inheritors create for the people they have turned into refugees, foreigners and non-citizens in their own country, subjects of a military regime and freedom fighters in an anti-colonial struggle, terrorists, murderers" (ibid.). Note: the descendants of the victims of Auschwitz, in particular, have made murderers of their victims. Not only have they – that is, we – made them victims – that is, victims of the victims of the Holocaust – not only are we guilty of the suffering we have inflicted on them, we are also responsible for, and in effect guilty of, the murders the Palestinians commit against us. For the buses blown up in our streets, for example. How did Rassinier put it? The Jews invented their own death. Over and above the factual inaccuracy of this statement, there is also an obscene paternalism to it: the Palestinians are not responsible for their own actions.

The philosophy this book offers the reader is moral philosophy. Theories of moral philosophy have, as a rule, tried, first of all, to answer the question, What is the good? Ophir wants to begin with the concept of evil. It is a somewhat original approach, and it could have been philosophically fruitful. The "ontology of evil," clearly linked with utilitarianism on the one hand and Marxist materialism on the other, but also to the pessimism of the Frankfurt school, seeks to locate evil in the here and now, to remove the "spiritual," that is, what can merely be thought of, not gauged or experienced, from the moral calculus of evils. The economy of harm to be prevented and "presences" to be banished – or, the other way around, of "presences" the banishment of which is to be prevented, as Ophir puts it – are the economy of the man, or perhaps the body, who suffers or benefits from what is present to him, either in the proper measure, in excessive measure (pain), or in insufficient measure (privation or deprivation). What cannot be included in this calculation under any circumstances is what Ophir himself defines as the supreme moral scandal, superfluous death. We shall come back to the matter of superfluity; but what this implies about death itself is that it can be included in the calculus of moral costs and benefits only if there is a living person for whom another's death would be superfluous. From the point of view of the dead, death itself, whether it is pointless (as it almost always is to the dying person) or not, ceases to be a moral issue. It ceases to be an issue at all.

"The first, most ancient, and most general moral command" is "Thou shalt not kill" (p. 508). Can this imperative be justified in the secular ontology of *The Order of Evils*? Ophir's answer to this question, which he does ask himself, is quite weak. In the last analysis, he cannot say why murder is a pure evil or why it is always, under all circumstances, forbidden to commit murder, without regard to religion, race, sex, or class. The murder of the solitary nomad whose absence will be felt by no one, who knows no one who will mourn his death, is apparently not to be considered evil once it has occurred; or at least Ophir cannot explain why it should be, even after the fact. All he has to say about this is that "it is impossible to dismiss everything a solitary, kinless person stands to lose without first killing her, and until she is killed, it is prohibited to cause her superfluous loss"; and "because this loss is not yours to calculate, you don't bear this suffering, this life is not yours to take" (p. 512). While Ophir speaks ironically of the imperative, as it were, that Auschwitz imposes, he seems to be speaking of his own imperative with complete – prophetic? – seriousness. He couches it in quasi-religious terms, perhaps because he cannot explain or justify the supreme moral certainty, according to which murder is always – even ex post facto – evil.

If it were a matter of philosophical difficulty, if it turned out that the philosophical structure Ophir erected stood on shaky ground, on inadequate assumptions, there would be no point in discussing this issue here. But the difficulty is more likely to have arisen not from the inadequacy of his philosophical thinking, but from the harnessing of his thinking to nonphilosophical purposes, from his obsession with blaming Israel, in the name of Auschwitz and despite Auschwitz. In this case, the nonphilosophical purposes philosophy is being made to serve are also immoral, not just bad philosophy. "And indeed," we are told a few lines previously, "from the point of view of the economy of evils in general and that of superfluous evils in particular, it is impossible to take the dead into consideration. The dead are the disaster of the living. When the living whose disaster this death is die, the disaster ends. This is the terrible paradox of the loss named Auschwitz ... and of the loss in every catastrophe of similar dimensions" (ibid.). In a word, then, Ophir simply dismisses all those who would give voice to the *différend* of the dead of Auschwitz. There is no one left to speak in their name, because no one misses them, mourns them, or is angry at their death. Death, murder, and decimation are thus no longer, in themselves, moral evils, because the damage, the suffering, the absence of those who were present and the presence of their absence – all these are gone.

But there is more. The effort to preserve the voiceless *différend* is itself to be considered evil. This conclusion may seem perverse, the author admits, but there is no way "to escape it." The Nazi evil "exists to this very day, due to and by virtue of memory" (p. 546). In other words, for Ophir, the Nazi evil itself – this very evil, and not just an offshoot or consequence or metaphorical representation of it – continues to exist. It does so because we remember it. The dead are gone, and nothing is left of them. Even their bodies, the detritus of the industrialized process of slaughter, were disposed of as part of that process, the nature of which was, in fact, "the total spiritualization and idealization of Evil" (p. 543). Or, to be more exact: spirituality is not itself a source of evil but "the result of an outbreak" of evil. It is "a spirituality of vacancy," that is, of turning the victims into a nullity. For, after all, it is not only that they burned the bodies, but that no one is left who misses those who were killed, because their relatives and friends and the witnesses to their murder were killed as well and their bodies burned. "The [Nazi] decimation was an evil to end all evils," and thus it lives on only in memory. To rid the world once and for all of the evil of Auschwitz, now that the dead are dead and their bodies have been disposed of, we must put an end to the spiritual existence of Evil as well. The *memory* of the material evil must be erased. Once again here, the reader is confronted with an unexpected reversal: the evil that persists in memory is no longer evil; the real evil is the memory of the evil.

Why is the memory such a bad thing? Because, by an inexorable logic, it becomes a mechanism for generating real, material evil. The Nazi destruction was absolute, and the memory of it represents a refusal to recognize that absoluteness. How is that done? Because there are no longer any real subjects, that is, living Jews, an imaginary subject must be invented. One sets up "a non-personal subject whose life is eternal or at least spans an entire history; the Jewish people, humanity, Europe, various types of 'us'" (p. 547). And, of course, "the victims became the alibi of this subject" (ibid.). And, of course, this happens in a way that is particularly harmful in Israel, for here the imperative of asserting the absoluteness of the Nazi evil and thus, in fact, denying the absoluteness of the real victim (the Palestinians, evidently) has been turned into a state religion. "[M]echanisms of public ritual ... have been nationalized and ..., for one day every year, turn the citizens into hostages of memory, trapped in a sticky web of hollow hyperbole and sad tunes" (p. 548). These, then, are not only the obscene ways in which public memory is expressed – as Zuckerman, for example, has taught us – but the locus of the actual appearance of evil, where it takes material and not just spiritual form. What is the remedy? To forget? Not really. No, Ophir is not trading denial for oblivion. He simply thinks there is a "satanic choice" here between the price of forgetting and that of remembering. "This satanic choice is the final victory of the Nazis over the Jews" (p. 552). What makes it such a great victory? Apparently because, if we forget, Nazism has achieved its aim of eliminating the Jewish people; but if we remember, we ourselves become Nazis. The memory of the Holocaust is the reason for Israel's moral blindness, hence the source of and excuse for all the evils it commits. This is what makes Israel a "paradigmatic example" of the global continuum of catastrophe, of which Nazism is another example (p. 591). Nuclear weapons and the manufacture and sale of armaments are two important components of the potentially catastrophic character of the Israeli state. Between the two are the Occupation, the apartheid (national, not racial), the "methodically deploy[ed] mechanisms of domination and control, practices of violence, ideological discourse" (ibid.). Soon enough, we come to this conclusion: "At the bottom of the gaping slope [*sic*] of this space is the methodical and controlled removal – either through transfer (as it is commonly called), deportation, or destruction – of a 'superfluous' group that is part of the governed population" (ibid.). The industrialized destruction of the Palestinians, the Israeli Auschwitz, is, Ophir thinks, right at the doorstep. And even if it be delayed, it will surely come. The extremist "hilltop youth" settlers and their rabbis might well agree with Ophir on this point, though they would disagree with him as to whom the victims will be.

The conclusion to be drawn from all this seems clear and inescapable: we must forget Auschwitz after all. The way out of our dilemma is no less terrible than the dilemma itself, but it is necessary. If there is such a close causal connection between remembering Auschwitz and ignoring the evils that require our urgent attention, then evidently Auschwitz has to be forgotten. Morally speaking, it is better to prevent the killing of more Palestinians, who are ontologically real and whose presence is not merely the "presence of an absence" than to remember those who are dead and gone and in whose absence we clearly have, ontologically speaking, no real interest. If that be the case, would it not be better for us to grant Pierre Guillaume victory than to allow more targeted assassinations? However, it turns out there is an honorable way out of this dilemma: not only can we find a way to talk about Auschwitz, but talking about it can even help root out the present evils. Not altogether in the manner of Guillaume, but not altogether differently either. Bitter can give rise to sweet, as we know, and the failure of the ontology of morals to explain why murder is murder is murder; why it always has been and always will be wrong; and why the evil that was done there (at Auschwitz) and then (sixty-odd years ago) retains its standing here and now as pure evil – this failure makes it possible to speak philosophically about Auschwitz, so as to clarify the nature of what the evil Israel is doing and, in fact, embodies. We must speak about Auschwitz in order to neutralize the evil generated by "the religion of uniqueness." We must also speak about Auschwitz in order to reduce the damage done by the belief of many Israeli Jews that they belong to a historical subject (an imaginary one, it will be recalled) that identifies historically with the victims and thus has the right not only to speak in their name but also, and especially, to relate to their catastrophe in a unique way.

An attempt to do this is made in the third part of Ophir's study of evil, which takes up almost half the book. This attempt, which is the conclusion reached by the first two parts of the book, renders *The Order of Evils*, in the main, a detailed, systematic, argument *against* the Jews' right to their own point of view on the Holocaust. This negation, in turn, is meant to justify the negation of the Jews' right to a state of their own, and thus to deprive them of their ability to do evil. Like other members of the international *resentiment* community, Ophir, as we have already seen on more than one occasion, makes use of the historical and moral connection that undoubtedly exists between the Holocaust and the

State of Israel. In a typically questionable manner, he turns this connection, first of all, into the principle underlying the very existence of the State of Israel. It is the principal, if not exclusive, basis of its claim to legitimacy; and it is the basis of its moral character, that is, it explains its moral blindness and exceptional capacity for harm. It is for this reason that we need to challenge the "religion of uniqueness," to "profane the holy name," to speak about Auschwitz (like Agamben, Ophir prefers this term to "Shoah" or "holocaust," and certainly to "the Holocaust"), that is, actually to speak about it, in a "secular" way. Ophir is trying to profane the holy name and speak about Auschwitz in order to show how close to our present situation, here and now, it is.

Hence, we do need to speak about Auschwitz. Hence, too, we need to restore a conceptual continuum that would allow us to compare it to other catastrophes. Such a comparison would show that Auschwitz has, after all, a certain uniqueness. The latter is to be found in the fact that Auschwitz combines *all* the factors common to other man-made disasters, factors present in Western democratic societies as well. In this sense, Auschwitz is just the most extreme case of something that has occurred in all the other places in lesser measure, but it is just for this reason that it stands out. Auschwitz differs from all the other sites of evildoing not in the type of evil done there but because "it is the first time that Evil appears in its most purified, distilled form as superfluity itself, superfluity without limits or measure, for Evil appears as its own end" (p. 556). We shall return presently to the notion of superfluity. As for the distinction between "type[s] of evil" and evil "purified" and "distilled," and the idea that Auschwitz represented the latter, even some of the most zealous adherents of the "religion of uniqueness" would agree (on the assumption, possibly unfounded, that this is a real conceptual distinction).[84] If we can agree, for example, that no state, as such, has ever mobilized itself to undertake the total elimination of a more or less defined human group in the way the German state, with all its institutions, its army, and most of its citizenry, did; and if we can agree (as most Holocaust scholars, including Bauer and Katz, do) that this mobilization was an important element in the German destruction of the Jews, then what difference does it make (except, perhaps, to some fastidious ontologists) whether we say it was the quintessence of evil in general or, as Hannah Arendt, for one, put it, the invention of a new and unprecedented form of evil?

---

[84] Yehuda Bauer – widely attacked for defending the uniqueness of the Holocaust – concludes a wide-ranging comparative discussion by calling the Holocaust "the most extreme form of genocide." See his *Rethinking the Holocaust* (New Haven: Yale University Press, 2001), 270.

On the other hand, to say that Auschwitz was a unique manifestation of "evil ... as an end in itself" would be an inadequate and even misleading way of expressing an idea that, while not entirely new, is of considerable value. Quite a few commentators on the Holocaust – historians, theologians, and philosophers – think one of its unique features was the noninstrumental nature of the crimes committed against the Jews. Arendt, incidentally, was one of the first, if not the first, to make this argument. Unlike most crimes and even most cases of genocide, the murder of the Jews brought no benefit, real or imagined, nor did the perpetrators expect to profit in any tangible way from the execution of their task. The motives for what they did were not benefit or profit. It is true that the destruction of the Jews opened the way to every possible kind of plunder, greed, cowardice, and opportunism; that quite a few individuals and institutions were enriched by the murder of the Jews and the looting of their property; and that the Germans found all sorts of methods of profiting from the Jewish dead – collecting gold teeth, cutting off hair, stoking the fires that consumed the bodies of emaciated, longtime prisoners with the fat of the newly arrived. But it was not material profit or any other kind of benefit, in any possible sense of these words, that drove the Thousand Year Reich to do what it did.[85]

In the historiographical literature on the Final Solution, there is a debate over this issue. One of the principal ways of looking at it as a concrete subject of research, an approach originated mainly by German historians, is to ask how the anti-Semitic policies of the Third Reich led to systematic killing; what stages led from the harassment of the German Jews, to a government policy of restriction, to their systematic exclusion from the economy and public life, to the physical expulsion of the Jews from the Reich, to the slaughter of entire communities in the places where they lived, to the concentration of the Jews in ghettos, and finally to the establishment of extermination camps, the deportation of all accessible Jews to these camps, and the industrialized process of putting them to death. It was at one time (especially in the 1980s) customary to distinguish between two main kinds of answers to these questions. There were, on the one hand, the "intentionalists," who claimed that the destruction of the Jews was the result of the more or less explicit aims of the Nazi leaders – Hitler, in particular – but also of those who planned

---

[85] Bauer develops this idea more fully in ibid., 47–48. Lang cites, among other sources, Hitler's will, written only a few hours before his death: "Above all, I charge the leaders of the nation and those under them to scrupulous observance of the laws of race and to merciless opposition to the universal poisoner of all peoples, international Jewry." Lang, *Act and Idea*,19n.

and carried out the program; and the result of racial anti-Semitism and an ideology that made it possible to consider a priori the elimination of the Jews and, once the right conditions were created, even made this elimination necessary. On the other hand, there were the "functionalists" or "structuralists," who held that the extermination policy grew without a master plan, in accordance with more or less localized, more or less contingent developments and in response to the constraints of the war and the reality created by earlier decisions – such as the "resettlement" policy – and their failure. This debate should be approached with caution because of the ideological and apologetic character of some of the "functionalist" writings: if it turned out that there was no prior intention to destroy the Jews, German guilt might seem to be mitigated.[86]

Nevertheless, this controversy is undoubtedly of historiographical interest, and some of the issues that arose between the intentionalists and the functionalists continue to reverberate in contemporary scholarship. As we learn from Christopher Browning's monumental work on the extermination policy against the Jews during the early years of the war, the debate is not yet over, yet the functionalist (in effect, developmental) approach does not necessarily, in and of itself, lessen German culpability or open the way to apologetics. This impressive work of scholarship, among other things, makes it possible to distinguish clearly between the ideological and historiographical questions.[87] Browning tries to show how the extermination policy gradually developed amid German bureaucratic chaos, out of attempts to Germanize the western part of Poland, which had been annexed to Germany after it conquered the country, and to resettle there, in place of the Poles, Jews, and others living there, hundreds of thousands of ethnic Germans (*Volksdeutsche*) brought from the east. This was linked to the policy of expelling Jews from the Reich. He gives no indication that the absence, before the war or during its initial stages, of an explicit plan for the systematic physical extermination of the Jews had the least effect on the character of the crime.

Another, more problematical example is to be found in the work of the historian Götz Aly. He and his colleague Susanne Heim have published a series of studies aiming to show that the extermination policy developed on a rational economic basis.[88] The term "economic" is to be understood here

---

[86] See Ulrich Herbert's introduction to *National Socialist Extermination Policies.*

[87] See Christopher Browning, *The Origins of the Final Solution: The Evolution of Nazi Jewish Policy, September 1939–March 1942* (Lincoln: University of Nebraska Press, 2004).

[88] See Susanne Heim and Götz Aly, "The Holocaust and Population Policy: Remarks on the Decision on the 'Final Solution,'" *Yad Vashem Studies* 24 (1994): 45–70; Ulrich Herbert's

in a special way, according to which a given area of human activity can be characterized by the kind of rational thinking that shapes it. What is meant is a limited kind of rationality, dictated by specific, simple, prior aims – maximizing profits, reducing costs, making the means of increasing profit as efficient as possible – what is sometimes called "instrumental rationality." The latter term originated with Max Weber, who used it to characterize the capitalist ethic, in which, according to him, we see the sort of rationality that is concerned with the efficient adaptation of means to the attainment of given ends, objectively and without being influenced by factors external to the calculus of ends and means.

Aly and Heim make frequent use of the term "rationalization," as well as "modernization," to describe the sequence that begins with the expulsion of the Jews from German economic life and ends with Auschwitz. They try to show that these actions were part of a conscious, intentional process – though not necessarily fully planned ahead of time – of concentrating the means of production, making production and trade more efficient, matching production to need, reorganizing industry, and other such steps in the direction of sweeping economic rationalization, especially as concerned the planning and management of the "resettlement" of whole populations. A large group of economists, sociologists, other social scientists, technocrats, and bureaucrats oversaw the "rationalization" process in Germany in its first stages. After the Kristallnacht pogroms, anti-Semitism made its way from the streets to the Reich's planning and administrative offices. After the outbreak of the war and the great conquests of its first years, these technocrats went to the occupied areas, where they tried to carry on with their ambitious modernization and rationalization programs. In this way there gradually developed, out of the expulsion of the Jews from the economy and as a continuation of the original "rationalization" program, the policy of total physical annihilation.

One source of this policy was the racial theories and the well-known attempts at racial improvement (eugenics) and systematic murder of people "whose lives were not worth living" (the physically and mentally handicapped and the mentally ill) that these theories inspired, which were a prelude to the mass murder of undesirable populations. Another source of the extermination policy, according to Aly and Heim, was a socioeconomic theory of surplus population in Europe, or parts of it, and the means that were chosen "rationally" to thin out unwanted populations, unproductive elements,

introduction to *National Socialist Extermination Policies*; and Götz Aly, "'Jewish Resettlement:' Reflections on the Political Prehistory of the Holocaust," in ibid., 52–82.

and so on. The surplus population theory rationalized reducing the number of mouths being fed by the German and reorganized European economies, through the expulsion, starvation, and extermination of many millions of people. For example, in a 1941 report by the "Reich Council on Industrial Rationalization" on "The Profitability of the Jewish Quarter of Warsaw," the author, a Dr. Gater – one of the young technocrats put in charge of rationalizing the economic and demographic organization of the Reich and its *Lebensraum* – calculates how much a single Jew is worth. In order to "balance the figures," the doctor recommends "allowing a scarcity situation to develop, without regard to the consequences," that is, the systematic starvation of the Jews concentrated in the ghetto. This council still exists in Germany today, though under a different name, the authors stress, and Dr. Gater appears in the German *Who's Who* as one of the most important experts on rationalization in the Federal Republic.[89] Thus far, Aly and Heim.

Evidently, no one suspects Aly of having an apologetic or revisionist agenda like Nolte's, for example. Many also value his scholarly contributions and the important discoveries he has to his credit. Nevertheless, he has also been widely criticized for his main theses, his methodological principles, and the way he has interpreted his findings. Particularly harsh criticism has been leveled at him and Heim by the Israeli-German historian Dan Diner.[90] He finds methodological flaws in their approach to archival material they uncovered and essential weaknesses in their interpretation of facts they discovered. He accuses them of presenting the Nazi annihilation of Jews and others as a natural, if extreme, manifestation of bourgeois capitalism, so that these acts lose their distinctiveness and historical specificity (p. 149). As Diner notes at the end of one article, Aly and Heim's original motivation was ethically significant: they tried to do what the judicial system had failed to do, namely, expose the deep involvement of "experts" – intellectuals who worked in the service of the Third Reich and middle-level administrators of the Nazi state – many of whom, unlike the leadership and the ideological Nazis, continued in their professional roles after the war. But eventually Aly and Heim's original motives gave way to impossible generalizations. Eventually, Diner claims, the absolute violation of the moral bounds and limitations accepted by even the most merciless capitalist rationalism – that

---

[89] Götz Aly and Susanne Heim, *Architects of Annihilation: Auschwitz and the Logic of Destruction* (London: Weidenfeld and Nicholson, 2002), 24.

[90] Dan Diner, "On Rationality and Rationalization: An Economistic Explanation of the Final Solution," in Jerry Z. Muller, ed., *Beyond the Conceivable: Studies on Germany, Nazism, and the Holocaust* (Berkeley: University of California Press, 2000), 138–159.

violation which Aly and Heim use to interpret the Final Solution – is like applying culinary standards to cannibalism.

If so, any attempt to discern rational motives for the German murder of the Jews is problematical, to say the least. Nor does Ophir think this murder was a means to any other end: it was neither the ethnic cleansing of territory the Germans coveted, nor an attempt to counter rival national claims, nor a simple matter of plunder. And as we see in, for example, Himmler's notorious speeches calling on the men of the SS to remain stalwart in the face of the terrible deeds they were being called upon to commit, even sadism was not the motive for the crime against the Jews.[91] They were murdered, it seems, out of a kind of idealism of murder.

Whether or not one accepts this characterization of Auschwitz's uniqueness, it must be noted in this connection that, contrary to what Ophir thinks, it was the murder, the annihilation of the Jewish people, and not evil per se that was an end in itself. It is a fine distinction but an important one, first of all because the concept of evil as an end in itself is not likely to be a cogent one, or at least one that is possible in terms of the phenomenology (or ontology) of evil. In the Western philosophical tradition, evil does not generally appear as the symmetrical opposite of good. For philosophical and not just theological reasons, most Western philosophers have rejected Manichaeism as a cogent possibility. Thus, it is generally not said that evil can be desired as one desires good (in a simple inversion, as it were). This asymmetry between good and evil is sometimes defined in terms of "negation" or "absence" (*privatio*). What this means is that evil does not enjoy the positive ontological status that good does, that what we call "evil" is merely the absence of the real entity we call "good." One can agree or disagree with this ontology, of course; but to the extent that Ophir is referring (as he almost certainly is) to Kantian ethics when he speaks of Auschwitz as a place where evil was "an end in itself," the matter calls for some clarification.

At the center of Kant's ethical doctrine is the idea that the good is an end in itself, that is, we desire it because it is good and not because it serves some purpose independent of it (e.g., happiness, utility, profit, health). In essence,

---

[91] A number of the descriptions provided by Browning, *The Origins of the Final Solution*, for example, demonstrate this well. See also Ulrich Herbert, "Lehashmid et ha'oyev beli lisno oto: Sin'at hayehudim bitemunat ha'olam shel mefakdei ha-SS ha'intelektualim bishnot ha'esrim vehasheloshim" (To Wipe Out the Enemy without Hating Him: Jew-Hatred in the Worldview of Intellectual SS Commanders in the Twenties and Thirties), in Jacob Borut and Oded Heilbronner, eds., *Ha'antishemiut hagermanit: Ha'arakha mihadash* (German Anti-Semitism: A Reconsideration) (Tel Aviv: Am Oved, 2000), 174–187. See also Berel Lang, *Act and Idea*, ch. 1.

the good is *defined* by Kant as the thing that is desired for its own sake. This definition of the good is a formal one; but it necessarily implies that evil cannot be similarly defined. For that which we want in and of itself is, by definition, the good, and whatever we want for its own sake is good. Evil cannot be desired as an end in itself, for if we so desired it, it would be good. In fact, the traditional asymmetry between good and evil appears in Kant again, but it passes from ontology and theology over to mere conceptual analysis. That is why Kant thought it was possible to speak of "radical evil" but not "demonic evil" – that is, something very bad but not on the same level, or with the same structure, as the good. Because the good is defined as something we desire in and of itself, by virtue of the fact that it is good, and an obligation is something we desire to fulfill because it is an obligation, the concrete content of the good or the obligatory is not, as long as we are speaking in terms of their general definition, an essential component of these two concepts or of the phenomenology of the ethical attitude. Evil cannot be defined this way. We cannot speak of evil will in the same way that Kant speaks of good will; and radical evil, as distinct from pure moral good, cannot be defined as the will or intention to do evil because it is evil. Evil always has well-defined, concrete content – as, for example, the desire to kill the Jews.

Although the return to the familiar position that the destruction of the Jews was utterly noninstrumental, so that it was evil pursued for its own sake, is questionable philosophically, it does have some literary basis. For example, the French writer Jean Genet, whom we have already mentioned, posited evil as the existential ideal of a life of humiliation, destruction, and self-abuse. It is probably no accident that he was a great supporter of Hitler and the Nazis, an avowed anti-Semite, a great hater of the State of Israel, and a lover of the Palestinians, not only for their refugee condition and their suffering, but more specifically for their desire and ability to murder Jews and Israelis. If not among philosophers, the ontology of "the Occupation" as absolute evil may find support among French writers. At any rate, Ophir fails here, not only as a philosopher but also as a historian. Himmler, in the speech we have mentioned that he gave to the SS, did not exhort them to pursue some abstract idea of evil or to desire evil as an end in itself. What he told them was that they would have to overcome their good inclinations and humanity for the sake of a concrete objective: racial purification. But because "racial purification" is a meaningless phrase, it was, in fact, the destruction of the Jews (something quite clear and unambiguous) that was the ultimate objective. The motivation came not from some inverted theology or notion of evil as an aesthetic ideal, but from the simple goal of destroying the Jews, in all its ugliness.

Thus, Ophir, too, thinks the suffering and death inflicted on the Jews at Auschwitz "were not means for achieving any other goal, military, political, or economic" (p. 557). But even if the Holocaust had this noninstrumental quality, and even if that quality distinguishes it from other catastrophes, for Ophir this is of no significance. It is a "phenomenological" attempt to characterize the Holocaust, he thinks, based on a retrospective view of the murderers, using knowledge now in our possession. But no one, today, is entitled to decide whether the problem for which the Germans found a "final solution" was real or imagined. It might be of interest to cite here one argument among the many made by Dan Diner in his article on Aly and Heim. Their treatment of the thinking of the Nazi experts and technocrats as a kind of "rationality" and the means adopted by the regime as steps toward "modernization" is unfounded, Diner maintains, partly because the documents they analyze transparently reveal an elaborate pattern of self-deception and colossal bad faith. The same is true of Himmler's "idealism" and the readiness of many others to take part in the terrible mass murder committed by their country in the name of the antivalues, so to speak, of race and the extirpation of harmful elements. In other words, the purposelessness and noninstrumentality of the Holocaust were not, in Diner's view, a matter of awareness. On the contrary, Aly and Heim's research reveals that the murderers were highly goal oriented. The problem for which they sought a final solution was, to them, quite real, and they managed to persuade themselves that they were considering it rationally. Can we really say today, in the context of a discussion that presumes to be moral, that no one is entitled to decide whether or not the problem was real, that is, whether the destruction of the Jews was instrumental or not?

Ophir seems to have confused phenomenology and psychology here. That is, he has confused an objective description of the phenomenon symbolized by Auschwitz with reflections on the mentality of the perpetrators. It may well turn out that "the need to get rid of the Jews – and perhaps also of the Gypsies – lay beyond the principles of pleasure and utility" (p. 558). But, for him, this psychoanalytic finding is of limited significance. Evidently, because the ontology of ethics does not recognize thought or motivation as having a distinct moral standing, the following conclusion is to be drawn: "This phenomenological singularity should not be given a transcendental status; it should not be employed to derive theological meaning or a criterion for moral comparison; and it should not be used as grounds for claiming the privilege or precedence of Jews as interpreters of the Shoah, as those authorized to give it meaning" (p. 562). In other words, what Ophir sees as the main distinguishing feature of the Holocaust is, for him, of negligible ontological significance, and, what is more, Jews and Israelis should not be granted the right to make any special claims on the basis of it. We must again insist on the real meaning of these statements, their falsity, and their consequences: the destruction of the Jews was, indeed, not psychologically but ontologically, that is, in a fully *real* way, an act with no utilitarian explanation of any kind, however criminal. On the other hand, "the Jews" have, in fact, never claimed any special right to interpret the Holocaust or any monopoly over its meaning, certainly not today, when German scholars, too, and others, are studying it, after many years when the subject was ignored academically.[92] What Jews have always insisted on, and what it is to be hoped they will continue to insist on, is their right to relate to the Holocaust as a Jewish catastrophe, that is, their own catastrophe. What is really at stake here, again, is the right of Jews and Israelis to their own distinct, particular, and particularistic view of the Holocaust.

Ophir fails here, first in terms of factual accuracy. He also fails to understand the noninstrumental character of the Holocaust philosophically. But, above all, he fails morally, because he is trying, if not to erase the memory of Auschwitz, then to suppress the viewpoint of its victims, their descendants, and their people. He is also trying to use Auschwitz to buttress a moral claim against them, a claim of metaphysical proportions, an accusation of unmitigated guilt. Let us follow Ophir's thinking closely: he argues that restoring the right conceptual continuum will show us how unfounded the Jewish and Israeli claim to a special status vis-à-vis the Holocaust is, and how guilty they are. Instead of the conceptual and legal continuum based on the category of genocide, Ophir wants to base his continuum on the concept of "evil." The ninth and final chapter of *The Order of Evils*, "These Times," is an attempt to arrive at a non-Jewish "understanding," an understanding in which Auschwitz, too, will have a place. That is, it is an attempt to construct a conceptual continuum of "evils" that includes Auschwitz and allows it to be compared to other locales of catastrophe – Biafra, Kolyma, Hiroshima, and on and on – in a way that transcends the Jewish point of view and, in effect, nullifies it. According to Ophir, "understanding, in this context, doesn't mean reconstructing the experience or just analyzing the conditions that made it possible. It means grasping its novelty as a human experience that changes

---

[92] One example out of many: in Ian Kershaw's introduction to his biography of Hitler, where he sets forth his motives in writing the book, he notes, "It is surprising, in retrospective, for instance, how little the anti-Jewish policy and the genesis of the 'Final Solution' figured in such earlier biographers." Ian Kershaw, *Hitler, 1889–1936: Hubris* (London: Penguin, 1998), xiii.

the historical conditions of being human" (p. 523). It is an attempt to "give the catastrophe ontological meaning, not just to explain, in the manner of historians, the conditions that made it possible and the causes that generated it" (p. 527). There seems to be a difference, in his view, between historical and "ontological" conditions of possibility, although he does not really enlighten us as to what that difference is. At any rate, the understanding we are seeking "must begin from the place where the historical narrative ends, or from the place where it transcends itself and turns into an analysis of the kind or kinds of human existence that appeared within, and out of, the catastrophe, those for whose appearance the catastrophe was a necessary condition" (ibid.). So far so good, as the man who fell from the fiftieth floor said when he passed the twenty-fifth. Thus far, the argument sounds reasonable enough. But let us go further along Ophir's tortuous path.

It is indeed hard to talk about Auschwitz. There are numerous pitfalls awaiting those who try to do so: the sanctification and instrumentalization of it (on this Ophir, on p. 529, cites, of course, Tom Segev, Idith Zertal, and Moshe Zuckerman), the cynicism, and the clichés. But one cannot remain silent, among other reasons because that would enable the deniers to go about their work unhindered. How, then, should one speak of Auschwitz? "Only if one circumvents the sanctifying discourse and desecrates the name" (p. 530). Our old friend, the theological metaphor-*cum*-provocation serves to introduce the central historiographical claim: Auschwitz is not a distortion of the human, nor does it stand out among the long list of horrors human beings have committed. Rudolph Rummel has estimated that some 170 million people were killed by government action during the course of the twentieth century, Ophir points out, enumerating a number of the atrocities and mass murders that were committed. This brings him to his main conclusion. The "continuum" on which Auschwitz is placed is not one of distortion or outrage but of humanness: "If Auschwitz is a 'model,' this is surely not because it established a new quantitative apex of killing and destruction, in either absolute or relative numbers. If Auschwitz is a model, perhaps this is because it was not a symbol of human distortion and perversion but a symbol of human excellence, a model in which killing was brought to a perfection of efficiency and precision" (p. 531). Thus, like Agamben, Ophir thinks Auschwitz is a paradigm for what all of us, hangmen and victims, democratic and totalitarian regimes, death camps and "camps" in general, are: human. While others try to make of Auschwitz something divine, Ophir is trying to anthropomorphize or humanize it.

In an effort to concretize his general arguments, Ophir uses the concept of "superfluity." Evil always resides, as we have seen, in superfluous death (or suffering, or loss). The concept of evil is thus defined by superfluity. Hence, Auschwitz can be characterized by the utter superfluity of the killing of the Jews there. And what defines the essence of Nazism is that it turns this superfluity into necessity. As we have pointed out, there is not much new in these ideas, not even in their language, and to some extent they are even admissible. The same is not altogether clear in the case of the conclusion Ophir draws regarding Auschwitz: if we understand the uniqueness of Auschwitz as a function of its superfluity, he writes, "it is obvious that this singularity does not necessarily entail a claim to being the sole historical instance of its kind, and it is clear that it is not novel in moral terms" (p. 563).

Couching the matter in terms of "superfluity" is meant to make it less subjective, less phenomenological, and more "ontological" than speaking in terms of the motives of the murderers, thus supporting the contention that the killing done at Auschwitz and the suffering inflicted there have no special moral meaning. What distinguishes Auschwitz is the absoluteness of its superfluity, quantitatively speaking, in comparison with other, less absolute superfluities, but this difference, the reader is informed, carries no moral advantage. Yet things are not so simple. It is not at all clear, for example (and Ophir offers no argument to clarify this point), that superfluity can be quantified and, if so, how. It is also not really clear why placing Auschwitz at the far end of the continuum of superfluity has no moral meaning or why the limit Auschwitz represents should be so much more meaningful morally when defined otherwise. Furthermore, it is doubtful that the concept of superfluity can bear the theoretical weight Ophir places upon it. If not, the fact that this concept is so critical for his theorization of Auschwitz and the evil it represents means that his attempt to "rethink" Auschwitz is a failure. And given the centrality of rethinking Auschwitz in Ophir's scheme, his whole theory of evil could well be a failure too.

Defining "evil" with the concept of "superfluity" is a kind of inversion of the concept of utility or pleasure, and Ophir's ontology of evil is a sort of inverted utilitarianism. Like utilitarianism, it refuses to base its definition of what is moral and immoral on the concept of "intent." "Moral outrage is always the result of superfluous death" (p. 339 in the original Hebrew; mistranslated in the English version); accordingly, the evil of Auschwitz is also defined in terms of the perfectly superfluous death and suffering inflicted there rather than in terms of the intentions, motives, thoughts, or ideology of the perpetrators. But there is a difficulty here. Superfluous death is a common occurrence, and not only from the point of view of the dying person, for whom it is always superfluous. Sometimes death is terrifying and infuriating in its superfluity. But it is not always an outrage, much less a moral outrage.

The death that suddenly befell thousands of the inhabitants of Lisbon in the earthquake that destroyed the city in 1755 was absolutely superfluous, in that it brought no benefit to anyone. But it cannot be described as a moral outrage; aside from a reckoning with God, it had no moral meaning. The same is true, on a larger scale, of the victims of the recent tsunami in Southeast Asia. Even the superfluous death of a child in a car accident – if we assume no one was at fault and it was caused by an unforeseen mishap – can be described as an outrage only from a theological point of view.

It turns out, then, that the concept of "superfluity" is insufficient to define evil's conditions of possibility. The definition must therefore be circumscribed and constraints added: "[T]he superfluity of the evils … is determined according to the possibility and the price of their prevention, not according to the intentions of the massacre's authors, collaborators, or bystanders" (p. 562). Evil is not simply superfluity but superfluity that can be prevented at a reasonable price. Note: it is not that it is simply unnecessary but that it is unnecessary in a very specific sense: that it could have been prevented. But the fact that a given death is preventable does not, by itself, philosophically justify, much less necessitate, the obligation to prevent it. It is even less clear that one must be prepared to pay a price to prevent what is preventable. And how is preventable evil to be weighted against the price of preventing it? What would Ophir have said about *Sophie's Choice*, for example? The use of the term "moral outrage" suggests that the imperative of preventing death is in full force, even if we must sometimes prevent it "at any price." The concept of "moral outrage," a serious one, applies, not to that which is simply superfluous, but to that which is unacceptable and cannot be assented to under any circumstances and *therefore* must be prevented. From a moral point of view, the concept of "outrage" precedes that of "superfluity," and Ophir's argument is circular. It is not superfluity that defines outrage but the opposite; it is outrage that turns the superfluous – sometimes, as in the case where superfluity is preventable – into moral evil. In fact, the concept of superfluity itself becomes superfluous.

The deaths of thousands of people in the Lisbon earthquake were not an evil, because, even if they were superfluous, they could not have been prevented. But in a certain sense these deaths *could* have been prevented. Had the houses in Lisbon been planned and built differently, to withstand earthquakes of a certain magnitude on the Richter scale, many lives could have been saved. Is this claim anachronistic? Of course. But it shows that the concept of "superfluity" does not deliver the theoretical goods it promises. It does not describe an independent ontological object. Had the city fathers only been aware of the danger, and had they had the means of preparing for it and thus preventing those deaths, we could weigh the price of prevention and say that the deaths were superfluous and outrageous. Even then, the degree of superfluity and of outrageousness would be measured against the quality of knowledge, the technical sophistication, the economic power, the capacity to act politically, the neglect that allowed unsafe construction, and so on. The relative nature of the concept of "superfluity" also becomes apparent in light of the fact that death can serve a useful purpose for one person and be superfluous for another. For example, how are we to judge, on the basis of the concept of preventable superfluity, a death induced to enable organs to be transplanted and save a life? And how are we to judge the benefit Germans derived from the deaths of many Jews, for example, the tons of gold they extracted from the mouths of the dead? Should we conclude that the deaths of those who had healthy teeth were more superfluous than the deaths of those who had gold teeth? It turns out that Ophir does not entirely escape the subjectivist assumptions he had tried to reject and that the conceptual basis for the theory of the objective economy of evils is quite shaky. It turns out that the concept of "superfluity" is an intentional, subjective, relative one. What makes something superfluous is that we think it so, that there is someone for whom it is superfluous. Superfluity always has a context and is always in relation to the person for whom death, or whatever, is either superfluous or useful. Nothing is superfluous in the abstract, independently of the interests, desires, uses, ends, or benefits people pursue. From the point of view of eternity, or nature, it is not only that nothing is superfluous, just as nothing is really necessary or useful, but that these concepts are meaningless. In other words, the concept of "superfluity" cannot serve as the basis for an "ontology" of evil or, more simply put, for a concept of objective evil. "Superfluity" leaves us in the realm of the spiritualization of evil, no less and perhaps even more than the concept of "intent." Most of all, superfluous death is an outrage, because what Ophir wants to dispense with, the viewpoint of the dead, cannot be dispensed with.

The failure of the concept of superfluity is seen most clearly when applied to the understanding of Auschwitz. In what sense was the death of the Jews there completely superfluous, if this perfect superfluity depended on their death having been absolutely preventable? In what sense can the construction and use of the murderous gas chambers be described as preventable? Leaving aside the possibility that the Allies could have bombed them and thus at least slowed down the killing process, it is hard to see in what sense the Jews' death could be regarded as superfluous in that it could have been prevented at reasonable cost. It could have been prevented if the Nazis had not decided to exterminate them, that is, if they had not been Nazis; or if they had not had the cooperation of the inhabitants of the occupied countries; or if the victims had not been Jews. It seems to me quite difficult to draw from all this any particularly profound insight into the moral value of killing the Jews.

But that is not all. For Ophir, superfluity plays a semidialectical role: it defines not only the moral essence of evil (superfluity that should be prevented) but also the inner logic of how evil is committed. Auschwitz was not only superfluous; its superfluity was based on the Nazis having made the Jews absolutely superfluous. The superfluity of death is the basis of evil; the superfluity of life is the basis of the evil of totalitarianism. Like many other bad dialectics, this one turns on a misunderstanding of the multiple meanings of a term. The Hebrew term Ophir uses, *meyutar,* can mean a number of different things, of which "superfluous" is but one. For example, it can also mean "redundant" or "useless." A "redundant" thing is what Occam thought his razor should cut away, namely, something – a hypothesis, for example – not needed to reach a desired result. But this "cutting away" is metaphorical, not only because it is not people we are talking about, but because the superfluity is not actually harmful; it simply does not make any difference. "Superfluous," is stronger, implying something one would prefer to get rid of, while "useless," means ineffective. But when, for example, we say that something a person did was "be'emet *meyutar,*" "*quite* unnecessary," what we usually mean is that it was harmful, and it would have been better if he had not done it. We are not saying, in most cases, that it was forbidden, that is, should have been prevented, but there is unquestionably something more substantial here than mere superfluity.

The Jews in Auschwitz were not really superfluous, or not only so. Their superfluity cannot, by itself, explain the positive act of extermination or the absoluteness of the Nazis' devotion to their total elimination. Ophir has borrowed this usage of superfluity from Hannah Arendt, he tells us, citing a passage from her well-known, important book on totalitarianism (p. 569 in Ophir, pp. 154–155 in Arendt). But he misses the main point. Arendt is calling our attention to a real and significant trait of totalitarianism in general and Nazism in particular. But this trait (in the Nazi case) is paradoxical. She speaks of it in connection with the role of ideology in totalitarian regimes: on the one hand, ideology completely takes over the state and all life (naked or otherwise) within it; but on the other hand, ideology can be of no consequence at all, as we see in what happened to Röhm and his cohorts.[93] Ophir

---

[93] Ernst Röhm, a German officer in the First World War, was one of Hitler's earliest and most loyal allies. He headed the SA (Storm Troopers), the most militant, ideological element

might have done well to quote the preceding passage in Arendt: "What makes conviction or opinion of any sort so ridiculous and dangerous under totalitarian conditions is that totalitarian regimes take the greatest pride in having no need of them or of any human help of any kind. Men, insofar as they are more than animal reaction, and fulfillment of functions, are entirely superfluous to totalitarian regimes." Arendt is not speaking of extermination – which for her is the most terrible thing of all, something about which she really has nothing to say except that it should never happen under any circumstances – but of the utter cynicism and nihilism of totalitarianism. What she sees as utterly superfluous in this system is everything human – thought, and commitment of any sort – not existence per se. What Arendt is trying to show is the exact opposite of what Ophir (and Agamben and others like him) mean by their notion of the "continuum": there is no continuity between totalitarian and democratic regimes, because the basis of democracy, the nonsuperfluity of the human, is the opposite of that of totalitarianism. In one place (p. 8 in *The Origins of Totalitarianism*), she writes that totalitarian rule is impossible in countries with small populations. It needs people, many people, more than democracy does. It needs them so that it can kill some of them. But, in her view, this superfluity is not merely the opposite of the nonsuperfluity of human beings under democracy, for all its flaws and weaknesses, but something essentially different. In any event, extermination, especially the extermination of the Jews, is another matter. The Nazis did not exterminate Jews because they saw them as superfluous but for other reasons, and "thought" was not one of them – another of Arendt's main theses.

Ophir presumes to "refine" Arendt's concept of superfluity, but in fact he simply lifts it out of its context (as they say), thereby missing the point. His reason for doing this may be the pressing and characteristic need he has to construct a continuum on which both Auschwitz and, say, the closures and restrictions imposed by Israel on the Palestinian population can both be placed. His philosophical failure stems from a desire to harness thought to an attempt to disprove what cannot be disproved, the special nature and significance of the extermination of the Jews. Nazism, in his view, was "the final extermination of the moral, not because it exterminated the Jews but because it identified superfluity in specific groups of others

in the Nazi movement, which achieved great military and political power before Hitler's accession, and even more during the first year of his regime. In 1934 he and many of his officers were liquidated in what came to be known as the Night of the Long Knives. On Röhm, see, e.g., Kershaw, *Hitler*, 172–175, 499–517.

ruled by it and posited these others as superfluous" (p. 569). But it was
not morality for which the Nazis sought a final solution; it was the Jewish
question. It was not morality that the Nazis wiped out; it was the majority
of the Jews of Europe. Morality, of which Ophir provides a good example,
is alive and well – indeed, it is handsomely remunerated; in Europe, the
Jews are gone.

In four or five quick pages, Ophir sums up the event symbolized by
Auschwitz. We should mention here that he has nothing especially interesting to say about it. Perhaps this is because what is really important to
him about it is the other matter to which discussion of Auschwitz quickly
leads him: Israel. He quotes (again, inaccurately) something Yehuda Bauer
once said, that the Jewish historian has a unique role to play: reconstructing
Jewish life as it was on the eve of the great destruction and while the destruction was underway. Ophir cites this in order to register a general complaint
about the "division of labor" that has, as it were, freed Israeli historians of
the need to wonder at the fact that an entire society can be mobilized for
genocide. The truth is, of course, that Israeli historians, and not only historians, have thought a great deal about this; but Ophir's complaint gives
him the opportunity to express what is really bothering him, it seems: that
the children and grandchildren of the victims – they and no one else – have
a special responsibility to understand this evil. So in the end Auschwitz can,
nonetheless, be invoked in support of moral attitudes or political stances.
In any case, the children of the victims not only have special responsibilities
but also a special destiny: "A historical coincidence has turned their society,
the society within which I am living and writing, into a terrible laboratory
testing the response of the survivors and their offspring to the emergence of
conditions that allow – with their full, partial, or tacit collaboration – both
the industrial mass production of death and the precise and detailed selection of its victims" (p. 542). No more and no less.

We should ponder this statement, perhaps even deconstruct it. Can we
say that it is entirely false? "Industrial mass production of death"? "Precise
and detailed selection of ... victims"? After all, Auschwitz does not exactly
resemble Rafah, Jenin, or even Deir Yassin – and even Ophir is not really
claiming it does. And the "murderous" gas chambers that were used at
Auschwitz – and they actually were – are not really the same as targeted
assassinations, for example. Even the inspections and refusals Palestinians
undergo at the checkpoints are not identical with what Dr. Mengele did at
Auschwitz. But Ophir does not tell us this. He merely tells us about "the
emergence of conditions" making industrial killing possible. How can
one argue with such a claim? What counterarguments could be brought to

disprove it? What exactly does it mean? But in any event, the point is not whether the claim is true but the fact that it is used to make an accusation. If this were just an apocalyptic warning, one could either be impressed or shake one's head, according to predisposition and common sense. But this is more than a warning; Ophir is leveling an accusation. Mass murder is still only a possibility, something that could happen, a short- or long-range threat (or promise). But the guilt is already here, and it is utterly real. It is so heavy – after all, we are speaking of systematic, industrialized slaughter – that it can be described only in terms of Auschwitz. Legally, it might be difficult to sustain an accusation on the basis of a mere possibility (after all, not even intent has been proved here); but we are dealing with ontology and ontological meaning, and as every second-rate ontologist knows, possibility is a part of reality. Israel is already on the continuum of evil, and if it is not uprooted altogether, Israel is bound to move along the continuum until the worst comes to pass.

Over and above what can be said about this Auschwitz-in-the-offing apocalypse, it raises another question of fundamental importance. This question has to do with the claim regarding Auschwitz's "human" character, the claim that it was no less than the quintessence of humanness. Ophir apparently regards this argument as having special philosophical weight. Leaving aside the philosophical pessimism that could be behind this, we should point out here that he is not the first to make this argument. To be precise, he carries to an extreme (more rhetorical than philosophical) certain kinds of arguments raised in the literature that deals, directly or indirectly, with the Holocaust and other mass crimes. To take one example, Christopher Browning, in his book *Ordinary Men: Reserve Police Battalion 101 and the Final Solution in Poland*,[94] tells the story of a group of German policemen who carried out, with great efficiency, a lengthy series of systematic killing operations against Jews in Poland. Much has been written about the mode of killing they employed, which was initiated before the gas-extermination industry got underway and continued alongside it: the slaughter of hundreds of thousands of men, women, and children in or near their own towns. What distinguishes this book is that it is based on the highly detailed testimony of the perpetrators themselves. These were, as the title implies, "ordinary men." They were not particularly young or especially committed to the Nazi ideology, but family men who, in normal times, would just be trying to make a living – ordinary men indeed.

---

[94] Christopher R. Browning, *Ordinary Men: Reserve Police Battalion 101 and the Final Solution in Poland* (New York: HarperCollins, 1992).

As Yehuda Melzer, the editor and publisher of the book's Hebrew version and himself a philosopher, writes in his foreword, the name of the reserve unit, Battalion 101, is like a slap in the face, a blow to the solar plexus. There is an immediate association with Ariel Sharon's famed Commando Unit 101, which, in the early 1950s, carried out reprisal raids that became a model for later such operations but also sparked a discussion of war crimes and the killing of civilians. And in fact, not long after the book was published in Israel, many letters appeared in the newspapers in which the obvious comparison was made: here in Israel, too, ordinary people do terrible things: in Hebron, at the checkpoints, throughout the occupied territories. (As a rule, the writers began with the accepted disclaimer: it isn't the same thing, and Hebron is not Ponar.) These associations, as we have said, are inevitable, and there is nothing wrong with them. In this case, it is a way of expressing moral outrage that is undoubtedly justified to a large extent. What is happening in Hebron is indeed outrageous, unacceptable, and unforgivable. On the other hand, people who are concerned with such things could be expected to apply the same comparison, and the same moral outrage, to Hamas's suicide bombings, for example. These, too, are, as a rule, carried out by ordinary people.

But philosophically speaking, such comparisons have a serious pitfall, one that is less obvious in the case of Browning but right out in the open in that of Ophir. In an appendix to the Hebrew edition of his book, Browning takes issue with Daniel Goldhagen over what Yehuda Melzer, in a felicitous phrase, calls "the adjectival question": to whom should the adjective "ordinary" be applied, "men," as Browning would have it, or "the Germans," as Goldhagen asserts? Were these murders committed by "ordinary men" or by "ordinary Germans"? In a book published a few years ago that made use of the same empirical material Browning had used and aroused fervent responses pro and con,[95] Goldhagen tries to show that, indeed, many ordinary people, essentially the majority of Germans, willingly participated, either actively or by assent, in the extermination of the Jews. But in his view, the fact that these ordinary people were, first and foremost, Germans was crucial. German history had, in a unique way, unlike that of other peoples, turned the Germans into willing accomplices in mass murder. Browning denies this. He sees the quality of "ordinariness" as universal. The men of Brigade 101 took part in the slaughter, some enthusiastically and some simply obediently (and some even refused to some extent to participate in the actual killing), not because

---

[95] Daniel Jonah Goldhagen, *Hitler's Willing Executioners: Ordinary Germans and the Holocaust* (New York: Knopf, 1996).

they were ordinary Germans but because they were ordinary men. In other words, the lessons of this story apply to all of us.

Goldhagen's book has been widely criticized (and widely read), not only for this central thesis but also for the way it is couched. Some think – no doubt with considerable justification – that the book's scholarship is not rigorous enough. It is not careful in its methodology or precise in its terminology. Nevertheless, in a narrow perspective, there is more to be said for Goldhagen's thesis than for Browning's. It is safe to assume that many, perhaps most people, finding themselves in circumstances similar to those of Reserve Brigade 101, would act as they did. But – and this is crucial – the circumstances in which those "ordinary men" found themselves were the circumstances of the Nazi regime, with its propaganda and indoctrination and, in particular, its policy of exterminating the Jews. And if these were unprecedented circumstances, as indeed they were, it is no wonder that the behavior of the policemen was unprecedented as well. One need not make the essentialist assumption that there was in this instance some age-old, murderous German entity or essence. Goldhagen himself, incidentally, does not think so; in his view, Nazism no longer poses a threat to the German people. But even without making the essentialist assumption, one can recognize the specificity of the German experience, as it is sometimes referred to. It is a historical, not a metaphysical specificity (or, again, uniqueness!), but that does not make the Germans any less specific (or unique). In the end, it was only the Germans who tried to destroy European Jewry and nearly succeeded. There is no escaping this simple fact. Nor need its significance be downplayed.

Browning's thesis would seem to carry with it a general anthropological and moral warning, an insight into the moral character of human beings in general: were we to find ourselves in the same circumstances – you, we, everyone, but especially, it turns out, Israelis and Jews – we would behave no differently. Possibly. And possibly not. How can one know this or prove it one way or the other? We might mention here that several decades ago a well-known attempt was made to answer this question scientifically. Between 1960 and 1963, the American psychologist Stanley Milgram did a series of laboratory experiments testing the willingness of "ordinary men" to carry out orders to do things that were patently immoral. These experiments, and the resulting findings, have become a classic example of social-psychological research, much commented on and interpreted, and to this day they continue to be both interesting and disturbing. To sum up briefly, Milgram created a situation in which people in "authority" instructed others to inflict extreme pain on a third party. The high degree of readiness shown by the subjects – a majority, in fact, complied – astonished Milgram himself and continues to surprise others who have since studied this phenomenon.[96]

It is not clear how much one can generalize from the Milgram experiment to the situation Browning describes. What is clear is that, statistically, a very high percentage of Germans who were confronted with the choice between killing and not killing did kill. In fact, almost all of them. Although this is impossible to prove, the Milgram experiment, and episodes like Kafr Kassem and My Lai,[97] show that Germans are not the only players in the terrible game of killing under orders. One may assume that Milgram's findings give us a characteristic statistical distribution, that is, that in any group of people in a similar situation, the percentage who agreed to kill would be similar to that in the German police brigade. Such "if" statements are called, in philosophical parlance, "counterfactual." They have interesting logical properties and can play an epistemological role. Under certain conditions, they may give us a clearer understanding of the reality to which they run counter. What aspect of that reality we want to understand better is up to us; in this instance, the reality is one in which the criminals were Germans, not Jews or Israelis. Does the statement "If we/I had been there, we/I would also have committed murder" have any real epistemic value? Does opening up a counterfactual possibility – such as Browning does by implication and Ophir does explicitly in predicting that the Israeli occupation will lead to exterminating the Palestinians – give us a better means of understanding reality? Does it help us to fathom what the German policemen did in Poland if, in addition to describing their actions in detail and emphasizing their ordinariness, we also make this "if" claim, putting ourselves in their place? Shall we understand the occupation better if, as Ophir suggests, we put ourselves or our children in the counterfactual situation of industrial killers of the Palestinians?

There are good reasons for saying that the answer to these questions is negative, that such hypotheses do not give us a clearer understanding of

---

[96] See Stanley Milgram, *Obedience to Authority* (New York: Harper & Row, 1974); and Adi Parush's instructive summary in *Tziyut, aharayut, vehahok hapelili: Sugyot mishpatiot bire'i pilosofi* (Obedience, Responsibility, and Criminal Law: Legal Issues in a Philosophical Perspective) (Tel Aviv: Papyrus, 1996), ch. 1. Parush deals here, and throughout the book, with legal and philosophical questions arising from criminal obedience – as this type of crime has recently been called – in relation to the shocking 1956 massacre in Kafr Kassem. Milgram bases his findings on Hannah Arendt's thesis of the banality of evil and her analysis of the personality of Adolf Eichmann (Parush, ibid., 42–49). The third chapter of the present book deals with Arendt and Eichmann.

[97] The village in Vietnam where a unit of United States Marines massacred dozens of men, women, and children.

ourselves, the conflict, or its victims. But what is worse, and what undermines Ophir's argument (and, to some extent, Browning's), is that he turns his counterfactual hypothesis, his imaginary Nazi-Israeli-Palestinian apocalypse, into the basis of a factual accusation, a judgment about the here and now. What makes Browning effective is that he arouses in his readers a sense of guilt and insecurity: had we been there, would we not have become murderers too?[98] This is an unsettling thought, and his choice of rhetoric leads us straight to it. Yet this guilt is ill-founded, because we were not there, and we did not commit murder. Browning's description puzzles us and provokes us to grave suspicions about human nature in general: is this what people are really like? This was Primo Levi's question, too (although he asked it about the victims, in particular the prisoners and *Muselmänner*). The answer, apparently, is yes, although no less and perhaps more important is that it was, in fact, the Germans who were there and committed the murders. As we have seen, Ophir thinks such behavior is, indeed, the very essence of being human (which is not quite the same as saying that, yes, we would all have acted as the "ordinary men" did); but he goes a small but significant step further than Browning: he transposes the universal guilt of being human into the more focused guilt of being Israeli. The continuity between Browning's argument and Ophir's thus enables us to grasp deconstructively the meaning of what the latter is doing. He exploits the terrible story, one small part of which is related by Browning, and the astonishment, incomprehension, and shame it arouses, in order to direct a harsh accusation against Israel and Israeli society. He turns what is, at bottom, nothing more than a counterfactual reflection into an extrapolation from our present situation (bad enough in itself) to a foregone conclusion, as it were. But this prophecy is no less counterfactual than Browning's implied "if" arguments, and, like them, it cannot serve as the basis of a moral judgment. To raise the counterfactual possibility of a systematic slaughter of Palestinians on the basis of the factual slaughter of Jews by the Germans is a way to place blame for a crime that has not yet been committed. And it almost certainly never will be.

Never will be? Ophir thinks it already has. What he predicted in *The Order of Evils* has come to pass. Or so he says in the introduction to *Zman emet: Intifadat Al-Aksa vehasmol hayisraeli* (Real Time: The Al-Aksa Uprising and the Israeli Left),[99] a collection of articles he edited just after the second Palestinian uprising broke out. This uprising did not embarrass or confuse him or those he included in his book. They knew exactly what

[98] See also Parush, *Tziyut, aharayut, vehahok hapelili*, 14.
[99] Jerusalem: Keter, 2001.

would happen – perhaps because he had already established for them, as he has for us, the conceptual continuum on which Auschwitz and the Israeli occupation could be considered together, thus showing what was in store. In the global, well-nigh cosmic economy of evils Ophir tries to catalog, one stands out above all the rest: "the Occupation." This, not Auschwitz, becomes the code word for the ultimate evil. Still, we must remember Auschwitz, not in order to rehash it ad nauseam but to give "the Occupation" its proper moral and ontological weight. With its mythic proportions, it is no wonder that this evil has only a mythic remedy. In one way or another, this means abolishing the political expression of Jewish nationhood and eliminating Jewish national identity. It is just the solution advocated by the Vieille Taupe circle.

THE EICHMANN TRIAL AND THE ISRAELI CATASTROPHE

Another member of the community of Holocaust abusers is Idith Zertal. In a series of publications, the most recent being a volume already translated into many languages,[100] she investigates the Israeli Holocaust "discourse," focusing on its role in shaping Israeli identity. In its main outlines, the picture she paints is very much like that painted by Boaz Evron, Ophir, Zuckerman, and their comrades, and it serves the same purpose: the use of the Holocaust as a ploy in an ideological, political, and cultural battle. As far as one can tell, Zertal's agenda is not explicitly anti-Zionist, but it is clearly on the continuum (to use Ophir's term) of denial, obliteration of memory, and disparagement of Israel and Israelis. Zertal's book, unlike those of Zuckerman and Grodzinsky, is written in a cultivated Hebrew and shows professionalism and historiographical acumen. But in her case, too, the picture is clouded by ideological resentment, and rigorous scholarship becomes pseudoscholarship, which enables her to be clever, to manipulate facts and interpretations, to mingle truth and fiction, and to play games with what is said, unsaid, ignored, or simply not recognized. It also thumbs its nose at a rich and wide-ranging scholarly literature. Zertal uses a lot of up-to-date jargon to construct a theory, the main virtue of which is that it cannot be disproved – not that it is necessarily valid. Thus, for example, the fact that a well-known scholar like Benedict Anderson is echoed in the following statement does

---

[100] I. Zertal *Ha'umah ve'hamavet. Historia, Zikaron ve'Politika* (The Nation and Death. History, Memory, and Politics) (Tel Aviv: Am Oved, 2002); translated as *Israel's Holocaust and the Politics of Nationhood* (Cambridge: Cambridge University Press, 2005). References are to the English edition.

not make it a scholarly one: "An essential stage in the formation and shaping of a national community is its perception [of itself] as a trauma-community, a 'victim-community,' and the creation of a pantheon to its dead martyrs, in whose images the nation's sons and daughters see the reflection of their ideal selves" (p. 2). One could show the falsity of this statement, but who has the patience? Yet the notion that one can speak of Israel's memory of the Holocaust in such terms is not only baseless; it is malicious. Zertal brings little empirical evidence, and what she does cite is careless and tendentious, serving to shore up sweeping generalizations and imaginary edifices. Like the omniscient narrator who sees into the recesses of the mind of his imaginary hero, she tells us the hidden motives and thoughts of the subjects of her research. The main point is to set up, on the shaky basis of this ostensible research, a moral, even theological superstructure, meant, in the last analysis, to accuse. Not to uncover historical truth or even to criticize, but to establish guilt and identify the guilty.

More than a thesis or theory, Zertal's book is a collection of articles (published at different times and in different places), the organizing principle of which is the notion that Israelis as a people have developed a sense of victimhood around the trauma of the Holocaust. This is the local version of a pattern that is universal in the formation of national groups and thus provides a key to unraveling the deeper character of the Israelis. But even if this pattern does not in every case produce a nation that is morally flawed – the Danes, for example, have apparently not turned their victimhood into a tool of wrongdoing – in our case it is a source of much misconduct. It is, in fact, the source of all the Jewish state's sins and distortions. For example: "According to circumstances of time and place, the Holocaust victims were brought to life again and again and became a central function in Israeli political deliberation, particularly in the context of the Israeli-Arab conflict, and especially at moments of crisis and conflagration, namely, in wartime" (p. 4). Because it is Israel that was guilty of all those wars – the myth of power and irrational existential fears drove it to belligerency and occupation – the Holocaust, or the instrumentalization of it, is the source of all the evil. We see here the same, old, false dialectic: in the name of the Holocaust, as it were; out of opposition to the outrageous use of it to bad ends; out of the shame of having made it serve the army, militarism, "the nation and death"; out of moral resentment at its trivialization and commercialization, the Holocaust is enlisted in a polemic against Israel, not just a particular Israeli policy but the Israeli character as such and the bases, as it were (have we not already referred to the "victim community"?), of Israelis' collective identity.

The tone is set by pronouncements like the following, which are meant not only as statements of fact or even "interpretations" of facts, but also as moral judgments: "In relation to the Holocaust the Zionist collective [*sic*] in Palestine had not lived up to the demands it made of others in the face of the Jewish catastrophe. In contrast to its self-image, it did not risk its all, as did the Polish disciples of the Zionist movement, in order to try and save its fellow Jews from destruction" (p. 29). Once again, the question of rescue is turned, offhandedly and frivolously, into an indictment. Once again, we see the characteristic discourse of the community of opprobrium, a recycling of the same concerns and arguments that recur, in much the same terms and, above all, in the same spirit, driven by the same self-righteousness, the same contempt for and arrogance toward anyone who disagrees, the same obliviousness to the complexity of the question, and, especially, the same total alienation from its painfulness. Zertal's argument trivializes the Holocaust much more than do the tactics she criticizes. Her description of the way the leaders of the prestate Jewish community in Palestine related to the Holocaust makes a caricature of what was, in fact, one of the weightiest moral and political dilemmas leaders have ever faced anywhere. Out of ignorance or malevolence, Zertal tries to minimize the fact that what hung in the balance for people like Ben-Gurion was the most difficult decision imaginable. As we saw in the case of Grodzinsky, there is some disagreement about the facts and about what decision Ben-Gurion actually made. But even if he was impervious to the cry for help from Europe (and according to other readings, this is far from clear), what is truly obscene is the way Zertal attacks him.

Even if we assume Ben-Gurion decided, in the end, to turn all available resources and efforts to establishing the state, this does not justify the terrible accusation Zertal and others have leveled at him. Of course, that decision is debatable. But one might have expected a historian like Zertal to take a more historical approach, that is, to show greater understanding of the way such decisions ought to be analyzed, the factors that should be taken into account. Perhaps we need not expect her to be as indulgent as she is when she portrays as morally relative the charges against the kapos and other collaborators with the Germans in the camps and ghettos; but the utter lack of forgiveness she shows toward Ben-Gurion and the leadership of the Yishuv and the state could be an indication that what really motivates her is not just scholarly curiosity. Her historical understanding leaves off where the motives of "the Zionists" are concerned. Perhaps because she herself is so immersed in rhetoric, she cannot see past the rhetoric of others (e.g., Ben-Gurion or Berl Katznelson) to the historical, political, and moral realities with which they lived and which they helped shape. The reader gets the impression that the behavior of the Zionist leadership was intolerably frivolous or that they acted out of wickedness and a monstrously selfish disregard for the terrible suffering of their brethren being incinerated in Europe. On the other hand, Zertal denies any moral stature or moral judgment – in fact, any moral substance at all – to the amorphous community of "Israelis" who were so easily taken in by the cynical, malevolent manipulations of the Zionist agents, as she calls them, and their leaders. This approach (a legacy of historical materialism?) is also to be found, by the way, in her book *Zehavam shel hayehudim* (The Jews' Gold),[101] where she treats the displaced persons as nonsubjects with no will of their own.

Israel's Holocaust and the Politics of Nationhood revolves around the Eichmann trial, which serves as the main source of evidence for Zertal's indictment. Two important chapters are devoted to the trial, chapters in which she displays her remarkable ability not to be confused by facts. For, as she tells us, she is not interested in the "respective historical events themselves" that led from the trial to the Six-Day War but only in the "discursive dimensions" of these two occurrences (p. 92). For her, the Eichmann trial was the watershed in the formation of the Israeli victim-community. Until then, Israeli society, which had just emerged from a bloody war of survival, had been deaf and blind to the Holocaust survivors in its midst. And if the trial did not "break the officially prescribed silence concerning the Holocaust," at least it raised discussion of it to a new plane (p. 138 in the Hebrew edition). Zertal has no real proof to offer of the charge of indifference. She makes it again and again in more or less the same words. Perhaps it is because, as an expert on narratives, she knows that anything repeated often enough comes to seem like the truth, or perhaps she knows others have already done the work for her and that the narrative about the suppression of the memory of the Holocaust has already gained enough of a foothold that it need only be stated to be accepted. It might be appropriate here to quote Hanna Yablonka, another historian of the Eichmann trial, who investigated the matter and found that, "in complete contrast to the widely held attitude that the Holocaust survivors constituted a marginal community in Israel before the Eichmann trial and to a certain extent after it, the truth is that, due largely to their demographic attributes, from the moment of their arrival in Israel the survivors were an exceptionally active

---

[101] Translated as *From Catastrophe to Power: The Holocaust Survivors and the Emergence of Israel* (Berkeley: University of California Press, 1998).

and – more importantly – influential group of immigrants."[102] No doubt the Holocaust was not discussed in the same way after the trial as it had been before, either in Israel or elsewhere. The trial clearly had a tremendous impact, radically transforming attitudes toward the Holocaust not only here but also in Europe, the United States, and elsewhere. But there was no "officially prescribed silence," certainly not in Israel of the 1950s, where the Shoah was already ubiquitous, though as yet only under the surface and without the organized and institutionalized memorialization that came later, largely under the impact of the trial.

In any event, after the trial and as a result of it, things changed; no one disputes this. The Holocaust was now not only ubiquitous but openly so. But only, of course – and this is Zertal's great contribution – as a result of manipulation and instrumentalization. We Israelis thus find ourselves in a bind, passive and infantilized, the victims a double manipulation: if we are constrained to keep silent, it will be a crime against those who perished, for they and their suffering will be forgotten; but if we feel compelled to talk about the Holocaust and keep the memory of it alive, we will also be committing a crime against the victims, because we will thereby be instrumentalizing them and using their memory and that of their suffering in order to send our children to kill Arabs. Either way, there is no way to get Israeli society, Zionism, the Jewish Agency, or the establishment off the hook. And certainly not Ben-Gurion. It is he, in Zertal's story of the trial, who embodies absolute evil. He serves as the ultimate anti-antimetaphor (to borrow her expression) for probing the innermost nature of the state he established and ran, for seeing it as it actually is: a Holocaust-exploitation factory. Zertal presents the Eichmann trial as a one-man show, Ben-Gurion's personal undertaking, without (in her typical fashion) bringing any real proof. She contents herself with repeating this charge ad nauseam, buttressed with quotes that do not really substantiate her accusations. The trouble is, the facts are quite otherwise. Thus, for example, she presents the decision to kidnap Eichmann and bring him to Israel as having been made by one man, and she sees the roots of it in the Kasztner trial. At that time, Ben-Gurion and his party (Mapai) had suffered a tremendous blow that was the beginning of their historic downfall. The Eichmann trial, she asserts, "was intended as, and indeed became, the great redress for the Kasztner affair, the show of power of the

---

[102] See Hanna Yablonka, *The State of Israel v. Adolf Eichmann* (New York: Schocken, 2004). 6. Yechiam Weitz, Anita Shapira, and Dalia Ofer, for example, do not accept the myth of the organized suppression of the memory of the Holocaust before the Eichmann trial.

new [Israel], 'another' Israel." And, in case we have missed the point, she explains, in a footnote, that the reference is to the expression "another Germany." It was "Ben-Gurion's last great national undertaking" (p. 90, see also 103ff.). Do other historians see it completely differently? A lady of Zertal's stature is not to be deterred by them from her mission of exposing the evil Ben-Gurionist discourse.

For Zertal, the trial was almost entirely the handiwork of Ben-Gurion. He gave the order to capture Eichmann and "was the architect, director, and stage manager of the preparations for the trial and the trial itself." He thus became the "guiding spirit in the process of creating the new Israeli discourse of the Holocaust from the perspective of power" (p. 96). As we have said, the facts were evidently completely otherwise. So Hanna Yablonka claims, at any rate, in the book we have cited, where she describes the almost accidental way the decision to capture Eichmann and bring him to Israel was taken and the utter unpreparedness (so typically Israeli) of the establishment and of Ben-Gurion himself for the great event. The same conclusion is reached in an unpublished study of the way the media, especially Israel Radio, treated the trial. If someone had really intended to stage the Eichmann trial as a show trial, the preparations for it were amateurish in the extreme.[103] The pressure for press coverage came "from below," and in fact it would seem that in this case not only did the calf want to suckle more than the cow wanted to give suck but the calf did not even get its fill. Thus, there were only a few direct broadcasts from the courtroom in Jerusalem's Beit Ha'am. One of the amazing facts this research has brought to light, by the way, is that the direct broadcasts were undertaken by a radio staffer, Nakdimon Rogel, only by skirting the opposition of other authorities. Of course, Zertal makes no mention of any of this.

The way Zertal speaks about Ben-Gurion is typical of her historiographical approach. She asserts as a proven fact, an indisputable historical truth, that it was Ben-Gurion who ran the trial, that he turned it into a show trial, and that, even before Eichmann was captured, he decided that the trial would have a "discourse-shaping" educational significance. But she brings not a shred of proof for this assertion, except for repeated quotes

---

[103] Ora Herman, "Shiddurim min haplaneta ha'aheret: Mishpat Eichmann, hamemsad, ukhlei hatikshoret ha'elektroni'im" (Broadcasts from the Other Planet: The Eichmann Trial, the Establishment, and the Electronic Media) (master's thesis, Hebrew University of Jerusalem, 2003). The organizers of the trial, she maintains, were constantly afraid they would be suspected of staging a show trial. "In the end ... there was no proper television or radio coverage, but this fact did not prevent the idea [they] feared most from taking root, that the Eichmann Trial was in every respect a show trial" (p. 20).

from an article by the British historian Hugh Trevor-Roper in the *Sunday Times* of April 9, 1961,[104] and observations on the trial and on Ben-Gurion by Hannah Arendt. Incidentally, Arendt herself relied on Trevor-Roper's article to say what Zertal is now saying. To complete the picture, Zertal cites Ben-Gurion's own written and oral remarks, and it is on this basis that she constructs her thesis of Ben-Gurion's manipulation and conspiracy. As usual in the *resentiment* crowd, she recycles arguments made by others in the group, such as the claim that the Kasztner trial influenced Ben-Gurion's decision to capture Eichmann, a claim she seems to have taken from Tom Segev. He does not prove that contention in his book either, relying instead on some kind of mysterious insight into Ben-Gurion's mind and on no less mysterious scholarly knowledge that the latter recognized that "something was required to unite Israeli society – some collective experience, one that would be gripping, purifying, patriotic, a national catharsis," and he wanted to exonerate Mapai in the wake of the Kasztner trial (*The Seventh Million*, p. 328).

   Zertal's treatment of the Trevor-Roper article is interesting in and of itself. On the one hand, she draws from it the claim about Ben-Gurion's role in bringing Eichmann to Israel and putting him on trial, that is, she regards him as a reliable source in this matter; but at the same time, she also presents Trevor-Roper as an obedient, unquestioning lackey who relays the great manipulator's message without comment (*Israel's Holocaust and the Politics of Nationhood*, pp. 104–105, inter alia). The Holocaust dimension, she says, "was inserted systematically into the collective talk and imagination in Israel" after the trial (and in the lead-up to the Six-Day War; p. 115). Let us assume that such things were, in fact, "inserted" into our consciousness, that we, our teachers, our parents, our journalists and jurists – all of us except Zertal and her cronies, that is – were manipulated by Ben-Gurion; but can the same be said of as eminent a historian of the Second World War as Trevor-Roper? No doubt there was something almost satanic about Ben-Gurion. And because he is the anti-antimetaphor of Zionism and the fully formed State of Israel, we evidently will have to conclude that they, too, are almost satanic.

---

[104] That is, not, as she says, on the day it opened but two days beforehand (Zertal, *Israel's Holocaust*, 141, 146). This is just a detail, of course, but it shows how seriously Zertal took her work. Although a full translation of the article was published in the newspaper *Davar* on the first day of the trial, Trevor-Roper published several other articles, not translated, during the days that followed, and Zertal does not even mention them. They shed further light on his position. I thank Ora Herman for making photocopies of these articles available to me.

Discourse theory enables Zertal to understand everything: "The desire to legitimize the will to power was the subtext of the entire trial and of the discourse which grew out of it" (p. 108). This desire, then, underlay all (!) the aims of the trial. How does she know? Because Ben-Gurion, in one of his speeches, made a "mythical link" between the Land of Israel and heroic power, or he said the Jews had to be taught they were no longer like sheep to be led to the slaughter but a people that could fight back. Dayan, for his part, derived from the trial "the sanctification of every square inch of the soil of [the land of] Israel for Jewish settlement" (p. 109). This, of course, leads directly to the growth of the Israeli cult of power and the Six-Day War. The rest is sheer pornography: "Ofer Feniger,[105] ... one of the golden youths of the Israeli Zionist utopia," writes, in a letter to his girlfriend Yael, that, in the face of the horror and impotence, "the terrible need grows within me to be strong; tearfully strong, strong and ferocious like a sword; serene and cruel" (p. 112). According to Zertal, this letter was written after the Eichmann trial and because of it. In fact, it was written after a visit to the Holocaust museum at Kibbutz Lohamei Hageta'ot (the name means "Ghetto Fighters"), both of which were established by survivors of the Warsaw ghetto – who were also, incidentally, Ben-Gurion's political rivals – long before the Eichmann trial. She also fails to quote the author's statement that he is alone among his friends in having these feelings. For her, he is a paradigm, and "four years after this letter was written, Ofer Feniger was killed during the 1967 war, in the battle for Jerusalem" (ibid.).

We thus leap from a discussion of the Eichmann trial, to the Six-Day War and the phony, contrived talk of imminent catastrophe that preceded it, to the obsession with the Holocaust that characterized the Israeli mentality before, during, and after the war. Israel would soon begin to settle the territories, and then Rabin would be assassinated. To be sure, Zertal does not concern herself with the "unfolding of events" but only with the discourse, yet the unfolding becomes clear from the discourse: Ben-Gurion kidnapped Eichmann and had him tried; the "subtext" of the trial was a will to power; Israelis saw the war threat as one of annihilation (meaning, they, too, were after power); Feniger died in the war. Ben-Gurion, then, by virtue of the show he had put on in the courtroom, was guilty of Feniger's death, all the more so of the messianic madness that seized so many after the war, and, apparently, of Rabin's death as well (pp. 197ff.). The Six-Day War itself was,

[105] Ofer Feniger was born in 1942 and grew up in Kibbutz Giv'at Hayim. After serving in the regular army, he studied painting and sculpture. In 1966, he married the woman to whom this letter is addressed.

of course, an unnecessary war. Israel faced no real threat, and ultimately
it was Holocaust hysteria that explains Israel's having launched it. That's
all there is to it. We have the key to understanding the history – sorry, the
discourse – of the past fifty years: Ben-Gurion's decision to capture and try
Eichmann. It is hard to believe that something like this can be written, let
alone read, translated, taken seriously, and quoted as authoritative.[106]

But the *pièce de résistance*, the outstanding example of the way Zertal's
discourse works, is yet to come: "The Holocaust also served [Ben-Gurion]
in his secret drive for the development of the ultimate weapon – an Israeli
nuclear bomb – starting in the early 1950s" (p. 99). The Holocaust, the
ultimate weapon (Final Solution?),[107] Ben-Gurion – thus is a discourse
concocted. Zertal stresses the importance for her argument of a letter Ben-
Gurion sent President John Kennedy in 1963. In it, he tried to persuade the
president, who saw preventing the spread of nuclear weapons as one of his
main foreign-policy aims (Zertal does not say this), not to oppose Israel's
efforts to acquire them. Ben-Gurion does mention there, among many other
things, the Jewish experience of the Holocaust, and it was mainly he (along
with Shimon Peres, it seems) who was responsible for Israel's acquiring a
nuclear military option. But what Zertal is implying, both by the context of
her remarks and by the way they are couched, is that Ben-Gurion's controversial decision to give Israel this option stemmed from an irrational lust for
power and entailed a manipulative use of the Holocaust on a massive scale.
Nowhere in Zertal's work do we find anything remotely resembling a real
discussion of the important question of Israel and nuclear power, but there
is a good deal of subtext: Ben-Gurion's unbridled cynicism, the manipulativeness and blackmail, the catastrophic will to power, the construction of
an all-encompassing Holocaust neurosis, and the shaping of reality to fit
it. There is also the obvious superfluousness of the Israeli bomb and, consequently, the absolute moral evil it entails. Out of all this there emerges
an Israeli threat to world peace, the apocalypse that, according to Ophir,
is waiting in the wings – and it all stems directly from the "Holocaust discourse" Ben-Gurion invented when he decided to kidnap Eichmann.

Concealing and ignoring facts are not necessarily the most interesting ways of creating this subtext. How does one go about constructing
the appearance of scholarly authority, for example? In an act of academic

[106] Again, the fact that a Jacqueline Rose, a Tony Judt, or an Esther Benbassa takes her so
seriously reveals more about a lack of judgment than it does about the reality of Israel.
[107] In Hebrew, the association is immediate: Zertal's choice of word for "ultimate," *sofi*, is
the same as the word usually used to mean "final," as in the "Final Solution."

generosity, in which there might also be a hint of esoteric knowledge not accessible to ordinary mortals, Zertal thanks the historian Avner Cohen for giving her Ben-Gurion's letter to Kennedy. But Cohen himself quoted this letter at length in his book on Israel's policy of nuclear ambiguity,[108] and even in those references, Zertal notices only one thing, Ben-Gurion's Holocaust complex. She ignores something else that Cohen also speaks about, the great complexity of the decision and the multiplicity of motives that led Ben-Gurion – and not only him – to the conclusion that Israel needed a nuclear option. She does not even pick up the fact that Ben-Gurion thought about this option as early as 1948 and not, as she writes, just in the 1950s. Were she interested in history and not just discourse, she might have learned, from the extensive literature on Israel and the bomb, about the whole range of considerations that led to the decision to acquire a nuclear capacity. It was a historic decision, among the most important that Israeli leaders have ever made. Many opposed the decision; even today there are those who see it as a mistake. Quite a few people are busy trying to disarm Israel of its nuclear weapons. Others see the decision to develop the bomb as one of the essential conditions for realizing Ben-Gurion's vision of a sovereign Israel with recognized borders, living in peace with neighbors that are unable to defeat it in battle.

The idea of pronouncing judgment in this matter and drawing up a historical indictment on the grounds of a scrap of correspondence is typical of Zertal's approach to history. Were she to glance at Shlomo Aaronson's book about Israel's nuclear policy, for example, she would learn that there are other ways of reading the discourse on Ben-Gurion. Aaronson thinks, and tries to show, that contrary to Zertal's "cult of power" discourse, Ben-Gurion wanted the bomb because he did not believe in the ability of Israeli society to maintain its military superiority over the Arabs over the long term and because he hoped the nuclear deterrent would lead to the end of the armed conflict and to Arab recognition of Israel within its 1949 frontiers. Others, like Yigal Allon, had reservations about the nuclear option because they believed in Israel's ability to maintain a conventional military advantage and feared that the nuclearization of the Middle East would restrict Israel's freedom of military action. In many respects, Allon was much closer

---

[108] Avner Cohen, *Israel and the Bomb* (New York: Columbia University Press, 1998). The letter to Kennedy is quoted on p. 169 (where the lines cited by Zertal, too, appear). Had she read Cohen more carefully, she would have learned that these words were written only after many years of diplomatic efforts to dissuade Kennedy and the Americans from stopping Israel's nuclear program, efforts in which the Holocaust rationale never arose so blatantly.

than Ben-Gurion to what Zertal calls the "cult of power," but the conclusion he came to was, in fact, to forgo the nuclear option. One should also mention here that, despite Allon's belief in the importance of military power for Israel, he was one of the first Israeli political leaders to come forward after the Six-Day War with a peace plan based on the idea of ceding most of the occupied territories back to the Arabs. But what bearing does this have on Zertal's discourse?[109]

The half paragraph Zertal devotes to Ben-Gurion and the bomb is of interest because we see there, in concentrated form, most of the features of her smear tactics: glibness; superficiality; feigned erudition; removal of the subject from the realm of rational discussion; sweeping delegitimation of Israel's nuclear policy; symbolic demonization of the figure of Ben-Gurion and, through him, of the whole history of Israel since its founding; clever use of the Holocaust; and ahistorical discussion of the entire subject. No doubt the "lessons of the Holocaust" played an important role in shaping Ben-Gurion's conception of the country and its defense policy. How could it have been otherwise? Why should it have been otherwise? But to separate this consideration from the many others, more important and immediate, that figured in the thinking of Ben-Gurion and his advisers – turning the "Holocaust neurosis" into the sole focus of the question of Israel and the bomb – is a good example of the way the Holocaust, not coincidentally linked to the possibility of a nuclear catastrophe, can be made to serve the purposes of anti-Israel propaganda.

To call Zertal's concoction pornography is to give pornography a bad name. The latter at least bears an occasional resemblance to reality. As is customary in her group of writers, Zertal lumps together left and right, Ben-Gurionism and messianism, Ofer Feniger and Rabin's assassin Yigal Amir. The messianism of the radical settler movement, for example, what she refers to as "messianic fever," has never been based on a "Holocaust discourse"; it is, in fact, opposed to such a discourse in many ways. But this fact does not trouble Zertal. The role played in that movement by the Holocaust, the ethos of the victim, and the justification of power based on the threat of another Auschwitz is quite different from, and even opposed to, the role they play in the secular Israeli ethos, certainly as the latter is portrayed by Zertal. But this does not prevent her from exposing the one, distinct discourse that draws all of Israeli society together. Left and right, religious

---

[109] See Shlomo Aronson and Oded Brosh, *The Politics and Strategy of Nuclear Weapons in the Middle East: Opacity, Theory, and Reality, 1960–1991; An Israeli Perspective* (Albany: State University of New York Press, 1992), 22–25.

and nonreligious, the security-minded and the messianists – all have been mindless, helpless victims of Ben-Gurionist manipulation and the Eichmann trial, which have led them willy-nilly, by a twisted logic, to disaster, for them and, even more so, for their victims. As we had the opportunity to point out earlier, the truth is that the theology and theodicy of the disciples of Tzvi Yehuda Kook reject the analogy linking Auschwitz with the sanctification, as it were, of military might. The logic of this analogy is a secular one of taking one's fate in one's own hands and relying on worldly power. But the logic of religious messianism in relation to worldly power is that the latter must serve a divine plan. This logic does not derive from the Holocaust; rather, the latter serves only as a confirmation, a further confirmation, of it. Kook's distinctive theological dialectic turns the Holocaust into the very opposite of what the secularists think it is. What really happened after the Six-Day War was that Ben-Gurion's heirs failed to stand up to the determination, sophistication, and cunning of the messianists, a small sector of the public, and have allowed them to set the country's political agenda ever since. Though Zertal's smear culture does not recognize it, there is in the story of the movement to settle the occupied territories, which has been Zionism's greatest calamity, a difference between the period preceding the 1977 political upheaval that brought the right wing to power and the period that followed it. Only then, in fact, were the stops pulled out and the broad-scale settlement policy put into effect. This is significant for our discussion here, because the systematic questioning of the moral validity of the Ben-Gurionist worldview by Zertal and her friends may well have contributed to their weakness, both moral and political, in the face of the settlers and their supporters.

A while back, someone called my attention to a review by Yitzhak Laor of Alona Frankel's book *Girl*.[110] The book is a memoir of the author's childhood, how she and her parents barely survived the Holocaust and what happened to them afterward. It is the wonderful and terrible story of a little girl whose parents found problematic shelter for her, after the person who had saved their lives by taking them in refused to take her as well. When their money ran out, and there was no more gold to be extracted from the mother's teeth to pay for the child's keep, the Polish woman who had been looking after the girl took pity on her and did not send her to her death, as she had done to another child entrusted to her care. Instead, she brought her back to her parents, to the hideout where the owner had not wanted her. In the end, the girl and her parents were saved nevertheless. As Laor rightly

---

[110] Alona Frankel, *Yalda* (Girl) (Tel Aviv: Mappa, 2004). Laor's article was published in the "Culture and Literature" supplement of *Haaretz*, June 25, 2004.

points out, Frankel's book is extraordinarily beautiful, heartrending, "and also remarkably optimistic."

Yet despite the book's beauty, Laor actually says very little about it. The title of his article tips us off as to what is really on his mind: "This Girl Is Not Us," he or the editor calls it. And in fact, most of the article consists of a single statement, which the author deems so important that he repeats it over and over again throughout: there, in that (quite dreadful) place where the book's young heroine stood, there, before the hideout of those parents who had given her up and abandoned her, she stood alone. None of us was there, he stresses. "It is not that the place is holy but that this good, brave, beautiful story makes it impossible to generalize it." Thus, instead of talking about the book, Laor offers us some general observations about the unacceptability (aesthetic? moral? political?) of generalizing, about the one-time nature of the episode, and about the manipulative way "the state apparatus turned the Jewish girl from the Holocaust into 'our little sister' and 'our daughter,' finally asserting that 'we are they' or 'we are all the second generation [of survivors]' or any of the other vain pronouncements of the [university] Hebrew-literature departments, which proclaim such utter inanities as 'identity' and 'trauma.'" He tells us, too, of the long road taken by "Israeli ideology" – a clever but, in fact, silly allusion to "German ideology"? – ever since the 1950s, a road of appropriation and exploitation that is one big fabrication and act of denial (!), done in order to create a "generality," meaning "us," at any price.

Frankel's book is truly wonderful. It merited a serious review, rather than exploitation for ideological purposes. It deserved an article that delved into the singularity (as Laor rightly calls it) of the story it tells, not one that appropriated it for an ideology that pretends to be anti-ideology and anti-appropriation. It did not deserve to be exploited to settle scores with the universities that Laor – to judge from a long interview with him in the Jerusalem weekly *Kol Ha'ir* (September 3, 2004) – had never forgiven for having failed to recruit him to the ranks of those professors he so despises.

Still, with all its viciousness, condescension, and nonsensicality, Laor's article is an interesting one. Not so much because of its metaliterary or historiosophic ruminations, or even because of the aspersions it casts upon the Hebrew-literature departments. Nor is it because it is not at all clear what amazingly efficient and energetic government mechanism turned Alona Frankel into a national treasure the moment her book appeared, or how the one-time character of the events can be detached from the public, inclusive character of the text. Nor is it because one might well wonder where Laor – a well-known literary figure versed in modern French thought, the secrets of deconstruction, and the various philosophies of *difference* – got the pedagogic authority to forbid us to read this text, understand it, or speak about it as we wish, to think, for example, about something the author herself speaks about: that the little girl who experienced the horror she describes (in Hebrew, i.e., the language common to all Hebrew-speakers) experienced it for one reason only, that she was (and is) a Jew? Even the fact that Laor regurgitates the usual slogans of the chorus of *resentment* is not especially interesting. We already know it all: the manipulation, the power of the "state mechanisms," the intellectual poverty and moral frailty of the academic establishment, the amorphousness and homogeneity of the Israeli character, the appropriation, the exploitation, the falsification, even the denial – we have heard about all these things ad nauseam. What is really of interest in Laor's article is how clearly it reflects the immediacy and ease with which the conditioned reflex of Holocaust *resentment* operates. The ink was hardly dry in this book before Laor sallied forth to do battle against the appropriation and exploitation of it to advance Israeli interests. There is something about the Holocaust, it seems, that arouses the bloodlust of Israel's *resentment* community. They cannot pass the subject up without saying a malicious word about Israeli ideology, the travails of the litera-ture departments, the state apparatus – in short, without casting aspersions on the Israeli and Jewish collective and complaining bitterly about its con-nection with the Holocaust. They react to such an extent that they permit themselves not only to exploit the poetic power and human ghastliness of Alona Frankel's story but also to distort its meaning completely – because Frankel's book is a very Jewish one, explicitly and intentionally. But at the same time, obliquely but quite clearly, the book reserves judgment about the Israeliness into which the girl narrator abruptly finds herself cast.[111] The appropriation for the common good of which Laor speaks is thus evidently quite sophisticated and dialectical as well as invisible to the naked eye, at least the eye that is not equipped, like Laor's, with an ability to expose the manipulative wiles of the establishment/academy/state apparatus. Or per-haps, as with Guillaume, any mention of the Holocaust is like a red flag that provokes a massive attack, tasteless and crude, on the Israeli collective.

[111] It is hard to imagine that an alert critic like Laor did not read the book through to the end; yet, on the ship that brought her and her family to Israel, right in front of Mount Carmel, the girl discovers on the bridge a group of boys (with a girl named Tzippi among them) who have rolled their shorts up so far that the pockets stick out and on whose tanned, muscular legs there are golden hairs ("even on the black-haired ones"). In short, Sabras, native Israelis. They throw oranges onto the deck below, apparently to give the newcomers to the country a chance to taste them. "With a little kick, I sent the orange flying into the depths of the ancient sea, the Mediterranean" – so the book ends.

Yitzhak Laor is a talented poet, a mediocre writer, a failed playwright, and, above all, a tireless manufacturer of politically committed literary criticism and one-dimensional ideological cant. Of late, he has also become a cultural entrepreneur, editing and publishing a literary and political journal, *Mita'am*, which is one of the venues most hospitable to the Israeli *resentiment* community. It is not difficult to find Auschwitz used there as a weighty argument in the ideological polemic against Zionism. The important British literary weekly, the *London Review of Books*, thinks Laor is important enough an intellectual to give him a platform. Its January 26, 2006, issue carries a review by him of the book by Idith Zertal mentioned earlier, *Israel's Holocaust and the Politics of Nationhood*, the English translation of which had appeared two or three months previously. It is interesting that the *London Review* gave Laor a platform. For if Laor's polished Hebrew makes up for the thinness of his writing, his English cannot conceal it. There would be no point in going over the review at length. In fact, it is not a review: not only is there no hint in it of criticism of Zertal's book, but he does not really talk about the book at all; he mentions only some items in the book's indictment of Israeli culture – the Kibia massacre, for example, and the lies Ben-Gurion told when a storm arose in its wake – and ties them together with the matter of the "Israeli Holocaust." This he does so as to inform the English reader (and this is his ultimate conclusion) of our urgent need as Israelis to pinch ourselves in order to break free of the spell Ben-Gurion cast with the Eichmann trial, that is, to abandon our obscene custom of seeing ourselves as the victims of the Holocaust.

In fact, and contrary to the impression given by Laor and his comrades in the community of opprobrium, the real obsession with the Holocaust is theirs, much more than that of Israeli society, the Israeli establishment, or Israeli academia. Worse still, it is the former who really abuse the memory of the Holocaust in their effort to show that Israel is the guilty party in the endless conflict with the Palestinians. A quick look at the contents of the twelve or thirteen issues to date of Laor's journal *Mita'am* shows a constant preoccupation with the Holocaust, well beyond that of any other nonspecialized literary or political journal in Israel. Because it is a journal of "radical thought," all the articles on the Holocaust in it happily agree with one another and present a composite picture of opprobrium orthodoxy. We have mentioned Amira Hass's article, in part a eulogy of her parents, in part an ideological denunciation of Israeli conduct toward the Palestinians. In another piece, Idith Zertal – like Agamben (whom she quotes) and Garaudy (whom she does not) – expresses serious reservations about the use of the term "Shoah." Yes, she concedes, the contamination of "Israeli language" and moral character makes her task risky; but she will do her duty anyway, insisting that some other word – she prefers "genocide" – be used. This will put an end to our complicity in the Nazi practice of concealing the true nature of what happened with such euphemisms as "final solution" and "evacuation" (*Mita'am* 8, 2007, 144–148).

In issue number 11 of his review, Laor includes an article of his own, "Hashoa hi shelanu (kol halo-muslimim)" (The Shoah Is Ours [All the Non-Muslims']). The article explores the "deep crisis" of European society, a crisis in which the Holocaust and its memory play a decisive role. The Israelis – the "less-than-brilliant," if not "completely foolish" Holocaust historians, but also "this philosopher Yohanan [*sic*] Yakira," who knows a lot about one thing and nothing at all about many others (I am not so sure about the first part, but the second is certainly true) – rejoice in the sudden European Shoah-consciousness. He is not fooled by such pronouncements as Nicolas Sarkozy's "I was changed at Yad Vashem" or by the deep sympathy Israel enjoys nowadays in Europe (despite the complaints of the Israelis that they are not well liked there). He knows that Israel, through its newly acquired role as symbol of the "West's" past crimes, is simply being used to cover up Europe's current hatred for Arabs and Muslims and complacency in the face of the new crimes being committed against the latter, in Europe and especially in Palestine.

Laor, I must admit, makes a few valid points about the complicated and often very problematic ways in which the Allies dealt with the destruction of European Jewry during the war and the Jewish displaced persons immediately afterward; and the way Americans and Europeans, particularly Germans, addressed the moral questions they faced during the first decades after the war. We have touched upon these questions earlier, and Laor does acknowledge that there is a vast literature dealing with them. In fact, he has little original to add, and his arguments are marked by confusion, arrogance, and the already familiar mélange of Shoah, anti-Zionism, and adulation of, and pity for, the Palestinians.

Laor also wants to enlighten the "West" about its "deep crisis." The previously mentioned article appears, with minor changes, in a recent volume of Laor's meditations, *Le nouveau philosémitisme européen et le "camp de la paix" en Israël* (The New European Philo-Semitism and the "Peace Camp" in Israel).[112] The title is revealing. Laor warns his French readers against drawing a distinction between Israelis such as the writers Amos Oz, A. B. Yehoshua, and David Grossman, who call for Israeli-Palestinian compromise

---

[112] Paris: La Fabrique, 2007.

based on a "two-state solution," large-scale withdrawal from the occupied territories, and the massive dismantling of settlements, on the one hand, and, say, the settlers, on the other. Both are too "Zionistic" for him. The writings in this little book oscillate between two poles: a wholesale denunciation of all Zionists, both of the right and of the left, and another version of "Auschwitz, or the great alibi," on the other. The two are blended into a single, surrealistic horror story: the "West" and Israel/Zionism have concluded an unholy alliance, based on a newfound memory of Auschwitz, with the aim of perpetrating all these atrocities against the Arabs, the Muslims, and the Palestinians.

Here is one small illustration of Laor's way with the facts. The Bar-Ilan University historian Ilan Greilsammer wrote in *Le Monde* (September 11, 2003) that "it is now enough to be an anti-Zionist, a-Zionist, post-Zionist, or New Historian describing the massacres perpetrated by the Jews during the 1948 war to be accepted with open arms." But Laor, for his part, informs his French readers that in Israel today it is not easy to conduct research into atrocities committed by Israeli soldiers in 1948. A few, he says, have even lost their university posts as a result. This is pure defamation and falsehood. The number of articles and books on these questions by Israeli scholars (notably Benny Morris, but also Yoav Gelber and Ilan Pappe, to mention just a few) is considerable, and the issue is debated openly. Perhaps the best proof is Laor himself, who edits his own journal in Israel and publishes constantly in *Haaretz*, the most influential Israeli newspaper. The latest example of the Israeli reign of terror against academic freedom of speech is to be found, perhaps, in the award given at the Hebrew University for a master's dissertation dealing with the interesting question of why Israeli soldiers refrain from raping Arab women. The prize-winning answer is even more interesting. It is because of Israel's infamous dehumanization of the Arabs and its demographic struggle, or attempt to carry out ethnic cleansing, against them: the fewer the rapes, the fewer the Arabs.

Laor is what is called an "intellectual." Like the other heroes of this chapter, they make their living from mental exertion, as a rule, rather than manual labor. They teach in universities, do research, write, and think. But at times the term "intellectual" takes on another meaning: we tend to regard him as having a civic responsibility. The "intellectual" is to be distinguished from the ordinary writer, scientist, or teacher in that he speaks out on a more or less regular basis, plays a public role, and is politically engaged. Though his professional expertise may not be in the matters he speaks about, he often enjoys the status of a moral authority. The intellectual is also the one who feels obligated to be involved in these matters and to lend his extra moral weight to causes he sees as worthy and just.

The term "authority" used here alludes to the French term *clerc*, as it appears in the title of the well-known book *La trahison des clercs* (1929),[113] by the French Jewish historian and humanist Julian Benda. The term is usually translated "intellectuals" (the English title, for example, is *The Treason of the Intellectuals*). The use of the term "intellectual" to mean someone who belongs to a more or less well-defined social category and has a non-professional involvement in public affairs originated in France at the end of the nineteenth century. The phenomenon, and the term describing it, came to the fore in the wake of the Dreyfus affair, when writers, pamphleteers, and other people of the mind became involved in the controversy. This was undoubtedly the intellectuals' finest hour. Or, to be precise, the finest hour of some of them, for there was no lack of intellectuals in the anti-Dreyfusard camp either. In France, more than in other countries, there developed an ideology of public involvement and commitment on the part of the intellectuals as well an anti-intellectual ideology (generally identified with the right wing). There also developed a whole genre of literature dealing with the nature and effect of intellectuals' involvement in political life. The best-known articulation of the theory of intellectual "involvement" (*engagement*) and civic responsibility is that of Jean-Paul Sartre. In his case, at least, the degree of personal risk entailed in such involvement was inversely proportional to the intensity of the involvement. While France was under German occupation, Sartre minded his own business; but right after the war he became a highly engaged intellectual, achieving unprecedented public prominence. His influence on French public opinion, especially that of the more educated classes, and the impact of his pronouncements abroad made him (some say) the best-known and most influential intellectual of the day. A whole era, the two or three decades after the war, was even called "the Sartre years."

Sartre almost always identified with the wrong causes. A man who saw the world situation, and especially the nature of the Soviet dictatorship and international communism, more clearly was his one-time fellow student Raymond Aron. Aron, too, saw himself as "involved," but he based his involvement on an attempt to understand French and world political realities as rationally and objectively as possible. He referred to his attitude to current affairs as that of an "engaged spectator" (*spectateur engagé*), that is, one who looks at things with objective detachment but feels himself to be a part of what is happening and takes a stand in relation to it. In retrospect,

[113] J. Benda, *La trahison des clercs* (repr., Paris: Grasset, 1990); translated as *The Treason of the Intelllectuals* (New York: W. W. Norton, 1969). References are to the French original.

in nearly all his stormy and sometimes bitter debates and confrontations with Sartre, Aron turned out to be right.[114] He also made an important and recognized contribution to the literature about intellectuals. In his book *The Opium of the Intellectuals*, which appeared in 1955, at the height of the Cold War and Sartre's advocacy of the Soviet cause, Aron probes the sources and character of this advocacy. Although the book belongs to a very specific historical, cultural, political, and even personal context – that of the Left Bank in the 1950s – much of its analysis and many of its insights are still of use at the beginning of the new millennium, here on the eastern shore of the Mediterranean Sea.

The question Aron (like Benda before him) poses is how to explain the phenomenon of educated and, as a rule, intelligent people – writers, artists, philosophers, scientists, and others – who align themselves so readily with the most murderous regimes, the most bloodthirsty dictators, the most dubious political ideologies. Sartre and a whole generation of French intellectuals were fellow travelers of the French Communist Party, perhaps the most dogmatic in the West, and defended Stalin and Stalinism even when they knew, or could have known, the true nature of that regime. Heidegger, Schmitt, and, in fact, the whole professorial rank of German academics, including, in particular, philosophers and jurists, participated enthusiastically in the Nazi adventure. The Italian philosopher Emilio Gentile was enchanted with fascism. And there are numerous other examples to be found among the *clercs* of the late twentieth and early twenty-first centuries.[115]

Benda sees the betrayal of the intellectuals as a surrender to what he calls *passions politiques*. In this passion of the intellectuals, he explains, we see all the signs of lust: the urge to act, the expectation of immediate results, the extreme exaggeration, the hatred, the *idée fix*. The intellectuals, he says, forgo their role as people of the mind, those who pursue universal

---

[114] A comprehensive analysis of the relations between the two and an account of the debates between them can be found in J. F. Sirinelli, *Sartre et Aron: Deux intellectuals dans le siècle* (Paris: Hachette, 1995). The English-speaking reader can read about this in some of Tony Judt's studies; we shall come to Judt in the Postscript.

[115] Aside from the two works previously mentioned, many studies have been published in recent years, some in Hebrew, that seek to explain how those whose profession is to think can make such colossal mistakes. Among them is Shlomo Sand's *Ha'intelektual, ha'emet, vehako'ah* (The Intellectual, Truth, Power) (Tel Aviv: Am Oved, 2000), which has as its context the Parisian debates on the subject of intellectuals and takes a stand on some of them – a bit strange, considering that the book is addressed to Israeli readers. Two chapters in the book presume to judge the Israeli intellectual and his vices, although the latter consist only of taking a political and intellectual stand, as it were, that is typical of the Israeli community of opprobrium.

truth, scientific fact, goodness, and beauty and allow national or class considerations to take over the entire intellectual enterprise, subordinating the transcendent to the worldly. Following this line of reasoning, we could say that just as totalitarianism – that is, the domination of the entire public realm by "the political" – is a danger specific to the modern state, "political passion" – that is, the domination of all thought by politics – is the modern intellectual malady. We see the first signs of this danger in Hobbes, who, in effect, elevated the theory of the state to the status of *philosophia prima*, that is, primary theory, the theory of theories, a status that, since the ancient Greeks, had belonged to metaphysics.

Yet Benda does not see the ability to resist political temptation and passion as an abdication of good citizenship or patriotism. His criticism of nationalistic *passion politique* should not be confused with his remarks on good citizenship. He sees nationalism, be it in the Italian or German or French (or, he adds, Zionist) versions, as a prelude to disaster. It represents a betrayal by the humanist not only of his universal task but also of his civic responsibility. But just as he condemns the nationalist writer Maurice Barrès for saying, at the time of the Dreyfus affair, that his country was always right even when it was not, he also condemns those who find fault with their country even when it is not at fault, and those – the pacifists – whose mystique of peace, just like their opponents' mystique of war, smothers their sense of justice (p. 187).

The main philosophical lesson to be drawn from Benda's analysis – a lesson at least worth considering seriously – is that "the political" is not the locus of the universal. Unlike the nationalists he abhors, he does not deny that there are such things as universal truth, universally valid moral principles, or the universal applicability of norms of justice and beauty. What he does deny is that this universalism can be imported in any simple, direct way into the realm of the worldly, the temporal, the partial, and partisan. Max Weber makes a similar distinction. In two well-known essays, he distinguishes between the vocation of the politician and that of the scientist. The politician is involved in historical (i.e., one-time, contingent) events as they occur. He can make use of scientific knowledge for an understanding of the general laws governing these events. But these two different ways of relating to reality must not be confused. And just as the scientist betrays his vocation and risks intellectual bankruptcy when he abandons the pursuit of the universal, the politician who imposes generalities and abstractions on his way of dealing with reality risks disaster for himself and those with whose well-being and security he is charged.

The way nation and class have been made into the subjects of universal doctrine (by nationalists and communists, respectively, as well as their heirs) is, in Benda's view, a kind of betrayal. This is the betrayal of those intellectuals whose political urges have gotten the better of them, who have given in to "political passion" and allowed the political to encompass every-thing, to dominate the entire world of the mind, as if it were possible for the political to be universalized. The result is – and this is ultimately the main point – that the domination of the intellectual realm by the political distorts not only the former but also the latter. Seeing everything from an exclusively political perspective becomes what we have called a "political perversion." What is then sacrificed is the intellectual's ability not only to deal properly with matters of the mind but also to understand the political and historical reality in which he lives. He can thus be led to support the worst, most venal and criminal regimes and rulers.

How are we to understand, Aron asks in his book on the intellectuals, that it is precisely "those who devote themselves to genuinely creative work – whether scientists, philosophers, poets, or serious novelists – [those who] enjoy real prestige and an almost total freedom" (p. 220) who so abhor the society they live in and that grants them that status and freedom? Even if "the West" – or what Menahem Begin and other right-wing demagogues like to call "the free world" – is not paradise on earth, we can still concur with Aron, Arendt, Leo Strauss, and many others that the democracies of our day are quite different from the dictatorships; that, contrary to what Agamben and his followers think, all types of regime cannot be lumped together under the single, all-inclusive heading of "sovereignty," thus blurring the differ-ences and making it possible to extend the hatred of tyranny and injustice to democracy as well. By the way, Israel, too, is a democracy, an imperfect one, but a democracy nonetheless. And so the hatred of Israel, on the part of people like Laor, for example, is a riddle. In Aron's view, the intellectu-als cannot accept the fact that reality does not conform to their theories. As a rule, teachers are displeased when their pupils do not obey them, and when the pupil is society as a whole, or history, the anger and frustration take on an almost metaphysical character. This is only a partial explana-tion, of course. It applies particularly to the Paris intellectuals whose blind-ness and arrogance are the object of Aron's critique. No doubt the reality in which the average member of the Israeli community of *resentiment* lives and works is quite different from that of the Parisian intellectual. There are also differences in the way the two –usually master and disciple – respond to and interpret reality in the two cases. For example, even in the darkest, most difficult hours of the colonial war in Algeria, no one, apart from a few anarchists, thought of doing away with France or its French character. Even when Sartre, influenced by Franz Fanon among others, called for the killing of French soldiers, there was no question of the fundamental character of the French republic. No one, not even France's harshest critics, ever thought the establishment of that republic was a historic mistake. Some diehard monarchists still talk about turning back the wheel of the French Revolution, but even they do not advocate abolishing French identity as such. The criticism of Israel, on the other hand – of its policies, its conduct, the occupation – has grown into a negation of the very idea of Zionism, which is the notion that there is a historic need and moral and political justification for the existence of a Jewish nation-state in the Land of Israel. Along with the Zionist idea, Israeli identity, as a concept and as a historical and political reality, has been completely negated.

France in general, and its intellectuals in particular, have still not come to terms morally with their recent past. One chapter in that past is that of French colonialism. Only recently have the extent of the killing in the Algerian war and the means employed by the army and the French settlers come to light. Another chapter in this reckoning has to do with the period of the Nazi occupation, the Vichy government, the collaboration with the occupiers, and the treatment of the Jews. There are those Frenchmen who dare reckon with their past – but it turns out that the reckoning is sometimes done with the Jews. This has been done most blatantly and perversely in the case of the Holocaust deniers. It has also been done in a subtler and more complex way by the negators of Israel. A comparison between the anti-Israel, anti-Zionist, and anti-Jewish arguments of the deniers, especially those on the left, and those advanced as part of the ostensibly legitimate criticism of Israel[116] reflects a dangerous family resemblance between the two "discourse regimes" (to use the current terminology). Above all, this resemblance is reflected in the permanent presence of the Holocaust in anti-Israel discourse and the obscene dialectic that turns the Holocaust into an effective anti-Israel argument. Here we see that these two phenomena – Holocaust denial and the systematic use of the Holocaust as a weapon against Israel and Zionism – are manifestations of a single perversion.

As we have said, the historical reckoning with their country that the French intellectuals have undertaken has not led to a delegitimation of the French republic as such. Even if at other times it was possible to ignore it or cover it up, the connection between "Frenchness" (and even "Catholicity") and "republicanism" is especially strong now that the French are faced with the challenge of militant Islam and millions of Arab immigrants. In the

---

[116] Of course, there can be legitimate criticism of Israel, as of any other country in the world; but that is not what is being spoken of here.

American case, too, the reckoning with the past – the Vietnam War, slavery, the decimation of the continent's original population – has not entailed a questioning of the legitimacy of the Union. Even the German intellectuals and writers on the left do not contemplate a dismemberment of the Federal Republic or an obliteration of its German character. But in Israel, the historical reckoning in which the Holocaust plays a central role has become the main rationale for a systematic campaign to undermine and demonize the Zionist cause and the state.

Judging from his poetry, Laor is an intellectual whose "political passion" has taken over his poetic field of vision. In his play *Ephraim Goes Back to the Army*, this passion appears to have led to a complete loss of creativity. Its dramatic quality is on a par with the semantic depth of the allusion in the title, and the associations it evokes – with the well-regarded novella *Ephraim Goes Back to the Alfalfa*, by S. Yizhar, who also wrote the story "Hirbet Hiz'a," for example – are as shallow as the scene of oral-sex-for-beginners in the play. Aside from this, the one thing in the play worth mentioning is its comparison of – what else? – Israeli soldiers with the Nazis. In case anyone did not get it, he spells out the point of this comparison in the interview cited earlier. The time has come, Laor says, for the world to be rid of the State of Israel, Zionism, and all their misdeeds. He is impatient, in a way: enough of this, enough damage has been done, let us put an end to this adventure once and for all. Nor does he forgive his professors, either, as we have seen, for failing to provide him with a livelihood in their midst or for collaborating with the Zionist project. For example, Professor Menahem Brinker, who taught Laor about Sartre and whom he apparently admires greatly: unlike this Israeli professor, who did not refuse the prestigious Israel Prize, Sartre, it will be remembered, turned down the Nobel Prize. We have already spoken here about Sartre and his colossal political blunders. But aside from being an important and original philosopher, we must say that Sartre was not always wrong about political and public issues. He said, for example, that anti-Semitism was not an opinion but a crime. Anti-Zionism is not a crime. Unlike anti-Semitism, there is no law in Israel or anywhere else that forbids calling for the elimination of the political entity that was created by the Zionist movement. Nevertheless, following Sartre, we may say that this, too, is not just an opinion, a stance, or a claim. It is plain villainy.

ONE MORE REMARK

Dealing with post- or anti-Zionists is like mountain climbing: one develops a strange need to see what the next summit hides, an irresistible curiosity about the never-ending productivity of the opprobrium community. It also resembles mountain climbing for its constantly frustrating nature: every time you think you have arrived to the last peak, you find out that there is yet another one ahead of you. Every time you think you fathomed the deepest abyss of malice, ignorance, or stupidity, something new comes out, and one has to concede again that he had been too optimistic in thinking that he has already seen the worst.

While preparing to send the absolutely last version of this book to the publisher, I found out from the *New York Times* that another book has just been translated from the Hebrew and appeared, or is about to appear, in English. Its author was interviewed for the *Times* and was accorded a rather favorable presentation in it. The book had already appeared in France a few months earlier, and with another recent book of another Israeli, also translated into French immediately after its publication in Israel, the collection of anti-Israeli books written by Israelis, has become somewhat richer. The two books bring the opprobrium to new heights of artistic and academic sophistication. Both also think, albeit in different ways, that Zionism, and Israel as a Zionist state, are continuing Hitler's work. One of them makes such an idea into the core of his book, the other only says so in passing, but both are convinced that in order to make the Israeli phenomenon intelligible, it is necessary to bring Hitler into the discussion. The first is due to Avraham (Avrum, as he is known in Israel) Burg, the second written by Shlomo Sand, a professor of history at Tel Aviv University. Both are already translated and available to readers outside Israel,[117] and both figured high on the best-seller list in Israel for weeks. Sand's book is, when these words are being written, already on its third printing in France.

Burg's book reads like a parody on the things dealt with in the present essay. It is an outstanding patchwork made of all the possible and impossible Shoah clichés and platitudes and of all the possible and impossible myths of the anti-Israeli opprobrium community. It is written in journalistic pseudo-high language; it is pretentious, pompous, self-righteous, utterly confused, and at times self-contradictory; and it is also deeply false in most of the claims it makes, both factual and nonfactual. He even cites Hannah Arendt – a must in this genre – although it is quite obvious that he does not have the vaguest

---

[117] See A. Burg, book *Lenazeah et Hitler* (Winning against Hitler) (Tel Aviv: Yediot Aharonot and Sifrei Hemed, 2007). The book appeared in France shortly after its publication in Israel; its English title is *The Holocaust Is Over, We Must Rise from Its Ashes* (New York: Palgrave Macmillan, 2008). Sh. Sand, *Matai ve'eich humzah ha'am ha'yehudi* (When and Where Was the Jewish People Invented?) (Tel Aviv: Resling, 2008). The book has already appeared in French.

idea what she is all about. The book though has some undeniable literary qualities: it is very artistically woven of two parallel narratives, sort of a mirror reflection of the actually existent evil of the Israeli reality, on the one hand, and its failed humanistic possibilities, told through the figure of Burg's late father, on the other. To add to the already apparent sophistication of this creation, the two tales are even written in different characters.

Burg grew up with a Zionist silver spoon in his mouth. He comes from the very heart of the Israeli/Zionist/Jewish establishment, both by parental and by his own merit. His father, Yossef Burg, had had one of the longest careers as Knesset member, minister, and head of the National-Religious Party (the *mafdal*, as it is called in Hebrew). His son tells about him then – with a sticky, embarrassing sentimentality – as a model of old Jewish wisdom, common sense, humanity, and, of course, religion, as a sort of symbolic counterpart to the present Israeli political, cultural, and moral bankruptcy, to its current nationalistic, violent, corrupt, too secular – you name it – reality. A reality that Burg the son denounces as an (almost) victory of Hitler and as (almost) hopeless. Unless, of course, we (and the readers outside Israel) listen to him – like the children of Israel who had to listen to the biblical prophets lest a catastrophe would overcome them – and go back to his father's ways. The truth of the matter, however, is that Burg the father was one of Israel's most opportunistic and mediocre politicians ever. His greatest gift was an endless capacity to survive, in all possible coalitions and under all possible prime ministers, be they from the labor or the nationalistic right. His most notable display of lack of integrity was, perhaps, they way he – depicted by his son as a man of peace and compromise – remained the head of his party while it was becoming nationalistic, messianic, and the political expression of the most extreme "greater Israel" religious ideology. It was not a sheer hazard that Begin made him responsible for the implementation of the part of the peace agreement with Egypt that was meant to achieve a compromise in the West Bank. Under the title of proposing the Palestinians an "autonomy," what was really happening then is that Jewish settlement within heavily populated Palestinian areas became the name of the game. The son was the speaker of the Knesset, one of the Labor Party's main leaders, and the head of the Jewish Agency, an institution that, among other things, is known for the very generous way it treats its executives. The fact that this is where Burg comes from – the most Jewish-Zionist of all places – apparently gives the things he says an extra power; no wonder that non-Israeli "critics" of Israel – Tony Judt, for example – cite him as a reliable source corroborating their own apocalyptic picture of Israel. This is just one illustration of the real value – intellectual and moral – of the book.

Sand's book is very different, and yet very similar. It is not a book of an ex-politician but of a man of science. It has a very simple and straightforward message, which gets down to the roots of it all, making all the debates, discussions, and argumentations obsolete a priori: the Jewish people are not a people (or an ethnicity). They are nothing more than a more or less ingenious invention, inculcated into the heads of naive Jews and non-Jews alike – the whole world in fact – by Zionist historiography, literature, politicians, whatever. Even medical-scientific research has been recruited by the Zionists to give to their invention more substance: Israeli geneticians have been busy studying hereditary properties of different Jewish communities, and other populations, trying to show that all the Jews have common ancestries. But they do not, because Ashkenazi Jews are descendants of the Kazars. So there is no biological basis for the Zionist claim for national, historical, or other rights in Palestine.

The whole thing is so utterly absurd, indeed hallucinatory, that reading it, let alone the idea that one would need to try to refute it, is almost an insult. What is true in this book is long known, and what is new is complete nonsense. Although Sand is described usually as a historian (he is a professor in the history department of Tel Aviv University), there is no historically independent work in this book – it is mainly a compilation, and most of the historical data brought in it, notably the Kazars story, are taken from the very same Zionist historiography he denounces as the inventor of imaginary history. Reading Burg and Sand, as well as the other members of the community of the opprobrium, Israeli and non-Israeli, one gets the feeling that the ensemble of Auschwitz-Israel-Zionism-Palestinians-Territories-Occupation-Arendt constitutes a guarantee for a severe loss of any sense of truth, honesty, academic integrity, even simple common sense – that it is an entry permit to a culture of the *everything goes*, of what the French call the *n'importe quoi*.

3

On the Political and the Antipolitical

Hannah Arendt, Eichmann, and Israel

ARENDT AND THE COMMUNITY OF OPPROBRIUM

The name of Hannah Arendt has come up several times in this discussion. In fact, her spirit hovers over this whole book. Her name and her writings are connected in one way or another to the whole range of questions, the pain and guilt, the anger and the self-righteousness surrounding the relationship between Israel and the Holocaust. Because she was an important thinker (some say the most important political philosopher of the twentieth century); because of her sustained interest in totalitarianism and the Nazi regime in particular, on the one hand, and in Jewish matters and Israel, on the other; because of her influence on political theory, which has only grown in recent years; because of her personality and biography; and, above all, because of her book on the Eichmann trial, Arendt is an obligatory reference point for any consideration of the question with which we are concerned here. A further reason is that she made a real, if only partly intended, contribution to the use of the Holocaust in the ideological struggle against Israel.

The Arendt literature has become of late so rich, if not always in quality at least in quantity, that it is practically impossible to cover it all. Some good work has been done in this vast field, and some less good, both serious scholarship and ridiculous hagiography. Until recently, the English-language literature on Arendt has suffered from a certain schizophrenia, a tendency of scholars interested in the general philosophical or political-theory aspects of her work to ignore its more Jewish sides. Recently, it has become more common for scholarship to take into consideration the Jewish as well as the universal aspects of her work, and there is a growing awareness of the importance of her Jewish experience for the development of her

entire opus. In this context, her involvement with the Zionist movement and
her subsequent criticism of it are, of course, regularly mentioned. What is
more or less ignored or suppressed, however, is the crucial, in fact constitutive, role, Zionism played in her *Jewish* experience and, consequently, in
her general philosophical and theoretical outlook as well. In fact, Arendt's
Jewishness found concrete expression almost exclusively in her complex,
always ambivalent relationship to Zionist ideology, the Zionist political program, the Zionist movement, and the State of Israel. What is paradigmatic
here is, on the one hand, her criticism, even rejection, of Zionism, and the
centrality of this rejection in her universalistic political doctrines; but also,
on the other hand, the general scholarly disregard for this factor in her thinking and the much more general crisis of which it is emblematic.

The French scholar Martine Leibovici has been trying, in a number of
studies, to do justice to the role of Jewish experience in Arendt's larger theory. In Leibovici's principal work, she deplores, at one point, the use by the
philosopher Alain Brossat (another French writer who has dealt extensively
with her writings) of Arendt to attack "those who affirm the singularity
of the Jewish genocide."[1] Brossat, a writer of some notoriety in left-wing
circles in France, interests us here only because he helps us see how widespread elsewhere the anti-Israel images, themes, clichés, and myths prevalent in the Israeli community of opprobrium have become, probably without
direct influence in either direction; how easily they cross borders of all sorts
to constitute the core of an international ideology of opprobrium; but also
how easily they fit into Arendt-inspired critiques of modernity, legitimate or
otherwise.

In *L'épreuve du désastre*, Brossat in fact is against the thesis of the singularity of the Holocaust.[2] However, he mobilizes not only Arendt but also
Foucault to buttress his arguments. As with many of his kind, his motives
are not merely theoretical but much broader and also, of course, much
nobler. He is worried, above all, by the danger of singling out the Holocaust,
absolutizing and fetishizing it, as grounds for a theoretical understanding
of modern violence. For there is a continuum in the forms of violence, and
even if the Shoah is its most extreme manifestation, what is really important
is not to let the latter – or those who have made of its memory a dogma, not
subject to rational discussion – eclipse all the other victims of violence. One

[1] See Martine Leibovici, *Hannah Arendt, une juive. Expérience, politique et histoire* (Paris:
Desclée et Brouwer, 1998), 150.
[2] See Alain Brossat, *L'épreuve du désastre. Le XXe siècle et les camps* (Paris: Albin Michel,
1996).

remarkable thing here, let us note first, is the similarity, even in phraseology, to Ophir and other Israeli writers we have considered, as well as to Garaudy. Some English-language writers, too – we shall say a few words about Tony Judt later on – share Brossat's concern. But what Brossat and Ophir, for instance, share is not only a universalistic concern about the negative effects singling out the Holocaust (that plague of the modern world) can have on non-Jewish victims of violence. And it is not only their "mobilization" of Arendt in service of this concern, or even the distortions in their respective readings of Arendt. They also share, in a more particularistic manner, a recourse to all the myths, clichés, half truths, and outright lies characteristic of the anti-Israel opprobrium. In the semi-autobiographical, semi-ideological preface to Brossat's book, one can read, for example, that "the spoliation and oppression of the Palestinians [is] seen as a compensation for the crimes of Auschwitz" (p. 23); or, "[Arendt's book on the Eichmann trial] hits directly the politico-memorial consensus [that] is being built on the Auschwitz-Jerusalem axis" (p. 46); or, "It was Arendt's autonomy in the face of the constraints determining the dominant discourse (the massive legitimating of the Zionism in power)" (p. 46). No doubt, great minds think alike, and we find the same ideas coming from Idith Zertal; Brossat too goes so far as to take Tom Segev to be an authority on the "Auschwitz-Jerusalem axis."

ARENDT AND THE ISRAELI OPPROBRIUM

Idith Zertal's contribution in bringing Arendt to the attention of Hebrew readers should not be overlooked. Several other Israeli scholars had taken an interest in Arendt previously, but hardly anything had been written about her.[3] In the past few years, we have been enriched by a Hebrew translation of her book on the Eichmann trial[4] as well as several works that have sought to make amends and give Arendt a respected place in Israeli intellectual discourse.[5] Contrary to the impression Zertal and a few others try to give, the situation among Israeli intellectuals is quite similar to that in Europe or the

[3] The work of Steven Aschheim, of the Hebrew University of Jerusalem, is especially noteworthy here. In 1997, a large international conference on Arendt was held in Jerusalem. See Steven E. Aschheim, ed., *Hannah Arendt in Jerusalem* (Berkeley: University of California Press, 2001).

[4] Hannah Arendt, *Eichmann in Jerusalem: A Report on the Banality of Evil*, revised and expanded ed. (New York: Penguin, 1994); Hebrew translation by A. Uriel (Tel Aviv: Babel, 2000).

[5] Moshe Zuckerman and Idith Zertal, eds., *Hannah Arendt: Hatzi me'a shel pulmus* (Hannah Arendt: Half a Century of Polemics) (Tel Aviv: Hakibbutz Hameuchad, 2005). This volume is based on a day-long symposium devoted to Arendt's thought, held in Tel Aviv in 2003.

United States: many think that Arendt was an important thinker of the first order whose depth, originality, insight, and understanding of modern society and the modern state in general and of Judaism, Zionism, and Israel in particular give her thought great significance. In the view of the community of opprobrium, this is especially the case for us here and now, in Israel, which stole the Palestinians' land, and which is preparing for the Shoah's victims' victims, whose land it stole, the dreadful fate described by Adi Ophir; the state whose Zionist character Yitzhak Laor hopes to see effaced; the state whose malevolent discourse has been analyzed so skillfully by Idith Zertal.

If I am not mistaken, nothing on Arendt was published in Hebrew, or at least nothing of a popular nature, before Zertal's *Israel's Holocaust* (or rather, the articles it contains),[6] except for a few polemical items that came in response to Arendt's volume on the Eichmann trial. So it is good that Zertal has brought Arendt's work to the attention of the Israeli public. But the truth is, Arendt deserves more serious consideration than Zertal offers us. It is not only that what the latter has to say is tendentious or that she manages to avoid any real discussion of the serious criticisms that have been leveled at Arendt, both here and elsewhere. What is worse, Zertal seems not to have understood Arendt's political philosophy. And without understanding it, especially without understanding it critically, one cannot understand Arendt's observations about the Eichmann trial, the Jewish people, the State of Israel, or Zionism – neither what she gets right nor what she does not. But Zertal, basing herself on some correct and even important arguments, has little to offer us beyond a provincial, moralistic defense of Arendt and a sweeping rejection of all criticism of the latter. With this as her point of departure, she proceeds to a radical critique, bordering on delegitimation, of Zionism and, especially, of Israel as a political and cultural phenomenon.

Zertal blames the "establishment" for preventing the publication in Israel of Arendt's book on the Eichmann trial. She also, of course, sees this as a serious infringement on freedom of speech. In a short footnote, she cites a conversation with the first Hebrew translator of the book, who, she says, raised the possibility that an "invisible hand" had prevented publication of his work, done many years before. The Israeli publisher who then had the rights to the translation said he had not published it because the Schocken publishing house in New York, which owned the rights to the original, was asking too high a price. Arendt's voice may not have been heard in Hebrew public discourse, but it is far from clear that she was actually silenced. Talk of conspiracies

---

[6] *Israel's Holocaust and the Politics of Nationhood* (Cambridge: Cambridge University Press, 2005).

helps in the construction of myths but usually bears little relationship to
truth. Arendt's absence from the Israeli scene is certainly regrettable, but it
is neither more regrettable nor more mysterious than her absence from intellectual discourse elsewhere, notably in Europe, where it was only with the
collapse of the USSR and the weakening of the grip of Marxist ideologies on
intellectual life that she began to be read seriously and widely. It usually takes
a few years for intellectual fashions to cross the Mediterranean, but, in fact,
Arendt did land in Tel Aviv scarcely a decade later. Israel has never been the
kind of ghetto Zertal wants her readers to believe it is, only somewhat provincial – and Zertal is a perfect example of this.

Besides, Arendt was not the only one. Leo Strauss and Raymond Aron,
for example, political philosophers whose importance is, perhaps, no less
than Arendt's, were also absent, to one degree or another, from Israeli academic discussion, not to mention the wider public forum in Israel. The same
can be said of "Heidegger's children," as a relatively recent book called four
of his disciples, all of them, of course, Jews: Hans Jonas, Herbert Marcuse,
Karl Löwith, and Arendt herself.[7] All are important thinkers, though until
recently they were hardly known in Israel and are still much less known than
Arendt. It is appropriate to make mention of them, as opposed to the many
others who have not been translated into Hebrew, because they belong to
Arendt's generation, went through similar experiences, and, like her, were
Jews with a complicated relationship to their Jewishness and to Israel. They
all knew each other, incidentally.

The most interesting chapter in Zertal's book is, indeed, the one on Arendt,
not necessarily for its quality but for its subject matter. The acridness, hostility, arrogance, and condescension are completely absent from her discussion
of Arendt. On the contrary, what we see here is the typical combination of
provincial self-effacement and overenthusiasm, on the one hand, with haughtiness and scorn for all those who do not share their insider knowledge and
enlightenment, on the other – the same that we see in Grodzinsky, Ophir,

[7] Richard Wolin, *Heidegger's Children: Hannah Arendt, Karl Löwith, Hans Jonas, and
Herbert Marcuse* (Princeton: Princeton University Press, 2001). The story of Hans Jonas
(1903–1993) is particularly interesting in this context. A German-born Zionist, he settled
in Palestine in 1934. He served in the Jewish Brigade during World War II and then as a sol-
dier in the newly created Israeli army during the 1948 war. After teaching for a while at the
Hebrew University of Jerusalem, he emigrated to Canada and, eventually, the United States.
Only lately Jonas's collection of his essays *Mortality and Morality: A Search for Good after
Auschwitz* (Evanston: Northwestern University Press, 1996) was translated to Hebrew. See
also his lately published *Memoirs* (Eng. translation) (Waltham, Mass.: Brandeis University
Press, 2008). Marcuse's *One-Dimensional Man* and *The End of Utopia* were published in
Israel, both in 1970.

Laor, and others. The completely uncritical attitude toward writers who are in vogue, be they more important or less so, and the treatment of these writers with something approaching religious awe are always accompanied by righteous indignation toward "establishment" scholars, mere mortals who are considered at best naive, victims of manipulation, and mindless products of "canonical" or "hegemonic discourse," who collaborate with the powers that be and the kinds of evil they embody or produce. And hovering over all this is a metatext of self-satisfaction, a bit of narcissism, and even a certain megalomania. "Conscious of defying established power, our tone of voice shows that we know we are being subversive, and we ardently conjure away the present and the appeal to the future, whose day will be hastened by the contribution we believe we are making" as Foucault put it in another context, a description that also applies to many of his would-be disciples, who think their ostensibly critical haughtiness is his legacy.[8]

All this applies particularly well to Zertal's discussion of *Eichmann in Jerusalem*. This book comprises, with minor changes, a series of articles Arendt wrote about the trial for the *New Yorker*. Zertal has not one critical word to say about Arendt or the book, and when she implies any reservation at all, it is gentle and forgiving. Thus, for example, concerning the harsh, ugly things Arendt writes to Karl Jaspers about the policemen posted outside the courtroom, who speak only Hebrew (!), look like Arabs, and obey orders (like Eichmann himself, perhaps), and about Jerusalem, which looks to her like Istanbul (to her, a less-than-flattering comparison) – these remarks Zertal sees as "disturbing" and "tainted" – heaven forfend – "with a note of racism" (p. 132, n. 19). Such "troubling" expressions are, incidentally, quite common in Arendt's writing, though confined mostly to private correspondence, for example, in letters she wrote to her good friend Mary McCarthy and, especially, to her husband Heinrich Blücher, to whom she confided her feelings without inhibition. These letters bespeak a great deal of love and intimacy for those they address but also contempt and scorn for many other people. Reading them, one sometimes gets the impression that Arendt is almost physically repelled by everything in Israel that is not Mittel-Europ, particularly in the conduct of the trial itself.[9] No less ugly than what she has to say about the Arab-looking policemen (which rightly troubles Zertal)

---

[8] Michel Foucault, *The History of Sexuality* (New York: Vintage Books, 1985), 10.

[9] The Eichmann trial opened on April 11, 1961; on April 20, Arendt, in Jerusalem, wrote her husband: "The trial and everything surrounding it is [*sic*] so damned banal and indescribably low and repulsive." Lotte Kohler, ed., *Within Four Walls: The Correspondence between Hannah Arendt and Heinrich Bluecher, 1936–1968* (New York: Harcourt, Brace, 2000), 357.

are Arendt's comments about Israelis of East European origin, comments that Zertal seems to embrace warmly. Yet the problem is not the ugliness of Arendt's words but their fallaciousness. In a later article that recycles the chapter in her book devoted to Arendt (and includes the story of Ofer Feniger, which she sees as directly connected with the Eichmann trial and Hannah Arendt), Zertal voices a further reservation, perhaps because of all the criticism heaped on her book. She admits that Arendt's work contains "too many factual and historical errors."[10] But she does not retract anything said in her own book, for example, about the fact that Arendt was "brilliantly erudite, uncompromising, and unexpected in the paradoxical nature of her arguments" (p. 145).

The statement that Arendt's writings are full of "paradoxes" appears from time to time in the extensive literature devoted to her. On the other hand, it is not at all clear that she was really "erudite" or that there is such great depth in her work. But she was without doubt one of the most important intellectuals of the second half of the twentieth century. As we have said, she was, and still is, tremendously influential. Since what I am about to say will be mostly critical of her, I must put it in proper perspective. Many of her writings, in particular her great book *The Origins of Totalitarianism*, were pioneering

[10] Idith Zertal, "Hannah Arendt neged medinat Yisrael" (Hannah Arendt versus the State of Israel), in Adi Ophir, ed., *Hamishim le'arba'im ushmone* (Fifty since Forty-Eight: Critical Moments in the History of the State of Israel) (Jerusalem: Van Leer Institute, 1999), 158–167. Zertal returns to Arendt in another article, "Bein 'ahavat ha'olam' le'ahavat yisrael': Hakol hehasser befulmus Arendt" ("Love of the World" versus "Love of the Jewish People": The Missing Voice in the Arendt Debate), in Dan Michman, ed., *Hashoah bahistoria hayehudit: Historiografia, toda'a, ufarshanut* (The Holocaust in Jewish History: Historiography, Consciousness, and Interpretation) (Jerusalem: Yad Vashem, 5765 [2005]), 357–398. This article recycles her biography of Arendt for the umpteenth time but also repeats her carelessness. She thinks "[Arendt] spent two periods of time, amounting to several weeks, in Jerusalem following the procedures against Eichmann at Beit Ha'am" (pp. 362–363). The truth is, Arendt was in Jerusalem from April 10 to May 7, and she attended only a few sessions of the trial (which began April 11 and ended August 14; a verdict was not handed down until December 15). She returned to Israel for four days in May 1963, to visit her old friend Kurt Blumenfeld, who was on his deathbed. He died May 21. After the publication of the Eichmann "report," she came to Israel, incognito, on a number of other occasions, mainly to visit her family. It is curious that, although Blücher sometimes accompanied her on her tours, he never followed her to Israel, waiting for her in Athens instead. As related by the daughter of her cousin Ernest and her good friend Kaethe (who married and immigrated to Palestine), Blücher seemed to "exercise a strong influence on his wife." But, she adds, he always maintained "a noticeable distance from us as a Jewish family. His Communist background prevented him from coming to terms either with us Jews or with the State of Israel." Edna Brocke, "Big Hannah – My Aunt," afterword to Hannah Arendt, *The Jewish Writings*, ed. J. Kohn and R. H. Feldman (New York: Schocken, 2007), 512–521.

works, and others are still of real value. She had a sharp eye, an outstanding ability to grasp what was important and speak about it in ways that others had not managed to do. She had the courage to speak out, for example, on anti-Semitism as a European – and Jewish – problem, when others (apart from the Zionists and certain other Jewish circles) were afraid to do so; and there are many other things one can say on her behalf. Nevertheless, the stature she enjoys in contemporary culture does not derive entirely from what she wrote or from the quality of her writing – perhaps because, as Zertal so nicely put it, her work is full of "paradoxes."

Arendt's special status is largely a symbolic one. To put it another way, it derives not only from the content of her books and many articles, or even from their distinctive style, but also from the whole constituted by her oeuvre, her life story (including the fact that she was a woman), and, to a considerable degree, her extraordinary personality. It might be apt here to quote part of the eulogy given at her funeral by Hans Jonas, who had gotten to know her in Heidegger's seminar, when, as a girl of eighteen, she came to Marburg to study philosophy. Jonas, who was her friend all through the years, was so exasperated by her book on the Eichmann trial that he broke off relations with her, only to mend them not long before her death.

Shy and distant, with striking, beautiful features and lonely eyes, she stood immediately out as "exceptional," as "unique," in an as yet undefinable way. Brightness of intellect was no rare article there. But there was an intensity, an inner direction, an instinct for quality, a groping for essence, a probing for depth, which cast a magic about her. One felt an absolute determination to be herself, with the toughness to carry it through in the face of great vulnerability.[11]

ARENDT AND ZIONISM: A STORY OF MISUNDERSTANDING

Jonas's description of Arendt here is almost certainly accurate. In his recently published *Memoirs*, her exceptional moral qualities and intellectual gifts, but also the severity of the quarrel over *Eichmann in Jerusalem*, come across even more clearly. One gets a similar impression from her writings, from her letters – mainly to her husband, but also to Karl Jaspers, her friend Mary McCarthy, and even Heidegger – and from things said about her by friends, students, and numerous admirers. Even Elisabeth Young-Bruehl's biography does not entirely manage to contradict this impression. A highly captivating, fresh, sometimes surprising, and even moving image of Arendt emerges from

[11] Published lately in Christian Wiese, *The Life and Thought of Hans Jonas: Jewish Dimensions* (Lebanon, N.H.: Brandeis University Press-UPNE, 2007), 179.

Edna Brocke's little portrait of her Aunt Hannah from America, mentioned
earlier. Arendt's relations with her family in Israel are a relatively unknown
chapter of her life. Warmth, intimacy, love, and admiration are all there. A
certain familiarity as well, which not only is a matter of family closeness but
also makes one think of the immediacy and simplicity of human relations in
Israel in the fifties. But there were also misunderstandings. Brocke relates
that she sometimes played the intermediary between her parents and her
aunt: "[Hannah] often repeated the criticisms of Israel current among many
leftists in Europe and the United States, which were usually based on scant
knowledge of the real situation, and this caused tension and needed to be
overcome, because they had been so close to one another since childhood"
(p. 515). On the one hand, there was a great closeness, a feeling of being
almost at home, tenderness, and esteem; on the other, disagreement, exas-
peration, even anger. This tension marks all her relationships with her Israeli
friends and relatives, even the closest and the dearest, like Kurt Blumenfeld.[12]
One has to keep this background in mind when speaking of the alleged campaign against her following the publication of *Eichmann in Jerusalem*. If
her friends spoke out against her, in private or in public, it was *despite* the
establishment rather than in its service. As Gershom Scholem wrote to her in
his second letter, she should have known better.[13] She knew all too well that
neither he nor her other critics in Israel were acting on behalf of the Zionist
or state establishment.

The most significant testimony, perhaps, is Hans Jonas's. Toward the end
of the period in which I have been working on the last additions, revisions,
and changes to the English translation of the present book, there appeared
the fascinating and extremely interesting *Memoirs* of Hans Jonas. For whoever is interested in the famous Jewish-German dialogue, especially during

[12] The correspondence between Arendt and Blumenfeld appeared a few years ago: *In keinen
Besitz verwurgzeit* (Berlin: Rotbuch Verlag, 1995). There is a French translation: *Hannah
Arendt – Kurt Blumenfeld, Correspondance, 1933–1963* (Paris: Desclée de Brouwer,
1998).
[13] The famous correspondence between Arendt and Scholem after the publication of her
Eichmann is longer than the two letters – one of each – usually published. There were in
fact a few more letters, at least two of which are not less interesting than the first ones. The
first two letters are published, for example, in the collection of essays and letters *The Jew
as Pariah*, ed. R. H. Feldman (New York: Grove Press, 1978), 240–251. I am not aware
of any publication in English that contains the other letters. They have been published
lately in French translation in the remarkable edition containing Arendt's *Totalitarism* and
Eichmann, as well as much more supplementary material, a very helpful introduction and
notes by Pierre Biuretz, notes, bibliographies, etc. See H. Arendt, *Les Origines du totalita-
rismem Eichmann à Jérusalem* (Paris: Gallimard, 2002). Scholem's second letter is on pp.
1370–1374 ; Arendt's reply to it on pp. 1374–1376.

the period between the two world wars; in the rise of Nazism and what it did to German philosophy; and in German Zionism, in all the great figures of the first decades of the existence of the Hebrew University, of its department of philosophy, of the Jewish Brigade, of Hans Jonas himself, this book is a precious document. It also makes a particularly pleasurable reading, very often amusing, especially for those who have some acquaintance, even indirectly, with the figures whom Jonas interacts with and describes. It is also very interesting for anyone who is interested in Hannah Arendt.

The great, life-long friendship between him and Arendt has been a well-known fact. But only now, with the publication of his memoirs, has it become possible to get an idea of how deep and close it was, ever since their first meeting in Bultmann's seminar on the New Testament in Marburg. In this extraordinary book, Jonas tells the story of a fascinating friendship and of a fascinating woman. But he also relates his great anger with the report of the Eichmann trial and the breach that lasted many years. Jonas was perhaps Arendt's closest friend. He leaves no doubt that he had not only held her in the highest esteem as a thinker and as an intellectual (second perhaps only to himself), but also had had the most deep feeling of friendship toward her. It had been most probably mutual, although with Arendt it is sometimes difficult to know. What he had to say about *Eichmann in Jerusalem*, its publication, and about Arendt as its author is worth citing at length. When she returned to the States from Jerusalem, tells Jonas, she said, "I think what I have to report will create quite an uproar in Jewish circles" – which means that she was perhaps less surprised by scandal than we are usually told. Jonas continues: "From the initial article on, I was shocked – first at the tone she'd adopted, second at the explicitly anti-Zionist tenor, and third at Hannah's ignorance when it came to things Jewish. ... In fact, her knowledge of Judaism was minimal. Her awareness of Jewish history didn't go farther than Moses Mendelssohn. ... Everything before that was surrounded by general fog, lost in the darkness of the past and the Old Testament, which she didn't know and probably hadn't even read, unlike the New Testament, which she'd studied with Bultmann" (p. 178).

After reading the first article in the *New Yorker*, Jonas recounts, he tried to dissuade her from publishing the rest of her report, or at least to change them. "But now I discovered that you couldn't talk to Hannah once she'd made up her mind. No argument, no persuasion, no correction of factual mistakes could shake her basic conception or even get her to entertain other possibilities. ... She had the temerity to assert that the history of eternal anti-Semitism was a Zionist invention ... she tried to convince herself and others that the notion of anti-Semitism's being a natural component of Jewish existence was a Zionist invention" (pp. 180–181).

The "tension" Edna Brocke talks about was not just a tension between her parents and her aunt; it was also one expression of great tension and great ambiguity within Arendt herself. This is what comes out also – paradoxically, if you like – from another anecdote told by Edna Brocke. Accidently or not, Israel's Independence Day fell during the time Arendt was in Israel covering the trial. It was celebrated then with much pomp and included a military parade. "It was impossible not to sense Hannah's ambivalent reaction to this ceremony. It awoke in her an earlier identification with the Zionist idea, while at the same time returning her to the contradiction that she had adopted as her own" (p. 514). This ambiguity comes out in what she wrote before and immediately after the Six-Day War.

Of this tension, there is not much left in *Eichmann in Jerusalem*. It explodes in a violent attempt (only partly successful) to overcome an ambivalence that had been waiting for an opportunity to resolve itself. The result, Arendt's series of the articles in the *New Yorker* and then the book, does not deserve the praise Zertal and others heap upon it. While in many respects interesting, even fascinating, and written with the fluency and acuteness that always characterized Arendt's work, it is probably the worst thing she ever wrote. In fact, it is just a bad book. What is more, the book is morally scandalous, and the reactions not only of Scholem, Blumenfeld, and Brocke's parents – all great admirers of Arendt – but also of the New York Jewish intelligentsia in general were justified, especially that of Hans Jonas, who tells of his great anger at the "report" on the Eichmann trial and the breach between them that lasted many years. This should not be taken lightly, as most Arendt scholars, and particularly her hagiographers, usually do. There must have been something to these reactions. Not all these people were stupid, blind, establishment lackeys or Arendt haters. The book, we know, has been translated into many languages and printed in countless editions. But the wide circulation it has enjoyed, its considerable influence on intellectual opinion, and the fact that it has aroused in many people the same enthusiasm it aroused in Zertal are further indications of the suspicious propensity of her crowd to embrace anything critical of Israel. More than signs of the book's quality, they are symptoms of a perversion. The very first lines reveal its true character and how Arendt came to devote a book to that terrible trial: she sneers, condescends, hands out marks right and left, makes pronouncements about how the trial should have been conducted and who should have said what, and fumes that it was done differently. In her essay about Arendt in the volume *Hamishim le'arba'im ushmone* (Fifty since Forty-Eight), Zertal writes, with her usual wit, that Arendt "burst … into the national classroom that the State of Israel had set up in Jerusalem's Beit Ha'am [the auditorium where the trial was held]" (p. 161). To carry this brilliant image further, we might say that what infuriated Arendt was that this particular class was not devoted to her book on totalitarianism.

Arendt was angry. It was finally mainly this that has remained of the tension. Even Zertal says so. She was particularly angry at the Jews: the *Judenräte*, the leaders, the parvenus. She did not especially like the East European Jews and did not really understand them. Only the Jews of German origin, like herself, merited a kind word here and there, but if they were Israelis she looked down on them, too. She had no mercy or compassion for the Jews, the Israelis, or the Zionists.[14] Above all, she was angry at Ben-Gurion. She was so angry at him that she allowed herself to tell stories about him that can be described, at best, as not quite factual. She may have been overly impressed by the aforementioned article by Trevor-Roper,[15] for what she has to say about Ben-Gurion – as the architect of the state and conductor of the trial, as the person who decided on his own to bring Eichmann to Israel and organize a show trial of him for the education of the Children of Israel and the world as a whole – is quite inaccurate but reminiscent of that article, which was, incidentally, written out of great admiration for him. She contributed thus in a significant way to the invention of a whole mythology around this trial.

Arendt's anger at Ben-Gurion was not unrelated to the Zionist chapter in her own life. As happened more than once, her Zionism was connected with one of the men in her life, Kurt Blumenfeld, a leader of the German Zionist movement. Her first male landmark, and in many respects the most important, had been Martin Heidegger. What she learned from him continued to influence her all the rest of her life, and, intellectually speaking, the

---

[14] By contrast, she shows a good deal of indulgence for the Germans. Much has already been written about her affair with Heidegger, both before and after the war, and there is no point in dwelling on it here. Arendt not only renewed her ties with him after the war, when he was forbidden to teach at the university for having been a Nazi, but was also the main driving force behind the translation of his works into English and the making of him into a central figure in American academic culture. Shlomo Avineri wrote a short article a while back (*Alpayim* 26 [5764 (2004)]: 281–285) describing the "correct, professional" relations Arendt had with Dr. Hans Roessner, the editor of her works at the respected Piper publishing house in Munich. Roessner had been a member of the Nazi Party and the SD. Arendt evidently never took any interest in his past, despite his belonging to a certain generation and despite signs, in his letters to her regarding her books, that might have aroused her suspicion. And if, in fact, she had taken an interest, Avineri asks, how could she have gone on working with him for twenty years?

[15] This is Ora Herman's surmise in "Shiddurim min haplaneta ha'aheret: Mishpat Eichmann, hamemsad, ukhlei hatikshoret ha'elektroni'im" (Broadcasts from the Other Planet: The Eichmann Trial, the Establishment, and the Electronic Media) (master's thesis, Hebrew University of Jerusalem, 2003).

encounter with him was undoubtedly the most important "consciousness-shaping" one she ever had, to use Zertal's phrase. Before she had reached the age of twenty, Arendt was already one of Heidegger's star pupils, and she was at the same time his lover, as is well known. Quite a banal story, in fact. The famous, charismatic professor, a husband and father, who carries on a secret love affair with his brilliant, young, beautiful – and, of course, Jewish – student. When the romance ended, as expected, in disappointment, the student decided to give up the study of philosophy. She had moved to Marburg and written a doctorate (on Augustine's concept of love) under another distinguished professor, Karl Jaspers, with whom she also had a deep, formative connection until he died. After her divorce from philosophy (a temporary one, as it turned out), she began to take an interest in the phenomenon of Jewish assimilation and its failure, and she wrote a biography of Rachel Varnhagen. Around this time, she met again Kurt Blumenfeld, an old family friend, who became her lifelong friend and, for a time, turned her, if not into a full-fledged Zionist, at least a *compagnonne de route*. For, as she said many years later, for whoever had wanted to act politically as a Jew, the only available possibility had been Zionism. A funny kind of explanation, if one thinks of it for a moment, which reverses the order, and which turns the end into means, and vice versa.

Be that as it may, it was more or less at the time she met Blumenfeld that Arendt decided to express her nonassimilation by becoming active in Zionist circles and organizations. This involvement lasted for several years, in Berlin, Paris (where she had fled in 1933), and then New York. But by then she had married Blücher, a non-Jewish communist and left-wing activist, and this marriage, which combined a great love with a strong intellectual bond, changed her worldview once again. She now took an interest in political questions, first and foremost the phenomenon of totalitarianism, from a more universal perspective. She no longer considered anti-Semitism and the "Jewish question" from a specifically Jewish point of view but rather as part of an attempt to grasp, theoretically and objectively, modernity in general and the new phenomenon she called totalitarianism in particular.

The Origins of Totalitarianism

The Origins of Totalitarianism is undoubtedly the best known of Arendt's books and the mainstay of her reputation. It is unquestionably a very important book, and in some respects – which even most of her disciples find difficult to pinpoint – it may even be a great book. It is, in fact, a compilation of three more or less independent essays. The first deals with anti-Semitism, or rather one aspect of it, limited both chronologically and thematically. The second deals with European colonial expansion, which Arendt sees as the principal cause of the decline and disintegration of the nation-state. The third analyzes the Nazi regime, and to some extent the Stalinist one, as the two main manifestations of what she regards as a completely new phenomenon, the totalitarian state. The analysis of totalitarianism is certainly the most important part of the book and the one that gives it lasting value. If one could summarize this rich, complex composition in a single sentence it would be that totalitarianism has three main components: the amalgamation of ideology with terror, the complete atomization of society, and the great symbolic importance of show trials and internment camps.

Many critics have seen the book as important for, among other things, having placed the question of totalitarian regimes on the agenda of the West, for the important (though not always entirely original) insights the book contains, for its great intellectual sweep and daring, and for the deep moral concern that informs it; but they have also noted its great flaws. The main point was made by Raymond Aron as early as 1954 (in the journal *Commentaire*): Arendt does not grasp the profound differences between Nazism and communism, and she does not really understand Stalinism; and her approach to Nazism is an essentialist rather than a historical or sociological one.

A further comment is in order. The book on totalitarianism must be seen in a specific ideological, intellectual, and sociopolitical context, one that gave rise to a whole literature that represented Nazism and Stalinism as different manifestations of a single historical phenomenon. Writings in this genre frequently played a role in the Cold War–era ideological struggle against communism. The other school of ideological or quasi-ideological historiography, that of the left, depicted Nazism as a variety of fascism, a subcategory of capitalism and imperialism. In the meantime many things have changed. Most historians, and to a lesser extent political scientists, now seem less enthused about the idea of putting Nazism and Stalinism (or communism in general) into one sociopolitical category and see only limited theoretical value in doing so. The term "totalitarianism" does retain a certain vitality for an assortment of ideologues, and it can probably still be used fruitfully for some serious purposes, but on the whole it is doubtful whether it has yielded much in the way of theoretical fruit. While Arendt's book does not fit squarely into this genre, and she did not write it as a Cold War apologia for liberal democracy, one cannot detach it entirely from this context.[16]

---

[16] On the vast literature dealing with the Nazi phenomenon and the development of various approaches to it, see Pierre Ayçoberry, *The Nazi Question: An Essay on the Interpretations*

Be that as it may, a further comment must be made about Arendt's book on totalitarianism and its treatment of the Nazi version in particular: there is hardly any mention in it of the Nazi extermination of the Jews or, for that matter, of the Gypsies, the handicapped, or the mentally ill. This is the ultimate paradox. The "tension" that was still somewhat veiled in the essay on anti-Semitism in this book comes out into the open in the essay on "The Totalitarian System." Arendt hardly mentions the Holocaust, yet it is this and nothing else that she is speaking about. As she says on many occasions, it was the need to understand this event – which nothing had prepared us to understand – that was the main, perhaps even the only, moving force behind the book. It was necessary to understand "this." Except that "this" has disappeared from the book.

It seems that "the camp," the hallmark of totalitarian regimes (and, according to Agamben, of the state as such) was, for Arendt, the Gurs detention camp, where the Vichy government held thousands of Jews and others prisoner, Arendt among them, rather than Auschwitz. Or, as M. Leibovici suggests with more nuance, seeing that Arendt's main sources were David Rousset, Bruno Bettelheim, and Eugene Kogon, all survivors of Nazi concentration camps but none of them of an *extermination* camp, it is in fact of the *universe concentrationnaire* (as Rousset called it) that she speaks, not of the extermination. She thus helped make it possible – there were undoubtedly other reasons for this – for a French Jewish intellectual like Vidal-Naquet to say on several occasions that it took not only French public opinion and intellectuals in general but even him, whose father had been deported and assassinated by the Nazis, some twenty years to understand that the Shoah was about extermination, not deportation. The theory of totalitarianism should make it possible for us to understand the crime, but of the crime itself she makes hardly any mention.

In fact, beside a few cursory remarks, there is practically no direct reference anywhere in Arendt's work to the destruction, to the crime of exterminating the Jews as it was actually carried out. The omission from the

of National Socialism (1922–1975) (New York: Pantheon, 1981). See also Enzo Traverso, *Le totalitarisme. Le XXe siècle en débat* (Paris: Seuil, 2001), 92. This is an important anthology, which follows, in a chronological order, the development of the uses of the notion of *totalitarisme*. As the author says (p. 92; his reference here is Claude Lefort), this notion "has been used most often as a suitcase-word, as a *passe-partout* meant mainly to evade the 'complication' represented by each totalitarian [case] insofar as it is a 'total social fact.'" A monumental work comparing the Nazi regime (which was coterminous with Hitler's rule) and the Stalinist regime in Russia (which was *not* coterminous with Communist rule in the Soviet Union; Arendt failed to notice this difference) is Richard Overy, *The Dictators: Hitler's Germany, Stalin's Russia*, 2nd ed. (London: Penguin, 2005).

Totalitarianism book of any direct reference to the actual extermination of the Jews prepares the ground for what is to come fully to light in her book on Eichmann. There, we find a virtual suppression (as well it might be called) of what has been spoken of publicly and explicitly for the first time, arguably the trial's true significance. For in her "report," she refused – as we shall see – to follow the course of the prosecutor, who, she would say, has founded his claims on suffering, that is, in fact, on the actual unfolding of the crime seen through the victims' experience. Thus, to take just one example, when she speaks of the ultimate stages of the crime, in chapters 6 ("The Final Solution: The Murder") and 13 ("The Death Camps in the East"), she talks of many things, but never really of the actual killing of the Jews (or others, for that matter): she talks of what Eichmann had seen or not seen in the east, of the juridico-philosophical problem of conscience, of the conspiracy against Hitler, of the fact that the court had to listen to testimonies about the extermination in the extermination camps – but not of the actual "Shoah by Bullets"[17] or, in particular, of the gas chambers.

Although Arendt scholars generally ignore this peculiarity of her work,[18] there are a few who do not. But, as it has become one of the rules of the game in much of the Arendt literature, the latter often try, so to speak, to save Arendt from herself. For example, M. Leibovici, in *Hannah Arendt, une juive,* the book mentioned previously, raises the possibility that there has been a displacement in Arendt's thought: in the *Origins,* she has embarked on a road that leads to misconceiving the nature of the Holocaust, yet, immediately after the war, she had "an astonishingly lucid understanding of it" (p. 147). In a 1946 conference entitled "Remarks to European Jewery," she said that in the camps only the Jews went to the gas chambers, or that because of a criminal lack of imagination we did not make the distinction between persecution and extermination: whereas others were persecuted, we, Jews, were exterminated. She expressed this view even more passionately when she accused the authors of the *Black Book,* published in 1946

---

[17] See the absolutely incredible Patrick Desbois and Paul A. Shapiro, *Holocaust by Bullets: A Priest's Journey to Uncover the Truth behind the Murder of 1.5 Million Jews* (New York: Palgrave Macmillan, 2008).

[18] Two recent examples are two reviews of the volume of her Jewish writings – the one by Steven Aschheim (in the *Times Literary Supplement,* no. 5452, September 28, 2007), who depicts nicely the "deep yet ambiguous" aspects and the "complexity" of her Jewish experience, yet sees in her "one of the earliest and most concerned analysts of the Final Solution"; the other, by Judith Butler (in the *London Review of Books,* May 10, 2007), typically entitled "I Merely Belong to Them," which is largely a curious gloss on modish anti-Zionism but which ignores completely the "complexity" of Arendt's Jewish experience, let alone her problematic dealing with the Holocaust.

by the Jewish Anti-Fascist Committee, of treating the extermination in an insufficient manner, though she admits that there is no more difficult history to tell in all of human history than the history of the extermination.

It is true that if one reads these words of Arendt's in light of pronouncements such as the one by Pierre Vidal-Naquet cited earlier, or of what Annette Wieviorka says in the introduction to her *Déportation et génocide*[19] – and what holds for France certainly holds for other European countries, and also for the United States – one may admire Arendt's early "lucidity." In truth, though, these more or less sporadic remarks by Arendt are neither particularly lucid nor very astonishing. What is perhaps astonishing is the lack of lucidity of so many others. Léon Poliakov in France and Raoul Hilberg in the United States are just two examples, out of numerous others, who had the same kind of early insights about the nature of the German accomplishment in Europe. To judge by the fact that they have devoted their life to research on this topic, one may assume even that they too thought that it was an extremely difficult – but also important – story to tell.

There was one more place, though, where the distinction between deportation and extermination was not so carefully done. In Israel, too, for many years, it was blurred to some extent. Unlike for French (and other) intellectuals, however, the Holocaust was conceived in Israel from the very beginning as essentially a business of extermination, the deportation being seen as a relatively secondary and subsidiary part of it. In the Yishuv and then in Israel, everybody – leaders, ordinary people, intellectuals – knew way before the end of the war, when Arendt and her husband were still refusing to believe, that what was going on in Europe was neither persecution, pogrom, nor deportation, but extermination. Practically everybody in the Yishuv had family or friends in Europe, information was arriving relatively early, and "lucidity" about what was happening was not such a rare commodity. If I insist on this matter, it is because a whole mythology, made, once again, of ignorance, bad faith, and sheer malice, has been constituted around the question of the reactions of the Yishuv to the Shoah. We dealt with it already, and there is no need to repeat it here. Arendt, through her way of presenting the Jewish Councils, for example, or her telling of the Kasztner affair, in other ways as well, has contributed significantly to the establishment of this mythology. Zertal, Grodzinsky, and Tom Segev, among others, who cultivate the story of negligence, indifference, insensitivity, miscomprehension, and lack of lucidity on the part of the Yishuv, are taken too often as real authorities on the matter, which they are not. Worth emphasizing here

[19] Paris: Plon, 1992.

is that a serious Israeli historiography deals, often quite critically, with all these questions; and that Israeli historians were practically the first to institutionalize lucidity, that is, to create an organized and not sporadic research, to establish the infrastructure necessary for this research and to teach systematically the extermination of European Jewery.

Arendt, in any case, and after her short period of lucidity, ignores the extermination. In the *Origins*, as we saw, it practically disappears. The gas chambers are mentioned twice in the whole work (according to Leibovici, p. 148) and in the third part, "The Totalitarian System," they are presented as the extreme form of the concentration camps (ibid., p. 149). As to the *Eichmann in Jerusalem*, Leibovici (p. 153), in what can be described as a quasi-heroic attempt to save Arendt from herself, thinks that the means exist in Arendt's work to "reintroduce" the lost distinction between deportation and extermination. To this one can make two remarks: First, it is more than evident that the theoretical resources for such reintegration exist in Arendt's work, which makes her non-reintroduction of the extermination into her writing only a graver sin; second, if she lacked these resources, she would, or should, as every serious theoretician does, forge them. What was lacking there was not theoretical tools, but the theoretical motivation to use them or, if need be, to forge them.

The End of a Zionist Adventure

Since, as we have seen, there were actually no more urgent motives than to understand the unprecedented crime, a real, bothersome question raises: Why didn't Arendt talk of the extermination in the *Origins*? Why did she choose not to talk of the horror that unfolded in the courtroom in Jerusalem? Is it possible that the already familiar "tension" had some old roots? This, in fact, was the case; it was not, however, a matter of psychological or merely biographical factors, but something of a paradigmatic nature. Arendt, in fact, was a Zionist, when she was involved with the Zionist movement, in one traditional sense, that is, as a Jew who asks money from another Jew to send a third Jew to Palestine. When she was a refugee in Paris and then in New York, Zionist involvement gave her a framework of belonging – and a livelihood, too. But for all her loyalty to and activity in the movement, she always kept a certain distance from it. For example, her activism never prompted her to consider *aliya* (ascent) (as immigration to Palestine/Israel is referred to in the consciousness-shaping discourse of the Zionists). A visit she paid to Palestine in 1935 did not leave her with pleasant memories (except for the admiration she felt for the young kibbutz pioneers). And though she did not say so when speaking to Jewish activists upon her return from Palestine, when writing about the trip to her friend Mary McCarthy shortly after the Six-Day War, what she mostly expressed about it was reserve. She did, however, add one sentence that became famous: "Any real catastrophe in Israel would affect me more deeply than anything else." In this sense, too, she thus proved to be a classical Zionist. Her Zionism was mainly one of catastrophe rather than of nuts and bolts, as some other Zionists referred at that time to the project of building a state.

Behind all these small anecdotes looms the same tension and ambiguity, and it is even quite easy to tell today that it was already very old when she was still working in Alyat Ha'Noar,[20] busy sending young boys and girls to Palestine. Perhaps the most interesting piece in the recently published volume of Arendt's Jewish writings is, as Steven Aschheim rightly says in his aforementioned review (note 3), is a previously unpublished draft of an essay on anti-Semitism. It contains many elements that would later figure in the first part of the *Origins*, but there are also several notable differences between the two texts. It was written probably toward the end of the thirties, and it provides an opportunity to grasp Arendt's preoccupations during the last years of her French exile.[21]

In the introduction to this piece, Arendt defines her position in relation to the only two options of Jewish existence she has ever seriously considered, and rejects them both: assimilation and Zionism. She understands both of them as parallel and at bottom very close reactions to anti-Semitism, and she even qualifies Zionism as the heir of assimilation. Yet, notwithstanding her deep reserves in regard to Zionism, she could write to Blücher, roughly at the same time (in a letter from 1936), that Palestine is at the center of "our" national aspirations, and this is so not because some ancestors of the present-day Jews had lived on this piece of land, but because for this craziest of all peoples the ruins of Jerusalem are rooted in the heart of time.[22] This instinctive, if one may call it thus, or completely pretheoretical, Zionism has in fact never left her – a fact that too many writers, like Judith Butler in her absolutely amazing review (see Postscript), ignore or choose to ignore – as is seen from the things she would say many years later, such as that the right of the

---

[20] The organization Youth Aliyah was established in Germany in 1932, in response to the deterioration of the situation of the Jews in Germany. It has been dealing ever since with helping the youth to make their Aliyah to Palestine, then Israel, to get proper education, and to integrate into their new country.

[21] Although unpublished before, it was not completely unknown. M. Leibovici is one of the rare scholars to have known it and to refer to it.

[22] Cited in *Jewish Writings,* in the preface by J. Kohn, p. xviii.

Jews to a national home in Palestine results from the potential immortality of the Jewish people.

What is remarkable, however, in this early text, is not only the fact that at this early stage she had such deep reservations about Zionism (as Aschheim remarks in his review, as late as 1941 Scholem was still seeing her not only as a wonderful woman – which she was in fact – but also as "an extraordinary Zionist" – which she was perhaps too, but certainly not in the sense meant by Scholem), but also, and chiefly, that she held already to the main themes of her ulterior criticism. Thus, for instance, her principal historiographical thesis, according to which Zionism was exclusively a result of anti-Semitism and of the failure of assimilation, is simply false. Even in regard to Herzl, the emblematic figure of this simplistic cause-and-effect history, things are more complex. At least according to one distinguished political scientist – true, Israeli and Zionist – the creation of a Jewish public or political space was not less important than the acknowledgment of the perpetuity of anti-Semitism and of the failure of assimilation.[23]

The Zionist nationalist historians have shown, she writes, as against the assimilationists, that the Jews formed a people. But they understand this peoplehood by a "theory of substance," according to which the Jews and the European nations were different "substances," irreconcilably strange one to the other, which, she adds perfectly conformed to the National Socialists, who "crystallized" this conception of *Volksgemeinschaft* into anti-Semitism. What is perhaps most remarkable about this doctrine, if one may consider it to be one, is not only its completely surrealistic nature – the nationalist-Zionist conception of Jewishness is the source of Nazi anti-Semitism – but the fact that respected academics, such as J. Butler, are not ashamed to repeat it as if it was in the least bit serious.

Notwithstanding a few attempts to offer a political – that is, not sub-stantialist – definition of "people," the truth is that the distinctions between "people" as a natural or "national" entity, or as a political choice or partici-pation, on the one hand, and between substantialist and political conceptions of peoplehood, on the other, are very vague. What is important, however, is not so much the theoretical weakness of these distinctions but the following double fact. First, Arendt's "political" conception of the Jewish people is, if not simply taken from Zionist thought, at least so close to it as to permit the hypothesis that it was her main inspiration. The truth is that most Zionist thinkers, at least the nonreligious among them, conceived the Jewish people in historical and political terms, even if they did not know – and even this

---

[23] Shlomo Avineri, *Herzl* (Jerusalem: Zalman Shazar Center, 2007) (in Hebrew).

had not always been the case – to cast their thought in that form and give it a theoretical sophistication like Arendt gave hers. Differently put, the Zionists' conception of Jewish peoplehood, insofar as it was the basis for their concrete program and action, was not more mythical, or substantial, than Arendt's own use of the notion of "people." Second, and more important, Zionism has provided, certainly during and immediately after the war – as she acknowledged herself on more than one occasion – the only real opportunity for free, active, and concrete *participation*, that is, to take part, according to her very own conception, in the political life and political power of the "people." If one wanted to seriously and honestly follow Arendt's line of reasoning, the conclusion forces itself: Zionism was then, and Israel is now, the only specifically Jewish space of freedom and responsibility.

This is a presentation of Zionism done completely in Arendt's terms. One can accept them, and the theoretical presupposition on which they are based, or reject them. One can say that Arendt both accepted and rejected them. For freedom, both personal and, in particular, political, one has sometimes to pay quite a high price. The Zionists were ready to pay very highly, in many different ways, for it. Some people are not ready to pay the price. But Arendt thought that freedom was worth the price – and she also knew that this sometimes means a moral price. This is why her critique of Zionism is so "paradoxical" or, more precisely, unacceptable. Unacceptable also because it is simply false: there is practically no truth at all in her depiction of Zionism as a monolithic movement, guided by one, unique, and mainly simplistic, substanialistic orthodoxy. All this was, in the last analysis, a rationalization, perhaps not much more than an excuse, cast in theoretical form, of a non-participation in the real Jewish political life. It was also what had permitted the adoption of several claims, which had been already then, and with an ever-growing force later, the common place of all the criticisms, in general misplaced and unfounded, of Zionism, and to supply the opprobrium community with a false appearance of honesty and intellectual respectability.

What is typical of this criticism of Zionism is not only its superficiality but also the political and historical blindness it involves. In this text, Arendt reproaches the Zionists not only for their failure to deal with the fact that the Soviet Union (and, let us recall, this was written at the late thirties) had accorded equal rights to the Jews but also for their willingness to deal at the same time with enemies and to have signed the famous "transfer" agreement with the Nazis.[24] Unable to distinguish between friend (Stalin's USSR) and

---

[24] In 1933 Nazi Germany and Zionist leaders signed an agreement – the "transfer agreement" – in which, in return for an agreement by world Jewry not to boycott Germany,

enemy, Zionism is not – do we hear Schmitt here? – a political fact. Beside
the amazing lack of lucidity, what is also unacceptable here is the mixture
of malice and frivolity in the denunciation of the transfer agreement, which
had made it possible for many Jews to leave Germany with some of their
money and to immigrate to Israel. One could draw from this text some other
examples of deep historical blindness.

All, or most, of the themes of Arendt's later criticism of Zionism are
already there. It will become public toward the end of the war – the timing
is also a significant matter – but its full radicality will not burst out until the
report on the Eichmann trial. In any case, over a period of several years,
the years before and immediately following the establishment of the state,
Arendt's was a critical voice in Zionist affairs. She was close to the views of
Brit Shalom (which numbered among its members Gershom Scholem and
Akiva Ernst Simon, who were among the harshest critics of her book on the
Eichmann trial) and, in particular, of Judah Magnes and the Ihud group
he had just founded. At the time of the historic debate over the partition
plan, Magnes, who spent the last months of his life in America, recruited
her to the movement and its last-ditch efforts to prevent the plan from
being adopted.[25] This was Arendt's last real Zionist political involvement.
Whatever one may think of this, it might still be argued that, as movingly
and honestly as she cared about the fate of the Zionist undertaking, unlike
the Brit Shalom people, who lived in Palestine and went on living here even
when their views were rejected and who would have paid a price had their
views been accepted and then proved wrong, she continued to express her
ideas and worked to implement them, even when she no longer bore any
responsibility and would not have to bear the consequences of miscalcula-
tion. In retrospect, her adherence to Zionism seems to have been conditional:
when the movement did not listen to her, she turned her back on it. The more
it departed from her way of thinking, the more Ben-Gurionist it became,
that is, the more it sought to establish a Jewish state in the Land of Israel,
the further Arendt distanced herself. One way or another, her activism in

some sixty thousand German Jews and about $100 million were transferred to Palestine.
The agreement was very controversial and provoked bitter disputes within the Zionist
movement. It is still evoked nowadays for polemic purposes. It figures highly in the Web
sites of the holocaust deniers, and A. Burg sees in it – he learned about it from Moshe
Zimmerman from the Hebrew University, a prominent member of the community of
opprobrium – another sign of the highly questionable moral character of the Zionist
movement.
[25] On this, see Joseph Heller, *Mibrit shalom la'ihud: Yehuda Leib Magnes vehama'avak
limedina du-le'umit* (From Brit Shalom to the Ihud: Yehuda Leon Magnes and the Struggle
for a Binational State) (Jerusalem: Magnes, 5764 [2003]), ch. 9.

Zionist and Jewish affairs diminished rather quickly. The more famous she became – her book on totalitarianism (1951) established her in much wider circles as an important political thinker – and the less she needed the support of a Jewish environment, perhaps, the more she cut herself off from the American Jewish community. She stopped writing in Jewish periodicals or on Jewish topics and was no longer involved in organized Jewish life. She had expressed her final break from the Zionist movement openly in a highly critical article, "Zionism Reconsidered," a kind of writ of divorce.[26] More than just a historical analysis of Zionism, it is filled with accusations and angry prophecies, most of which did not come to pass. Unless, of course, one regards as evidence of originality and political perspicacity, as Zertal does, the prediction that a Jewish state established in the Land of Israel would find itself in a protracted, bloody conflict with the Arabs.

But there is more to it. One of Arendt's claims in this article is that the Zionists, and in particular the Halutzim of socialist Zionism, have not had "the slightest suspicion" of a national conflict with the inhabitants of the "promised land" (*Jewish Writings*, p. 349). One of the founding myths of the systematic and theoretical anti-Zionism is the notorious myth of "a land without a people to a people without a land." According to this myth, the Zionists ignored, innocently or not, the fact that Palestine was inhabited by another people, having its own national movement. Like most myths of this kind, it does not contain but a very partial truth. In fact, almost all the Zionist leaders, since the very first stages of the Jewish immigration to Israel, have had a more or less clear perception of the political, national, and demographic reality in Palestine – namely, not only of the presence of an important Arab population but also of its resistance to the creation of a Jewish national home in this land. This resistance, however, had not become "national" before the 1908 Young Turks revolution and became specifically Palestinian only with the demise of the Ottoman Empire and the beginning of the British Mandate.

Many admirers of Arendt, in Israel and elsewhere, praise this prophetic article, sometimes in superlatives. Seyla Benhabib, for example, thinks that Arendt's insights and predictions contained in it are "breathtaking." Once again, then, great lucidity. As if she saw something other Zionists, Ben-Gurion, for example, did not see. As if her perspicacity enabled her to understand better than the whole Zionist movement where its actions were leading,

---

[26] The article "Zionism Reconsidered" appeared in the August 1945 issue of *The Menorah Journal*. It was reprinted in Hannah Arendt, *The Jew as Pariah: Jewish Identity and Politics in the Modern Age* (New York: Grove Press, 1978), 131–164, and in the *Jewish Writings*, 343–374.

as if her views could have averted the catastrophe of the now more than sixty years of war with the Arab world. The truth of the matter, however, is that most Zionists foresaw precisely this. Some of them decided to forsake Jewish nationalism altogether. One of these was Hans Kohn, whose background was quite similar to Arendt's and, like her, would later teach in New York's New School for Social Research and become a respected authority on nationalism (among other things), and who, after spending several years in Palestine, decided, as early as 1934, that the realization of the Zionist project would demand too high a price, an ongoing armed conflict with the Arabs, in which he decided he could not morally take part. Several years before Arendt's article was published, Kohn wrote an article bearing the title "Zionism."[27] The history of the Zionist movement, the analysis of the actual situation in Palestine, and the prognosis for the future contained in Kohn's article are not very different from Arendt's. The tone, however, is completely different. While Arendt's is vindictive and recriminating, Kohn's is much more matter-of-fact and impassionate. But from his description a sense of tragedy emerges and, through this, a deeply compassionate attitude toward the Zionist adventure.

Another is Ze'ev Jabotinsky, the leader of the Revisionist camp (later to become Herut, then Likud, both right-wing parties), who, very soon after the First World War, was already saying, on the basis of a geopolitical and historical analysis of the situation in the Middle East rather similar to Arendt's, that the Arabs would never accept a Jewish national home in Palestine and an "iron wall" would have to be built. Only if the Jewish state were militarily strong would the Arabs be willing, one day, to accept its existence in their midst. Ben-Gurion, too, understood this, but in the early thirties he was still trying, through negotiations with moderate Arab figures, to reach some kind of agreement. The main stumbling block to achieving it, even on a theoretical basis, was the steady refusal, even of the most compromising Arabs, to accept free Jewish immigration into Palestine.

Ben-Gurion, Jabotinsky, Yehuda Magnes, Akiva Ernst Simon, or Gershom Scholem did not think otherwise – none of them thought either that the country was empty, or that its Arab inhabitants were going to vanish, or, in particular, that they were going to give up peacefully their opposition to the establishment of a Jewish national home, let alone, state, in the land of Palestine. None of them even thought that there was anything particularly evil, incomprehensible, or even irrational, in this opposition. The difference between all these and Kohn on one side and Arendt on the other

---

[27] It was published in H. Kohn, *Revolutions and Dictatorships. Essays in Contemporary History* (Cambridge, Mass.: Harvard University Press, 1939; 2nd ed., 1941), 299–330.

was neither about the facts nor even about their interpretation. The difference was that of a historical-political, mainly moral, decision. Kohn thought the price was not worth paying. More precisely, he thought that he was not ready, personally, to pay the price of being involved in the conflict to which he saw no easy solution. But he did not think he was in a position to become a judge looking at it from the height of absolute moral knowledge and, especially, to incriminate the Zionist side. The other persons mentioned here thought that there were extremely good moral reasons to go on, even if this demanded a high cost. The same kind of moral dilemma is still alive. Taking a stand on the Arab-Israeli conflict is basically a moral exigency. It is not dependent on the behavior and conduct of this or the other side. The extreme misrepresentation of the Israeli actions, and the parallel absurd lenience toward the Palestinian conduct, is often nothing else than a refusal to take the risk of an explicit moral position. The point of all this is that the real difference between Arendt (and Kohn) on the one hand and Ben-Gurion (and Jabotinsky, Blumenfeld, or Scholem), on the other was not one of political acuity but of moral position. To depict her or her article as being especially perspicacious is either manipulative or ignorant or both. In both cases, her authority is being used to foster an ideological attitude in the guise of an objective judgment.

A significant milestone in Arendt's estrangement from the Zionist movement and, in fact, all organized Jewish life in the United States was the Biltmore Conference in 1942. Here the Zionist movement as a whole, and the American Zionists in particular, adopted Ben-Gurion's comprehensive political program for the establishment of a state. In the run-up to the conference, Arendt was still trying to persuade delegates to oppose this idea, but she was completely unsuccessful. From then on, she was unforgiving of Ben-Gurion, and not only of him but of Zionism itself for disregarding her advice and establishing the state. Her anger at Ben-Gurion is the subtext, to use Zertal's favorite lingo, of *Eichmann in Jerusalem.* Put plainly, it was a need to settle accounts with Ben-Gurion, as a symbol of the historic decision to establish the state, that, in significant measure, underlay Arendt's decision to come to Jerusalem and cover the trial. But presumably the anger at Ben-Gurion and Zionism that we see in the book came from a deeper rift, which we might describe as a chronic Jewish dilemma, her failure to solve her own Jewish question. This rift was apparently healed only after the trial; she later described her presence there in a phrase that became famous: *cura posterior,* a belated cure.[28]

---

[28] The expression appears in a letter to Meier Cronemeyer, written in July 1963 (i.e., after the trial): "The writing of [the book] was, for me, somehow, a *cura posterior.* And that it was the beginning of 'laying the foundations of new political morality' is certainly correct.

The Unresolved Jewish Dilemmas and the Limits of the Theory of the Political

What exactly was the ailment that the Eichmann trial cured? We can trace its development to some extent. One diagnostic key is the matter of assimilation. Arendt had been greatly concerned with this question. Much had also been written about her book on Rachel Varnhagen, which we have already mentioned. Varnhagen was a Berlin Jew who, at the beginning of the period of the Jewish Enlightenment, tried to shed her Jewishness and make her way in enlightened German society. She learned too late that this attempt at assimilation would be futile. Many thought, correctly, that Arendt saw Varnhagen's life as a mirror image of her own: her experience with non-Jewish society and her choice to live on its periphery. This choice, incidentally, was related to her affair with Heidegger, her feeling that her Jewishness was somehow connected to the way the affair had begun and ended, as well as what happened to German society, and Heidegger himself, in the years that followed. It was related to the marginality imposed on Arendt after she completed the book, during the years when she carried the manuscript with her from one place of refuge to another. Arendt always liked to think of her life as marginal, even when she was no longer a refugee.

Arendt describes this choice to live on the margins as a decision to be a "pariah." The latter is a Hindu term borrowed by the sociologist Max Weber to describe the Jews of Europe. Arendt also takes it from Bernard Lazare, who, like Weber, used it to speak about the Jews.[29] For Arendt, ostracism, or nonacceptance by what she calls "society," is the permanent condition of the modern Jew, one that has continued even since he was granted emancipation and equal rights, as it were. But unlike the Zionists, she does not see this pariah status as a consequence of "exile" as such. In her view, premodern Jewish life was not a life of ostracism. It was only when the Jews were given civil rights without at the same time being accepted socially that they became pariahs. Hence her conception of the "political": it is in the overcoming of "society" by politics that the Jew can find his place in humanity. But until this

---

However, modesty prevented me from ever putting it this way." See Elisabeth Young-Bruehl, *Hannah Arendt: For Love of the World* (New Haven: Yale University Press, 1982), 374. Young-Bruehl uses this expression as the title of her chapter on the Eichmann trial.

[29] Arendt devoted herself a good deal to Lazare. She edited the English edition of his articles in 1948 and spoke of him at length on various occasions, among others in her essay on anti-Semitism and her article "The Jew as Pariah." Lazare symbolized for her the "willing pariah." It is typical that the application of the term "pariah" to the Jews is generally attributed to Arendt and not to the sources from which she took it.

happens, as it apparently did to Arendt in America, emancipation impels Jews to seek ways of "integrating" – in vain, as historical experience shows – into non-Jewish society. The pariah out of choice is the Jew who keeps his sense of worth and dignity, as opposed to the parvenu, who embodies, for her, all that is contemptible and futile about assimilation, a Jewish life based on the desire to be accepted by "society" and to resemble the non-Jews. This polarity of the possibilities of Jewish existence is one of Arendt's best-known ideas. It, too, she borrows from Lazare, but she expands it into an entire theory of postemancipation Jewish life.

Besides the questionable historical schema (anti-Semitism as a purely modern phenomenon), the attempt to reduce all the possibilities of modern Jewish existence to this either-or dichotomy seems a bit exaggerated, and the theory of Jewish modernity Arendt bases upon this dichotomy is not especially persuasive, even if we disregard the superficiality of her observations about East European Jewry. But two additional comments, one less important and one more so, could be made about it. First, Arendt herself was much less a pariah than she liked to think, certainly once her international reputation was established and respected universities and institutes began to invite her to teach and do research at their expense. This is how the American essayist Susan Sontag, for example, saw Arendt's whole relationship with Mary McCarthy. Here, Arendt revealed her own weakness, her aspiration to be something she was not, an American rather than a serious European intellectual. The American writer, for her part, was pleased to be connected with this learned and sophisticated European. In light of this, Sontag observes, their correspondence was at times amusing, at times touching – and at times merely ridiculous.[30]

Second, despite the refusal of the post-Zionists – who reject the Zionist "negation of exile" – to recognize it, Arendt's critique of assimilationism is very close to, and in fact based upon, the Zionist critique of Diaspora life. One need not be particularly astute to note this similarity, and Arendt never actually denied it, although on various occasions she stressed that, however much she appreciated the self-criticism of the Zionists – that is, their criticism of Diaspora Jews – she never identified with the former politically. What must have been some instinctive and yet completely nonpolitical malaise with Jewish existence in between-the-wars Germany crystallized, so to speak, into political awareness through her passage through Zionism. What she did not accept was the Zionist identification of *diaspora* and *exile*. She did not think, like the Zionists, that the *pariah* situation was a more or less

[30] Interview with Susan Sontag, *Magazine Littéraire*, November 1995, 36.

inevitable outcome of life without a homeland and without the – specifically Jewish – institutionalization of freedom. She has not followed them thus but for the polemical side of their journey: like them, most probably because of them, she had understood that one had to transcribe nonassimilation to a political discourse and action; that, like Bernard Lazare before, the dignity contained in the choice to refuse the refusal was not sufficient, that one had to transform feelings into political existence. Only she thought that that transformation could be accomplished without real engagement in Zionist concrete political action; her personal itinerary shows that this was not possible. Instead of offering a real alternative to Zionism, she simply denied that it was "political," which is absurd, especially in terms of her own theory, and cut herself completely from any involvement in Jewish affairs. It is certainly not uninteresting that, out of some 510 text pages of the recent *Jewish Writings*, only 90 contain pieces written after the establishment of the State of Israel, mostly things connected with the Eichmann trial. One can risk the hypotheses that the very questionable aspects of her criticism of Zionism, her inability to solve the inner contradiction of her attitude toward it, are not unrelated to the weaker aspects of her general doctrines.

The inspiration for her critique of assimilationism came, as we have said, much under the influence of Kurt Blumenfeld. Or, more precisely, her relationship with him contributed greatly to turning her personal awakening from assimilation into political consciousness and political thinking. For Blumenfeld, Zionism and Zionist activity, the negation of exile and, finally, the decision to emigrate to Palestine, were a moral matter: not only an admission of the "objective" failure of the Jewish attempt to go on living in Europe and the historical necessity of finding a homeland for the Jews, but also a recognition that political life, hence the creation of a Jewish polity in the Land of Israel, was the choice incumbent on the individual Jew who aspired to be a moral person. Arendt's own enlistment in the Zionist cause was also a matter of morality (which she defined as political). In a famous German broadcast interview, published as "Was bleibt? Es bleibt die Muttersprache" (What's Left? The Mother Tongue),[31] she explains that, after Hitler came to power, she understood that if one is attacked as a Jew, he must defend himself as a Jew – not as a German, a citizen of the world, or a supporter of human rights. It was this recognition that prompted her to become active in

---

[31] In 1964, German television broadcast an interview with Arendt. Asked what was left for her of the Germany she knew before the war, she replied, "What remains? The Mother Tongue remains." See the interview with this title in Peter Baehr, ed., *The Portable Hannah Arendt* (New York: Viking, 2000), 3–24.

a Jewish organizational framework, and the only one she could consider was
that of the Zionist movement.

In spite of all this, Arendt became a harsh critic of Zionism, not only of the
policies adopted by the movement toward the end of the Second World War
but of the entire Zionist undertaking. In the 1945 article, she makes public
her most far-reaching claim, based, as it were, on the history of Zionism from
its inception: Zionism is the twin sister of assimilationism and, like it, has
failed the most important test, that of making Jewish existence "political."
Her history of Zionism is of limited interest. Though, as usual, it contains
some interesting points and deep insights, it is marked by considerable ignorance and is not a real historical analysis. The article belongs to a peculiar
genre that Arendt perfected: a cross between the journalistic, the academic,
and the political. In any event, what is interesting in the article is the pairing
of Zionism and assimilationism and the critique of both as a flight from traditional, apolitical Jewish existence, from "worldlessness" (*Weltlosigkeit,*
her favorite term), to yet another apolitical existence. One could challenge
this interpretation of Zionism as a denial, or rather a misunderstanding, of
its very essence, namely, the aspiration to make Jewish existence political,
to build a Jewish "world" in which, alone, Jews could decide their own fate.
The most revelatory aspect of all this is the claims she makes about the kibbutzim: an exaggerated admiration on the one hand; the reproach of being
just yet another form of worldlessness, on the other. This later claim, and
without offering here anything of an apology of the kibbutz, is undoubtedly one of the most bizarre elements of her attitude toward Zionism. These
remarks betray, however, something important: her inability to get past her
concern, not to say obsession, with assimilation, that is, the Jews' failure
to become part of the wider European, and specifically German, "society."
Beginning with the book on Varnhagen, she was preoccupied with this subject. But the central, almost exclusive role the failure to assimilate played in
Arendt's life represented a failure on her part: in the end, it was all that really
interested her. Unlike the Zionists, for example, she never learned to take a
real interest in Jewish history or Jewish life beyond the failure of assimilation, and in the last analysis her own political activity in the realm beyond
nonassimilation was marginal.

Arendt's moral and political philosophy echoes these concerns in a round-
about way: it accepts the Zionist critique of the impotence and apolitical
character of Jewish life as well as the Zionist ideal of making Jewish life
political. But it also reflects her own failure as a thinker to address Jewish
life politically. Arendt's thinking took many twists and turns over the
years, but through all of them – at least up to the last turn, in *The Life of the*

Mind, where she no longer insists on the priority of the political but restores "thought" to its lost stature – one can discern a single thematic focus, which is existential no less than theoretical: the attempt to delineate a "political" realm, or to formulate a concept of "the political," that is not reducible to other aspects of human existence. Arendt identifies "the political" as the realm of freedom, as distinct from two realms of necessity, that of physical life (the biological) and that of "society" (the historical, sociological, and economic). Again, the sharp distinction she draws between "the political" and "the social" underlies her whole political philosophy as well as her interpretation of modern Jewish history: "society" is where the Jews tried and failed to give concrete meaning to the abstract, formal equality they had been given. The responsibility for this failure was their own, no less than that of others. It derived from their inability, or perhaps unwillingness, in her view, to take on a *political* existence and give *political* meaning to their emancipation.

The political, then, is the place of freedom. It is what the time-honored Hebrew phrase calls *motar ha'adam* (roughly, the human advantage) or, in more philosophical terms, the clearest expression of what is specifically human. The condition for its appearance – and it does, indeed, "appear," not being given at the outset – is "action," living in "the world," that is, in the public realm. This notion, as formulated mainly in Arendt's book *The Human Condition* (which many regard as her main theoretical achievement), is based on a partly philological, partly literary analysis of several concepts in political and social theory, mostly drawn from Greek sources, which she uses for her purposes with considerable disregard for their original meaning. She tries to generalize and broaden these concepts into a comprehensive description of "the human condition" or what might be described as a hierarchy of forms of human existence and the inner human values they embody. This hierarchy of values is based mainly on a gradual movement from the primary stage of "labor," more or less that which is needed for physical survival; to the higher stage of "work," namely creative activity; and then to the political stage of "action," which, alone, is where the specifically human manifests itself. In a way unmistakably reminiscent of Heidegger, Arendt uses the Greek terms and their etymology to construct a general critique of Western philosophy (political theory, not ontology) from Plato to our own time and a sweeping condemnation of the disregard for "action" in favor of labor, the marketplace, consumption, and the accumulation of wealth, on the one hand, and thought, inquiry, and modern science, on the other.

Arendt's philosophy is a rehabilitation of the political life, that is, of action in that unique sphere where large numbers of people meet to determine together the character of their common life. She acknowledges that such a political sphere has existed only two or three times in all of history: in ancient Greece (Periclean Athens), at the time of the American Revolution, at the time of the Hungarian uprising, and, to some extent, during the student disturbances in the late 1960s. Perhaps it existed in the kibbutzim as well, though she does not say this in so many words. Her reconstruction of these happy moments in human history is undoubtedly more romantic than serious historiography, but leave that aside. What matters is that for Arendt the Greek model of political life, as she reconstructs it and as it actually was to some extent, can serve as the basis of a general, normative theory of political life for all times and places. The place of "the political" is the multitude. The diversity of the multitude cannot be papered over with an all-encompassing definition or concept. This is what makes the political sphere unique and reveals its essence: it is not only the place where diverse individuals act in concert but, precisely because their differences cannot be encompassed by a single concept, name, or definition, it is also a sphere that must be *constructed* by joint deliberation and action, in a way that is always unpredictable. "Natality," as she calls it, that is, radical novelty, is a paradigm of the unpredictable diversity of life in the realm of "the political." Hence, totalitarianism is the opposite of "the political" (and not, as Agamben and his epigones think, the quintessence of it): in totalitarian systems, there is an "atomization" of the public sphere, and it disappears, along with the possibility of speaking and acting in concert. It is no longer possible to take a position on matters of common concern or to participate actively in exchanges of views or open-ended debate (the content of which is left somewhat vague in Arendt's presentation), which would be the basis of what she calls "action." But, as we have pointed out, this is not only a theory of "the political" but also, and perhaps principally, a theory of the human *qua* political: speech and action in the political sphere are the true expression of individual autonomy and freedom. Humanness can be fully expressed only through action in the public sphere, outside the home and the sphere of private, familial, and economic pursuits – that is, only in the *vita activa* (the title of the German edition of the book) and not in the inaction and ineffectuality of the *vita contemplativa.*

Arendt draws some rather Zionistic conclusions from her general theory of "the political." For example, she believes freedom has a price and that action – that is, political life that gives no assurance of order or of any particular outcome – entails forgoing absolute moral purity. One must dirty one's hands if one wants to do something. Unlike George Steiner, for example, she sees no moral advantage in foreswearing political action, only moral weakness and human wretchedness. One of her best-known – and most controversial – arguments is that a major component of the crime committed at Auschwitz, in the case of both the perpetrators and the victims, was the total collapse of the moral personality. In the victims, moral disintegration was the final manifestation of their passivity and helplessness. In her view, the refusal to resist, that is, to exercise one of the key elements of the political, was immeasurably worse than real political struggle, even if armed, would have been.

The limitations of Arendt's political philosophy are also a reflection of her Jewish failings. An example is the centrality of dignity or honor in her thinking. Just as her sense of her own Jewishness and her turn to Jewish political action were based largely on a recognition that action was a condition of human dignity, the latter plays a major motivating role in her general theory as well. But human dignity is a matter of personal self-worth, and it is always connected with the way we are perceived by others. Arendt's concern for Jewish dignity is something very different from the Zionist desire to ensure Jewish survival, for example, or even the republican concern for the common good.

This is but one example, specific but typical, of the way Arendt's political theory remains, in the last analysis, at a remove from the truly "political." One of the "surprising paradoxes" in her work is that her interpretation of the human-as-political as being action within the sphere of human multiplicity remains so remote from the concrete reality, or historicity, of political action. Though she was an involved observer (in Raymond Aron's phrase), sometimes perceptive, always critical, of the political events of her time, her attempt to understand "the political," to decipher the nature of modern "anti-political" regimes and to pronounce judgment on modernity and modern man in general, is only partly successful. The concepts that form the matrix of her philosophical program are quite arbitrary and sometimes vague, and the theory itself is too general and abstract to provide a real understanding of the phenomena with which she is concerned. She is extremely articulate and offers the reader a number of interesting and original insights, but along with them are ideas drawn from a wide variety of other sources, which she repeats without always making clear how conversant she is with their original meaning. Although her conclusions are not supported by any real scientific research, and most of her sources (other than classical philosophy) are secondary ones, she permits herself to speak authoritatively about all aspects of the human condition, even though what she has to say can sometimes be distinctly amateurish.[32]

---

[32] A salient example of the way the need to encompass all aspects of "the human condition" led Arendt to make pronouncements about matters with which she was not really familiar

But the main criticism that can be made of her is that what she gleans from going back to philosophy is not political theory but an idealized perspective, more literary and imaginative than scientific, for assessing – and judging – the modern (and perhaps the perennial) human condition. Her view of things is more existential than political or even sociopolitical, a moralistic perspective more concerned with judgment than understanding. The concept of "action," on which Arendt's critique of modernity is based, is very vague, most likely anachronistic, and, in any case, more moral in the eudemonistic sense (i.e., aimed at human happiness) than political. It belongs in the category of what Foucault calls self-concern more than in that of concern for the general good. The perspective this concept opens is so broad and inclusive, on the one hand, and so concerned, in an almost narcissistic way, with individual self-fulfillment, on the other, that the specificity and concreteness of the political are nearly lost. The reflection on human existence made possible by the nonteleological concept of "action" – it is purposiveness that defines the realm of "work" and the production of goods for consumption and the accumulation of capital – is not, ultimately, really political. It is motivated not by the question of joint action – in which human beings seek to improve their common condition and realize such shared objectives as general well-being, justice, equality, or freedom – but rather by a concern to enable the individual to live a "good life," to achieve redemption (in the traditional philosophical, not theological, sense). Although Arendt's critique of science and technology is similar to Heidegger's, her "concern" is not, like his, with the authenticity of being, but with life in the world, that is, life within the context of human multiplicity, and the loss of this "world" in modern times. Yet this does not mean that her concern is a political one; again, it is a concern for the individual and not the common good. Her main philosophical criterion for judging modernity is the value of individual life.

This analysis applies mainly to *The Human Condition*. In the years that followed, Arendt's views changed somewhat. Aside from her many pronouncements on current affairs, her theoretical writings during these years belong more clearly to the political realm and less to the phenomenology of the timelessly human-*qua*-political. *On Revolution* (1963) is her most important book from this period, and, apart from her study of Rachel Varnhagen,

is to be found in her statements about the scientific revolution and about Galileo in particular. In this instance, she also quotes other sources – especially her friend Alexandre Koyré, E. A. Burtt, Whitehead, Schroedinger, and others who wrote about modern science and the scientific revolution – but what she takes from them is very general and, in the end, detached from the concrete context of the scientific revolution. See Hannah Arendt, *The Human Condition*, 2nd ed. (Chicago: University of Chicago Press, 1998), 257–268.

it is, to my mind, her best book. The theoretical presumption here is more restrained and the program more modest than in her previous philosophical works. Her writing style has also become more indulgent, perhaps, as some other commentators think, because she is dealing with the American Revolution, about which she has many positive things to say. (This may be due to a sense of gratitude to the country that gave her refuge, welcomed her with extraordinary warmth, and took her to its heart.) But precisely for this reason, some of the more problematical aspects of her concept of "the political" stand out in the book. It deals, in fact, with two revolutions, the American and the French, not historically but in terms of the modern phenomenon of revolution per se. According to her analysis, the hallmark of revolution is not necessarily liberation or the violence it entails, but rather the creation of a politically free space. The concept of "revolution" should be reserved, according to Arendt, not for the violent overthrow of one regime in favor of another but for the creation, following the violence, of a constitution that becomes the basis of the state. The failure of the French Revolution, in contrast with the American, stemmed from its having been taken over by "the social," that is, the subordination of the political interest to the interests of equality and social justice and a desire to relieve abject poverty. Arendt sees "the social," in this sense not only as outside the bounds of "the political" but as actually opposed to it. For her, "the political" is not the locus of compassion or even solidarity. One even senses in her a certain impatience with the mob – violent, poor, and ignorant – that, in her view, caused the failure of the French Revolution. She exhibits the same impatience toward the masses of Jews who did not live politically, even when they became victims of the Nazi regime. As Jonas tells in his *Memoirs*, she was "tough," less affected than he was by the horrors of the world (p. 62).

What remains of the theory of *The Human Condition* in Arendt's later works, and in her political philosophy in particular, is thus a theoretical rejection of compassion. The latter is not an appropriate motive for political action. Neither compassion nor the objective conditions that give rise to it – the various forms of human suffering, wrongs, and injustice – figure in her thinking about "the political" or its foundations. On several significant occasions, she gave this theoretical position concrete expression, for example, in her attitude toward the status of women or her controversial stance on the civil rights struggle then at its height in the American South. After the violent events in Little Rock, she wrote an article opposing efforts to desegregate the schools. The article caused a major scandal, and Arendt later retracted some of its arguments, though not the main point, which was that the school belongs to the social realm, and in this realm people (such as whites) should not be forced to keep company with those whose company they do not want (such as blacks).[33]

Both the inner contradictions of Arendt's political Jewishness and the limitations of her political thinking are somewhat pathetically evident in her intensive activity – more in the realm of words than of concrete action – on behalf of the creation of a Jewish army to fight the Germans, during the Second World War.[34] Because, as we have seen, the Jews were attacked as Jews, they needed to fight back as Jews. The opportunity to fight as a Jew, or at least to struggle so that young Jewish men could fight as Jews, presented itself to her, in New York, during the years 1941–1942. Arendt, after assisting in a public conference in which Blumenfeld raised this proposal, published a number of articles in the *Aufbau*, the journal of the Jewish German-speaking New York community, in which she expressed her support for the establishment of such an army. It should not confine itself, she thought, to defending the Jewish community in Palestine but become part of the general struggle for the freedom of the entire Jewish people – although it is not altogether clear what "freedom" it would have won, beyond the honor that would be achieved by the death in combat of some Jewish soldiers. This plan failed, of course, and it is no coincidence, perhaps, that Arendt found herself working hand in hand at this time with the Revisionists (a militantly nationalist faction of the Zionist movement), who also wanted to establish a Jewish army. It was not only she who sought honor and dignity. It is no accident that the critics of Labor Zionism from both the left and the right found themselves working together on a plan that, even if it had succeeded, would have amounted to little more than a demonstration. In truth, it is doubtful that such an army could even have restored the Jews' lost honor, while what

---

[33] Arendt's article was originally written for *Commentary* magazine, which in fact refused to publish it. (It was published a year later, in 1959, in *Dissent*). Norman Podhoretz, who was to become the editor of *Commentary* and one of the principal spokesmen of the new American Jewish right wing, relates the incident amusingly – and illuminatingly. Podhoretz was a young member of the magazine's editorial board, which then had a leftist orientation. He left the board after its refusal to publish Arendt's article (though he completely disagreed with it), and as a result of this courageous stand became one of her closest friends. Or so he thought, until the exchange of letters between Arendt and Mary McCarthy was published. There, he learned what she really thought of him, it seems. Her comments about him to her friend show nothing but contempt, condescension, and scorn. See Norman Podhoretz, *Ex-Friends* (New York: Free Press, 1999), 139–177.

[34] Several articles Arendt wrote in 1941–1942 on the idea of a Jewish army are now available in her *Jewish Writings*, 136–160. They make for fascinating reading, showing her in her most Zionistic phase. She is still speaking here about the Zionists as *us* and making statements like "We [Jews] have only one truly political organization: the Zionist Organization" (143).

was really at stake was not their honor but their lives. In the end, the plan turned out to be a pipe dream, even from the point of view of general political theory. For just as there can be no sovereignty without an army, there can be no army without sovereignty.

However, a Jewish army did fight, in the end, against the Germans. The Jewish Infantry Brigade Group (better known as the Jewish Brigade) was formed in 1944 and fought in Europe during the last stages of the war as a unit of the British army. It was created as the result of strenuous efforts by the leadership of Palestinian Jewry. It was Chaim Weizmann who, when the war broke out in 1939, first offered the British the full cooperation of the Yishuv. We have already referred to this "declaration of war" of the Jewish people on the German Reich when speaking of the deniers. However, it was more than four years before the British accepted the offer and only after the nature of the Final Solution became known to the Allies. Some five thousand soldiers fought in the brigade. (In all, between thirty thousand and thirty-eight thousand Jewish soldiers from Palestine–Eretz Yisrael, as it was officially called under the British mandate, fought in various units, some of them defined as Jewish, of the British army. More than seven hundred died in action). They actually saw combat for only three weeks, during the last stages of the Italian campaign. But they were quite active in the rescue of Jewish survivors after the war and in the illegal immigration to Palestine, were involved in some revenge operations against a number of prominent Nazi criminals, and played an important role in the newly born Israeli army and in the 1948 war. But by then Hannah Arendt was not seeing herself anymore as part of the Zionist movement, although, in the last analysis, it was the Zionists – the Zionist movement, the prestate organized Jewish community in Palestine, the State of Israel, and Arendt's nemesis Ben-Gurion – who realized certain aspects of her political philosophy, and they did so in a specifically Jewish way. As it turns out, it was only in the State of Israel that Jews could fight as Jews and take political action as Jews – that is, live a real *vita activa*, an active, political life in the full sense of the term and in all spheres of their existence. In the view of many Jews, and not only Israelis, it was the establishment of the State of Israel that restored their lost honor. In any event, what she knew and said during her Zionist period – that for Jews political action, that is, human life, is possible only in the framework of a Jewish polity – turned into opposition to the idea that a Jewish polity was possible only in a Jewish state and, as we have said, her more or less complete disengagement from organized Jewish life.

To put it differently, Arendt's theory of "the political," her main philosophical achievement, is closely tied to her view of Jewish life. Paradoxically, this theory is at the root of her understanding of the latter as being apolitical and of her own way of expressing her Jewishness. The honor Arendt's pariah guards so closely is always a matter of how he relates to non-Jewish society. In the last analysis, even the political idea, as it were, of a Jewish army is, for her, anchored in a concern for personal honor, a stance that does not transcend the personal, may even be narcissistic, and, in fact, amounts to nothing more than reverse assimilation. Her charges against Zionism apply to her much more than to Ben-Gurion, for example. Though she writes passionately about her own Jewishness and her interpretation of Jewish existence, there is nothing revolutionary about them, nor does she advocate real change. It is no accident that her book on revolution fails to mention the Zionist revolution at all, and, characteristically enough, her Jewishness was completely abstract, perhaps even imaginary. Arendt never got to know Jewish history or the Jewish heritage, and in refusing to recognize the concrete political content that Zionism sought to give Jewish existence, she was turning her back on the possibility that that could be done.

In contrast to the gratitude Arendt felt toward America, in relation to her Jewishness she never exhibited the same respect or loyalty or commitment that Leo Strauss (her compatriot and acquaintance), when asked "why we remain Jews," called simple, human "decency." Strauss spoke of this on various occasions, but most explicitly and interestingly in the introduction to the English edition of his book on Spinoza's critique of religion.[35] For him and many others, Spinoza exemplifies Arendt's pariah: though he ceased being a part of organized Jewry, he refused to become a parvenu among the non-Jews. Like Arendt, though to a lesser extent, he did not remain completely marginal. But unlike Arendt, Spinoza, knew that he was living an apolitical life. And in sharp contrast with Arendt, he thought human life could sometimes be lived fully through a special kind of philosophical understanding that was completely personal and utterly apolitical. In light of this, and in light of Arendt's view that the philosophical life, the *vita contemplativa,* was seen by her (until her very last, unfinished, book) to lie outside the "world" – an object of criticism and not an ideal to aspire to – the lack of human "decency" toward the Jewish people of which Strauss, citing Hermann Cohen, accuses Spinoza was not as serious as that of Arendt herself.

The "decency" of which Strauss speaks is the very foundation of the polis, the Greek form of political life, and its theoreticians, the Greek philosophers and historians, were for both Strauss and Arendt a major source of inspiration in their thinking about "the political." But for Strauss, Athens

---

[35] See Leo Strauss, *Spinoza's Critique of Religion* (New York: Schocken, 1965), 6ff.

was always connected with Jerusalem. His whole intellectual life, and to a great extent his ethical and personal life, moved between these two poles. And by the way, as Ehud Luz, the editor of a recent collection of his writings in Hebrew translation, points out, Strauss always placed Jerusalem ahead of Athens. For Arendt, there was nothing left in the end but Athens. And of Strauss's "decency," very little was left. For her, even more than for Strauss, this "decency," being the basis of "the political," is possible only in a real polity, a state. Because she opposed a Jewish state, and because being Jewish had no other positive meaning for her, this "decency" was, in the end, absent from her Jewish experience; or, to put it in a more balanced way, even though at certain times in her life such decency played a dominant role, even overshadowing other aspects of her life as a Jew, it gradually disappeared as Arendt became a more universal thinker and as she restricted her Jewish "politicality" to claiming the right to criticize.

THE EICHMANN TRIAL: A STORY OF FAILURE

In the last analysis, Arendt's Jewishness was apolitical, abstract, and sentimental. It was thus a failure, not only from a Zionist or even a Straussian point of view, but also, and above all, from the point of view of her own theory – her philosophy of "the political" and of action within "the world," which is, by that very fact, public action. This is the focus of her whole worldview. Arendt's failure is existential, political, and philosophical, but above all it is a moral one. That the Jewish Condition in modern time was that of apolitical and abstract life was exactly what the Zionists have always thought. They too have understood that the only way out of this situation was the politization of Jewish life. Maybe they were all wrong, Arendt and the Zionists alike; maybe the Orthodox were right. Maybe George Steiner is right. Many others say it, ever more loudly. However, and as she acknowledged and said during a certain period of her life, the Zionist politicization of Jewish life was the only available possibility; this has become more than evident after the war, precisely when she decided that she wanted no part in it. What she could have never acknowledged, though, was that the Zionists have succeeded, against all odds – this was more or less her opinion – to realize their program, namely, that they have managed, for the best or for the worst, to create a Jewish *world*.

The clearest indication of Arendt's Jewish failure is, in fact, her book *Eichmann in Jerusalem*. As has been suggested before, it is also a bad book. It is bad, however, in a very special way, worthy of its author. This is a failure of a great woman and, as we know, great men's and women's failures are great as well. The book is superbly written, with an extraordinary intelligence, with great passion and keen eye. Not only its success in the bookstore was immense, but it has also contributed more than anything else to turn the Eichmann trial into a historical event. This, at least, is what David Cesarini thinks, who has recently published a remarkable biography of Eichmann. Yet, according to Cesarini, the success of the Eichmann book is paradoxical; one more paradox then: the press's interest in the trial, very intense at the beginning, dwindled rapidly. If the Jerusalem process constitutes nevertheless a turning point in the attitude to the Holocaust, both of the public opinion at large and of the academic community, it was largely due to *Eichmann in Jerusalem* and to the scandal it caused.[36]

Why would it be a paradox? Because contrary to what many think, the book is far from being a truthful and clarifying presentation of the Final Solution. This is not only because of the many factual inexactitudes it contains – the chapters in which Arendt outlines the general process of the extermination are, despite its insufficiencies, admirable, and they even conserve a certain value as an initiation to the story of the Holocaust; not only because we have at our disposal nowadays a great many excellent general or monographic studies of the Holocaust that are much more accurate and up-to-date; not even because of the distorted and extremely problematic description and evaluation of the role played by the *Judenräte* in the Final Solution, or of the role of Eichmann himself, for that matter. The book fails because Arendt refused to understand that which was going on in front of her, namely, first and foremost, the irreducible value of the story of the extermination as it was told by the witnesses; also because the research on the Holocaust was already then, and more so afterward, developing in directions completely different from those she envisaged, becoming a discipline on its own, independent of the study of the general forms of totalitarian regimes; but also because her book has become an almost canonic text for the opprobrium crowd, for its Israeli members like Zertal, Ophir, Laor, Burg, or Eyal Sivan, as well as for its other members like Judith Butler and Tony Judt.

Arendt's failure in this book was first of all theoretical. She fails in the same way she accuses those who ran the trial, in reality or in her imagination, of doing: with the possible exception of the German-born judges, they missed the historic opportunity the trial provided to clarify the "true" meaning of Eichmann's crimes. But the book fails in other, less theoretical ways, as well. As we have said, the trial was, for Arendt, a kind of delayed

[36] D. Cesarini, *Becoming Eichmann: Rethinking the Life, Crimes, and Trial of a "Desk Murderer"* (2004; Cambridge, Mass.: De Capo Press, 2006).

healing. It turns out there were medical reasons, if we can call them that, for her decision to come to Jerusalem for the trial. To describe it this way is not just a matter of clever phrasing. When Arendt explains what prompted her to propose that the *New Yorker* send her to cover the trial, why she so much wanted to go, and what was so important to her about the show about to be staged in that faraway, unloved city, she speaks about herself, not about the trial. She is not especially interested in the historical aspects of the trial, for example, or what could be learned from it about the destruction of European Jewry. The journey to Jerusalem, she explains apologetically in a letter to the Rockefeller Foundation, is something she owes herself. Not the Jews who were killed, not the readers of the *New Yorker*, but herself. To Karl Jaspers she writes that she hopes she won't have to spend more than a month on "this 'pleasure'"; but she would never be able to forgive herself if she "didn't go and look at this walking disaster face to face in all his bizarre vacuousness." For Jaspers knows "how early I left Germany and how little of all this I really experienced directly."[37] Incidentally, Jaspers had serious reservations, some of them matters of principle, about Israel's conduct in this affair and about the whole undertaking. Arendt would repeat some of them – though without citing their source – in her report on the trial. But knowing, as he evidently did, the mind of his former student, he cautioned her to keep her criticism to herself, lest she cause damage to Israel. Needless to say, she did not take Jaspers's advice. S. Aschheim, in the review of the *Jewish Writings*, brings another example, a citation from a letter to Mary McCarthy: writing the book, she tells her friend, was "morally exhilarating … a means of transcendence.… I wrote this book in a curious state of euphoria. And ever since I did it, I feel … light-hearted about the matter. Don't tell anybody; is it not proof positive that I have no 'soul'?"

The fact that she was unable to restrain herself and used the occasion to settle accounts with Ben-Gurion and the Zionist movement he led explains much of the book's weakness. As Zertal, too, is aware, Arendt did not really come to Jerusalem to cover the trial, though that was what she repeatedly claimed. And as another critic, the political philosopher Judith Shklar, has pointed out, Arendt did not come to Jerusalem looking for truth, either.[38] She knew ahead of time what she wanted to say and was only looking for

[37] Letter from Arendt to Jaspers dated December 2, 1960, in Lotte Kohler and Hans Saner, eds., *Hannah Arendt Karl Jaspers Correspondence: 1926–1969* (New York: Harcourt Brace Jovanovich, 1992), 409–410.
[38] Judith N. Shklar, "Hannah Arendt as Pariah," in Shklar, *Political Thought and Political Thinkers* (Chicago: University of Chicago Press, 1998), 362–375.

support for her views, which were, as always, fixed. The testimony of many of her acquaintances in Israel, some of them close friends and relatives, all conveys the same impression: Arendt came to Jerusalem with preconceived ideas and would let nothing change them. As she wrote to Jaspers, she knew long before seeing Eichmann– this "walking disaster" – that he was "bizarrely vacuous." The only thing she changed was the terminology: from "vacuous" to "banal."

The book also contains numerous inaccuracies. But these are just a mild indication of the book's failure. One might also forgive Arendt's colossal (and typical) presumption that in the guise of covering the trial, and instead of just criticizing the prosecution for using the occasion to tell the whole story of the catastrophe, she tried not only to make a final reckoning of the destruction of European Jewry but also to draw from it all the relevant philosophical conclusions.

It is not only Arendt's presumption that is typical but also her feigned innocence. Responding to criticism of the book, she claims things were attributed to her that she never said, for, in fact, all she set out to do was cover the trial.[39] Nevertheless, it is fair to assume that the book's long shelf life has not been due to its presentation of the trial alone. Unless, of course, one wants to regard the legal failure, as it were, of the prosecutor Gideon Hausner – which even Arendt, by the way, saw as merely relative – or, even more, the manipulations of his master David Ben-Gurion – whom she never forgave – as shedding light on the phenomenon known as Israel. Unless, that is, one sees these things as keys to unraveling all Israel's crimes and all Zionism's sins and, like Zertal, thinks Arendt provides us with these keys.

At the same time, Arendt's feigned innocence was one of the strangest and most revealing aspects of this whole affair. Her reactions to the furor caused by her book are to be found in many different places: in an afterword she appended to the book, in newspaper articles, in various published exchanges (the best known being with Gershom Scholem), in personal letters (particularly to Mary McCarthy), and elsewhere. In these responses, she expressed her anger and amazement at the witch hunt that followed the book's publication. The occasion evoked her polemical skills and showed what she was capable of when no holds are barred. She knew how to attack ad hominem, how to kick in the most sensitive places, but also how to dodge the most difficult questions and bring an appropriate measure of *mauvaise foi* to the confrontation. Most astonishing of all, she seems really not to have understood

[39] See, for example, her comments on Jacob Robinson's *And the Crooked Shall Be Made Straight* in *The Jew as Pariah*, 260.

why her book has stirred up such a storm or what all the fuss was about. She apparently really thought she had been the victim of, on the one hand, an organized campaign of persecution, an actual conspiracy, undertaken by groups with vested interests, and, on the other hand, some kind of irrational current of thought. It apparently never occurred to her for a moment that, at least here and there, her critics might be right or, if not right, at least addressing real issues. In light of, among other things, Jonas's testimony or her letter to McCarty, referred to previously, one is at a loss to explain this attitude. At the same time, one can sometimes discern an inadvertent, indirect admission to some of the charges leveled against her. This is most evident in the effort she makes in her last, unfinished book, *The Life of the Mind*, to explain and rationalize philosophically some of the terms she tosses around in her book on the Eichmann trial, terms that became the focus of the controversy and brought it to public attention, such as "thinking" (and "the absence of thought"), "evil," and, above all, "the banality of evil."

One of Arendt's standard replies to her critics is that most of the issues on which she is attacked were not even discussed in the book – although the book's reputation grew from the notion that it contained, for example, a philosophical theory of "the banality of evil," Arendt does not think it did. Unfortunately, she says, the subject she considered was quite limited, and it is in the nature of a report on a trial that it should discuss "only the matters which were treated in the course of the trial, or which in the interests of justice should have been treated" (p. 285). The notion that a journalistic report on a trial should be able to make pronouncements about what the trial should adjudicate is in itself a question worth pondering. One of the things the court should have considered, in Arendt's opinion, a lapse she complains about bitterly, is the collaboration of the *Judenräte* and the Jewish leadership with the Nazis. Though she is harshly critical of the prosecution's efforts to broaden the scope of the deliberation beyond the narrow legal issue of Eichmann's guilt or innocence, she thinks ample consideration should have been given to the Jewish leaders' contribution to the destruction of their own people, however unclear the relevance of this question to that of Eichmann's culpability. This charge against the *Judenräte* is the aspect of the book the critics always find most infuriating. Here, too, Arendt makes use of things said by others, without attribution.

It was Raul Hilberg, in his large, important work on the destruction of European Jewry, who argued that the fact that the Jews were organized and lived in more or less orderly communities made it easier for the Germans to annihilate them. He also discusses the ways the Nazis used the Jewish leadership to facilitate their work. Among other things, Eichmann and his people were, as we know, able to get the Jews to finance their transportation to the death camps with their own money. While one might see this as diabolical cleverness, it was, of course, simply a matter of economy and bureaucratic efficiency. Yet Hilberg did not jump to the conclusion Arendt so readily does, that had it not been for the collaboration of the *Judenräte* so many Jews could not have been killed. He also knew that, as a historian, he had to beware of making the kinds of sweeping generalizations of which Arendt was so fond. For example, it was important to see the differences between one place and another, to recognize that the vast territories in the east, the General Gouvernement, and the occupied areas of Russia, were not like the countries the Germans ruled through indigenous governments, such as France and Bulgaria. In any case, the view generally accepted today, which Hilberg more or less shares, is that even without the collaboration of the leaders – and, after all, they did not always collaborate – the Jews would have been killed anyway.[40] Questions of "what if" can be debated endlessly, precisely because they are of no consequence. What is of consequence is that Hilberg never used this argument to pronounce moral judgment on the Jewish leadership or to draw the moralistic conclusions Arendt does. He also knew that what was really important for the process of expulsion and mass killing was the complicity, not of the Jews, but of the governments and populations of the countries where they lived. Similarly, in his view, there was nothing banal about Eichmann or the evil he committed.[41]

---

[40] The most comprehensive study of the *Judenräte* is that of Isaiah Trunk, *Judenrat: The Jewish Councils in Eastern Europe under Nazi Occupation* (New York: Macmillan, 1972). A brief summary of the principal scholarly and interpretive approaches to this matter, as well as numerous bibliographical references, are to be found in Dan Michman, "Jewish 'Headship' under Nazi Rule: The Evolution and Implementation of an Administrative Concept," in his *Holocaust Historiography*, 159–175.

[41] Hilberg, incidentally, has an interesting story to tell about Arendt. Having borrowed his idea about Jewish collaboration with the Nazis, and having cited him as an important authority on the destruction of the Jews, she saw him as an ally. When the uproar arose following the publication of her book, Arendt was angry that he did not come to her defense. But Hilberg would have nothing to do with this alliance: he resented her use of what he had written and stressed his differences with her. Despite the lavish praise she gave his book and the fact that it was her main factual source concerning the destruction of the Jews and especially the role played by the *Judenräte* (which did not prevent her from heaping vulgar abuse on him, in her typical fashion), it was she, Hilberg relates, who was the anonymous reader who advised Princeton University Press not to publish his book. She had been asked, as an authority on totalitarianism and Nazism, to read the manuscript, and she evidently decided the subject had already been exhausted by other studies. The story of Hilberg's travails finding a publisher is interesting in its own right, with quite a few lessons to teach, regarding Israel as well (Yad Vashem, too, refused to publish the book). As Hilberg bitterly

But Arendt is not content to argue that the court should have considered this question, an argument that is debatable; she also does the judges' work for them and announces a verdict. It is, as we know, a harsh and merciless one: the Jewish leadership, she declares unambiguously, was guilty of unforgivable moral dereliction. It aided, if it did not abet, the mass killing. The many studies that have since been done on the question of the Jewish leadership during the Holocaust show that, for the most part, Arendt's accusations are baseless. The communal leaders sometimes cooperated with their murderers and at other times opposed them in different ways; but whatever cooperation or lack of cooperation there was had no real bearing on the scale or pace of the killing. The sweeping generalizations and moral judgments on which Arendt bases her accusations represent, at the very least, extreme intellectual recklessness. The glibness and harshness of her judgment, her many errors of fact, and, in fact, her complete ignorance regarding the history and sociology of the communities about whose destruction she writes have all been discussed ad nauseam. The same is true of the tendentiousness of her report, which appears to be a direct outgrowth of her theory of anti-Semitism and the Jews' responsibility for it. But over and above the question of collaboration and of the historical accuracy of her charges, there is another question, that of the legitimacy of the role of judge that she arrogates to herself, the moral validity of her judgment. A comment might be in order here, along the lines of one made with great delicacy by Judith Shklar, that the moral authority on the basis of which Arendt pronounces judgment on the Jewish leaders should be seen in light of the fact that she herself escaped from Germany in 1933 (after being arrested briefly by the Gestapo for Jewish and Zionist activity) and the fact that later, when the war broke out and the Germans invaded France, she managed to flee to Spain and emigrate from there to the United States. Unlike others, she and her husband were helped to enter the promised land. Already then, she belonged to a select group that enjoyed privileges denied to ordinary mortals.

At any rate, despite the storm raised by Arendt's remarks about the *Judenräte*, it is not because of them that the book is a failure. Her indictment of the *Judenräte* is usually seen as the most outrageous part of the book, as an attempt to place part of the blame for the Holocaust on the Jews themselves and an expression of Arendt's own self-hatred. The latter point aside – she

---

notes, it did not occur to anyone to ask him to help with Eichmann's prosecution. See Raul Hilberg, *The Politics of Memory* (Chicago: Ivan R. Dee, 1966).

did not hate herself or her Jewishness – there is some truth in this criticism. Still, it was not the book's major failing.

The Philosophical Failure: The Banality of Evil

The real failing of this book is philosophical and moral. First, however, a remark about the purportedly philosophical nature of the book. Its subtitle, *A Report on the Banality of Evil*, proclaims its philosophical pretensions. The reservations Arendt expresses in the afterword did not and do not prevent readers from seeking, or thinking they have found, in it a profound and original philosophical discussion of the question of evil. Zertal is certainly not the only one to be overawed by the philosophical achievement of the book, in which, she thinks, Arendt introduces a new concept into the lexicon of political philosophy, the famous "banality of evil." I don't know how familiar Zertal is with this lexicon, but it is regrettable that she does not give us even the slightest explanation of this concept or what exactly is new about it. For Arendt herself does not do this either. And, in fact, the concept is not fully transparent to all readers of the book, and some may not even be convinced that it represents such a great innovation. We might point out here that, even if it were Hannah Arendt who "introduced" the concept to the previously mentioned lexicon, she was not the one who coined the term. The idea of using "banal" as an adjective modifying "evil" in the book's title was apparently that of Blücher; what is more, the whole matter came up many years earlier, in her correspondence with Jaspers. The more hidden source of all this was probably Joseph Conrad's Kurtz of *Heart of Darkness*, which deeply impressed Arendt and to whom she refers numerous times in *Imperialism*.

Shortly after the war, in 1946, Jaspers sent Arendt his book *Die Schuldfrage* (published in English as *The Question of German Guilt*), which deals with the question of collective German guilt for the crimes, some of them committed during the war. Incidentally, this book remains one of the most interesting and penetrating discussions of this question to have been written. Although Jaspers naturally does not take up questions of historical guilt or responsibility, the book is more relevant than ever today, when many Germans are trying to shake off the collective guilt and responsibility for the crimes of their parents and grandparents. In a letter reacting to the book, Arendt raises several points about the nature of the Nazi crimes, calling them "monstrous," that is, incapable of being adjudicated (*Hannah Arendt Karl Jaspers*, pp. 51–56). Jaspers replies that to speak of "satanic greatness" in the Nazis "is … as inappropriate … as all the talk about the 'demonic' element in Hitler. ... We have to see these things in their total banality, in their prosaic triviality, because that's what truly characterizes them. Bacteria can cause epidemics that wipe out nations, but they remain merely bacteria" (pp. 60–63).[42]

Nevertheless, the really interesting question here is not who has the copyright on the expression "the banality of evil," for it is not at all clear that this expression conveys anything philosophically profound. Arendt herself – and here we have reason to take her word for it rather than that of her interpreters, including, unfortunately, Zertal – says the following in her introduction to "Thinking," part 1 of her unfinished book *The Life of the Mind*:[43] "The immediate impulse" to deal with mental activity "came from my attending the Eichmann trial in Jerusalem. In my report of it I spoke of 'the banality of evil.' Behind that phrase, I held no thesis or doctrine, although I was dimly aware of the fact that it went counter to our tradition of thought – literary, theological, or philosophic – about the phenomenon of evil" (p. 3). The literature on Arendt, serious and otherwise, has dealt extensively with the meaning of "the banality of evil." The opinion of the present writer is that it is essentially an empty term and that Arendt's presumption of opposing "the Western philosophical tradition" with it is quite exaggerated, as, indeed, the concept of a single "Western philosophical tradition" (as Heidegger and many of his disciples, for example use it) is itself overblown, presumptuous, and condescending. In any event, even if Arendt herself did not claim philosophical originality for her book on Eichmann or its thesis of "the banality of evil," there would be room for some additional comment on it, if only because of the high rating it gets from Zertal and others.

Our first comment touches on the fact that the concept was used at all. One must keep in mind the context in which Arendt (without giving it much "thought," as she puts it) introduces it: at a trial that was the first great public expression of the Jewish catastrophe and an occasion of great pain. She was well aware, as Jonas tells us, that her "report" on the trial would cause

---

[42] Kohler and Saner, *Hannah Arendt Karl Jaspers Correspondence*, 127. Years later, Arendt often spoke about Nazi and totalitarian evil as a kind of fungus that spreads and takes over everything in its path. The contrast between the representation of evil as "banal" and its earlier literary representations – in Shakespeare, for example – can be found in these letters of Jaspers to Arendt. See his letter of October 19, 1946, in ibid., 60–63. Arendt may have forgotten this or not thought it important, but, in any case, she does not mention it in the Eichmann book. Nor does Zertal take the trouble to indicate the actual source of this daring expression, which, it will be recalled, she says Arendt introduced into the philosophical lexicon.

[43] Cited according to the one-volume edition: H. Arendt, *The Life of the Mind* (New York: Harcourt Brace, 1978).

an uproar, though she was perhaps surprised at how big it turned out to be. She should not have been surprised, though. The famous *ton* of her report hit right. The court hall in Jerusalem was, after all, a bit more than the scene of great manipulation. It was also the place where a great pain unfolded, a pain to which there has not been then, or ever since, a *cura posterior*. As usual, it is advisable to look at what Scholem wrote. Her irony, he writes to her in his second letter, is so *rafinée*, that only he can understand it; however, he adds, he can't think of a less appropriate place to display her skills in writing ironically. Thus, it was not only "thought" that was absent here but also caution, a modicum of sensitivity, and, above all, compassion. If there had been a real thesis or theory, one might have admired the courage of the *New Yorker* correspondent. But because, as she herself tells us, there was neither, what we are left with is arrogance, recklessness, condescension, and intellectual ostentation. In a word: moral failure.

Our second comment is a bit more complicated. It also entails more distressing reservations about Arendt's honesty and discernment. In fact, even if there was no "theory" behind the concept of "banality," there was certainly a rhetorical purpose. The impression the term gives – of being subversive, provocative, and original; and of being paradoxical, in drawing the surprising contrast between "evil" and "banality" – explains the sometimes ludicrous way various commentators and would-be commentators treat this whole nonissue.

Neither a real concept nor anything new, the term "banality" does not float in a vacuum. Even if there is no theory behind it, and it does not – as Arendt writes to Scholem – really herald some profound change in her way of relating to the question of evil,[44] it definitely has a context. That context is the psychopolitical portrait of Eichmann that Arendt thought she could draw on the basis of what she saw and heard in Jerusalem, by silencing the narrative of the victims and highlighting the role of the *Judenräte* in the destruction of the Jews.

---

[44] In her book on totalitarianism, Arendt uses the expression "radical evil" when speaking of the crimes of Nazism and Stalinism. The expression was coined by Kant in *Religion within the Limits of Reason Alone*, but Arendt, in her typical fashion, uses it in an entirely different sense. Gershom Scholem, in his well-known letter to her following the publication of the Eichmann book, notes the change, from the previous book, in her treatment of evil, and Arendt admits to this. If we can believe the statement quoted earlier from the introduction to *The Life of the Mind*, this admission was a bit hasty. As Richard Bernstein has rightly pointed out, there is, in fact, no significant difference between the two books in their treatment of evil. See his *Hannah Arendt and the Jewish Question* (Cambridge, Mass.: MIT Press, 1996), ch. 7.

Be that as it may, the Eichmann book purports to be a report on the trial; it is this that Arendt defines as "a report on the banality of evil." The main burden of the book is a partial narrative – an intelligent, illuminating synthesis of materials drawn from, among other places, the testimony given at the trial – of the destruction of European Jewry in terms of the role Eichmann played in it. The book can be seen as a kind of alternative indictment, corrected and updated, that Arendt thinks the prosecutor Gideon Hausner should have presented at the trial. She has made several additions to this narrative that she thinks the court should have considered. The most important of these, as we have said, is the matter of the contribution of the Jewish leadership to the extermination process. By the same token, she omits from the narrative other things that, in her view, were raised extraneously in the trial. Thus, her revised indictment hardly relates to the testimony of the survivors. She adds a psychobiography of Eichmann and, of course, her feelings, criticism, and legal and philosophical commentary. All these should have contributed to her definition of evil as something banal.

Contrary to Arendt's later declarations, she does not try only to clarify what should and should not have been done in the trial. Had she done so, there would have been no point in reconstructing Eichmann's personality or psychologizing his motives. For, from a purely juridical point of view, all that is important is whether Eichmann was responsible for what he did, whether he should be judged, and whether he deserves to be punished. On this question, Arendt says many times she has no doubt the court did its work well. But she is dissatisfied that it did not probe Eichmann's mentality or, what is more important, the paradigmatic significance of this mentality for a general theory of the nature of evil. What this has to do with a mere report on the trial, only the god of journalism knows. Though Arendt takes to task all those involved in the trial for not confining themselves to the question of the defendant's criminal guilt, she herself goes well beyond this question. She finds banality in one particular place, Eichmann's personality, and what she tries to do is reconstruct that personality showing the inner "essence," or something like that, of the way he worked and the evil he caused or facilitated. In a way not unlike that in which she reconstructed the personality of Rachel Varnhagen, Lessing, Kafka, Lazare, and others, she tries to give a picture of Eichmann "from within," as it were. She describes the Varnhagen biography as an attempt to tell the woman's story as she herself would have told it. This is not possible with Eichmann, because he was a liar and a "mindless" individual; but, paradoxically, there is a similar presumption here of being able both to see inside and to draw generalizations from what is seen there. It is not clear, as a rule, what she has taken from where: what she learned from Eichmann's own testimony, or at least from looking at him during the trial; what she has taken from the literature (she cites mainly Reitlinger and Hilberg, but only in a general way, without quotations or references); and what she reconstructs from the kind of empathy and understanding the judges, for example, not to mention the prosecutor and his staff, did not have (especially p. 145). But the conclusion is drawn unhesitatingly: the psychological, political, and moral portrait of Eichmann is presented to us as an established fact. And this portrait is supposed to have philosophical implications, too, of a general nature. One needs to read Arendt's answers to her critics in this light as well. There is not much integrity in these answers.

One of the strategies Arendt uses to bolster her theory of banality is to minimize the importance of Eichmann. She contends that his role in the planning and execution of the Final Solution was "[exaggerated] beyond rhyme or reason" at the trial and in Israel generally (p. 210). Recent research shows that her judgment that the prosecutor exaggerated Eichmann's role even further might be somewhat hasty. A completely different picture emerges, for example, from Yaacov Lozowick's book on Eichmann and the Nazi apparatus of which he was a part and, in an even more straightforward way, from Cesarini's biography of Eichmann, who has only the harshest things to say about the Eichmann profile by Arendt.[45] Another example is in the research by Susanne Heim and Götz Aly mentioned in Chapter 2. These two scholars are hardly part of the Zionist political or academic establishment, which, in fact, is quite critical of their work, as we have seen.

Eichmann's role in the deportation and murder of the Jews of Hungary should have carried some weight against the theory that he was just a cog in the machine. After all, just a few months before the end of the war, when it was obvious to everyone that the Thousand Year Reich was heading for defeat, Eichmann, defying even Himmler, managed to organize the speedy deportation – in less than two months, Arendt tells us – of hundreds of thousands of people from there to Auschwitz, where there was still time to murder most of them. Arendt devotes just over half a page to this organizational feat, noting, to be sure, that, "thanks chiefly to the Zionists," the deportation of the Hungarian Jews got more publicity than the other phases of the Jewish catastrophe (p. 200). Yet she devotes five pages to the relations between Eichmann and the Hungarian Jewish leadership, including the Kasztner affair.

---

[45] Yaacov Lozowick, *Hitler's Bureaucrats: The Nazi Security Police and the Banality of Evil* (London: Continuum, 2002).

The brevity of Arendt's description of the Hungarian deportation, and the fullness and venom of her description of the Hungarian Jewish leaders – Eichmann and his people she describes objectively and without emotion, as befits the coverage of a trial – is not just a rhetorical ploy meant to reinforce the impression of Eichmann's marginality. After all, the Hungarian episode has just provided her with an opportunity to ponder – in what she calls a modest journalistic report on the trial, let us recall – "the central moral, legal, and political phenomena of our century" (ibid.): the relationship between positive law and conscience, the limits of obedience, and the obligation to refuse to do things above which "a black flag [signifying 'absolutely forbidden'] flies as a warning." Of course, the disobedience in question is Eichmann's ignoring Himmler's order not to deport the Hungarian Jews. The conscience is Eichmann's, too, that which leads him – this servile bureaucrat, lacking initiative and worried only about his own advancement – to defy his superior. And the "black flag" is the one that, according to the judge who tried the case, should have flown over the illegal order given to the Israeli border guards who carried out the massacre at Kafr Kassem.

Did Eichmann, then, act like those border guards in obeying a patently illegal order, or, unlike them, did he obey his own conscience? Hard as it may be to believe, this is the question Arendt asks about Eichmann's actions in Hungary. No wonder her comments about "the central moral ... phenomena of [the twentieth] century" are neither especially wise nor, in fact, notably different from adolescent patter. At any rate, she has no precise answer to the question of what motivated Eichmann to do what he did in Hungary. Nor is such precision called for, she tells us. He had two motives, loyalty to the Führer and the conscientiousness of a law-abiding citizen, and it doesn't matter which was more important. What apparently sets Eichmann and his "conscience" apart is that, in his contribution to the Final Solution, these two opposing factors – superior orders and the law – came together, for the Führer's will *was* law.

The leader (or *Führer*) principle, according to which the leader's will is not only the law but also a tacit guide to action, is the very principle, so to speak, underlying the political theory, or nontheory, of Nazism and, even more, of its chaotic mode of governing. Arendt could have learned this from, among others, Franz Neumann's *Behemoth*, to which we have previously referred.[46]

---

[46] See also Ian Kershaw, *Hitler: 1889–1936 Hubris* (New York: Norton, 2000). The last chapter, "Working towards the Führer" (pp. 527–591), treats this question at length. Kershaw also deals extensively with Hitler's mythical leadership role in Nazi culture in general. See

This "principle" has generally served to rationalize every imaginable kind of corruption, opportunism, and violence; the complete absence of institutional or moral restraints; and political, legal, and administrative disorder. This is the way the German state was run from the moment the Nazis seized power and increasingly as the war drew to a close and their regime crumbled. What happened in Hungary must be understood against this background. To describe Eichmann's conduct in terms of "conscience" is no doubt original, but more than anything it is baseless.

In any case, Arendt concludes after fewer than twenty lines, if in civilized countries the law assumes that conscience will dictate "thou shalt not murder," in Hitler's Germany conscience dictated just the opposite. There, things were turned upside down: "Evil in the Third Reich had lost the quality by which most people recognize it – the quality of temptation" (p. 150). Whereas "temptation" generally refers to a desire to violate the law, an attraction to that which is evil, forbidden, and shameful, in the Third Reich it became an attraction to that which is usually seen as being in the spirit of the law: *not* killing, stealing, or despoiling, *not* murdering the Jews. But, as is widely known, the Germans have a unique ability to resist temptation and control themselves. Most of them did, in fact, withstand the temptation to save Jews or to refuse to kill them. The irony in these lines is certainly biting. But the philosophy is less than convincing.

How is this strange discussion to be understood? It is no doubt meant to prove the unprovable, that even in Hungary Eichmann's behavior was "banal." For, as Arendt tells us, he was merely, in some perverse sense, a man of conscience who was able to overcome the temptation to spare Jews. It was not anti-Semitic or ideological fanaticism that motivated him and kept him fixed on his goal, even at the price of disobeying Himmler, but an inverted loyalty to the law/will of the Führer. All this was apparently "banal," because the "temptation" to spare Jews from death had a different "quality" than ordinary "temptations," and thus overcoming it had a different quality too: there was no heroism in overcoming the desire to save Jews. This was a banal kind of resistance to temptation.

This argument is really strange, not only because Arendt's reconstruction of Eichmann's personality and motives is undoubtedly fragmentary and may, in part, be just a figment of her imagination. More recent research shows that in this, too, she was wrong. That, at least, is what emerges from a personality test administered to him in prison and recently analyzed by Georges

his *The "Hitler Myth": Image and Reality in the Third Reich* (Oxford: Clarendon; New York: Oxford University Press, 1987).

Bruner.[47] Even lacking this evidence, it is clear to anyone who reads Arendt's book that it is based more on her personal impressions than on any objective analysis, not to mention scientific inquiry. But the real problem with her portrait of Eichmann is not that it is so obviously stitched together out of whole cloth or that her use of him to substantiate her theory is so obvious. The real difficulty is a philosophical one. For even if we acknowledge that she carries off a psychological tour de force, it is nothing more than this: psychology. And psychology is not phenomenology, as this pupil of Heidegger's should know better than most. In other words, Eichmann's psychology – criminal or banal as the case may be – is not in itself and cannot be a comprehensive theory of the nature of evil. At most, Arendt managed to show that in this one instance, however dreadful, a person who helped carry out a crime of unprecedented magnitude was a "banal" individual. That is, he seems to have had a normal personality and might even have been simply pathetic.

The psychological portrait of Eichmann has, all the same, a paradigmatic value insofar, as they say, it is the portrait of an "ordinary man." In recent years it has become customary, in fact, to link Arendt's banality to the Browning-Goldhagen controversy about the question, Who was ordinary – the man or the German? To what has been already said about this earlier, I would like to add here the following remark: Eichmann was not an "ordinary man" in the sense the men of the Reserve Police Battalion 101 were. The latter were "ordinary" in the sense in which philosophers, or others, speak of "the man in street," which means here mainly that these men did not have any particular function, they did not enjoy any prerogatives, they were at the bottom of the chain of command, they did not make decisions, they did not take initiatives exceeding very limited ones, they were not responsible but for what they did themselves at the precise time and place where they were in person. They were also unknown, which means that they did not participate in what Arendt calls the *political*, be it democratic or otherwise. They were also ordinary in the sense of *normal*, which means that they lived more or less according to the norms of occidental societies, except that they killed thousands of Jews.

Now Eichmann was not "ordinary' in this sense. He was "normal," apparently, but – and this should have been the most relevant issue from an Arendt-like point of view – this normality was not a *political* property.

---

[47] See Georges Bruner, "Bikoret habanaliut hatehora: Al hadehumanizatzia shel Eichmann etzel Arendt" (A Critique of Pure Banality: On Arendt's Dehumanization of Eichmann), in Moshe Zuckerman and Idith Zertal, eds., *Hannah Arendt: Half a Century of Dispute* (Tel Aviv: Hakibbutz Hame'uhad, 2005), 81–106.

Politically, Eichmann was not at all "ordinary." As it is often remarked, the Eichmann Arendt saw in the glass cage was not the Eichmann either his victims or his comrades saw. This difference is due, however, not only to the passing time, advancing age, or even to the fact that he had been long preparing himself for the role he was now playing in Beit Ha'am. The uniforms that he once wore were a symbol of the power he had, which is a very real entity – a political entity; or, in the sense Arendt gave to this concept, and in his case, antipolitical. But the antipolitical is also a kind of political. Eichmann might have been, or perhaps not, an ordinary and banal *person*; as a *political agent* he was exceptionally nonbanal.

The philosophical question that seems to be under consideration here – and it is indeed a weighty one – is that of intent: the connection between evildoing and the intention behind it. Here is what Arendt says in summarizing her assessment of the banality of evil: "Foremost among the larger issues at stake in the Eichmann trial was the assumption current in all modern legal systems that intent to do wrong is necessary for the commission of a crime" (p. 277). Eichmann's case seems to disprove this assumption. In fact, the concept of law in general, and legal systems all throughout history (not only the "modern" ones), have been based on the fundamental assumption that the individual enjoys a certain kind of freedom. In legal thinking, unlike in theology or metaphysics, this assumption is always, to some extent, a necessary fiction. The concept of legal culpability (which Arendt claims is her sole concern, not theology or metaphysics) is based not on the intent "to do wrong" but on a claim of "responsibility" or "accountability" – that is, that the accused knew what he was doing, or at least what the likely consequences of his action would be, that he desired those consequences, and that he knew how to distinguish right from wrong; in short, that he could be held accountable for his actions.[48] Legal thought per se has never asked the question of intent in the way Arendt poses it. For a "legal system," it is enough that Eichmann knew that he wasn't Napoleon and that the trains he dispatched were not headed for the Florida coast but rather bringing their cargo to the death factories, as Arendt calls the extermination camps. For,

---

[48] Arendt herself, incidentally, sometimes distinguishes between "guilt" and "responsibility," although she sees the latter as being mainly political and the former psychological. See her article "Collective Responsibility," in J. W. Bernauer, ed., *Amor Mundi* (Dordrecht: Nijhoff, 1987), 43–50. This article is a reaction to a lecture (by Joel Feinberg) in a symposium held in December 1969. Two legal questions that came up here were the right of victors to try those they have defeated and the validity of retroactive legislation. But Arendt was not particularly troubled by these questions, for they had already been considered at length in relation to the Nuremberg Tribunal.

as she herself points out, citing a papal envoy, everyone in Hungary knew perfectly well what the practical consequences of deporting the Jews would be (p. 196). In other words, the people doing the deporting knew, too. The intent that had to be proved to the court was that of sending the Jews to the fate that actually awaited them, and no one has ever disputed the contention that this was exactly what Eichmann had in mind.

The intent Arendt thinks needed to be found in Eichmann's case, and that she was so provoked to discover was not there, is intent of the sort alluded to in the Kantian notion of "radical evil." Evidently she sees being evil in this sense as wishing to do evil *because* it is evil. As we have already had occasion to point out, this is not the real meaning of the Kantian term. Arendt uses the latter in her book on totalitarianism, but in a loose, general way that is more rhetorical than philosophical. Now, as she writes to Gershom Scholem, she has backtracked from the conception of radical evil she espoused in that book. In fact, though, there is very little difference between the two books in terms of what she has to say about evil and the "ordinary people" who commit it. We might also point out in passing that the notion of "radical evil" belongs to a moral theory, in fact a moral theology, not to a political or legal theory. In Arendt's book on totalitarianism, it appears as a political concept, a highly problematical usage to say the least. What is more, the concept as Kant uses it is, again, something else, not what Arendt seems to mean in her comparison of radical and banal evil. To the extent that any real conclusion can be drawn from the highly general, if not confused, things she has to say about this question, it is that radical evil is the diametric opposite of moral obligation, a kind of "pure" (i.e., formal) will to do evil for its own sake. But as we have already seen, this is an empty notion, even self-contradictory. In the book on totalitarianism, which she wrote at a time when she had foresworn philosophy, she uses the expression "radical evil" to say something quite banal: that there are types of evil that are intolerable, deeds that are unacceptable under any circumstances, things that are, in other words, unforgivable. If one takes at face value what she writes to Scholem, one could well conclude that the things Eichmann did, if they were indeed "banal" and not "radical" evil, were *not* unforgivable. Certainly she did not mean to say this, but if not, it is not clear what she did mean, aside from the observation that very bad things can be done by ordinary people. This adds absolutely nothing to our understanding of the nature of evil itself, on a legal, philosophical, theological, or even political level.

One way or the other, the *banality* of evil inherited its *radicality*. But in the latter as well as the former case, Arendt is unable to give a real explanation of what she means – first of all in her book on the Eichmann trial, but, in fact, in her later work on the life of the mind as well. She seems to think it quite important to show that Eichmann was neither a fanatic – either as an ideologue or as an anti-Semite – nor a "monster." Hausner and many others spoke, and still speak, of the monstrousness of the man and what he did. As if he had to be a monster or our claim and that of the prosecution in the trial would be undermined. "Monster," "monstrous," "monstrosity" are the kinds of words that are more expressive of our inability to speak – for example, about the Holocaust or Eichmann or what he did – than of things we actually want to say. By the same token, when we say of someone that he or she is an "angel" or "divine," or that a piece of music is "heavenly," we are really expressing an inability to speak. It is a kind of verbal hand-waving. Incidentally, Arendt herself sometimes used the adjective "monstrous" in speaking about the deeds of the Nazis, for example, in describing what happened the day that the Reichstag was burned and immediately afterward.[49] In any case, Eichmann was not really a monster – smoke did not issue from his nostrils, and he did not have horns. In fact, if we look at the matter a little more closely, it turns out that not only does Arendt have nothing of philosophical value to say, but she also contradicts herself. For whatever positive meaning the term "monster" might have involves an absence of moral sentiment. This kind of statement rests on a number of assumptions that are not obvious, such as that moral sentiment or insight is an essential element in the self-definition of the "human." Thus, a "monster" is one who lacks such sentiment or insight. Yet what is "banal" and even amusing about Eichmann, Arendt tells us toward the end of the book (p. 288), is his "sheer thoughtlessness." Again, it is not quite clear what she means by this new term or whether it is simply the replacement of one vague expression by another. If she means the utter lack of any moral fiber, of this indispensable element of humanness, we would have to conclude that Eichmann was indeed a monster, although it would then not be clear what she finds so amusing about him.[50] In only one place do we find even a feeble attempt at an explanation: his thoughtlessness, she says there, lies in his inability to empathize even slightly with his Jewish interlocutors. Might we not then conclude that this whole grand theory of the banality of evil amounts to nothing more than the claim that Eichmann had no talent for empathy or that perhaps he was simply stupid?

[49] In the interview entitled "What Remains? The Mother Tongue Remains," in Baehr, *The Portable Hannah Arendt*, 13.

[50] In the same broadcast interview, edited, by the way, shortly after the publication in German of her Eichmann book, Arendt says she read with great interest all 3,600 pages of the police report of his interrogation. "I do not know how many times I burst out laughing in the course of reading it," she relates.

Be that as it may, what underlies all this is a significant and typical philosophical failure: "With the best will in the world one cannot extract any diabolical or demonic profundity from Eichmann" (ibid.). Using almost the same words as Jaspers, she says Eichmann was neither a Macbeth, an Iago, nor a Richard III. In other words, if we are to see him as evil in a non-banal way, it is not enough to impute to him criminal intent of the kind every court of law imputes to one it convicts of a crime (after all, not all murderers, robbers, rapists, or defrauders are Richard III); he must be made out to be a Shakespearean figure. But of course that is impossible. The sad truth is that the mountain of banality becomes a molehill; it all boils down to the fact that Eichmann was a bureaucrat, that he could not understand the Jews, and that he was not Richard III. Arendt never transcended her German philosophical romanticism. This is the same romanticism she shared with Heidegger, incidentally, and that was one of the main philosophical sources of his moral and political blindness. It is the romanticism that is not satisfied with the fact that evil is, in reality, always abject, ugly, and despicable – always evil, in other words – but that tries to find in it something that is not and cannot be there – the profound, the diabolical (whatever that is), some sort of inverted greatness – and when it does not find it, it is disappointed. The opposite of greatness is lowliness, ugliness, and small-mindedness. It is the romanticism found, for example, in Hollywood films that depict mafia dons as "deep," and it is a close relative of the aestheticization of evil, which, as we know, has found fertile ground in Nazism.

Judith Shklar, in the article mentioned earlier, sees in the term "banality" an expression of the gulf between the causes and perpetrators of the Nazi crimes, on the one hand, and the consequences of those crimes, on the other. This is a valid distinction; but in this sense almost all collective human activity, not only the evil variety, is "banal." Presumably, a similar gulf exists between the NASA engineers, for example, and the "one giant leap for mankind" taken by the astronauts whom those engineers landed on the moon. Such a gap exists in other realms, even in philosophy. There are those who think Heidegger, for example, was in many ways a banal person. Even in joining the Nazi Party, he was neither deep nor demonic.[51]

---

[51] On Heidegger's membership in the Nazi Party, on the year he served as rector of the University of Freiburg (1933–1934), and on his attitude toward this episode after the war, much has been and continues to be written. See, e.g., Hans Sluga, *Heidegger's Crisis: Philosophy and Politics in Nazi Germany* (Cambridge, Mass.: Harvard University Press, 1993). This book is of particular interest because it places Heidegger's case in the more general context of the rallying of almost all of Germany's professors of philosophy to the Nazi cause. In this context, the case of Heidegger does, indeed, seem somewhat banal.

The sad truth is that "the banality of evil" has been overrated. In the last analysis, what the expression means is a good deal less than what Zertal evidently takes it to mean. Or, more precisely, the positive content of the expression is quite trivial and none too original. And whatever originality is to be found in it is empty and simplistic. As elsewhere, the most interesting aspects of Arendt's theory of the banality of Nazi evil are often borrowed from others. Many of the descriptions and factual assertions – some of them accurate and at times significant – on which the claim of "banality" is based are to be found in other works and other writers whom Arendt knew and sometimes even mentions. The expression is no doubt connected with important insights and distinctions in Arendt's theory of "totalitarianism," especially the part dealing with Nazism. But the theory of "banality" in and of itself, despite its pretenses, has no real philosophical depth.

Thus, if we look closely at the new concept Arendt is said to have introduced into the lexicon of political philosophy and try to pin down its precise meaning, it turns out to be an empty phrase with no real ideational content, a non-idea. Yet there is something catchy about the expression "the banality of evil," something in its apparent originality that captures the imagination. Of course, its philosophical elusiveness and emptiness do not make it easier to refute, but they are also why so many of her readers refer to it so often and why it is so important to the reputation of Arendt's book on the Eichmann trial. The expression has made a place for itself in Holocaust "discourse" and slipped into more or less learned deliberations on the question of evil in general. There, the concept has not proved particularly fruitful or produced any special insights. On the other hand, its influence on Holocaust research and the public image of the Holocaust has been fundamentally negative, unless we are to join Hilberg in taking some small comfort in the literature of denial, in the fact that the latter has forced historians to close gaps in their research and seek out firmer historical truths, beyond what was already obvious and well known. For all too often, those who concern themselves with the Holocaust treat "the banality of evil" as a veiled threat, a potential challenge to the intellectual validity of their enterprise and, especially, to their personal and moral commitment to it.

The Yaacov Lozowick book we have mentioned only makes explicit what is hinted at in many other places: as the subtitle of the book makes plain, it is concerned mainly with the banality of the evil represented by Eichmann and his henchmen. As Lozowick testifies in the opening lines of the book, he thought at first that this evil was indeed banal but after years of research came to recognize that it was not (p. 9). His disagreement with Arendt pervades the entire book and is most evident at the end, where he challenges the banality thesis explicitly and in detail. In fact, the energy Lozowick invests in showing that Eichmann and his wickedness were not "banal" is wasted. What he says about this question in the book neither adds much to nor detracts much from the (considerable) value of his historical and factual findings.

The Moral Failure: Arendt and the Story of Extermination

Arendt's moral failure in the Eichmann book is even greater than her philosophical failure. One of the main reasons for the anger she has aroused is the feeling that her thesis about the banality of evil diminishes in some way the significance of the wrong done to the Jews – not from the point of view of the perpetrators, which she did presume to do, but from that of the victims. There is good reason to feel this. Treating Eichmann as "banal" reflects the same theoretical, and perhaps emotional, ability to set compassion aside to which we have already referred. Just as Arendt had no compassion for the masses whose suffering, used to justify the French Revolution, brought about its failure, she had no patience for Eichmann's victims either. Perhaps it was because, as she set about reporting on the trial, she had an ideological agenda. Her stubborn (and historically dubious) attempt to minimize Eichmann's role in the extermination process; her repeated charges that the prosecution exaggerated, as it were, his position in, and influence upon, the process; her questioning of the importance of the trial and its deliberations; her claim that it did not clarify, as it should have, the universal legal, political, and moral significance of the Nazi crimes; and her questioning of the way Israel tried Eichmann – all these create the impression that the intention behind the book (and, indeed, it was an intention, for Arendt was surely not "thoughtless") was not to give an objective or even critical report but something else altogether. Another of Zertal's subtleties is the phrase "The State of Israel against Hannah Arendt," which she uses as the title of her account of the trial and its consequences, mentioned previously, an account that appears in the volume *Fifty since Forty-Eight*. But in this instance, too, Zertal, has things backward: it was not the State of Israel that sought to judge Arendt but the Jewish refugee from Germany who tried, successfully, to place organized Jewry, that is, mainly the State of Israel in the last analysis, in the defendant's box. And if Arendt was burned by the reactions of those she accused, it is precisely this that was meant by the ancient saying, "Because you have drowned others, they have drowned you" (Chapters of the Fathers 2:7). In any event, the way she used the trial to settle accounts with the State of Israel and Ben-Gurionism represents a moral failure.

One of the best-known documents of the Arendt controversy is the brief exchange of letters between her and Gershom Scholem, an exchange that, incidentally, brought their decades-long friendship to an end. Scholem's letter was published in Hebrew, but, as Zertal points out, Arendt felt he did not keep his promise to publish Arendt's response along with it. So Zertal took it upon herself to render this service to the Hebrew reader, providing commentary on it as well. From Scholem's statement that "[a] heartless, frequently almost sneering and malicious tone" pervades the book, Zertal concludes that "there can be no question that [Arendt's] secular, rational, critical, sometimes ironic, sometimes aloof, and wholly modern style was perceived by Scholem ... as evidence of her lack of awe, her contempt for the sublimity, the numinous sanctity of the Holocaust, the mystical, religious dimension attributed to the events, namely her contempt for all that was sacred to the nation, of which the Holocaust was now becoming a part" (p. 153). Of course, there is no hint of any of this in Scholem's letter. But this is an opportunity to repeat the canard we have already seen in Ophir (and Garaudy and Guillaume) about the theologization and sanctification, as it were, of the Holocaust. Scholem's brief allusion to the fact that he had devoted a lot of time to the study of Jewish history is the occasion for half a page of commentary by Zertal: it was unnecessary for him to say this, she declares, because Arendt had known him for more than thirty years. Rather, it is a sure sign for our commentator that Scholem's intentions were not pure and that he already had other readers in mind. It is true enough that the length of Scholem's acquaintance with Arendt is surprisingly similar to the length of Arendt's acquaintance with Scholem, but the autobiographical remarks *she* adds to her letter do not, in Zertal's view, betray any hidden motives. Zertal also explains to us that Scholem, in his comment, "segregated Jewish history as a whole within a sacred delineated space and denied Arendt access to it" (p. 151). For, of course, he saw in this history "a kind of mystic entity, whose depths could not be plumbed and whose full meaning was beyond human comprehension, and hence any attempt at analytical and rational examination was sacrilege" (p. 152). Arendt does offer us such a rational examination, as does Zertal herself, clearly. Zertal regards Scholem's remark that he saw Arendt "wholly as a daughter of our people, and in no other way" as patronizing and sexist (p. 149). Given what we know about Arendt's attitude to feminism and to women in general, it is not hard to guess what she would have said about this pseudofeminist bending over backwards.[52] Her own reaction to Scholem's remark was that she had never pretended to be anything else.

---

[52] Arendt's attitude to women and feminism may not have been completely unlike her attitude to Jews and Zionism; similarly, the attitude of feminists toward her was not unlike that

And this was no doubt true, although on some other occasions she said some things that were rather different. In a February 1950 letter to Heidegger, for example, she writes: "I have never felt myself to be a German woman and for a long time have ceased to feel as a Jewish woman. I feel ... like a girl from elsewhere [*Mädchen aus der Fremde*]." In 1952 Jaspers wrote her that he would never cease to regard or claim her as a German. I do not know if Zertal regards these comments as patronizing or sexist; but Arendt, at least, was not offended by them in the way she was by Scholem's. By the way, in his reply to her letter, Scholem remarks that Arendt misunderstood him completely: his intention was to dissociate himself from those who had accused her of being an "assimilated post-Zionist," a recent appellation, he says, which designates those who no longer consider themselves solidary with the Jewish people.

In fact, Scholem's letter to Arendt is a model of restraint, courtesy, and intelligence. Of irony, too, of course. It contains some harsh things, quite harsh. But it is not condescending. By contrast, there is plenty of condescension, scorn, and bad taste in Zertal. After all, Arendt's book itself has some harsh things to say, and she hardly needs the sort of defense Zertal offers her. Undoubtedly, there will be those who read this as male haughtiness toward a woman sticking her nose into public affairs, or some such thing, but Zertal seems not to be aware, or to understand, what Scholem meant when he told Arendt he saw her as a daughter of the Jewish people or to what issue he was alluding. Of course, Arendt knew Scholem's work and understood the allusion quite well, even if she chose to ignore it and to take offense.[53] Toward the end of the time she spent as a refugee in France, shortly before she managed to escape and Walter Benjamin died failing to do so, she took part in a reading group he had assembled in his room, in which Scholem's *Major Trends in Jewish Mysticism* was read. Zertal quotes the praises Arendt showered on the book after it was published in New York (by the Schocken publishing house, where she worked), including the statement that "Scholem has changed the picture of Jewish history." It was this subject that the group had discussed in Benjamin's Paris apartment. But, Zertal writes, while Scholem was concerned with the religious aspects of Sabbateanism, Arendt saw it as

---

of Zionists, as we can see from Bonnie Honig, ed., *Feminist Interpretations of Hannah Arendt* (University Park: Penn State University Press, 1995).

[53] One of the most interesting and revealing expressions of this offense is actually Mary McCarthy's. In December 1963, after reading Arendt's exchange with Scholem, she writes to her friend that "the net effect of all this controversy was to make me resolve never to set foot in the State of Israel." Carol Brightman, ed., *Between Friends: The Correspondence of Hannah Arendt and Mary McCarthy, 1949–1975* (New York: Harcourt Brace, 1995), 157. Arendt did not see fit to react.

"the precursor of the Zionist national movement," discovering in mystical messianism a potential for concrete political action (p. 147). There are two things to be said about this, one positive, the other less so. On the one hand, Zertal deserves credit for having shown us how farsighted Arendt was; unlike Scholem, who was always opposed to political messianism and even regarded it as dangerous, Arendt saw even then, in a positive light, what we all discovered only much later as "concrete political action" – for example, that of the Bloc of the Faithful settler movement. On the other hand, the notion that Sabbateanism was a "precursor" of Zionism was Scholem's and definitely not Arendt's. She only mentions it. Scholem did not, in fact, concern himself only with the "religious dimensions" of Sabbateanism but also with the way the crisis it generated led to a political secularization of Jewish life, that is, to Zionism. This is one of the main features of the new "picture of Jewish history" he painted. Arendt's review of Scholem's book is indeed a positive, even an enthusiastic one. Zertal apparently did not notice it, but Arendt is, on the whole, simply paraphrasing Scholem. Perhaps Zertal was misled by the way Arendt restates Scholem's ideas without reservation, adding, in her typical fashion, a few thoughts of her own. One needs to be familiar with Scholem to recognize what part is his and what hers.

Gershom Scholem was, as we know, the founder of a new scholarly discipline, the study of Kabbalah. In light of what Zertal says about him, it may be appropriate to mention this here and also to add, with all due caution, that his achievement was no less significant than Arendt's in placing the question of totalitarianism on the agenda of political thought. What is more, Arendt's use of the latter concept is far less original and groundbreaking than Scholem's research on Kabbalah and its role in Jewish history. Another difference between the two, we might add, lies in the fact that, whereas Arendt, in her work on totalitarianism and elsewhere, was writing mainly philosophical, phenomenological, or metahistorical commentary on facts she had gleaned from secondary sources, Scholem devoted most of his time to arduous empirical research, the deciphering of manuscripts, and the study of primary sources.[54] But the historiography of Kabbalah was, for Scholem, part of a whole historiosophy, perhaps the most important in twentieth-century Jewish thought. At bottom, what Scholem's research

---

[54] On Scholem as a scholar, and on his avoidance of the public sphere, see, e.g., Yosef Dan, "Gershom Scholem velimudei hakabbala ba'universita ha'ivrit" (Gershom Scholem and the Study of Kabbala at the Hebrew University), in Hagit Lavsky, ed., *Toldot ha'universita ha'ivrit: Hitbassesut utzemiha* (The History of the Hebrew University of Jerusalem: Consolidation and Growth), vol. 1 (Jerusalem: Magnes, 2005), 199–218.

seeks to demonstrate is that the concept of "Jewish history" has a concrete meaning and methodological, historiographical, and historiosophic validity. That is, there is room and full rational justification for scholarly research on Jewish history as such, that it cannot be dismissed merely as a sociological or institutional phenomenon or as a matter of manipulation. Put differently, all of Scholem's scholarship was meant to prove something that was for him a historical truth of the highest moral and existential significance: the irreducible specificity and sui generis character of Jewish history. Had I not read Zertal, I would not think it necessary to add here that Scholem does not sanctify Jewish history in the least.[55] Scholem thinks – and tries to show in his various scholarly works, especially his great study of Sabbateanism – that Jewish history unfolds according to its own inner logic, and though the influence of the non-Jewish world cannot, of course, be ignored, there is, in the final analysis, a historic Jewish identity that cannot simply be subsumed under "general" history. Scholem's understanding of Jewish history is dialectical, that is, historical and not theological, and this is the precise meaning of his attempt to show that Sabbateanism was the progenitor, or one of the progenitors, of Zionism.[56] The main import of this idea for our purposes is that the thing we call "Jewish identity" is not given or fixed, an eternal, unchanging essence, or substance, a closed realm of holiness, as Zertal thinks, but exists in history and has a historical character; Jewish identity is, according to Scholem, the unanticipated *outcome* of a history that, like all histories, is marked by coincidence, contingency, and human freedom. He thus sees Zionism as a political embodiment of Jewish history. That is why he immigrated to Palestine and spent the rest of his scholarly career at the Hebrew University of Jerusalem.

These were the very things Hannah Arendt could not accept. She did not immigrate to Palestine, and those who benefited from her talents were mainly American students. More important, for her, too, action was connected with theory, and there was a continuity and consistency between political and moral life and decision making, on the one hand, and scholarship, on the other. Arendt was concerned with Jewish matters, and not only in connection with the Eichmann book; early on, as we have seen, she was

---

[55] The question of Scholem's religiosity should be kept separate from that of the scholarly and historiosophic significance of his research.

[56] Steven Aschheim analyzes illuminatingly and at length the difference between Arendt and Scholem in this regard. But he describes Scholem's concept of Jewish history as "organic," which might be misleading. The development of an organism and dialectical development are two quite different things. See his *Scholem, Arendt, Klemperer: Intimate Chronicles in Turbulent Times* (Bloomington: Indiana University Press, 2001).

even involved in organized Jewish life. But in her purely theoretical writings, published after she cut her ties with organized Jewry and Zionism, Jewish matters always figure – that is, must always be *understood*, in the full, exact sense of that word – as a part of "general" history. That is, in complete contrast with Scholem's attitude toward Jewish history, she sees no theoretical validity – and thus, obviously, no moral or political justification – in the notion of Jewish history as sui generis. She is suspicious of attempts to make something substantial of Jewish history and of the tendency of Jewish nationalists, the Zionists foremost among them, to see themselves as part of a primordial (to use a current term), suprahistorical entity with an eternal, unchanging "essence." Although on various occasions she speaks of a "Jewish people" and a continuum of Jewish existence, through different forms, from early times to the present, she never sees fit to formulate this idea in theoretical terms. We are left with little more than feelings, instincts, scattered phrases, and clichés. She never proposes a real alternative to Scholem's complex dialectical (and anti-essentialist, nonsubstantialist) historiosophy. Her understanding of the politicization of Jewish life is ahistorical and, in the last analysis, as we have said, apolitical.

It is perhaps no accident that the main, indeed the only theoretical expression of Arendt's view that there is no eternal Jewish essence is her concern with the antihistory of the Jews, that is, with anti-Semitism. The sole theoretical support for her anti-essentialist position turns out to be indirect and implicit: as modern anti-Semitism is not just another stage in a long history in which a fixed essence takes on different forms, the same is true of modern Jewish existence in general. It is against this background that we must understand, for example, Arendt's scorn for Hausner's presentation of the Nazi mass murder of the Jews as just another chapter in the long history of Jewish suffering. Neither the court that tried Eichmann, she says, nor those present in the courtroom understood what was being unfurled before them. They saw Auschwitz as just another pogrom. But, in fact, it was something absolutely new and unprecedented. The crime committed there, genocide, was a new crime; the perpetrators – representatives of a totalitarian regime – were a new phenomenon; hence, Jewish modernity is something new, and its historical dimension is of secondary importance, or perhaps of no importance at all.

This idea is expressed most clearly in Arendt's essay on anti-Semitism, which is the first part of her important book on the origins of totalitarianism. In an introduction to the book (written in 1967), she quotes Jacob Katz's *Exclusiveness and Tolerance*, showering praise on the "younger generation of Jewish historians" working in Jerusalem (i.e., the very historians who became, in the view of Zertal and other disciples of Arendt, "the establishment"). Arendt takes as her point of departure what Katz writes about the gathering of the German Jews into ghettos at the end of the Middle Ages and the beginning of the modern era, a development that gave rise to an isolationist ideology and a sense of unbridgeable difference between Jews and gentiles.[57] She explains that these changes in Jewish life and Jewish self-awareness were a necessary condition and principal cause of the birth of modern anti-Semitism. This, according to her, ought to prove that there is no continuity between premodern and modern anti-Semitism and that, one way or another, it is modern Jewish existence, not the earlier history of Jew-hatred, that is the source, or at least the main source, of modern anti-Semitism. Were Arendt familiar with Katz's book on anti-Semitism, she would know that, while he regards modern anti-Semitism as a new phenomenon, he also insists that it has its roots in premodern religious anti-Semitism, that it is, in fact, merely a secular form of the latter, substituting quasi-rational images for religious ones without any change in its "essence" as Jew-hatred. In a methodological discussion included in the book, he even tries to show that modern anti-Semitism cannot be understood apart from the long, singular history of Jew-hatred and thus that it can be understood properly only through historical research.[58] Katz dismisses Arendt's theory in two brief critical notes: because she sees anti-Semitism as a reflection of internal tensions in non-Jewish society, she misses the former's true nature; and while her research does make some useful distinctions, it is full of contradictions and largely baseless, arbitrary pronouncements.

On the face of it, Arendt is engaged in the debate over the proper theoretical understanding of modern anti-Semitism: is it a result of traditional anti-Semitism or is it a new phenomenon to be analyzed in its own terms? Like some other historians, she seems to reject the notion that it is just another form of something fixed and unchanging, a permanent feature of European civilization or of Jewish existence. For her, anti-Semitism is not something primordial, as other scholars have held. It is something decidedly new, something modern that cannot be lumped together with the religious Jew-hatred of earlier times. A theoretical understanding of anti-Semitism is thus to be acquired, not by tracing a chain of historical causality that would account

[57] Jacob Katz, *Exclusiveness and Tolerance: Studies in Jewish-Gentile Relations in Medieval and Modern Times* (Westport, Conn.: Greenwood Press, 1980). Arendt draws upon chapter 11 and, to a greater extent, chapter 12 in Katz's book, but only selectively and tendentiously, and, in fact, distorts what he says.
[58] Jacob Katz, *From Prejudice to Destruction: Anti-Semitism, 1700–1933* (Cambridge, Mass.: Harvard University Press, 1980). However, the methodological chapter quoted here does not appear in the English edition.

Post-Zionism, Post-Holocaust

for its emergence from ancient roots, but by analyzing modernity itself, with its inner contradictions and characteristic dialectic. As we have seen, there is a debate among historians over this question, but it is doubtful that Arendt has made any real contribution to settling it. She accepts uncritically the assumption that there is no continuity between ancient and modern anti-Semitism, and aside from a rather blunt and categorical rejection of the opposing view, she has little to say.[59]

The debate over the nature of anti-Semitism is a legitimate one. But any serious investigation of the question is predicated not only on a definition, precise as possible, of the methodological principles of the inquiry and the concepts employed but also on a spelling out of the theoretical objectives. If we are to grasp the true meaning of Arendt's position, we must take into account not only her theoretical conclusions but also the question she set out to answer. The historiographical, phenomenological, sociological, or political question about the continuity or lack of continuity in the history of anti-Semitism derives its primary meaning, long before possible answers can be considered, from the point of view from which it is asked. The perspective of Arendt's work on anti-Semitism – which is a speculative sociopolitical essay more than a work of scholarly research – is that of the political history of modern Europe. In considering anti-Semitism, she is trying not so much to understand its history as to get at the roots of totalitarianism. It is in this context that her claim of noncontinuity must be seen: anti-Semitism, be it modern or premodern, is not the problem, not a subject of inquiry for its own sake. Her theoretical interest in it is not independent but rather a function of her theoretical interest in political modernity in general. From this point of view, anti-Semitism is not even a phenomenon in its own right, not something that exists independently, and as such it has no history.

It is quite clear that Arendt is not a real expert on the subject of anti-Semitism. But beyond this, it is sometimes charged that her essay echoes traditional anti-Semitic images and comes perilously close to being itself anti-Semitic. While she does lean more than necessary on anti-Semitic authors, it would be unfair to impute any anti-Semitic feelings to Arendt herself. What does seem to inform her approach to the subject is left-wing, quasi-Marxist ideology and theory. A general change in political conditions

[59] Despite this, she is sometimes honored as an authentic representative of the school of historiography that denies the primordiality of anti-Semitism. See, e.g., Omer Bartov, "Anti-Semitism, the Holocaust, and Reinterpretations of National Socialism," in Bartov, *Murder in Our Midst: The Holocaust, Industrial Killing, and Representation* (New York: Oxford University Press, 1996), 53–70.

in Europe would, in this view, lead to the elimination of anti-Semitism (the main aspect of the "Jewish problem"), which is a function of improper socio-political arrangements, "objective" conditions that are, in principle, ana-lyzable and subject to rational redress. Be that as it may, her discussion of anti-Semitism does not stand alone but is meant, rather, to shore up the main thesis of her sociopolitical theory, that totalitarianism is a new and unprec-edented phenomenon. It made its first appearance in history in the form of two modern totalitarian regimes, the Nazi and the Stalinist.

Jacob Katz, on the other hand, asks about the nature of modern anti-Semitism from a Jewish point of view, and his interest extends beyond the methodological and historiographical aspects of this question. If we con-sider anti-Semitism from this point of view, Arendt's arguments are of little importance. To put it crudely, it matters little to a Jew whether he is being killed for being of a different religion, if not the anti-Christ, or for belong-ing to an alien race that Europeans are purging from their midst the way a body purges itself of a disease. Even if, as Arendt thinks, these rationales are merely an ideological superstructure concealing an underlying socioeco-nomic reality, the difference between the two acts of murder would likely be of limited interest to the one being murdered. Looked at this way, the fact that a murder was committed before and is being committed now is sufficient to raise the issue of past and present as a single theoretical ques-tion, sufficient, that is, to justify treating Jew-hatred as a *historical* question. Treating it this way does not necessarily imply an "essentialist" point of view or a belief in the "primordiality" of anti-Semitism.

Katz's question can be answered in different ways. As he himself shows, it can even be answered in a way that stresses the uniqueness of modern anti-Semitism. The differences between him and Arendt are not over the facts or even the interpretation of the facts. What is at stake is the legitimacy of one or another point of view. The real meaning of Arendt's thesis of nonconti-nuity is that there is no room or justification for treating anti-Semitism in a distinct or specific way. There is reason for a Jewish army but not for the university departments dedicated to the study of Jewish history or sociology, for example.

Lest there be any doubt in the reader's mind, we are not talking here about the fashionable "discourse of narratives," about historicism or any other kind of relativism. The "point of view" we are speaking about here is not a matter of "narrative" but of theoretical motivation, the place where the questions arise. Katz's viewpoint is not the source of a "narrative" alongside which other, equally valid narratives could, as it were, be posited. The concern of his historiography, like all theory, is with historical truth – however elusive and difficult to define – as Arendt's undoubtedly is. Nor do the differences between Arendt's and Scholem's points of view abrogate the demand for historical truth. But the question of historical truth, the attempt to understand "what really happened," is, in this instance, being asked from a specific place, on the basis of a certain political and moral stance. This stance forms the real background of the dispute between Arendt and Scholem. What is at stake is the legitimacy of one or another point of view. The argument turns on the driving force behind the theoretical concern, not on any empirical data or the results of any hermeneutical inquiry. To be more exact, since the validity of the extra-Jewish viewpoint underlying Arendt's theoretical work cannot be questioned, what is really at stake here is the validity of the *Jewish* point of view, that is, the notion of Jewish history written by Jews as Jews (though not necessarily *for* Jews). And here we see the real import of Scholem's statement to Arendt that he always thought of her as a Jew.

Scholem's best-known charge against Arendt was that she lacked something that is "hard to define" but nonetheless real, something Jewish tradition calls *ahavat yisrael* (love of the Jewish people). Arendt's response was that, indeed, she did not feel such love. She never loved any ethnic group or human collective, she writes to Scholem. She only loved her friends, only individual people. As far as one can tell, there was some truth in this statement; although here and there her loves and fealties, for Heidegger, for example, raised eyebrows, there is no doubt that she had a real talent for love and friendship. This is evident from her disciple Elisabeth Young-Bruehl's comprehensive biography of her and also in her published correspondence, including with Martin Heidegger. Nevertheless, her reply to Scholem was condescending, insulting, and, above all, sophistic and unfair. Zertal nonetheless waxes enthusiastic over her, describing the dozen or so lines Arendt wrote about love as "a fundamental discussion of the connections between politics and love, and the issue of politics and compassion" (p.150). Zertal is particularly thrilled with Arendt's "love of the world" (the title of the Young-Bruehl biography), which she contrasts with Scholem's "love of the Jewish people." We can disregard the fact that Zertal says not a word about the meaning of the term "world," its place in Arendt's philosophy, its roots in Heidegger and in phenomenology in general, or Arendt's radical reversal of its Heideggerian meaning, that is, her transformation of the concept into a political one. But when Zertal explains to us that Arendt, in her reply to Scholem, makes clear that she, unlike him, loves only real people and not abstract entities like national groups, one can hardly help but wonder what makes her love of the world any less abstract than Scholem's love of the Jewish people.

Here too, it seems, Zertal does not quite grasp what is at stake. But Arendt understood all too well. That is why she points out, right after her "fundamental discussion" of love, that Scholem's question can be taken in "political terms," thus raising the question of "patriotism." In other words, Scholem's "love of the Jewish people" can be understood unsentimentally as a Jewish version of the political concept of "patriotism," or "love of homeland." She also knew that this concept was central for the Greeks and for the entire republican tradition and that it is fundamental to political theory. This is the name given to the highest virtue in public life, that which prompts people to act as citizens and in "the world" – in short, to realize Arendt's own ideal of the good life.

But, in a not uncharacteristic reversal, what the Greeks saw as love of homeland, loyalty, and decency becomes for Arendt something quite different. We agree with each other, she writes to Scholem, that there can be no patriotism without criticism or opposition. These are straightforward things that Scholem, who was always critical and oppositional and even saw himself as an anarchist in some ways, could certainly accept. But for her, she goes on, there is more to it. Patriotism is what distresses her in the wrongs committed by her own people, more than in the wrongs done by others. With her usual discretion, she adds that such distress is one of those things that cannot be shared with others. Perhaps she has forgotten her own discussion of the *Judenräte* in the Eichmann book, as public a discussion as one could imagine, or the fact that she began the book with the pronouncement that for the Jews this was the darkest chapter in the whole story of their extermination. Even darker than the gas chambers, apparently. At any rate, what she offers Scholem is no doubt quite an original definition of "love of homeland" or "love of one's people." I am quite sure that some of Israel's and Zionism's perpetual critics will be happy to adopt this definition for their oppositionism. Still, one might question not only whether it is the right way to define patriotism but also whether Arendt was a Jewish "patriot" in any other reasonable sense, however much she may have felt like one. We may also assume that she was not being dishonest with herself in feeling this. Sartre, of whom Arendt was not particularly fond, labels such lack of dishonesty with the hard-to-translate expression *mauvaise foi.*

The idea that a person should be especially critical of those closest to him is one that contains an important psychological and moral truth. Nevertheless, such a statement may conceal motives that are not at all "patriotic," and the suffering that goes with such criticism is not always that of love. After all, to take a critical or oppositional stance is no great achievement, and who does not have criticism of one "aspect" or another (as Zertal puts it) of the Zionist vision and its realization, or of Jewish behavior, even during the Holocaust? The most fervent Zionists have never hesitated to criticize their own movement and its leaders, since the very beginning. Few national movements have treated their leaders as they have been treated in the State of Israel or in the prestate Zionist community. But there are different kinds of criticism; and this is exactly the point made by Scholem, who was a patriot in the very sense that Arendt defines it, a harsh critic of "many aspects" of Zionist and Israeli policy, as we see from his membership, early on, in Brit Shalom and in statements he continued to make about the character of the state until his dying day.

In fact, what Arendt says goes beyond criticism. The very fact that, in a discussion of the destruction of European Jewry by the Nazis, she can compare wrongs done by her own people and wrongs done by other peoples or speak of the way the Jewish leaders' shortsightedness, cowardice, and even corruptness made the Nazis' work easier, as it were, shows that something is seriously wrong with Arendt's judgment. In this matter, she suffers from a certain moral blindness. We should not forget, either, that she said these things before "the Occupation" began. The fact that this comparison has now resurfaced in the pronouncements of Israel's critics and the negators of Zionism does not diminish her blindness. And here, too, the paradigmatic question of the origins and causes of this blindness arises. Arendt's patriotic indignation, whether directed at the *Judenräte* or Ben-Gurion (in the Eichmann book as well as the response to Scholem, the two are lumped together), is not moral outrage against iniquity but something else altogether, not uncharacteristic of her. It might be described as a deep unease with Jewish "particularism," that is, Jewish nationhood. In essence, it is the reluctance to adopt a specifically Jewish point of view.

This unease is shared by all the protagonists in the present work, from the Holocaust deniers on the radical left to the Jewish and Israeli post- and anti-Zionists. *Eichmann in Jerusalem* is clearly among the fruits of this unease, and the book gives us a picture of some possible consequences of it. It may even be that the *cura posterior* we spoke of earlier is merely Arendt's attempt to dispel this unease, to come to terms with it once and for all, and to display, in her report on the banality of evil as revealed in the Eichmann trial, that it has been healed. The most concrete and perhaps, in the end, most disgraceful expression of this disease and its healing appears in another connection that has gone almost unnoticed by Arendt's critics. As we have seen, she has a number of complaints about the way the trial was conducted. The main one, it would seem, is that it should have concerned itself with the actions of the defendant and not the suffering of the victims. This would seem to be a semiformal argument, and, true to form, Arendt presents it as if she were an authority on judicial procedure. But she was not really expert in such matters, and her argument can be disputed. The notion that the suffering of the victim is not merely a subjective matter of pain or of physical or psychic injury but an objective aspect of the criminal act itself is one that is gaining adherents among jurists and criminologists. In fact, some time ago a new discipline called "victimology" began to emerge, a field of research and treatment based on the recognition that the victim and what has happened to him are an integral part of the "crime," no less than the criminal or the criminal act. It is no accident that it is feminist thought that has taken the lead in this development, and as we have already suggested, there may be a connection between Arendt's inability to anticipate these changes, her sometimes strident disaffection from feminism, and the way she treats the testimony of the victims and survivors in the Jerusalem trial.

Who Should Have Judged Eichmann?

But the full significance of Arendt's position becomes clear, not only in her explicit argument about the judicial irrelevance of the testimony or in the appearance of academic seriousness and objectivity with which she dresses up this argument, but also in the form of her argument and, especially, in what she leaves unsaid: the testimony of the survivors is largely omitted. Arendt claimed repeatedly that her whole purpose in writing the book was to cover the trial. We can forgive her for having strayed from this intention and for instructing the court as to what it neglected to do, what it should have considered, and what it should not have. But the greatest gap between what she says she meant to do and what she actually did lies in her having omitted the most important aspect of the trial, the survivors' testimony. She explains briefly how the witnesses were selected and why Hausner erred in choosing the ones he did and not others. She sees the whole business of the witnesses as a kind of disgraceful circus. Haim Gouri, who, unlike Arendt, was present in the courtroom from beginning to end, thinks this testimony was the most important part of the trial. This is also the conclusion of Hanna Yablonka's research on the Eichmann trial (which, by the way, disproves all Zertal's contentions about the trial, virtually one after another). Perhaps because Gouri is not as up-to-date as Arendt in judicial matters (or so she thought), he understands what should have been obvious and what today, forty years later, is clear as day: that Arendt's quasi-formal nitpicking was, and still is, of no importance – except as an excuse to skewer Israel and Ben-Gurion. The question of whether this was or was not a show trial, or whether Eichmann should have been tried in Israel, or in what way the trial should have been conducted – all these are of little consequence compared to the thing that really made the trial important, historically important even beyond the borders of Israel and the Jewish world, even more important than the Nuremberg trials. What made the Eichmann trial what it was was precisely what Arendt could not accept, to such an extent that she almost completely ignored it: the testimony. All the rest vanished just as Eichmann's ashes vanished in the Mediterranean Sea.

It could be that language difficulties prevented Arendt from understanding what was happening before her very eyes. She did not know Hebrew, and the translation into German was so bad, she thought, that the choice of interpreter must have been dictated by a heavy dose of "vitamin P." (That is how people referred then to *protekstia,* or "pull," which, as we say, people with the right connections do not need, and she may have used the expression to demonstrate how familiar she was with Israeli folklore.) In any event, it is more likely that her attitude to the testimony and the witnesses was a matter of conscious choice. Apart from a few scattered notes, she confines her report on them to one chapter, number 14. There, she begins with the witnesses for the defense who were unable to come to Israel because they had not been granted immunity from prosecution. Then she speaks of the defendant's testimony. And finally she comes to the witnesses for the prosecution. We should note that more than half the sessions of the trial (62 out of 121) were devoted to the latter. Arendt has reservations of one sort or another about the way the witnesses were chosen; to her readers, at any rate, she speaks of only four depositions. She begins with that of Yehiel Dinur (Ka-tzetnik), whom she describes as the author of several books about Auschwitz dealing with brothels, homosexuals, and other such "human interest" stories (quotation marks in the original). Out of his testimony, she chooses three sentences that she presents as utterly ridiculous and then describes his fainting while on the stand as a pathetic show. After this, she mentions the testimony of attorney Aharon Hoter-Yishai dealing with the Jewish Brigade, which she describes as propaganda. She speaks highly of the appearance of the first witness, the father of Herschel Grynszpan, quoting the story of his deportation and that of his family from France as the fairest and most reliable (!) Holocaust account to be given at the trial.[60] And she tops it off with the story

---

[60] Herschel Feibel Grynszpan was born in Hannover, Arendt's birthplace, in 1911. While a refugee in Paris as well, he assassinated, in 1938, the German diplomat Ernst vom Rath. He was arrested, was later handed over to the Germans, and apparently did not survive the war. His family remained in Germany and was deported from Germany to Poland in 1938,

of Wehrmacht sergeant Anton Schmidt, who was executed for aiding the Partisans, as related by Abba Kovner at the trial. The heroic tale of this brave German soldier touched her more, it seems, than anything else she heard in Jerusalem. And this concludes Arendt's report on the testimony she heard at the trial.

As we have seen, it is customary in the voluminous historiography of the destruction of the Jews to distinguish among three categories of people involved: the perpetrators, the victims, and the bystanders. Anita Shapira, for example, who not long ago did a comparison between Arendt's coverage of the trial and that of Haim Gouri, sees the differences between the two as reflecting a methodological debate over the right way to understand the history of the Holocaust. Should the tools of scholarly research be directed at the perpetrators or the victims?[61] In fact, Shapira misses the point here. What distinguishes Arendt from Gouri has nothing to do with this debate, which appears to have been settled. Holocaust scholars are generally in agreement today that all three categories should be investigated. The historiographical debate is and always was superfluous, being largely the expression of more or less veiled political and ideological leanings.[62] Whatever her pretenses, Arendt was not a historian, and what she had to say about the trial, Eichmann, and the Holocaust was not based on scholarly research. Again, she relies mainly on the works of Hilberg and Reitlinger, that is, on scholars who investigated the Holocaust from the point of view of the perpetrators.[63] Gouri has never pretended to be a historian, though he has devoted a good deal of time to documenting the Holocaust. The debate between Arendt and Gouri is thus not a historiographical, methodological, or historiosophical one. It is not over historical truth or historical understanding. What is at stake, rather, is the legitimacy and validity of the victim's point of view and his right to make his unique voice heard – without apology and without any need to defer to the universal. This is what Arendt

---

in what was the first mass deportation of Jews and the first step of the final solution. The Grynszpan family survived the war and actually had not experienced the extermination itself. The father Zyndel was the first of the prosecution witnesses at the Eichmann trial.

[61] Anita Shapira, *Mishpat Eichmann: Devarim shero'im mikan lo ro'im misham* (The Eichmann Trial: Things Seen from Here Are Not Seen from There) (Jerusalem: Yad Vashem, 5762 [2002]), 13.

[62] A broad survey of the various historiographical approaches to and modes of "representing" the destruction of the Jews can be found in Saul Friedländer, *Memory, History and the Extermination of the Jews of Europe* (Bloomington: Indiana University Press, 1993). The articles in this volume, too, are now somewhat dated.

[63] See also Walter Laqueur's review of Robinson's *And the Crooked Shall be Made Straight*, reprinted in Arendt, *The Jew as Pariah*, 252–259.

could not accept. This is the assumption underlying her research into anti-Semitism and totalitarianism, this is the conclusion to which her critique of political Zionism led her, and this is what is reflected in the almost physical revulsion she felt toward everything in Israel that was not Central European or German.[64] There is no room for a specifically Jewish perspective on the Holocaust. Here at last, in the most painful spot, faced with the testimony of the survivors presented at Beit Ha'am in Jerusalem, we see the concrete significance of Arendt's historiosophic argument with Scholem over the nature of Jewish history, as well as her disagreements with Katz over the question of continuity or discontinuity in the history of anti-Semitism: in her view, the Eichmann trial should have been conducted without the testimony of the survivors. What they had to say was irrelevant to the question of the juridical and philosophical nature of Eichmann's crime. Though in her view the trial was meant to expose the true nature of this new crime, of which Eichmann was one of the perpetrators (among the least important of them, in her view), there was no place in it for the testimony of the survivors.

A great deal has been written about Hannah Arendt and her book on Eichmann. Even among her many devotees, few, if any, share Zertal's enthusiasm for the book. Most recognize its weaknesses. The American philosopher Seyla Benhabib, for example, who has written one of the more interesting works on Arendt, also contributed an essay on *Eichmann in Jerusalem* to an important volume surveying Arendt's work.[65] She is quite critical of the book, though her criticism is restrained and polite. Toward the end of the essay, Benhabib raises the question of Israel's legal right to bring Eichmann to trial. Arendt thought the United Nations Genocide Convention of 1948 granted such a right, although, of course, Israel did not claim it in the proper way. The convention grants jurisdiction over a perpetrator of genocide to courts located in the territory where the crime was committed. Arendt, in a passage Benhabib quotes at length (p. 78), explains that Israel ought to have claimed that "territory" is a political and legal concept, not just a geographical one. It refers not to any particular piece of land but to an interpersonal realm defined by shared language, religion, culture, law, and history. In other words, it is that nonterritorial "homeland" that she denies Scholem's right to feel "love of country" for. In any event, and without Arendt stating it in so many words, Israel had the right to try Eichmann precisely, and only, because it was the state of that people against which the crime was committed.

---

[64] See Leibovici, *Hannah Arendt, une juive.*

[65] Seyla Benhabib, "Arendt's Eichmann in Jerusalem," in Dana Villa, ed., *The Cambridge Companion to Hannah Arendt* (Cambridge: Cambridge University Press, 2000), 65–85.

What Arendt says may well seem strange in some ways, but in fact she is merely returning here to her concepts of "the world" and of "action," which were based, in turn, on the historical model of the Greek polis and the way she believed it saw "action" and language as the foundations of "the political." Greeks who lived outside the geographical bounds of the polis, for example in the colonies the Greeks established around the eastern shores of the Mediterranean, were still regarded as citizens of the polis, that is, of the realm constituted by shared action and speech (*The Human Condition*, p. 198). While it is quite doubtful that this interpretation of the nature of the political realm is of much value in regard to law, it does show that, in an odd way and despite the idiosyncrasies of her argument, Arendt was more of a Zionist –and more decent – than some of her Israeli devotees, let alone thinkers of Benhabib's ilk. For, in fact, Benhabib rejects this Zionism. What claim, she asks, does the State of Israel have to represent all Jews, wherever they live and whatever citizenship they hold? Thus put, and in the context of a discussion of the Eichmann trial, Benhabib's argument betrays not only very poor judgment but also the symptomatic nature of this kind of thinking. Who, if not Israel, would capture Eichmann, kidnap him in defiance of international law, and bring him to trial? A committee of Jewish professors at Harvard? What Benhabib says amounts to the retrospective judgment that Eichmann should not have been touched but allowed to live out his life in peace in Argentina.

What Arendt says about Israel's right to try Eichmann, Benhabib continues, runs "contrary to her otherwise careful distinctions between citizenship rights and national identity" (p. 78). She is right. The "tension" between Arendt's critique of nationhood, especially Jewish nationhood, and her recognition of a specifically Jewish "interpersonal realm" that justifies Israel's speaking in the name of the victims remains unresolved. This is so because, first of all, it is insufficient to speak, as Arendt often does, of a "Jewish people" rather than a nation, nationality, continual history, or constituting political subject. One must also clarify the difference between "people" and "nation" and why "peoplehood" cannot form the basis of a claim to national sovereignty. Arendt never makes this clear. She thinks there is room for a "homeland" for the Jewish people, in fact in the very land that was once theirs, at least according to the claims some of them make, but she opposes the establishment of a nation-state. In the end, her ambivalence heals of its own accord, or perhaps (as we have said) it explodes, inadvertently, out of sheer thoughtlessness; it is no accident that this happens just when Arendt gets a chance to speak directly and without intermediaries about the destruction of the Jews, that is, in her book on Eichmann.

The tension is also reflected in Arendt's confusion of categories. As we have pointed out, the Greeks, according to her own analysis in *The Human Condition*, thought of a nonjuridical, nonterritorial basis for participation, that is, for citizenship. It was, for them, based on shared speech and action. But they did not see the polis as representing the Greek "people" or any other prepolitical collectivity. Above all, they did not see "the political" in historical terms, that is, the sort of terms on which the Zionist claim to the Land of Israel and Israel's alleged claim to represent the entire Jewish people are based. But because, as Benhabib (like Grodzinsky, let us recall) rightly points out, there is no political realm of action or speech that is common to all Jews, Arendt's characterization of the Greek notion of political commonality cannot be used to justify Israel's claim. Arendt could only maintain that Israel had a right to try Eichmann on the basis of Israel's representing the Jewish people, wherever they might be, and the historical character of this representation, that is, on the same grounds on which Ben-Gurion, for example, justified kidnapping Eichmann, bringing him to Israel, and trying him before an Israeli court. The problem Ben-Gurion was facing, though, was not only that he could not count on anyone else to do the job but that there was no forum – no real "public space"– in which to get all the Jews' agreement or disagreement. Once again, Benhabib would have had Eichmann remain at home rather than let Ben-Gurion hurt both her sensibility and her sense of autonomy by imposing on her a representation she did not want.

In any event, there is something else that troubles Benhabib. She argues that the "unresolved tension between the universal and the particular" in Arendt's thinking is most clearly expressed in the latter's discussion of the legal concept that, in her view, should have been used to indict Eichmann, "crimes against humanity." Benhabib is right, but she bases her claim on different grounds than those I would use to make a similar claim. For what we have here is more than the familiar "unresolved tension between the universal and the particular." Once again we encounter this cliché; and once again we cannot but shake our heads at the fact that serious thinkers like Benhabib find themselves with no better intellectual ammunition for dealing with the "Jewish problem" than this shallow Pauline idea. What we have here is an intellectual and moral failure. Arendt thinks the Jerusalem court did not understand the uniqueness of the new crime of genocide, and if it had understood it, it would have known that "the physical extermination of the Jewish people was a crime against humanity perpetrated upon the body of the Jewish people, and that only the choice of victims, not the nature of the crime, could be derived from the long history of Jew-hatred and anti-Semitism. Insofar as the victims were Jews, it was right and proper that a

Jewish court should sit in judgment; but insofar as the crime was a crime against humanity, it needed an international tribunal to do justice to it" (*Eichmann in Jerusalem*, p. 269). One could dispute the historical and not only the legal validity of this argument, for, as we have seen, there are among the historians and interpreters of Nazism those who think that Jew-hatred was a constitutive element, not merely a consequence, of Nazi racism. In other words, it is probably wrong to say that it was "only the choice of victims" that stemmed from the long history of Jew-hatred; rather, this choice was actually the essence of the crime. If so, the murder of the Jews was irreducibly significant.

Arendt does not consider this possibility or the rationale that could be derived from it for Jewish judges trying Eichmann. But the real difficulty with her position does not lie in her misinterpretation of Nazism or the legal standing of its crimes but rather in her discussion of what are presumably mere technicalities of the conduct of the trial. She recognizes Israel's right to demand that Eichmann be tried *on its soil*. But she has reservations not only about the way the trial was conducted, the insistence of the prosecution on hearing the testimony of survivors who had no direct connection with the defendant, or Ben-Gurion's staging of the trial. She also has reservations about the legal framework within which it was conducted, the legal principles used to indict Eichmann, and, in general, the court's limited understanding of the issues. Above all, she denies the right of the State of Israel and its judges to try the defendant. Eichmann, as we know, was brought to trial on the basis of the Israeli law for the prosecution of the Nazis and their collaborators. The first four counts of the indictment were defined, on the basis of this law, as "crimes against the Jewish people": causing the death of millions of Jews in the framework of what was called the "Final Solution"; subjecting millions of Jews to living conditions likely to lead to their death through forced labor and deportation to ghettos and camps; causing severe bodily harm to millions of Jews through starvation, persecution, and torture; and preventing them from having children. These same actions were defined in the next three paragraphs of the indictment as "crimes against humanity."[66]

Israel recognized the concept of "crimes against humanity" by incorporating the principles of the United Nations Genocide Convention into its laws. But, on the basis of these same principles, it added the legal concept

---

[66] See Gideon Hausner, *Justice in Jerusalem* (New York: Schocken, 1968), 300–301. These are, in fact, the main paragraphs in the United Nations Geneva Convention of 1948, which Israel included in its law for bringing Nazis and their accomplices to justice.

of "crimes against the Jewish people," even placing it before the provisions
regarding "crimes against humanity." Of course, the concept of crimes
against the Jewish people does not exist in any other legal system. It is precisely this uniqueness that Arendt rejects. From her point of view, the trial
could well be held in Jerusalem, but it should have been conducted from the
perspective of the "international community" and not that of the Jewish
dead or survivors. It is true that Jews were killed and, if we are to be completely accurate, that it was *only* against Jews that genocide in the new sense
was committed. At least this is what Arendt thought, not having had, alas,
the privilege of reading Rassinier or Ophir. Nevertheless, she is also of the
opinion that the crime was not really against the Jewish people but against
humanity. The Jews must understand that the fact that they, in particular,
were killed in this distinctive way was marginal and accidental in relation
to the truly significant fact that they were killed differently from their being
killed in the past and that this new way of killing deprived them of their
status as victim, because it was a crime against humanity as a whole. They
may not make a particular claim of their own but must rather join all the
others, including, evidently, the Germans, Poles, Latvians, and Frenchmen,
for example, in protesting the crime committed against them. It is true that
this crime was committed by means of the murder of the Jews, but that, as
we have said, is coincidental and not part of the essence of the crime itself.
When the State of Israel defined the category of "crimes against the Jewish
people," it refused to do precisely what Arendt says it should have done:
represent humanity in the examination of the nature of the Nazi crime. This
refusal Arendt could not accept. She never forgave Israel for disobeying her
and insisting on being the spokesman of six million prosecutors, as the chief
prosecutor said in his opening argument, a statement for which the *New
Yorker* correspondent heaps abuse on him. In other words, Hausner's rhetoric aside, Arendt cannot accept the fact that the State of Israel assumed an
"essential," and not merely an "incidental" role in regard to the victims. If
pressed, we might put it this way: she does not recognize the existence of a
Jewish *différend*.

Thus, Arendt thinks the Jewishness of the victims of the Nazi crime was
merely a philosophical and legal parable. Bringing Eichmann to justice was
an opportunity to think about the universal meaning of this case in point,
not to think about the victims. She is unable to grasp why the State of Israel –
and, in fact, all (or almost all) Jewry – refuses to be a case in point. By the
way, she is not the only German Jewish refugee to have seen the history of the
Jewish people as a case in point. Leo Strauss, for example, whose fate and
life history were so similar to Arendt's, says that "from every point of view

it looks as if the Jewish people were the chosen people in the sense, at least, that the Jewish problem is the most manifest symbol of the human problem as a social or political problem."[67] "Chosenness" plays an ironical role here, of course. Strauss uses it to speak of the failure of all attempts, including that of Zionism, to solve the "Jewish problem." He was no less universal a political philosopher than Arendt, and throughout his life he dealt only with "the human problem as a social and political problem." But he dealt with this human problem *by means of* the Jewish question, in its own terms and from a specifically Jewish point of view. He never saw a need to forgo that point of view in order to be universal.

Despite all that we have said about Zertal's book, it sometimes offers the reader unexpected pleasures. One of the roles of the State of Israel and one of the justifications for its establishment, she writes in chapter 2 of *Israel's Holocaust,* is to give voice to those who survived the death camps, those who were rescued from the reality Arendt describes as being entirely new (p. 88). Zertal quotes from *Le Différend*, a book by our old friend, the French philosopher Jean-François Lyotard. Here, she learns a distinctly Zionist lesson, that Israel must provide "a verbal and legal framework for the survivors' cry for help and for their claims and charges," that by means of the state the survivors have "transformed the wrong into damages and the *différend* into litigation" (p. 57). But Zertal, like Ophir, manages by sleight of hand to turn Lyotard on his head and extract from a principled defense of Israel – its entitlement to reparations, its right to try Eichmann, and its obligation to speak out in the survivors' name as much as possible – a no-less-principled condemnation: the State of Israel has, to be sure, betrayed its destiny. Zertal does this in her discussion of the law for bringing the Nazis and their collaborators to justice. More precisely, she discourses, if one may say so, on this law, revealing that it was merely "Israeli society's" way of ridding itself of its "unease at what she considered to be Jewish conduct during the Holocaust." "Israeli society" has indeed felt unease, as well as a great many other emotions, about Jewish conduct during the Holocaust.[68] Arendt, too, feels such unease, it will be recalled. But, as Zertal well knows, there is unease and unease. Nor is it entirely clear that the law, passed to a large extent as a result of pressure from the survivors themselves, is the clearest expression of this unease – but why quibble? After all, we are talking not about historiography

---

[67] In the aforementioned introduction to the English edition of Spinoza's book. See Strauss, *Spinoza's Critique of Religion.*

[68] Hanna Yablonka tried to show this, among other things, in her moving book *Survivors of the Holocaust: Israel after the War* (New York: New York University Press, 1999).

but about discourse, and evidently we are expected to be delighted that facts, which might only have confused us, have been dispensed with.

It may be of some interest here that Lyotard, too, in another work, *Heidegger and "The Jews,"* sees in the Jewish people a kind of parable. For him, it is a psychoanalytical, philosophical, and political parable of European culture, and he sees in the destruction of the Jews the final working out of this parable. Nor does he see this destruction merely as an instance of the new, general crime of genocide but rather as a phenomenon in its own right. He makes various observations about the possibility of "representing" the Holocaust, among them that the victims, too, must be represented. But in the pictures and words that depict the killing, the humiliation, the despair, and the suffering, one thing is generally missing: that the men, women, and children whose extermination is being depicted were not exterminated merely as men, women, or children but as Jews.[69] Perhaps, in the last analysis, the State of Israel was right to add the legal category of "crimes against the Jewish people" to that of genocide.

Although the description of the post-Eichmann discourse in Israel that Zertal offers her readers is what it is – idle chatter – it turns out that quite a few otherwise serious people share her view of the role that the memory and "representation" of the Holocaust play in shaping Israeli consciousness. For example, Hanna Yablonka, whose views are usually diametrically opposed to Zertal's, thinks, in this case, that during the period of tension leading up to the Six-Day War, and after the war as well, Israeli society, including native-born Israelis who had served in the army, still harbored the feeling of "existential anxiety" that had been aroused by the Eichmann trial. Unlike Zertal, Yablonka does not see this anxiety as the result of manipulation by Ben-Gurion; rather, "one might call it a failure of Zionism that twenty years after the establishment of the Jewish state, and immediately after a military victory that astounded the world, a basic lack of confidence was still deeply etched in the [native] Israeli soul – like some Jewish genetic code."[70] I must admit I do not quite understand the significance of the cliché about "existential anxiety," nor am I convinced that the mood in the country during those weeks we call "the waiting period" was not, at least to some degree, a rational concern over the threat of war. It is hard to assess, too, whether this anxiety, if it existed, was inherited or acquired, and it is not clear how

[69] Jean-François Lyotard, *Heidegger and "The Jews"* (Minneapolis: University of Minnesota Press, 1990), 53.
[70] Hanna Yablonka, *Survivors of the Holocaust: Israel after the War* (Basingstoke: Macmillan, 1999), 195.

the role of the Eichmann trial in generating it can be measured. After all, as we have seen, Zertal thinks the trial was meant to nurture an ethos of power and violence. In any event, Yablonka categorically denies Zertal's claim that the whole matter was Ben-Gurion's doing, whether out of devilish or banal intent. According to her, the trial was only the spark that set in motion a process that turned the Holocaust into a major component of Israeli public "discourse" and collective consciousness. All was already in readiness, even without it (p. 201). All was in readiness because, whatever Holocaust consciousness is, it is not manipulation and invention.

Even as important a historian as Saul Friedländer sometimes recycles these arguments. In his book *Memory, History, and the Extermination of the Jews of Europe*, he writes about the possibility that the memory of the Holocaust would prove an obstacle to achieving peace between Israel and the Palestinians, an eventuality that would be a "tragedy." How serious this concern is can be seen in a story he cites as illustration: a journalist (Akiva Eldar, of *Haaretz*) relates that none other than Yitzhak Rabin concluded from the mass murders in Yugoslavia that Israel should not rely on foreign powers to save it in the event of a threat. How does this anecdote lead to the conclusion that the memory of the Holocaust could harm the prospects of peace? The god of clichés only knows.

Hannah Arendt, who was keen-eyed and sharp-tongued in all that pertained to the less pleasant aspects of Jewish and Israeli life, knew well how to hold up these things for public scrutiny. As she says of herself in the interview cited earlier ("What Remains? The Mother Tongue Remains"), irony is irony, and that is the way she writes; there is no getting around it. Leaving aside the discomfort aroused by her irony, and more often by her scorn, she is no doubt right in much of what she says, including about the Eichmann trial and more generally about Israel, Zionism, and the Jews. In a number of respects, the conduct of the prosecution at the trial, and perhaps some of the testimony it presented as well, deserved at least part of the criticism leveled against them. Hausner was histrionic, some of the witnesses' statements did not relate directly to Eichmann's actions, Ben-Gurion and other politicians interfered in the preparation of the indictment, and Eichmann could well have been convicted on the basis of the documents, without most of the witnesses who were called to the stand. These charges are valid, and no doubt others could be added. Yet, as we have said, none of this matters. It does not matter because this is the way things look – and it is unlikely they could look much better – when survivors, or those who speak in their name, are given the floor. The almost physical repugnance Arendt felt for the trial and everything surrounding it did not stem from any particular flaws that could have been rectified if only, for example, Hausner had been of German background or a better interpreter had been found. These flaws could have been corrected only if Ben-Gurion had not been Ben-Gurion, the survivors who wanted to testify had not been survivors, and the guards at the entrances to the courtroom had not been swarthy Israelis who spoke only Hebrew. In short, the flaws could have been overcome if Israel had not been Israel, and we had not been who we were.

Arendt's criticism of the conduct of the Eichmann trial, her refusal to recognize the legitimacy and importance of the survivors' testimony, and her rejection of the juridical relevance of the category "crimes against the Jewish people" amount to a rejection of the Israeli *différend*. Or, to put it differently, it is a negation of the right to an Israeli point of view. But a Jewish and Israeli perspective on the Holocaust is an essential component of Israeli identity. To negate the legitimacy of airing the testimony, of the way the trial was set up and even, let us say, staged, is to negate the legitimacy of Israeliness as such. Contrary to what critics of the Israeli culture of Holocaust commemoration say, there is no argument here between "universalism" and Jewish or Israeli "particularism." It is, rather, a dispute between two kinds of particularism: one upholds the right of the Jewish victim to have his say, and one denies it. This denial is universalistic to the same degree that the Nazi negation of Jewishness was universalistic. It is, in fact, particularistic, in that it is aimed in quite a particularistic and specific way at the right of the *Jewish* victims and their progeny to recall their catastrophe (not, as a rule, at the right of the Palestinians, for example, to remember their *Naqba*) and to live out this memory as they see fit, even if the commemoration is not always aesthetic, and even if there are aspects to it that not everyone likes. For it is not only catastrophes that are unpleasant; the memory of them, too, can be troublesome and even ugly.

The criticism of what is called *shoanut* ("Shoah business") is legitimate and even needed. But when this criticism is directed at the instrumentalization of the Holocaust or Holocaust consciousness *as the source of evil done by Israelis,* and when it sees in the Holocaust the source of the suffering of the Palestinians, using it to settle scores with policies of the State of Israel, it is only outwardly criticism of *shoanut*. This is so, in part, because in the last analysis these are not real arguments, because in fact Israeli society emerges quite well from a grappling with the Holocaust that is bound to fail. We have already had occasion to mention Peter Novick's book on the role played by the Holocaust in American culture in general and American Jewish culture in particular (see Chapter 2, note 73). We have also mentioned the criticism of Berel Lang. Novick's position is, in fact, quite similar to what we hear from the Israeli *ressentiment* community, though it should be noted that he does not use the Holocaust or his critique of American Jewry's attitude toward it as the basis of a sweeping negation of Zionism or American Jewish communality. Whatever one's reservations about the book, there are things to be learned from it, especially about the parallels and similarities – but also some important differences – between American Jewish and Israeli ways of relating to the Holocaust. Novick's description of the way the Holocaust has been turned into a central concern of American culture is critical, ironical, and basically unsympathetic. He deals with phenomena familiar to all of us from the Israeli reality: the demagoguery, the instrumentalization, the commercialization and sentimentalization of the Holocaust; the appropriation of it by everyone – rabbis, conservatives, the right, the liberal left – for his own purposes (p. 184).

But what we do not have here in Israel and the American Jews do is the use of the Holocaust to combat assimilation and reinforce Jewish ethnicity among the nonreligious, non-Zionist part of the population (see especially pp. 185ff. in Novick). The memory of the Holocaust is an important component of the Israeli ethos, of Israeli culture and public awareness. It seems that with the passage of time, as we get further and further from the events and those who were directly involved – the perpetrators, bystanders, and survivors – age and die, this memory becomes more and more important to Israeli Jews. But it is not the sum total of Israeli Jewish identity and never has been. It is not even a truly important factor in Israeli policy making. In the final analysis, the Israeli attitude toward the Holocaust has always been much more complex – and interesting – than one would assume from the sort of "discourse" study we get from people like Zertal. It will be recalled that she cites a letter from Ofer Feniger to his girlfriend Yael as strong confirmation for her thesis. Hanna Yablonka, too, quotes from this letter, though not in the manipulative way Zertal does and not in any direct relation to the Eichmann trial. Like Zertal, Yablonka sees the letter as exemplifying the role of the Holocaust in the formation of the Israeli ethos. Feniger, a paratroop officer, was killed in the battle of Ammunition Hill in the Six-Day War. His friends and acquaintances and the soldiers under his command regarded him as an outstanding young man. As a paratrooper, he learned to jump at a military base "somewhere in Israel," as we used to say. He jumped and rolled and dangled from various contraptions before going into the air for his first parachute jump. Everyone referred to the scariest of these contraptions as "Eichmann." No one thought this sacrilegious. And perhaps this little fact helps put into perspective the discourse about the religion of the Holocaust, the theology of anxiety, and the cult of power attributed to people like Feniger by those who would use the Holocaust as live ammunition in their ideological struggle against Israel and Zionism.

Israeli and Jewish anti-Zionism has made the misuse of the Holocaust one of its main arguments. Even in the context of internal Israeli and Jewish matters, this amounts, at times, to nothing more than an expansion of the use of the Holocaust to attack and besmirch Israel and, in the end, to delegitimate it. The claim that the Holocaust has been misused as a Zionist-Israeli-Jewish propaganda tool; that it has been so overused as to be cheapened; that it is being marshaled to serve the interests of the state, of nationalistic education, and of the formation of collective identity; that it is being exploited to justify the power-seeking policies of the Zionist state – this claim is no different in principle from the arguments used by the Vieille Taupe group and the Holocaust-deniers of the European radical left. Though there is a measure of truth – as there always is – in the arguments of those who use the Holocaust to criticize Israel, the whole truth is just the opposite: the real misuse of the Holocaust is being done mainly by them. Contrary to what people in certain circles think, the assault on Israel by means of the Holocaust is much broader and more effective than the use made of it by Zionism. Furthermore, the most common argument about Zionist misuse of the Holocaust is an important part of the use made of it by Zionism's enemies. Paradoxically, the effectiveness of anti-Israeli and post-Zionist propaganda using the Holocaust is largely based on what parades as criticism of the use of it for Israeli and Zionist purposes. Hannah Arendt's book on the Eichmann trial has played a decisive role in making this argument respectable, widespread, and effective among Israel's critics, from within and from without.

4

Postscript: 1967 or 1948?

By a strange coincidence, the beginning of the new millennium can be seen as a turning point in the history of the State of Israel. The year 2000 witnessed the most far-reaching attempt to put an end to the Palestinian-Israeli conflict, the failure of a long and complex peace process sponsored by the United States, and the outbreak of what is known as the Second Intifada. In this wave of violence, more than a thousand Israelis died, mostly civilians killed by suicide bombs, and between four and five times as many Palestinians died, many of them civilians, mostly at the hands of Israeli security forces. Since then, the region has experienced the withdrawal of Israel from Gaza and the evacuation of several thousand settlers there (along with the evacuation of a small number of Jewish settlements in the West Bank); the Second Lebanon War; and a radical restructuring of the Israeli political scene (with the creation of the Kadima Party by Ariel Sharon).

The peace process, which eventuated in the failed summit at Camp David, followed by more negotiations and more meetings, notably at Sharm e-Sheikh and Taba (both in Egypt), was led by Ehud Barak, then prime minister of Israel, and by Yasser Arafat, the late president of the Palestinian Authority, and closely overseen by U.S. president Bill Clinton. Barak was guided by a few simple principles: the process that had begun with the Oslo accords and that had been based on the idea of creating a political momentum toward settling the conflict by means of a series of interim agreements and partial steps had run its course, and the time had come to tackle the fundamental problems. Hence, the negotiations he was to engage in had to lead to the end of the conflict, which meant the end of the Palestinians' demands. The principle on which any agreement would be based had to be that of two states for two peoples – a sovereign Palestinian state alongside a sovereign Jewish state, the already-existent State of Israel. This meant, on the one hand, a complete Israeli withdrawal from the Gaza Strip and the West Bank, roughly to the pre-1967 lines, a "swap" of lands to compensate the future Palestinian state for territories remaining under Israeli sovereignty, the dismantling of more than one hundred settlements, a compromise over Jerusalem, and rejection of the Palestinian demand to recognize the "right of return" of the refugees. All this was, of course, conditional on satisfactory security arrangements for Israel and, perhaps most important, a full and formal recognition of the legitimacy of Israel as a Jewish state.

These principles were also the main guidelines in the proposals put before the two parties by Bill Clinton after the failure of the Camp David summit, the so-called Clinton Parameters, but the latter went beyond Barak's initial position on several points, notably the partition of Jerusalem. Barak accepted these additions, but Arafat rejected them. There are many versions of what exactly happened during the Camp David discussions and afterward, of the reasons and causes of the failure of the negotiations, and of the outburst of Palestinian violence that came to be known as the Al Aqsa Intifada. Numerous books and articles have been written about it, variously blaming the failure on the Israelis, the Americans, or the Palestinians. Although I do not wish to join this discussion,[1] I do want to emphasize one point that even some Palestinians and

---

[1] I believe, however, that the best description of what happened was given by Clinton himself: There was a proposal on the table of a fair compromise, indeed for a historical break-through; Barak accepted it, Arafat did not. All the rest is gossip. I was personally involved in the publication of one of the main players' versions: Yves-Charles Zarka, Jeffrey-Andrew Barash, and myself conducted, over a period of several days, intensive interviews with Shlomo Ben-Ami, who was, during the final stage of the negotiations, the Israeli foreign minister but a central figure in the negotiations all along. The outcome was a book that appeared in French (and was then translated into Spanish) under the title *Quel avenir pour Israël?* (What Does the Future Hold for Israel?). The most important part of our conversation with Ben-Ami concerned the peace process. His version of its failure was basically in agreement with Clinton's. Ben-Ami later published another book, much more comprehensive, on the same subject. This time, he revised his description of some of the details of the process, blaming Barak and the Americans more than he had when he was speaking with us and amplifying his own role in the negotiations. But the bottom line remained the same: Israel, under Barak's leadership, was ready to implement a very far-reaching compromise, but the Palestinians refused. See Sh. Ben-Ami, *Hazit lelo oref: Masa el gevulot tahalikh hashalom* (Battlefront without a Home Front: A Journey to the Limits of the Peace Process) (Tel Aviv: Sifrei Hemed, 2004). See also Denis Ross, *The Missing Peace: The Inside Story of the Fight for Middle East Peace* (New York: Farrar, Straus, and Giroux, 2004). Other participants in this peace process, like Martin Indyk and Aaron Miller, have also given their versions of the events. The latter is much more critical toward the Israeli side. The most critical approach toward Israel is to be found in series of articles, some of them part of a debate with Ehud Barak and Benny Morris, written jointly by Robert Malley and Hussein Agha and published in the *New York Review of Books*. Although Malley and

their supporters do not question: Israel had expressed willingness to reach an agreement based on compromise and on the idea of two states for two peoples. More important, there are many indications that at least at that point, and even after the beginning of the Palestinian violence, Israeli society as such, and most Israelis as individuals, accepted the same principles.

In this respect, the year 2000 can be seen as a turning point: it marked the demise in Israel of *Eretz Yisrael hashelema* (usually translated as "Greater Israel" but in fact meaning "the whole Land of Israel") as a political program. It was the full and formal acknowledgment that the political and demographic reality, on the one hand, and moral considerations, on the other, imposed a return to the classic, mainstream Zionist position favoring territorial compromise with the Palestinian people, a recognition of the basic legitimacy of their claim to self-determination and acceptance of a partition of the Land of Israel/Palestine between Jews and Arabs.

This turning point gave momentary satisfaction to many people on the Israeli left: politicians, ideologues, writers, and ordinary citizens. At last, it seemed, Israeli society as a whole had accepted the long-held views of such left-wing leaders as Shlomo Ben-Ami, Yossi Beilin, and Yossi Sarid and such left-leaning writers as A. B. Yehoshua and Amos Oz. But when, to their surprise and dismay, the compromise did not work out, important sectors of the left, the self-appointed "true left," renounced the two-state solution and vehemently espoused positions that are referred to in Israel as "post-Zionist" but in fact amount, as we have seen, to a kind of anti-Zionism. By this I mean an ideology that does not recognize the legitimacy of the Jewish claim to statehood, that refuses to accord the Jewish people the right of self-determination, and that flatly and a priori denies that Israel can be both Jewish and democratic. This refusal is, more often than not, accompanied by an unreserved acceptance of the Palestinian right of self-determination and "right of return." Here we have another turning point that occurred in 2000: it suddenly became acceptable to say in polite company and in respectable journals that Israel should cease to exist as a Jewish state.

This refusal to acknowledge the legitimacy of the Jewish state is not new. The Arab refusal to accept any kind of a Jewish national existence in Palestine was the reason for the outbreak of the 1947–1948 war and has been a central factor in the political reality of the Middle East ever since. There are good reasons to think this refusal also played a major role in the failure

Agha basically blame Israel and Barak for the failure of the Camp David negotiations, a careful reading of their articles show that they tell, in the end, the same version of Clinton, Ben Ami, and Ross.

of the Camp David peace process. It is highly significant, I believe, that the main stumbling blocks to an agreement were more symbolic than concrete: the Palestinian refusal to recognize any Jewish historical claim in Jerusalem, particularly on the Temple Mount – Arafat is said to have denied there had ever been a Jewish temple there – and insistence on the acceptance of the "right of return." It was clear to the Palestinian negotiators and even, to a degree, accepted by them that there would be no "return" of refugees in significant numbers to Israel itself. Their insistence that the "*right* of return" be recognized amounted to a demand that Israel acknowledge its own creation to have been an illegitimate, even criminal, act and that the international community, too, acknowledge as much. The symbolic significance of the denial that there had ever been a Jewish temple in Jerusalem – that the city had ever been a Jewish religious center – needs no comment.

A more common sentiment, voiced previously by some Western intellectuals, politicians, and others, was that Jews did not deserve to have a state of their own any more than followers of other religions did. Religions simply do not have states, it was argued. There had long been a murmur, growing ever louder as the situation in the Middle East appeared more and more hopeless, questioning the wisdom and the legal and moral justification of a Jewish state in the midst of the Arab world. But there was still a certain reluctance to say this too loudly in public. A critical, sometimes hostile attitude toward Israel had been a regular feature of the reporting and commentary of such media organs as the BBC, CNN, the *Guardian*, the *New York Times*, and *Le Monde*, but it was rare that explicit calls for the de-Judaization or de-Zionization of the State of Israel were heard. Now – and this is an important aspect of the turning point in question – it is no longer shameful in civilized circles to call for stripping Israel of its Jewishness.

In fact, a whole campaign has gotten underway not only to de-Judaize Israel but also to vilify and even demonize it. The enormity of the solution, its almost unprecedented radicality, demands weighty justifications: only if Israel is a hopelessly evil adventure can the extreme solution suggested be justified. It happened before with South Africa; Israel must be at least as bad as the former apartheid regime there. In fact, worse: the charges against Israel and Zionism have to be much weightier. No one has ever claimed that the whites have the same kind of claim to southern Africa as the Jews to the Land of Israel. Refuting the latter is harder and takes more lethal ideological weaponry.

The campaign of delegitimation and vilification that is fueled by this anti-Zionist ideology is a multifaceted one. I have chosen to concentrate in this book on two of its most remarkable features: the prominent role played in it by

Jews, Israelis in particular, and its use of the Holocaust as a major ideological weapon. Of course, anti-Zionism is by no means an exclusively Jewish matter. Over and above the persistent *Arab* rejection of any Jewish claim to Eretz Yisrael and denial of any legitimacy to the idea of a Jewish national home, anti-Zionism has, in the West, become the trademark of a whole intellectual subculture. For large segments of the Western intelligentsia – on the campuses, in the media, and in the arts – anti-Zionism of one sort or another no longer seems to require justification or explanation. In fact, most anti-Zionists are not Jews. But from an Israeli point of view, the participation of Jews and Israelis in the anti-Zionist campaign is of particular interest.

The second point is even more significant. The systematic use of the Holocaust in this offensive is meant – explicitly and intentionally by the Holocaust deniers, more implicitly and sometimes unconsciously by main-stream anti-Zionists – to bear the weight of their principal contention, which is, in effect, an annihilationist one, if only by implication. The State of Israel, as a Jewish state, is illegitimate and must cease to exist, they maintain. But that, in turn, would mean the Jewish population of Israel/Palestine giving up its present means of self-defense, thereby casting it into a physically precarious situation not unlike that of, say, the diminishing Christian minority in Lebanon or the Kurds in Saddam Hussein's Iraq. This is precisely why, from an Israeli point of view, it can never be allowed to happen, and this is also why it is in fact an annihilationist message.

Many Israelis thought they belonged to what is usually called "the left," the "peace camp," or to what is called in America the "liberals." They believed that as long as they advocated the establishment of a Palestinian state alongside Israel, were against the Jewish settlements and settlers, and supported an Israeli withdrawal from the territories occupied in 1967, their position was politically sound and morally defensible. They thought what was at stake in the domestic and international debate, however harsh or even violent, was the question of where to draw the boundaries; that "occupation" meant control of the territories conquered in the Six-Day War, that they themselves were, if not altogether "the good guys," at least not entirely "the bad guys" either. They awoke one morning to find that they were still fighting the first Arab-Israeli war; that the stakes were – perhaps had been all along – 1948 and not 1967; that "occupation" meant the very existence of their state, whatever party headed it; that they and the settlers belonged to a single amorphous and homogeneous, criminal crowd; that "Zionism" had become an ugly word. They found themselves inundated by an ever-growing stream of books, columns, and speeches telling them the most incredible things about themselves and about their country. They realized that they were facing the best and the brightest of the Western intelligentsia and, with them, many of their very own personal friends and colleagues. It was an incredible phenomenon. Even if Israel deserved some of the criticism (and it deserved it less than even some of its friends say), in the last analysis anti-Zionism – the denial to the Jewish people of the right of self-determination in Eretz Yisrael – is an outrage and a sign of moral bankruptcy.

ANTI-ZIONISM AND ANTI-SEMITISM

One of the ugliest aspects of the latest wave of anti-Zionism and anti-Israelism is the participation of Jews and Israelis in it. In preparing the English and French versions of this book, I got better acquainted with the growing phenomenon of anti-Israel sentiment abroad. Not that I did not know it existed, but having more important things to do, I never bothered to delve into it. Now I had to read some of the literature, and I must admit I was taken aback, especially by the central role played by Jews in smearing and delegitimizing Israel. It seems at present as if the country's main ideological foes, outside the Arab and Muslim world, are Israeli and non-Israeli Jews. The former are, of course, an appreciable asset to the latter, and the latter are no doubt much appreciated by the non-Jewish enemies of Israel. The so-called post-Zionists in Israel, insofar as they stress their country's moral and political bankruptcy, are translated, quoted, invited, and taken as authorities about Israel and its politics. If prominent Israelis like Burg, Sand, Zertal, Ophir, Kimmerling, and Zuckerman all say that Israel is so terrible, who are we to deny it? The sheer volume of anti-Israel verbiage, the intensity and unrestrained quality of the animosity, and the utter distortedness of the way Israeli society and the Middle East situation are depicted are all astonishing. Some of the writings I have had to read are so hateful as, in effect, to call upon Palestinians to kill more Israelis.

Of greater interest, however, are the parallels I have found between the reactions to this phenomenon in Israel and those elsewhere. It is not without significance that writings by authors like Alvin H. Rosenfeld, Phyllis Chesler, and Edward Alexander in the United States; Danny Trom, Pierre-André Tagieuf, Alain Finkielkraut, Yves-Charles Zarka, and Jean-Claude Milner in France; and Bernard Harrison, Paul Ignaski, and Barry Kosmin in the United Kingdom, among others, appeared more or less at the same time that my own book appeared in Israel.[2] It seems, indeed, that the beginning

---

[2] See, *inter alia*, A. H. Rosenfeld, "Progressive Jewish Thought and the New Anti-Semitism" (New York: American Jewish Committee, 2006); P. Chesler, *The New Anti-Semitism: The*

of the new millennium is a turning point in many ways. If the reactions before consisted mainly of documentation and apologetics, there are now some attempts at countercriticism as well. Although it is essentially the same debate – in fact, a real ideological war is taking place in Israel and elsewhere, within but also outside the Jewish world – the arguments move, so to speak, along parallel lines that do not meet. Understandably enough, in America and Europe the debate turns around the question of anti-Semitism: is anti-Zionism identical with anti-Semitism, is it a special brand of anti-Semitism, is it neo-anti-Semitism, or is it something else altogether? In Israel, again understandably, the question of anti-Semitism, or whether its own post-Zionists are in some sense self-hating Jews, does not attract much attention. Sometimes the post-Zionists are indeed accused of self-hatred. It is my personal impression, though, that most of them are rather narcissistic than anti-Semitic. For most Israelis, after all, the real or imagined prevalence of anti-Semitism in other parts of the world is rather a rumor, and what worries us in our everyday life, when we enter a coffee shop or take a bus for example, are other things. Many Israelis feel that living in Israel has freed them of this particular worry at least. But the question of whether anti-Zionism is a new version of anti-Semitism is interesting, and it merits some comment.

The first problem with using the term "anti-Semitism" in the debate about anti-Zionism is that it immediately becomes a new weapon in the hands of the anti-Zionists: as soon as someone dares to criticize the critics, even the boldest and most malicious, the latter turn into victims, whose

Current Crisis and What We Must Do about It (New York: Jossey-Bass, 2003); E. Alexander and P. Bogdanor, eds., *The Jewish Divide over Israel* (New Brunswick: Transaction, 2006), as well as some earlier works by Alexander; D. Trom, *La promesse et l'obstacle: La gauche radicale et le probleme juif* (Paris: Cerf, 2007); B. Harrison, *The Resurgence of Anti-Semitism: Jews, Israel, and Liberal Opinion* (London: Rowman & Littlefield, 2006). This remarkable book, the only one in the list written by a non-Jew, includes a useful appendix with some additional references. A knowledgeable refutation of many of the anti-Israeli allegations of the so-called new historians and others can be found in a work by Haifa University historian Yoav Gelber, *History, Memory and Propaganda: The Historical Discipline at the Beginning of the 21st Century* (in Hebrew) (Tel Aviv: Am Oved, 2007). The curious reader may get an idea of the quantity and quality of the anti-Israeli and anti-Zionist literature produced by Israeli academics from http://Israel-Academia-Monitor.com. Similar monitoring of anti-Israeli writing in the media is done in the United States by CAMERA (The Committee for Accuracy in Middle East Reporting in America), which recently published the proceedings of a debate on this subject, with the participation of Edward Alexander, Kenneth Levin, Andrea Levin, Cynthia Ozick, Alvin H. Rosenfeld, and Alex Safran, under the title "Israel's Jewish Defamers." A fascinating collection of some thirty or forty virulently anti-Israeli writings is T. Kushner and A. Solomon, eds., *Wrestling with Zion: Progressive Jewish-American Responses to the Israeli-Palestinian Conflict* (New York: Grove Press, 2003).

freedom of expression is said to be under threat. Similarly, although I was very careful to underline time and again that I did not consider the members of the Israeli opprobrium community to be Holocaust deniers, I was accused, after the publication of this book in Israel, of saying they were. As one of my adversaries put it, anyone who dares to criticize "the Occupation" is accused nowadays of being a Holocaust denier. This is false, and not only because I, too, am a critic of "the Occupation." As the Cossack who cries "Help!" knows, it is always useful for aggressors to make the noises of victims, especially if they lack better arguments. This book was said to be inquisitorial, and some of the post-Zionists were sure, or at least moaned publicly, that, tenured or not, they were going to lose their jobs. So far, none of them is unemployed. I have read the same kind of discourse in the reactions to Rosenfeld's essay, for example (many of them cited in a Wikipedia entry devoted to it).

Yet, the claim that there is an affinity between anti-Zionism and anti-Semitism is not without foundation. There are some interesting parallels between the two, though perhaps more structural than substantive. Until the Holocaust discredited anti-Semitism, it was considered a legitimate position. Many people described themselves openly as anti-Semites, in much the same way that many people – Israelis, non-Israeli Jews, and non-Jews – now openly declare themselves anti-Zionists. This is one important similarity between anti-Semitism (or Judeophobia) and anti-Zionism: both are shameful positions that at a certain moments in history find enough people who are willing to legitimize and defend them.

In the first part of this book, I elaborated on one specific kind of Holocaust denial, that which stems from and serves the purposes of anti-Zionism. I also tried to show that Pierre Guillaume and his friends are not anti-Semites in the simple sense of the word, exactly as the Jewish ultra-Orthodox participants in the deniers' convention in Teheran were not anti-Semites in any simple sense. Perhaps these deniers, too, are not anti-Semites but "only" anti-Zionists. The fact that Guillaume's obsession is anti-Zionist and not anti-Semitic does not make it less despicable than other forms of Holocaust denial; this, I am sure, will be generally conceded. More controversial, I suppose, is my claim that the anti-Zionism we find in those critics of Israel who do not deny the Holocaust is perversely close to Guillaume's. Put differently, either the Vieille Taupe circle is, aside from its denial of the Holocaust, perfectly reasonable in its views on Israel or there is something profoundly wrong with anti-Zionism in general. The onus of proof lies with the non-denying anti-Zionists: they must show that the similarities between them and Guillaume are superficial and immaterial, that their anti-Zionism is different from and better than that of, say, Serge Thion. It is not enough for them to lament being persecuted (which, in fact, none of them are).

The proof of the pudding is usually in the eating. Daniel Bensaïd teaches philosophy at a Paris university. He is also a militant, one of the main ideologues of what is usually referred to as the Trotskyite movement and an official member of the Ligue Communiste Révolutionaire – yes, this kind of thing still exists – which has gained some importance in the French left since the demise of the Soviet Union and the near disappearance of the Communist Party from the political map of France. He is a comrade and colleague, as he puts it, of the French philosopher Alain Badiou, who has recently achieved some prominence among the consumers of up-to-date French thought. Bensaïd has defended Badiou against the attacks of, notably, Eric Marty, a professor of literature at another Paris university, who dared to express public outrage that Badiou had written that the word "Jewish" was a Nazi invention and that those who insist on applying it to themselves or, in simpler words, insist that they *are* Jewish – like the State of Israel, most of its citizens, and the author of the present lines – commit a Nazi fallacy. I simplify a bit – Badiou, though not necessarily the most profound of living French thinkers, is a very sophisticated writer – but this is more or less the spirit of his thesis.[3]

Bensaïd has conducted his pro-Badiou campaign in, among other places, a polemical tract in which he defends himself and the French radical left in general against allegations, made notably by Bernard-Henri Levy, that they have committed seven major errors (which Bensaïd, with typical French finesse and irony, calls "cardinal sins").[4] The worst of these, and the one to which Bensaïd devotes the most attention, is the allegation of anti-Zionism. There is nothing bad, he explains, in being anti-Zionist. This is a perfectly legitimate stance. It means only that Israel has to cease to be a Jewish state. Its inner contradictions will, sooner or later, cause it to fall apart in any case, but not, it is hoped, at the cost of a new Massada. Serge Thion, whom we have already met, also thinks that the end of the Zionist adventure is inevitable; he only hopes it will happen sooner rather than later. In an article published in his online journal, he expresses his wish that Massada come as soon as possible. "Massada," it will be recalled, is the mythic name of a Jewish

---

[3] These articles, which contain Badiou's reflections on the meanings of the words "Jewish" and "Jew," as well as many other writings, are now available in English in a volume entitled *Polemics*, trans. S. Corcoran (London: Verso, 2006). For a devastating critique of Badiou and others (notably Agamben) for their postrevolutionary preoccupation with Paul's alleged invention of universalism, see Mark Lila, "A New, Political Saint Paul?" *New York Review of Books,* October 16, 2008.

[4] D. Bensaïd, *Un nouveau théologien – B.-H. Levy* (Paris: Lignes, 2007).

mass suicide. The problem is that, so far, the only ones committing suicide, in a political way so to speak, are Arabs and Muslims – as a means to kill as many Jews as possible, that is.

This is not the only similarity between Bensaïd and the deniers of La Vieille Taupe; like Guillaume, he takes Trotsky to be an authority on the Jewish fate, the nature of Zionism, and the prospects of Jewish settlement in the Middle East. As early as 1940, Trotsky said that Zionism would prove a fatal trap for the Jews. In fact, we find in Bensaïd's defense of anti-Zionism most of the anti-Zionist themes of Pierre Guillaume and Serge Thion: the State of Israel is a price paid for the Shoah; the theologization of the Shoah is meant to give to Israel a religious sanction; Israel is essentially a colonial phenomenon; and though it is undeniable that a "Jewish national fact" now exists in Palestine (as he learned from a Palestinian internationalist as early as in 1969!), the State of Israel itself is an anomaly, an outlandish, exclusive ethnic and religious pseudodemocracy; it continually commits atrocities against the Palestinians; and, although the wheels of history cannot be rolled back and Israel cannot be dismantled, it must cease to exist as a Jewish state and be turned into a binational one.

Badiou, as we have seen, does not approve of the use of the adjective "Jewish." Another Parisian comrade-colleague of Bensaïd's, Hannah Arendt's great admirer Alain Brossat, has used an interesting metaphor to express his reservations about the decision of several Jews, including Bensaïd, to speak out publicly as Jews: they are, he says, "restarred" Jews (*Juifs re-étoilés*). The occasion for this egregious display of bad taste was the publication in *Le Monde* (on October 19, 2000) of a manifesto by a group of French intellectuals announcing, *en tant que Juifs* (as Jews), that Israel did not speak in their name. A few things are worth noting in this remarkable document: it was published a few days after Ariel Sharon's visit to the Temple Mount and the beginning of the violence of the so-called al Aqsa Intifada, when negotiations between Israelis and Palestinians were still being held. The *en tant que Juifs* group nonetheless calls for the immediate resumption of the peace process. The latter should lead to the establishment of a sovereign Palestinian state, on the one hand, and the peaceful coexistence of Jews, Muslims, and Christians, on the other. Mentioning only the Arab right to a sovereign state, the appeal could well be taken to imply a denial of the right of the Jews to sovereignty. But the signatories feel entitled to make this appeal because they are Jews. The message is: as Jews we have both the duty and the right to tell the whole world, and the Israelis as well, how a solution to the tragic Middle East conflict should look. We insist not only on this prerogative but also on our right to dissociate ourselves publicly from Israel.

What is most notable about this petition, however, is the immediate appearance of the master postulate: Israel may not appropriate the Shoah for its own purposes or speak about it "in our name." But how can Israel speak about the Holocaust at all *without* speaking in their name? Besides, when did Israel ever pretend to have a monopoly on the Shoah? Paris itself has an impressive institution for Holocaust commemoration and research, the Mémorial de la Shoah, which, incidentally, was established before Jerusalem's Yad Vashem. And various other Holocaust memorials are to be found in the United States and elsewhere. None of these is questioned by Israel. More important, what need was there to bring the Shoah into this debate altogether? It is understandable that some Jews may not wish to be identified with Israel, especially when vicious attacks are being directed against Jewish individuals and institutions for their alleged ties to that country. But what does the Shoah have to do with it? In their dealings with Arafat, neither Sharon nor Barak made any reference to the Holocaust. The reason the Holocaust is invoked by these critics is clear: it adds to the moral and rhetorical force of their denunciation of Israel. Can the attitudes expressed in the manifesto, in Badiou's ruminations about the signifier "Jewish," or in Bensaïd's defense of anti-Zionism, be described as anti-Semitic? Comrade Bensaïd thinks not. He learns from Hannah Arendt that anti-Semitism is a racial notion, whereas anti-Zionism is merely a political one. One could suggest perhaps that if anti-Semitism had led to genocide, anti-Zionism, as a political concept, envisages only a politicide.

So much for France. In America, too, there are anti-Zionists among the ranks of the intellectuals. Some time ago, the distinguished scholar Judith Butler published two articles in the *London Review of Books*. The one is a review of the then-recent volume, *Arendt's Jewish Writings*; the second, an apologia for Butler's own anti-Zionism and for the divestment campaign against Israel.[5] Genuflection to Hannah Arendt is, as we have seen, an obligatory part of the anti-Zionist ritual. Butler, Bensaïd, Badiou, and Brossat, like Zertal, Ophir, and Laor, all regard her as an authority on all that concerns Zionism and Israel.

Bensaïd, for his part, quotes Butler. He learns from her review (translated into French) that the nonseparation of state and religion in Israel is disastrous. Why it should be necessary to quote Arendt or Butler on this particular subject is a mystery, especially because the review – which is, in fact, little more than an anti-Israeli, anti-Zionist diatribe – contains far more quotable,

[5] J. Butler, "I Merely Belong to Them," *London Review of Books*, May 10, 2007; and "No, It's Not Anti-Semitic," *London Review of Books*, August 21, 2003.

poetic, and profound insights. To take one example: "Paradoxically, and perhaps shrewdly," Butler says, "the terms in which Arendt criticized fascism came to inform her criticisms of Zionism, though she did not conflate the two." Butler actually gets it backwards: Arendt criticized Zionism *before* she dealt with fascism. But what is really important here is that Butler, "paradoxically, and perhaps shrewdly," accomplishes something that even Thion could not have pulled off more effectively: speaking of Zionism and fascism in the same terms. "Paradoxically, and perhaps shrewdly," we ourselves might well speak about Butler in the same terms we use to speak about Guillaume or Garaudy. Butler "does not conflate" Zionism with fascism; precisely in the same way, we do not conflate Butler with Guillaume.

Butler does, however, "paradoxically or perhaps shrewdly," conflate Zionism with apartheid. In the other, somewhat earlier article, she, like Bensaïd, defends anti-Zionism. No, she says, anti-Zionism is not the same as anti-Semitism, and the Joint Harvard-MIT Petition for Divestment from Israel is not overtly or even potentially anti-Semitic, as the ex-president of Harvard, Lawrence Summers, has claimed. What the latter in fact said was that profoundly anti-Israeli statements and actions were "anti-Semitic in their effect if not their intent." Butler completely misconstrues Summers's point. For her, "anti-Semitism" is what affects Jews outside Israel. Apparently, attacks against Israel and Israelis, whether physical or verbal, cannot, by definition, be anti-Semitic. When a government-controlled Egyptian television network broadcasts a series depicting *The Protocols of the Elders of Zion* as a factual account of how Zionism and the State of Israel arose, for example, this is apparently mere anti-Zionism and not anti-Semitism.

In typical fashion, the accusation of anti-Semitism becomes, in Butler's hands, a weapon for criticizing the critics: now Butler and the signatories of the petition are the persecuted ones. And this, in turn, provides an excellent excuse to evade the real question: not whether speaking out against Israel poses a risk to Diaspora Jews, but whether the anti-Zionist position *in itself*, or the call for divestment *as such*, is anti-Semitic. This is not a simple question. The fact that Jews take anti-Zionist positions does not, in itself, prove that such positions are not anti-Semitic. Jews – in earlier times mostly apostates – have always been busy spreading anti-Jewish notions. But the prominent role played by Jews (Israeli or otherwise) in current anti-Zionist activity is unprecedented in many ways. If such activity is anti-Semitic, it is certainly anti-Semitism of a curious kind, the kind that secures entree to the minions of universal truth and universal culture. If it is anti-Semitism, it is the emancipatory kind.

Internal strife among Jews, sometimes mean and even violent, is not new. Furthermore, I am convinced Butler is not a self-hating Jew. As an avowed "progressive Jew," she would certainly oppose any kind of racism, bigotry, or ideology based on hate. Maybe this is one of the reasons why her perception of Israel and her criticism of it are so similar to, say, Thion's, who also certainly considers himself to be a progressive thinker. Like him, she thinks that Israel has to change and become something other than what it is now. She does not agree with Thion that the only solution is for Jews to "go back where they came from," nor does she share his unabashed hatred for everything Israel represents. Maybe this is the difference between anti-Semitism and anti-Zionism. But she is sure of how the whole problem came about, and in this certainty she is indeed very close to Thion. Some people think, she says, that the significance of the 1948 war was "the violent appropriation of Palestinian land and the dislocation of 700,000 Palestinians" – certainly "an unsuitable foundation on which to build a state." Does Butler herself believe this? It soon becomes clear that she does: "Israel is now repeating its founding gesture in the containment and dehumanization of Palestinians in the Occupied Territories. Indeed, the wall now being built threatens to leave 95,000 Palestinians homeless." In fact, very few, if any, Palestinians have been made "homeless" by the construction of the security barrier, and only a small part of it is actually a wall. It is true that some Arabs have lost part of their land (not their homes). However, Israelis also have lost something: an unknowable number of them have lost the privilege of being killed by infiltrating Palestinian resistance fighters. In areas where the barrier is complete, suicide bombing and other attacks on Israeli civilians – in buses, restaurants, discothèques, and shops – have virtually stopped. Given the fact that Butler's article was written at the height of the suicide-bombing campaign, it is hard to avoid the suspicion that she is not, after all, immune to the kind of affectivity Thion exhibits toward Israel and Israelis.

The divestment campaign is also interesting. At the risk being attacked the way Chomsky attacked Pierre Vidal-Naquet and of being faulted on my knowledge of English, I would like, nonetheless, to question on linguistic grounds whether this campaign can accurately be characterized as "criticism." In my no-doubt-outmoded vocabulary, advocating action against someone is not quite the same as criticizing him or her; a slap in the face is not "criticism" but violence. The call for divestment is in fact a call for action, action meant to cause real harm. A strange way of "criticizing," indeed.

In fact, the campaign is little more than an expression of *resentment*, serving the *amour proper* of the signatories more than the interests of the Palestinians, of peace, or of morality. In concrete terms, it is unlikely to have any significant effect. Ostensibly, such campaigns are a form of direct action, meant to pressure governments to change their policies. But it is clear that this will not work in Israel's case. Not only is Israel too powerful – economically and otherwise – to be affected by such measures, but it has already shown its capacity to resist them. The Arab League boycott lasted for decades. Israelis could not buy Toyotas until the late 1970s. It did not prevent Israel's economy from overcoming dire straits, from growing and flourishing. How effective is a similar measure, the divestment campaign, likely to be today? Or the calls to the poorer European universities, which do not invest either in Israel or anywhere else, to boycott Israeli academics by not cooperating with them, not inviting them to conferences, and not publishing their papers? In short, neither of these boycotts will bring the desirable change, and using these kinds of measures will not turn Israel into a binational state or even remove as much as a single small settlement from the West Bank. In other words, it is not from a sense of autovictimization, fear, or paranoia that this criticism of the criticism is done. If I do share Summers's concerns, it is not because I worry about the possible concrete results of the appeal to divest – it will have none, even if it is accepted – but because I think it is necessary to say a few words on the act itself.

Unless the respected faculty, students, and graduates of MIT, Harvard and other high-ranking American and European universities are completely ignorant of the situation in the Middle East, the only possible explanation for all these proposals and appeals is that they are meant to be symbolic. Because such a boycott was previously undertaken against the apartheid regime in South Africa, its present significance is clear: Israel, the Zionist entity, the Jewish state – call it what you will – is *like* the former apartheid regime. Actually, the similarity is twofold: first, Israel conducts a policy of apartheid, and the Palestinian state that the Israelis pretend to be talking about is, in the best of cases, nothing more than a few Bantustans with no real sovereignty; second, and more important, the Israeli regime is, like that of apartheid South Africa, an illegitimate political entity. It is thus morally and legally justifiable to try to force its hand, even if it be against what is alleged to be the democratically expressed will of the Israeli people. It is also acceptable, and for a progressive Jew obligatory, to call for the state's destruction in its current form.

Whether anti-Zionism is anti-Semitism, neo-anti-Semitism, potential anti-Semitism, or something new, Butler's articles show that it has some interesting similarities to traditional Jew-hatred. The long history of Judeophobia is one of violence, persecution, pogroms, expulsion, robbery, murder, and rape. Besides its amazing longevity and its persistence all through Western history, it is not necessarily very different from other forms of racial or religious bigotry or hate ideologies. One distinctive feature of Judeophobia, however, is the fact that it has been espoused by some of the West's most refined, civilized, knowledgeable, and otherwise noble figures – including theologians, philosophers, artists, writers, scientists, statesmen, and social reformers. Needless to say, this does not attest to its validity. But the same can be said of anti-Zionism: while many outstanding members of the intelligentsia in the Western countries are today anti-Zionists or harsh critics of Israel, this does not in itself attest to anti-Zionism's or to that criticism's credibility or moral probity.

Another similarity between anti-Zionism and anti-Semitism is their potentially annihilationist character. When Butler and her ilk speak of changing the present form of the state in Israel, of resolving its inner contradictions by stripping away its Zionist and Jewish character, it is not always clear what they really have in mind. They often seem to be hiding behind an impenetrable separation wall – of ignorance, bad faith, self-righteousness, and simple malice – hiding from the fact that their own discourse is potentially exterminationist. One has to be blind to the reality in the Middle East and deaf to the real meaning of Summers's claim to write the kinds of thing Butler does – and she is far from being alone. Neither Voltaire nor Kant nor Pascal ever dreamt of anything remotely resembling Auschwitz. Yet their systematic discrediting of Judaism and the Jewish people is inseparable from what happened to the Jews in the twentieth century.

However, again, what is at stake in the present debate – and this is one of the greatest differences between anti-Semitism and anti-Zionism – is not the physical extermination of Israel's people. Such extermination is not a real possibility, whatever Israel's enemies do or say, even in the *London Review of Books*. Here, even Thion was wrong. Israel is too strong militarily, politically, economically, socially, culturally, and morally. This is not always the image of Israel projected in the media or in the writings that Butler reads and quotes, and Israelis certainly face grave dangers and difficulties. But its extermination is not around the corner. The calls for boycotting Israel or its universities do not carry much political weight. But they have a historic significance. Like traditional anti-Semitism, they are a symbolic and potential justification for genocide. If one kind of measure is justified, others might be too. Some of the anti-Zionists are already expressing sympathy for Hizballah and Hamas.

A third similarity is the following: like traditional anti-Semitism and other forms of anti-Judaism, anti-Zionism is not a stance, a theory, or a claim. It is also not a "criticism." Although it is mainly intellectuals who propagate it, it only appears to belong to the realm of ideas. It has been said that anti-Semitism is not a position but a crime. The reason is that Judaism, too, is not a position or a theory but a historical reality. The same holds for anti-Zionism. Zionism, too, is not merely an ideology but has developed, over a century and a half, into a historical, political, and cultural reality. Like the anti-Semitic negation of Judaism, the negation of the "Zionist entity" is nothing short of criminal.[6]

Butler is one of those – now legion – who not only preach against the Jewish state as such but also know a way to eliminate it: it must, in their view, become a binational state. Following a line that has become axiomatic, Butler refers frequently in her articles to the Palestinians' right to self-determination, to their own sovereign state. She does not mention even once a parallel Jewish right. While the Jews have a right to exist, in her view, that right does not imply a right to self-determination. She seems to think their existence can be assured in a Jewish-Arab state (probably alongside a sovereign Palestinian state) where all would live together in the civil harmony of an inclusive, nonethnic democracy. Along the lines of Lebanon, Iraq, Syria, and Saudi Arabia, perhaps. For, as everybody knows, no part of the world is more hospitable to multicultural, multinational, democratic, pluralistic, and tolerant state structures than the Arab Middle East.

To be sure, Butler does not invent her anti-Zionism out of whole cloth; nor does she lack arguments or empirical data to substantiate her claims. Her sources, however, seem to be limited to the Israeli opprobrium community. She insists that she is "emotionally invested" in Israel; but as this investment seems to be little more than a license for unbridled and unfounded "criticism," of the country, one would rather have her divest her emotional capital from Israel and put it elsewhere. Though she seems impressively ignorant, or at least silent, about the real situation in Israel, the history of Zionism, and the relations between Israel and the Jewish Diaspora, she is well acquainted with the "small but important" post-Zionist movement in Israel. More than anything else this "knowledge" only shows the international nature of this "movement"; at the same time, its presence in Israel provides a handy alibi for the most outrageous – and, at the same time, ridiculous – forms of anti-Zionism. The praises distributed with such generosity to Israeli post-Zionists, on the one hand, and the disregard of Israelis who think differently, on the other, constitute an implicit discrediting of the latter: one no longer considers them valid interlocutors, and no defense of Israel or Zionism is admissible

---

[6] See Jean-Claude Milner, *Les penchants criminels de l'Europe démocratique* (Paris: Verdier, 2003).

in legitimate discussion. The community of opprobrium is immune to any counterargument and sunk in a kind of intellectual autism.

A ONE-STATE SOLUTION

The idea that the solution of the Arab-Jewish conflict is to be found within the framework of a single state and not two – one Arab-Palestinian and one Jewish – is not new. As early as 1947, it was judged unfeasible by the United Nations Special Commission on Palestine (UNSCOP), which proposed the partition of Eretz Yisrael/Palestine into two states. We have already talked about Arendt's participation, alongside Judah Magnes, in last-ditch efforts to prevent partition. The stakes in the debate were very high, indeed a matter of life and death, not only for Zionism as an idea but also for the Jews actually living in Palestine. Not only would Arendt not have borne the consequences of any decision taken, but – unlike Magnes, who was part of the Zionist establishment and a resident of Jerusalem – her efforts to convince the Truman administration to back off from its support of the partition decision meant imposing a solution from without, against the will and better judgment of a democratic community, the Yishuv, whose overwhelming majority thought otherwise.

Yet, what might have been a legitimate position before May 5, 1948, the day the State of Israel came into being, became something completely different afterward. One could say Magnes's position was legitimate at the time – unrealistic and even silly, but legitimate. One could even claim he was right and that the establishment of a Jewish state in the Land of Israel was a mistake. It is always risky to engage in such discussions, which involve counterfactual speculation; but as an academic game, for those who have a taste for it, they are legitimate. What is much more questionable – politically, morally, and historically – is the proposal to annul Israel's Jewish character after the fact and to create a single binational, metanational, anational, or "secular democratic" state "from the river to the sea," or one that would live alongside a mono-national Palestinian-Arab state. Not only can the wheels of history not be turned back (as even Bensaïd seems to understand, although he suggests doing precisely that), and not only does the "one-state solution" mean the negation of the Jewish right to self-determination, but doing so would mean the destruction of the multifaceted reality that is coextensive with, and wholly conditioned upon, Israel's Jewish character.

In fact, the idea of a binational state has never been completely dead. It has been kept alive by some rather marginal groups of radical left-wing activists, mostly Israelis, who have continued to talk, mainly to themselves, about de-Judaizing and de-Zionizing Israel. These ideas have found a favorable reception in some equally marginal groups in Europe and the United States, who, like the Vieille Taupe crowd, triumphantly tout one obscure Israeli writer or another in support of their own anti-Zionist ideologies. Arab intellectuals and politicians, who have often adopted their rhetoric more than the ideas, also take great interest in these people. But except for an occasional reference in the more serious Western media, no one else seemed to pay much attention to these professional anti-Zionists. In Jerusalem, which is always rife with idiosyncratic visionaries, the ideologues of dismantling the "Zionist state" are known to practically everyone but taken seriously by practically no one.

Lately, however, the binational idea has resurfaced elsewhere and become part of mainstream discourse about the Middle East and the Israeli-Palestinian problem. It gained momentum after the failure of the Camp David negotiations, which left many thinking a peaceful solution based on the two-state principle was unrealizable. It was also then that, as suggested earlier, it became acceptable to speak seriously of the illegitimacy of a Jewish state. Ironically, all this was happening at the moment when Israel seemed willing to give up the dream of the "whole Land of Israel" and return to the two-state solution. Purportedly serious talk about a binational state has become very popular in post- and anti-Zionist circles, and the idea has gained some intellectual respectability. After all, Hannah Arendt was also for it, and it seems a reasonable way to negate the Jewish right of self-determination without advocating explicitly, as Thion does, that the Jews be "sent back where they belong."

It is perhaps mainly due to the efforts of New York University professor Tony Judt that this obsolete idea has regained respectability and found its way into mainstream academic discussion. In October 2003, roughly at the same time that the Butler article appeared in the *London Review of Books*, Judt published an article in the *New York Review of Books* (*LRB*'s American predecessor and counterpart) under the provocative title "Israel: The Alternative." It is probably the polemical character of the article, more than the idea of a binational state per se, that accounts for the scandal it provoked. It is, in fact, scandalous, and in more ways than one. Judt has spent his career studying French intellectuals in the first decades after the Second World War. Both the period and the theme have attracted a lot of academic attention (notably, of course, in France), and the truth is, Judt does not deliver much beyond what a number of excellent French historians have done. He is well acquainted with French writing of the period but seems not always to grasp fully the philosophical background out of which the political and ideological controversies of that time arose. This does not prevent him from taking sides and proposing a highly partisan view of the French intelligentsia of the period. True, it is hard to remain neutral toward the main figures – Sartre, Aron, and Camus, to mention only those to whom Judt gives extensive treatment – but his unabashedly judgmental attitude is quite exceptional in academic writing. Nevertheless, the main conclusion of his study is illuminating. He regards French intellectual culture of the Cold War era as one of irresponsibility. In light of his recent writings on Israel, this is an amazing insight.[7]

Unlike other members of the opprobrium community, Judt, who spent some time in Israel as a young Zionist and even served in a volunteer capacity in the Israeli army, seems not to reject Zionism as such. It just came too late, he contends, when the world had entered a post-national, post-state era, so that Israel, with its outdated nationalistic ideology, is thus an anachronism. So it has to be updated and become a binational state. Although this historical judgment is colossally oversimplified, if not altogether false, it does provide a foundation, however pseudoacademic, for the whole anti-Zionist structure of ideas. One can even find in Judt's recent writings the anti-Zionist master postulate, from which he proceeds to a far-reaching condemnation of Israel and a call for its de-Judaization.

Not surprisingly, Judt's obligatory reference to the Shoah-Israel nexus is connected with Hannah Arendt, appearing in the published adaptation of a talk he gave upon receiving the Arendt Prize.[8] There, Judt offers some reflections, inspired, he says, by Arendt's "banality" doctrine, on the question of evil in the modern world. He does not seem overly concerned about the danger of anti-Semitism in the democratic countries, and he is probably right. What worries him much more is that we – it is not altogether clear whom he refers to – overemphasize the uniqueness of the Shoah but then invoke it on every occasion and thus confuse the young. He is also worried that by attaching the memory of the Holocaust too firmly to the defense of one country – Israel – we risk provincializing its moral significance. He finds particularly obnoxious the fact that every criticism of Israel is nowadays censured because of the fear of a new Shoah. He himself has been chided for criticizing Israel. According to the Wikipedia article on Alvin Rosenfeld's

---

[7] See in particular, T. Judt, *Past Imperfect: French Intellectuals, 1944–1956* (Berkeley: University of California Press, 1994); and *The Burden of Responsibility: Blum, Camus, Aron and the French Twentieth Century* (Chicago: University of Chicago Press, 1998).

[8] T. Judt, "The 'Problem of Evil' in Postwar Europe," *New York Review of Books*, February 14, 2008.

essay, referred to earlier, Judt told the *New York Times* he "believed the real purpose of the outspoken denunciations of him and others was to stifle their harsh criticism of Israel and its treatment of the Palestinians." Like Butler, he apparently sees his call for the transformation of Israel into a binational state as mere "criticism" and, like her, sees the countercriticism as a form of persecution and as an attack on his freedom of speech. I may not sufficiently grasp the intricacies of Jewish life in the United States, but my impression is that he manages to evade the censors quite well and continues to publish his anti-Zionist criticism despite the attempts to "silence" him and his like.

Like other non-Israeli critics, Judt cites Israeli authors to bolster his argument. In his case, though, there is a particular irony in his choice of sources: this highly sophisticated scholar looks for support in the most pathetic and ridiculous writings of the Israeli opprobrium community. In another of his articles, for example, Judt chooses to cite, out of all the available Israeli literature, a piece by the politician Avraham Burg that contains in a nutshell all the themes the latter was to develops in his aforementioned book. As could have been expected, Burg's article was quickly translated and published by the *Guardian* and *Le Monde*. (Yet even Burg does not advocate the replacement of Israel, as terrible as it is, by a binational state.)

Judt conducts his offensive simultaneously on two fronts: the in-house Israeli/Zionist/Jewish debate and the international, mainly American one. His vise-like attack has two main themes: first, Israel is an anachronism. Even if the Zionist idea was not initially illegitimate, and even if Zionism has never been a colonial phenomenon, a Jewish state has become historically and politically unjustifiable, and Israel has to change the forms of its legitimation (to use once again Butler's sophisticated formula) and become a binational state. In addition, and if this is not enough, it should also be made clear that a *two*-state solution has been rendered unworkable by the now-irreversible settlement of Jews in the territories Israel occupied in 1967.

The truth is, the situation is very complex. No doubt the settlements would make a two-state solution very difficult to achieve. The Palestinians' violence and intransigence and their apparent inability to manage their own affairs would also be impediments. But the settlements are impediment enough. Has a two-state solution become completely impossible, then, as Judt thinks? Five years after Judt's article was first published, it seems a bit too apocalyptic. Writing with the authority of a historian back in 2003, Judt was telling his readers that a catastrophe was imminent. If nothing radical happened soon, he wrote, Israel would, in five years, be neither Jewish nor democratic. As it happens, the present lines are being written on the very date this reprieve, granted to Israel by Judt, was to have expired. What has happened during the intervening time, in the Gaza Strip, for example, cannot but remind us of the Talmudic dictum that, with the destruction of the Temple, prophecy was given to fools.

Judt published his article shortly before the Israeli withdrawal from the Gaza Strip. This move involved the evacuation of several Jewish settlements inhabited by some eight thousand people, among whom were children constituting a third generation in these communities. The evacuation was carried out, on the whole, with amazing ease, despite the dramatic pictures of resistance broadcast all over the world. Although the situation in the West Bank could prove quite different, the evacuation of the Gaza Strip alone was enough to show that Judt had profoundly misjudged the situation.

The withdrawal was, in fact, the transfer of a civilian population. However, Israeli public opinion – not to speak of the rest of the world – showed almost no compassion for the plight of the evacuated. Clearly, most Israelis – left, center, center-right, even right – had come to the conclusion that settling in the "territories" had been a bad idea and that the only way to resolve the conflict or at least to gain a certain measure of stability would be to undo it and acquiesce in the repartition of the country between the Arabs and the Jews. Many Israelis are skeptical even about the possibility of achieving a measure of calm and are also aware of the strategic price to be paid for further withdrawal – the incessant rocket attacks on Israeli towns and villages neighboring the Gaza Strip shows them that withdrawal would not necessarily bring calm – but they still support it. They often do so for moral reasons: they acknowledge a Palestinian right of self-determination and refuse to rule over another people. Contrary to what Judt thinks about Israel and Israelis, what happened in the Gaza Strip and subsequently was a sign of the maturity and moral sensitivity of Israeli society. Despite the cruelty of the suicide-bomb offensive against Israel, there was no Grozny in the occupied territories. There may be no other example of a state with such a highly developed military and technological capacity reacting with such restraint to the kind of violent assault Israel has endured for the past ten years. Butler gives Jenin as an example of Israeli murderousness, directed especially against children. But this is a libel: what happened there was the exact opposite of what she, and others like her, insinuate. But I shall not pursue this point.

Aside from Judt's erroneous prognosis, there is one more point in his 2003 article that is worth mentioning. Like Arendt's activity toward the end of her Zionist involvement, Judt's demand that the Jewishness of the State of Israel be annulled is not directed at Israelis but at Americans. But his call for American intervention, unlike Arendt's, is based not on fear for the fate of the Jewish national home but on a concern about the repercussions the situation in Israel might have on local Jews and American interests. Not only is Israel bound to explode but it has become a burden. Judt is not the only one to think so: as recent public opinion polls show, a majority in many European countries and elsewhere thinks that Israel constitutes the greatest threat to world peace, second, perhaps, only to Iran. On top of all this, America's support for Israeli policies erodes its credibility in the world. In short, enough is enough; we Americans should convince, perhaps force, those reluctant Israelis to give up their outdated dreams, de-Judaize their peculiar state, and accept a binational one instead. The ironical tone here should not mislead: Judt's article is outrageous, and not because he calls the Jewish state an anachronism. Trying to convince the Jews (or the Palestinians, for that matter) to give up their aspirations to self-determination may be silly, but it is not morally wrong. What is unacceptable is trying to force the dissolution of an existing political framework, be it Jewish or Arab, against the wishes of its citizens. This is imaginable only if the entity in question is not only illegitimate but utterly criminal. But that is precisely what anti-Zionism has, by various means, set out to demonstrate.

Judt has also addressed the Israeli public directly. In an article published in May 2006, in the English edition of *Haaretz* on the fifty-eighth anniversary of Israel's independence, entitled "The Country That Will Not Grow Up," the New York University professor gives the natives a quasi-biblical moral lesson. We Israelis, he lectures us, are politically immature, in fact infantile. We suffer from a "collective cognitive dysfunction." The proof: Israel's poor standing in world public opinion. One wonders if he would take the bad reputation Jews have – it is usually called "anti-Semitism" – among some observers of the recent Wall Street crash, for example, as proof of some Jewish, and not specifically Israeli, dysfunction. However, Judt has other proofs: he draws a portrait of Israel and of Israeli society and politics, already familiar to us from the growing body of anti-Zionist and anti-Israeli literature, written by Israelis and non-Israelis alike. It is, for the most part, an inaccurate, distorted, even scurrilous picture, not very different from the one we find in the literature of La Vieille Taupe. Interestingly enough, there is not one word in this article on the idea of a *one*-state solution; but this is perhaps understandable. Given the fact that Israel is an anachronism and a burden and that the Israelis are infantile, unreliable, and politically hopeless, it is appropriate that we – Jewish American intellectuals, in particular – take matters in hand and impose order on the Middle East. Nor need we take too seriously what the Israeli themselves say, except for a few outstanding figures who tower morally and intellectually above the rest of country, some of whom are depicted in the second chapter of the present volume.

Judt, Butler, Bensaïd, and many others whom we have not mentioned here are aware of the great difficulties that a one-state solution would present. Indeed, they know, or say they do, that the obstacles in its way could be well-nigh insurmountable. But they believe, or at least hope, that the difficulties can be overcome. In fact, they do not claim much more than that. But we have witnessed a number of attempts of late to address this question in a more serious manner, to investigate the real possibilities of building a binational state. Several "models" have been constructed and their applicability to conditions in the Middle East weighed. Could Canada, Belgium, South Africa, or some other existing multinational country serve as a paradigm for an Arab-Jewish state? Or should we take the bull by the horns and come to terms with the specifics of the local situation in its own terms?

I shall not dwell on these proposals, few of which seem to me much more than futile academic speculation. But one particularly ambitious program, proposed by Virginia Tiley, is worth a brief mention. In a number of articles and a book,[9] Tiley has proposed a solution based on a detailed study of the actual situation in Israel, the Israel-occupied territories, and the territories controlled by the Palestinian Authority. She is well acquainted with the history of the Israel-Arab conflict, and, in many respects, her model is well grounded. But her proposal still shows a failure to appreciate what is really at stake, and so it remains, ultimately, unacceptable.

Typically, and like Butler, she recognizes the Jews' right to exist. Typically, it is the recent history of the Jews, namely the Holocaust, that puts this right beyond any questioning. Typically, she thinks Zionism is about finding a safe haven for the Jews. Typically, she misunderstands completely the nature of Zionism. She ignores, out of ignorance or choice, the fact that Zionism had been, long before the destruction of European Jewry made it plainly clear that the Jews deserve a safe place to live in, a program for the reassuming of an overall responsibility to the life of the Jewish people in all its aspects. This is what is meant when it is said, in an Arendt-like vein, that Zionism is a program of repoliticizing Jewish life, or of reentering History, or of normalizing Jewish existence. This is what is meant when one speaks of the right of self-determination. All this is precisely what Tiley's model gives up. It amounts to a historic burial of Zionism: the State of Israel will have to be changed, the Jewish Agency transformed, and the electoral system altered, replacing the constitutional laws with other laws. Of course, all these changes will cause a

---

[9] See V. Tiley, *The One-State Solution: A Breakthrough for Peace in the Israeli-Palestinian Deadlock* (Ann Arbor: University of Michigan Press, 2005); "The One-State Solution," *London Review of Books*, November 6, 2003.

lot of opposition and will hurt the feelings of many people. Given the famous recent history of the Jews, this is comprehensible. So a way will have to be found to overcome them. After all, it is only feeling, perhaps not as infantile as Judt thinks, but certainly not a rational attitude that has to be reckoned with as such. In short, the Jewish insistence on the right of self-determination is something we should not take too seriously into account.

Other attempts have been and are being made to devise a working one-state solution. Not all of them insist, as Tiley does, that the essence of the Zionist project be abandoned. We shall have to wait and see what they have in store. Personally, I think they will all prove futile. This is also the opinion of Sari Nusseibeh, a leading Palestinian intellectual, now president of the (Arab) Al-Quds University in East Jerusalem. Interestingly enough, Nusseibeh is also one of the very few Arab intellectuals or political figures to have dared acknowledge, even semipublicly, that the Jews have a case, that their claim to Palestine is in any sense morally, historically, or legally valid. (He has since been silenced in this regard.) Lately, he has written that, despite the hopelessness of the situation in the "occupied territories," Arabs should not be tempted by the one-state solution. Some believe that the recent efflorescence of post- and anti-Zionist thinking creates a historical opportunity for the Arabs and that once a binational state replaces the Jewish state, their high birth rate will work to their demographic advantage, so that they can then regain control over their lost land. But they are wrong, he says, and instead of pursuing such illusory solutions they would do better to work toward the only one that stands a chance, that of two states. The Jews, he thinks, will never settle for anything else. He is right; and the most that Judt, Butler, and their Israeli friends can accomplish is to make the two-state solution more difficult to implement than it already is. Unfortunately, as usual, it is the Palestinians who will pay the heaviest price for this obstructionism.

THE MORAL DISASTER

Judt, as we have just seen, is concerned about the effects of Israel's failures – cognitive or otherwise – on the well-being of Jews elsewhere. Apparently, not only Israelis suffer from existential anxieties. But writing these lines in New York, I must admit that, with all my sympathy for his concerns, I cannot detect much discomfort among the Jews in this city. Even Jewish professors at the local universities do not seem to suffer unduly. His call for dismantling Israel because it poses a danger to Diaspora Jews is thus not only outrageous from a moral point of view – imagine Israelis calling Jews to convert because anti-Semitism makes life difficult for them – but also quite surrealistic. Moreover, if there is a threat of mounting, even violent anti-Semitism, blaming it on Israel and not on the anti-Semites is not only morally wrong but signifies a certain cognitive malfunction. (Here, too, we see a parallel between anti-Zionism and classical anti-Semitism: the Jews themselves are held responsible for being hated and persecuted.) Indeed, this concern about anti-Semitism only confirms the Zionist prediction that anti-Semitism would continue to be a factor in Western culture for a long time to come. After all, the Chinese living in New York do not feel menaced by what is happening in Tibet; widespread criticism of China does not affect them and or cause them to dissociate themselves from their homeland.

Another Jewish American intellectual with some Israeli background, Daniel Boyarin, a professor of Talmudic studies, has a better characterization of the kind of plight Israel brings upon American Jewry: it is a moral plight. As quoted by Rosenfeld, Boyarin writes that "just as Christianity may have died at Auschwitz ... so I fear Judaism may be dying at Nablus" or Hebron or the refugee camps on the West Bank. Actually, as we said apropos Ophir's similar grief about morality's death at Auschwitz, it was mainly Jews who died there; to say that Christianity did seems both exaggerated and premature. Similarly, if there is violent death in Hebron or Nablus, it is mainly that of Palestinians. Sometimes of Jews too. Judaism itself seems to be more under threat in California than in Israel.

Boyarin, though, speaks of moral, not actual death. In an article published in *Tikkun*, an American Jewish magazine that, modestly, pronounces itself dedicated to healing, repairing, and transforming the world, Boyarin gives us further insight into the roots of Israel's discomfiting immorality. The harm done to the Arabs is the greatest evil Israel is committing, of course; but we have already seen this. The Arabs are the innocent victims of the rude invasion of their land by a foreign population. It would be interesting to know if Boyarin also sympathizes with the opposition of some Americans and many Europeans to the immigration to their countries of poor and needy people from the Third World the way he sympathizes with the Palestinian opposition to Jewish immigration to Palestine; but I am sure he will come up with a good explanation of why these cases are different.

Boyarin is concerned not only with the evil done to the Palestinians but also (somewhat narcissistically, as he concedes) with the harm done by Zionism in another quarter: it is not only the Arabs, the Oriental Jews, the other peoples that have suffered genocide, and the Germans who are victims of the Zionists, but we must now also reckon with the harm done to Judaism itself. This time, however, it is not its death in Hebron – or is it Nablus? – that he is talking about, but the plastic hammers with which young Israelis, to provoke hilarity, used to hit each other on the head in the streets on Independence Day (a practice obnoxious to many that has now mostly disappeared). It is emblematic to him that "our way of celebrating has become an enactment of symbolic violence, a sign of the erosion of sensitivity to others that once was a vaunted hallmark of our culture." No more, no less. Of course, Jews have not been better than others as individuals, or even as a collective. But they had had this "cultural aspiration ... to a kind of gentle concern that precluded, in aspiration, violence." It might seem strange that, in his view, the unfulfilled aspiration is more important than the reality, but there is certainly some truth in this observation, and as a historian, Boyarin knows of what he speaks. It makes me think, though, of something my friend Alex once said to me. He, too, is a historian, a specialist in ancient history who grew up in the Soviet Union, a former Peace Now activist, and an incorrigible Zionist. When Jews had political power, as they sometimes did in ancient times, they were, he said, capable of behaving as violently as the others, killing, looting, and the like. Then they lost their political power and internalized an aversion to political violence and, indeed, to power itself. This is the sensibility that Boyarin so nicely describes. In modern times, Jews have attained political power twice, with the Bolshevik revolution and with the establishment of the State of Israel. In the first instance, as we know, Jews played a major role, and, among other things, killed, tortured, imprisoned, and exiled their opponents and others in great numbers. The Zionist movement and the State of Israel have done nothing of the sort. In fact, the only instance in Jewish history where Jews have had political power but did not use it for killing was in the Zionist movement. Zionists have never killed their political opponents. They fought – they still do – against their enemies, sure enough, but usually with more restraint than others. Even in Nablus, that den of terrorism, they mostly arrest, rather than kill, locals suspected of preparing the bombs destined for Israeli buses. I suspect it is for this that Boyarin cannot forgive us.

LAST WORD, OR THE LOGIC OF THE POT

An old story, probably Jewish, tells of a good lady who knocks on her neighbor's door and asks her to give back a pot she borrowed some time before. "Your pot?" says the neighbor. "First of all, it is broken; second, I have already given it back to you; and, third, I never took it." The neighbor's logic is similar to that of the anti-Zionist opprobrium community. It goes like this: the Holocaust never happened, and that is why Israel is illegitimate. If there was a Holocaust, Israel misuses it, manipulates it, and exaggerates its uniqueness in order to acquire a legitimacy it does not deserve. But Israel is, in fact, itself a Nazi state; or if not Nazi, then fascist; or if not fascist, colonial; or if not colonial, apartheid; or if not apartheid, anachronistic; or if it is not anachronistic, then the Jews are not a people; or if they are a people but call themselves "Jewish," they are Nazis after all.

It goes on and on in this vein. Having spent countless hours reading such arguments, I can vouch for one thing: although the main themes are repeated endlessly, the critics' inventiveness – in producing new versions of the old stories and in compounding the ignorance, the stupidity, the lies, the malice, and the bad faith – has not been exhausted. It probably never will be. Surveying this amazing production in its entirety, one gets an unexpected feeling. On the one hand, it is extremely exasperating, even depressing. But after a while it comes to seem, like so many perversions, almost comical. Israel, as it emerges from this literature – and not necessarily just from writings of the Holocaust deniers – is continuously engaged in genocide, politicide, ethnic cleansing, and the serial murder of children. It has robbed the Palestinians of their land and continues to do so. The Jews came to Palestine as colonialists and then only because of the Holocaust. They have exacted from the Palestinians the price of the suffering inflicted upon them in Europe, which, in any case, was not unique, and pretending it was serves to obscure the suffering of all the other victims of mass crime. The state the Jews built on stolen Arab land is not only morally but also historically and politically unjustifiable. It was not only a crime but also a mistake. Its continual existence is also both a crime and a mistake. Israel does not want peace, and in any case it is not a democracy. It cannot be a democracy because there is a contradiction between its Jewishness and its pretense of being a democracy. At best, it is an ethnic democracy, which is inclusive of one ethnicity – the Jewish – but exclusive of all others. However, the Jews do not constitute an ethnic group; the Zionists have simply invented a nonexistent Jewish peoplehood; and if they were an ethnic group, they should cease to be so, because there is no longer room for particularism in the global village. In Israel, Hitler actually won his war, in two senses: the Israelis, by applying SS and Gestapo methods in their war of aggression against the Palestinians, are carrying on the Nazi legacy; and in their stubborn particularism, their insistence on calling themselves "Jewish" and their peculiar state a "Jewish state," they are also Nazis. Israeli society is not only artificial, illegitimate, and criminal; it is also pathological, infantile, and cognitively challenged. The main cause of all these distortions is the Holocaust and the role it is being made to play in the collective psyche of the Israeli non-nation. There are other myths, like the divinely ordained conquest of Canaan and the massacre of its peoples;

but the Auschwitz myth, that of the Six Million, is a particularly efficient means of inducing the unique moral blindness that permits Israelis to kill all these Palestinian children; not to speak of their own children, whose killing by suicide bombers is also their responsibility, because they have driven the Palestinians to such desperation that the latter have no other way of fighting for their legitimate rights but to kill as many Israeli civilians as possible. Of course, the Palestinians rightly refuse to pay the price of the Holocaust, which, in any case, they do not believe ever took place and which, if it did, happened in Europe, which is very far from Palestine. The Israelis endanger Jews living outside Israel, who resent the fact that Israel speaks in their name. In fact, it should not bother to speak at all, because no one is any longer listening, and if someone is, it is only to Israel's small, courageous, morally superior, and politically lucid post-Zionist minority. Israel is also a liability to the United States and to other mature nations. The manipulation and infantilization of the collective Israeli consciousness is only one aspect of a gigantic – in fact, global – campaign that makes use of official historiography, hegemonic metanarratives and discursive regimes to foster a delirious misperception of reality. Israeli society is a neurotic society, plagued by irrational fears that are deliberately cultivated by a corrupt, cynical, expansionist political oligarchy. It has turned the Holocaust into a state religion and thus turned *homo israelicus* into a power-hungry paranoiac. Israel's war machine, financed by the proceeds of Holocaust blackmail, is solely responsible for what is going on in the Middle East, and the wall it is now building is only another means of confining the Palestinians in a single enormous ghetto or concentration camp. If nothing drastic happens soon, the Israelis are going to wipe the Palestinians out altogether, or at least those whom they have not yet eliminated through ethnic cleansing. Alternatively, they will destroy themselves, in a Massada-like mass suicide – or perhaps the whole world, in a final, Samson-like, apocalyptic act.

If the reader thinks I am exaggerating or caricaturing what is in reality a serious, intellectually sound, and morally honest criticism, I can only suggest that he or she do what I did: spend some time reading this material. It's best to do it in Jerusalem or Tel Aviv, where things usually look different than they do on CNN or the BBC or in the pages of the *Nation* or the *Guardian*.

Appendix: Biographical Notes

Yehuda Bauer (b. 1926) is a historian of the Holocaust and a professor at the Hebrew University of Jerusalem.

Azmi Bishara (b. 1956) was a member of the Knesset (Israeli parliament), representing the Balad (National Democratic Alliance) Party, from 1996 until his resignation in April 2007, following charges of treason and espionage brought against him by the General Security Services. He left the country and has remained abroad since then. Bishara received a PhD in philosophy from Humboldt University of Berlin in 1986 (his thesis was on the philosophy of Karl Marx) and joined the faculty of Bir Zeit University (in the West Bank), where he headed the Department of Philosophy and Department of Political Science. Since 1990, he has also worked as a researcher at the Van Leer Jerusalem Institute. His books have been published in Arabic, Hebrew, English, French, and German. Selected publications: *Die Jerusalemfrage: Israelis und Palätinenser im Gespräch* (with Uri Avnery, 1996), *The Palestinian Elections: An Assessment* (1997), *The Arabs in Israel* (2003).

Yosef Grodzinsky is a professor in the Department of Psychology at Tel Aviv University and the Department of Linguistics, McGill University, Montreal, working mainly in the field of neurolinguistics. He is interested in the neurological instantiation of formal syntactic and semantic knowledge, which he has been studying in both sickness and health. He also done research on the history of the Holocaust and published several articles on this subject. Selected publications: *Theoretical Perspectives on Language Deficits* (1990), *In the Shadow of the Holocaust: The Struggle between Jews and Zionists in the Aftermath of World War II* (2004), *Broca's Region* (ed. with Katrin Amunts, 2006).

Jacob Katz (1904–1998) was a prominent scholar of Jewish history, specializing in Jewish-gentile relations, the Jewish Enlightenment, anti-Semitism, and the Holocaust.

Baruch Kimmerling (1939–2007) was a sociologist at the Hebrew University of Jerusalem. His research was concerned mainly with Israeli and Palestinian societies and the Arab-Israeli conflict. In the 1970s, he began to analyze Israeli society from a postcolonial perspective. Selected publications: *Zionism and Territory: The Socioterritorial Dimensions of Zionist Politics* (1983), *Palestinians: The Making of a People* (with Joel S. Migdal, 1993), *The Invention and Decline of Israeliness: State, Culture and Military in Israel* (2001).

Yitzhak Laor (b. 1948) is a poet, playwright, novelist, and essayist. He writes literary criticism for the *Haaretz* daily newspaper and teaches in the department of literature, Tel Aviv University. He is known mostly for his poetry of political protest, particularly about the Israeli occupation that followed the 1967 Six-Day War and the Lebanon war of 1982. Laor was one of the first to refuse military service in the occupied territories (1972) and is well known as an acerbic critic of Israel's occupation policies. Selected publications: *Ephraim Goes Back to the Army* (in Hebrew, 1987), *The People, Food for Kings* (in Hebrew, 1993).

Hagit Lavsky has taught Jewish history at the Hebrew University since 1986.

Dan Michman (b. 1947) is a professor of modern Jewish history at Bar-Ilan University, Ramat Gan. He also works as an adviser to and chief historian of Yad Vashem, the Holocaust research, documentation, and commemoration center in Jerusalem.

Adi Ophir (b. 1951) is an associate professor at the Cohn Institute, Tel Aviv University, and a fellow of the Center for Advanced Studies, Shalom Hartman Institute, Jerusalem. His main areas of interest are modern and contemporary continental philosophy, ethics, political thought, and critical studies. He founded and edited *Theory and Criticism*, a journal for critical theory, published by the Van Leer Jerusalem Institute. As a fellow of the institute, he directed an interdisciplinary research project on "Humanitarian Action in Catastrophes: The Shaping of Contemporary Political Imagination and Moral Sensibilities." Selected publications: *Plato's Invisible Cities: Discourse and Power in* The Republic (1991), *The Order of Evils: Towards an Ontology of Morals* (2000), *The Worship of the Present: Essays on Contemporary Israeli Culture* (in Hebrew, 2001).

Eyal Sivan (b. 1964) is an Israeli film producer and director and a screenwriter, based in France since 1985. He has taught at various French and Israeli academic institutions. He has openly declared his anti-Zionism and called for civil disobedience in Israel. In 2006, after French intellectual Alain Finkielkraut called him a "Jewish anti-Semite," Sivan sued him for libel. Selected films: *Izkor: Slaves of Memory* (1991), *The Specialist / Un spécialiste: Portrait d'un criminel moderne* (1999, with Rony Brauman), *Route 181: Fragments of a Journey in Palestine-Israel* (2004, with Michel Khleifi).

Leni Yahil (1912–2007) was a historian of the Holocaust.

Idith Zertal, a historian and essayist, is one of the so-called new historians who have challenged conventional beliefs about Israeli history. Her fields of research include the Holocaust, Zionism, collective memory, and Israeli nationalism. Zertal has taught history and cultural studies at the Hebrew University of Jerusalem and at the Interdisciplinary Center, Herzliya. She has been a visiting professor at the University of Chicago and at the École des Hautes Etudes en Sciences Sociales in Paris, as well as the Institute of Jewish Studies at the University of Basel. Selected publications: *From Catastrophe to Power: Holocaust Survivors and the Emergence of Israel* (1996, 1998, 2000), *Israel's Holocaust and the Politics of Nationhood* (2005), *The Lords of the Land: Jewish Settlements in the Occupied Territories, 1967–2006* (with Akiva Eldar, 2007).

Moshe Zuckerman (b. 1949) is a sociologist, historian, and philosopher teaching at Tel Aviv University. An associate of the Cohn Institute there, he has also headed the university's Institute for German History. He has written on collective memory, the sociology of art, and the Holocaust in its historical and contemporary context. Zuckerman is well known in Germany, where he has taught and published extensively. In Israel, he is known as a critic of domestic politics and society. Select publications: *Zweierlei Holocaust: Der Holocaust in den politischen Kulturen Israels und Deutschlands* (1998), *Israel – Deutschland – Israel: Reflexionen eines Heimatlosen* (2006).

Index

Hacohen, Ran, 84, 85

Hagana, 131

Halevi, Binyamin, 133

Hamas, 84, 190, 317

Hancock, Ian, 162

Harrison, Bernard, 308

Hass, Amira, 95–97

Hatzalah. *See* rescue

Hausner, Gideon, 260, 267, 274, 282, 289, 296, 299

Hebrew University of Jerusalem, 47, 210, 229, 281

hegemonic discourse, 59, 126, 225

Heidegger, Martin, 141, 212, 224, 227, 231, 245, 249, 252, 265, 271, 275, 279, 286, 298

Heim, Susanne, 175, 180, 268

Herzl, Binyamin-Zeev, 32, 126, 239

Hess, Rudolph, 48, 49

Hezbollah, 317

Hilberg, Raul, 39, 117, 118, 146, 236, 261, 262, 268, 276, 291

Himmler, Heinrich, 178, 179, 180, 268, 269, 270

Hiroshima, 29, 54, 181

Hitler, Adolf, 10, 14, 15, 16, 23, 39, 48, 49, 50, 64, 72, 84, 85, 96, 109, 110, 119, 125, 126, 131, 164, 174, 179, 218, 329

Hobbes, Thomas, 145, 150, 151, 213

Holocaust

 Arab views, 98

 commemoration, 68, 70, 90, 300, *see also* United States Holocaust Memorial Museum

 cultural meaning of, 56, 93, 101, 104, 122, 166, 195, 198, 201, 207, 209, 210, 258, 276, 278, 298

 destruction of European Jewry, 288

 historiography, 26, 59, 100, 116, 127, 130, 136, 146, 153, 161, 174, 188, 236, 291

 instrumentalization of, 102, 107, 119, 120, 124, 132, 181, 204, 215, 300

 justification for Israel's establishment, 25, 26, 29, 49, 50, 55, 56, 57, 63,

65, 77, 78, 86, 88, 90, 95, 99, 127, 132, 173

 memory of, 102, 114, 121, 122, 125, 171, 181, 209, 299

 representatability of, 298

 Shoah, 49, 61, 127, 173, 208, 209

 shoanut, 126, 300

 survivors, 38, 85, 96, 109, 127, 205, 297

 terminology, 49, 61

 theological interpretations, 71, 76, 278, 312

 unique Jewish perspective on, 118, 300, 313

 uniqueness of, 8, 9, 58, 63, 75, 103, 114, 153–169, 172, 174, 178, 183, 187, 189, 221, 294, 296, 321

 victims of, 126, 168

Holocaust denial, 1, 2, 16, 64, 78, 81, 105, 114, 158, 160, 215, 288, 307, 329

 left-wing, 4, 26, 33, 52, 54, 86, 95

 in the Arab world, 26, 50

Horkheimer, Max, 74

Hungary, 130, 268, 269, 270, 273

Ignaski, Paul, 308

Institute for Historical Review, 51

Intifada, 96

Iraq, 106

Irgun (*EZEL* - Irgun zva'i Le'umi), 54

Irving, David, 2

Islam, 47

Israel

 as the Chosen People, 48, 159, 297

 comparison to Nazi Germany, 88, 89, 216, 329

 delegitimation and negation of, 52, 54, 56, 65, 66, 77, 88, 105, 121, 131, 320

 Eretz Yisrael, 136, 255

 historiography, 133, 136, 237

 Israelis, 30, 79, 82–89, 97, 108, 110, 135–137, 195, 198, 208, 298, 300, 306–310, 328